D1374540

A Reader's Guide to the development of the English novel in the eighteenth century

A Reader's Guide to the development of the English novel in the eighteenth century

Frederick R. Karl

THAMES AND HUDSON · LONDON

Originally published in the United States of America by Farrar, Straus and Giroux, New York, 1974, under the title *The Adversary Literature, The English Novel in the Eighteenth Century: A Study in Genre*.

First published in Great Britain in 1975 by Thames and Hudson Ltd, London

Printed in Great Britain by
The Camelot Press Ltd, Southampton

TO THE FIVE:

Charlotte, Deborah, Dolores, Judith, Rebecca

Contents

Introduction: The Novel as Subversion

Too often, critical studies and college courses in the eighteenth-century novel create the impression that the tentative fictional works of the seventeenth century were negligible and that, somehow, through some process approximating spontaneous combustion, the "novel" flamed suddenly in the work of Daniel Defoe. Even a glance at William H. McBurney's *A Check List of English Prose Fiction 1700–1739* will demonstrate how much fictional activity preceded and accompanied Defoe and how dependent Defoe was on techniques and experiments tried by these lesser writers. We tend to ignore them—Mrs. Mary Manley, Mrs. Eliza Haywood, Arthur Blackamore, Mrs. Mary Davys—because their work was ephemeral, but it fed into the huge reservoir of ideas and techniques that is the basis of later, more durable fiction.

Such early work, of course, is only of historical interest. The demands of quick publication, rapid writing, and the rivalries of competing factions and fictions from the Continent led to carelessness, sentimentality, platitudinous description, discontinuous narrative, and insufficiently motivated characters. As a consequence, the work received critical excoriation, which in turn hindered the development of the craft. Fiction was caught in a familiar cycle. Attacked by the press and by the upholders of cultural standards, like the chameleon it changed color; and yet the very qualities attacked by critics passed into the major novelists, who modified and metamorphosed them, and ultimately passed them on to still-later writers. William McBurney catches well the kind of fluctuating dialectic in which the early English novelist operated:

> Since novelty or sheer variety remained the chief criterion of fictional excellence, each imitation strove to surpass its original model. This soon tended to exhaust the possibilities of the type. As a consequence, the popularity of specific works was less lasting, and fictional vogues, discarded by upper-class readers, passed down through the social strata with increasing rapidity. Such acceleration of popularity prevented any stagnation of the novel, such as the heroic romance had experienced in the later seventeenth century, and to some extent eliminated the dangers of a similar discrediting. [*Four Before Richardson*, 1963, Introduction, xvi]

The comments of Mrs. Manley—a contemporary of Defoe—in a preface to *The Secret History of Queen Zarah and the Zarazians* (1705) are generally applicable to nearly all the major eighteenth-century novelists, although taken by themselves her remarks are self-serving. She speaks of the contemporaneity of fiction, asserting that ancient accidents and unknown heroes create boredom; that names should be chosen to indicate characters; that "there are truths that are not always probable," although probability is essential to "true History." In matters of sex, time, accidents, common sense, Mrs. Manley argued for verisimilitude of content and style. " 'Tis not by extravagant expressions nor repeated praises that the reader's esteem is acquired to the character of the hero's. Their actions ought to plead for them; 'tis by that they are made known and describe themselves . . . 'tis impossible they should not have some imperfections, seeing they are men, but their imperfections ought not to destroy the character that is attributed to them."

These remarks are applicable to the entire range of the English novel. And although we may dismiss Mrs. Manley's fiction (such as *Secret Memoirs and Manners of Several Persons of Quality of Both Sexes, from the New Atalantis*, 1709) as gossipy and superficially scandalous, nevertheless her *obiter dicta* suggest a meaningful view of fiction. Her remarks are part of an avalanche of commentary and third-rate fiction that came at the end of the seventeenth and beginning of the eighteenth century; and in passing into our major writers, such early work becomes a significant part of the novel's development.

These brief considerations show the danger in any attempt to simplify matters concerning the emergence of the novel. Definitions of the form, parallel developments, antecedents, shaping of the genre, quality of the audience—these and other aspects are all significant in the early development of fiction. Even more important, however, is to learn what this new form, still a nebulous, unshaped body of material, meant to the eighteenth-century reader. Because the problems in studying any genre are so involved, but are particularly evident with one as ambiguous as the novel, we must seek clarification in a number of ways. Although the eighteenth-century novelists themselves believed that they had embarked on a new and daring literary venture, we must note how synthetic the novel form is. Yet, at the same time, even while tracing beginnings, we must recognize the distinctiveness of the new form; it may not have been a spontaneous creation, but it was something new. Many-sided and many-shaped, armed almost with Argus's hundred eyes, the novel took an adversary position to accepted values even as it accepted many of its adversary's ideas. In such ambiguity and paradox, we seek a genre.

Chartings

From its start, the English novel has represented an adversary culture. Although it seemed to bow to the tastes and needs of the new bourgeoisie, it also stood for new and often dangerous ideas, criticized the predominant culture, and displayed what were often subversive forms of behavior. It upset familiar assumptions, questioned realistic presuppositions, and tested out, however sparingly at times, new ideas, forbidden desires, secret wishes. As it plumbed the subconscious and countered rational analysis, it touched, as Lionel Trilling has shown us, various areas of neurosis and psychopathology within the reader. If only for these reasons, the novel, we can say, ran counterproductive to a productively minded society.

In the very assumptions we make about a given novel's "reality," or the type of realism it must encompass, we reveal our ambivalence about fiction. The expectations in our lives are usually based on assumptions that some stabilizing force will provide continuity from one day to the next. We may call this stabilizing force social justice, or reasonable success, or general freedom from agony, or any of the names we use to indicate an attitude that precludes suicide. We normally seek reasons for continuing with our life rather than reasons for destroying it. Our will to survive remains fairly constant; and we rebound from defeat with a hardihood that defies logic. Many of us actually feel that such stability will continue to be possible even when events appear contrary to our expectations.

The novel upsets virtually every one of these assumptions. First, it must not reflect reality too closely or it becomes indistinguishable from reporting. Second, it must not support our version of social justice too strongly, or else it justifies a process that has no need of fiction. Third, the novel, as a result of placing several kinds of data under scrutiny, may provide "results"—however defined—considerably different from our own view of these data. Fourth, social and personal morality are generally more flexible in fiction than in our own lives or in the lives we plan for our children. Frequently the novel involves considerably more forgiveness than we may feel, and it sanctions far more commission of error than we may deem safe. Fifth, fiction offers dangers and experiences from which readers have shielded themselves. After all, reading itself is a denial of the novel's world of new characters, diverse events, and outrageous accidents.

The novel, then, creates a division between the cultural context in which we live and the context within the novel we read. This is part of its adversary nature. Yet cannot we say the same of any art form? Opera, for example: we experience opera while enjoying a well-cushioned seat, after a filling dinner, on an evening out that will cost us a considerable sum, which we can usually afford. And from this bourgeois vantage point, we delight in acts of raging jealousy, bloody revenge, and Machiavellian deceit; we applaud murder, incest, regicide, passions of the most irrevocable kind. If we can make this kind of adjustment in opera, from our own realistic comforts to the violent action of the art form, why should we not be able to make a similar adjustment in the novel, instead of feeling divided, anguished, and alienated by what we read?

The answer must lie in the difference between the exotic, spectacular quality of opera and the seeming ordinariness of fiction, even of exotic fiction. When we view opera, we make immediate distinctions between *them* and *us.* And then the passionate voices, elaborate scenery, violent stage movements—the color, sound, pageantry—make us react at the level of spectacle. While our passions may be touched, our deeper emotions are not seriously assaulted. None of this denies that a great aria or a well-realized scene will change our sensibilities; of course it will. That sensibility which may change, however, is a part we can consciously separate from our day-to-day lives. Opera does not threaten us. Fiction does.

The novel differs from opera and from all other art forms in the nature of its language, as well as in its realistic characters and recognizable events, in the ordinariness of its assumptions about life. These qualities are constant even in the experimental novel, where events may be screened, character split, language reshaped. The novel draws more closely on those elements related to our routines than can any other art form. It is at our elbow. Its language is the language we speak and its scenes are the shards of our consciousness. Even in *Finnegans Wake*, we seek those aspects of the novel we can relate to our routine activities: our dreams, our nighttime reflections, our subconscious languages. Fiction at its most bizarre is still wound up with our fortunes in ways different from any other art form. It is intimately connected to our philosophy of how things work and can be explained. And therein lies the paradox of the novel. For even as it illuminates our routine realities, it must attack them; even while it reflects our dreams and hopes, it must undermine, even mock, them; and even when it describes people like us, it must counter them, often savagely and ruthlessly. From its start, the novel has succeeded best in provoking just such a dialectic.

Not coincidentally, the eighteenth-century novel developed parallel with the growth of the "common sense" school of British philosophy. The social and commercial movements that made the novel possible also affected philosophy. In fact, the establishment of the novel in the eighteenth century helped to fix a new way of thinking and seeing, utilizing different ideas and images, all working inexorably against the expressed culture of the day.

Harbinger of a counterforce, Thomas Reid, the Scottish philosopher, broke with both David Hume's skeptical empiricism and George Berkeley's idealism. Reid condemned their reliance on ideas, laying his faith and his philosophy on the altar of things, senses, nature. A refutation of Berkeley's idealism needs little explanation when we recall that the bishop asserted that ideas alone are the direct objects of the mind's consciousness, a doctrine hardly acceptable to the mid-century Englishman, whose interests were money, status, and tangibility. Reid's refutation of Hume, however, is more significant and deserves greater attention.

Following John Locke, Hume began as an empiricist, refusing any knowledge on trust, asserting that knowledge is founded on experience and observation. So far, Hume's interests would appear synonymous with those of the mid-century burgher anxious to cut himself off from Platonic ideas, medieval realism, and other philosophical abstractions that deny the validity of primary human experience. Hume went further, however, maintaining that nothing is to be learned from experience and observation, that all rational belief itself—what one sees and hears—is unreliable. In Hume's view, empiricism is invalid for being founded on man's reason, an inference Hume's own skepticism would question. In another way, Hume rejected the principle of induction, the cornerstone of a means of reasoning based on fact.[1] Induction is fixed within a system of cause and effect; it strives for certainties and allays doubts. To question the principle is to disturb the very bases of eighteenth-century rationalism.

Reid's work, especially *An Inquiry into the Human Mind on the Principles of Common Sense* (1764), refuted the theory that ideas can supplant particulars and that ideas replace everything but themselves. Arguing for the common man, Reid said that all men are equal in their abilities to sense the qualities of things and to relate this sensory knowledge to their selves. This sensory knowledge he called the common certainties of existence. There are things that we all know to be true and accept as true; how we know them is of less interest than the fact that we do. Reid asserts that the individual is a continuous and identifiable being in his own mind as long as he can remember; that he uses this knowledge of himself and of others to argue for the materiality of things, for the fact that fire is hot, snow cold, that some things are sweet, others bitter, that sound, touch, taste, sight, and smell are not hypotheses but facts.

Unlike Hume, Reid felt it was futile to question these facts. Rather, we should stress those things we assume in common: our sense of choice, our expectations of the future based on our experiences of the past, our reliance on the principle of induction in our daily lives. Reid stressed that philosophy should concern itself with the meaning of this knowledge, not with whether it exists. The common-sense school as a whole emphasized that the function of

[1] Induction allows us to generalize about particulars. We may assume that if two items are allied together, and no instance is known of when they have not been so allied, they probably will always be allied. Such conclusions are general principles derived from particular observations, a process indispensable to the scientific method.

language is to define how we should know certain things, not to question if we know them.

In this respect, Reid and his followers (Adam Ferguson and Dugald Stewart, among others) sensed the needs of those large numbers of people, then coming forcefully to the surface, who felt traditional philosophy was mumbo jumbo; who sought in the novel, not metaphysical or epistemological questions about being and knowledge, but affirmations of their own sensations, of their own feelings of choice, of their hopes for a future based on rational principles of cause and effect. In a real sense, this bourgeois audience, like Reid's more academic group, had thrown off medievalism, whether Plato's or Berkeley's. Ideas and philosophical idealism had become discredited, as had Hume's philosophy of skepticism. Common sense offered certainties.

The novel is solidly based on such assumptions. Yet it would appear that any art form so closely identified with elements of the "scientific mind" is sure to be caught in a series of paradoxes, forcing the novelist to tread a very thin line between common sense and the improbable. The chief paradox is, of course, that the novel had to satisfy the very people who distrusted fiction and preferred the more practical things of life.[2] Furthermore, it would appear that the novel

[2] Ian Watt (*The Rise of the Novel*) draws analogies between realism in philosophy and in the novel, stressing the sense of particularity in both. "The general temper of philosophical realism has been critical, anti-traditional and innovating; its method has been the study of the particulars of experience by the individual investigator, who, ideally at least, is free from the body of past assumptions and traditional beliefs; and it has given a peculiar importance to semantics, to the problem of the nature of the correspondence between words and reality. All of these features of philosophical realism have analogies to distinctive features of the novel form, analogies which draw attention to the characteristic kind of correspondence between life and literature which has obtained in prose fiction since the novels of Defoe and Richardson." (p. 12)

Watt cautions that such an analogy does not mean that philosophical realism led to fictional realism. The novel's realism is part of a much larger movement involving the end of the medieval world, a post-Renaissance view of man as individualized, containing seeds of anarchy and alienation. This larger view of how the novel became realistic belongs more to cultural social history than to literary criticism; even the analogy with philosophy is somewhat arbitrary. All this is cautionary for the student who seeks causes and effects in anything as ambiguous and vague as the constituting of a new art form.

In his excellent study of the novel, *The Rhetoric of Fiction*, Wayne C. Booth provides, in effect, a lengthy reply to Watt. Yet Booth sometimes distorts Watt's point as he refutes it. Not the least of these exaggerations is Booth's narrow definition of realism. Thus, Watt says that realism portrays "the individual life in its larger perspective as a historical process." Booth relates this as: "Properly speaking, the novel for him [Watt] begins only when Defoe and Richardson discover how to give to their characters

would be hobbled ideologically by its common-sense role; that no strain of adversariness or subversion was possible in a form that catered to a scientifically, industrially, commercially oriented audience. Yet the novelist was able to subvert the culture he appeared to support. He could attack the foundation of respectability, status-seeking, stability in his audience, while at the same time appearing (sincerely) to share his readership's fears. The novel clearly was socially oriented, a forum for criticism, an advocate for justice, even when it moved toward imaginative areas of particular representation that preclude unrestrained righteous indignation or outbursts of social defiance.[3]

The novel was helped immeasurably by the adoption, starting in the early 1700's, of a new type of secular mythology. If we employ Mircea Eliade's terms, the "sacred" and the "profane," we can say that common-sense philosophy joined with an acceptance of the "profane" that marked the end of "sacred" assumptions, although not the forms. Eliade speaks of religious man traveling back periodically to his beginnings, to live amid the glories of the divine presence. Yet such a desire for the return to paradise is, in bourgeois

---

sufficient particularity and autonomy to make them seem like real people." (p. 41) While Booth states that Watt equivocates about Fielding because of the latter's deficiencies in formal realism, Booth ignores the social orientation of Fielding implicit in Watt's definition of terms. The fact is that realism is a very fluid term, and in its broadest sense, it indicates the novel has an orientation different not only in degree but in kind from other forms of literature.

[3] Eighteenth-century ideas of nature suggest other paradoxes within the novel. For Holbach (in *Système de la Nature*, 1770), for example, nature is irreligious, part of the secular world. In fact, Basil Willey speaks of Holbach's view of nature as a "defiant Titaness who would dethrone the established gods and overturn all earthly altars and thrones, the symbols of priestcraft and tyranny." (*The Eighteenth Century Background*, p. 156)

Yet Holbach is more ambivalent than that. Like the novelists, he is caught in the paradoxes implicit in any position stretched between received ideas and the need to redefine a new order. For Holbach, nature is all, and yet man, who is part of nature, errs. If that is so, then is nature at fault? The answer must be no, since nature is holy, faultless. Clearly, if nature is causality, as Holbach asserts, then nature cannot be both perfect and the source of human error. Also, nature and reason are allied, are congruent; then, once again, how can we explain human error if reason is God?

The contradictions are of great interest, for Holbach's "system" is an attempt to bridge several ideas that the novelist of the eighteenth century was also forced to confront. These are the ideas we call "received"—from custom, tradition, history, those elements we consider causative—and those ideas that appear to exist only in our time and place and are individualized, new, indeed novel. The novelist had to assimilate elements from the status quo even while his literary existence depended on criticism of the status quo. Holbach's view of nature as causality is appropriate. He maligns divine purpose, admires natural law—and yet must admit that *both* derive from nature.

eyes, tantamount to an evasion of responsibility. Eliade warns that the bourgeois view is wrong when it assumes that the desire for the eternal return must be an escape; in truth, he says, the wish for the return to beginnings is "*a responsibility on the cosmic plane,* in contradistinction to the moral, social, or historical responsibilities that are alone regarded as valid in modern civilizations." (*The Sacred and the Profane*, 1961, p. 93)

It is the profane society with which the novel is concerned. Within the profane experience, man feels responsibility only to himself and to society, and less to society than to himself. For such a man, the universe is not a unity but an infinite number of pieces like himself. There is little connection between his life and the life of the cosmos; he lives within much less ambitious terms, and his allegiances are to the familiar things that surround him in his daily life. Robinson Crusoe and Tolstoy's Ivan Ilyich are prototypical examples: for these men, each event, each activity, each choice is not attached to events and actions in the divine world; every move is made, as it were, for the first time, *by him,* in that time and in that place, unconnected to the past. That man is our man in the novel, our familiar protagonist, and he is, already in the eighteenth century, more alone in his self than any previous figure in English literature except the Elizabethan tragic hero.

Such a profane man has lost his sources. He is not as cut off as Kafka's K., *but within the context of his society,* he is comparably out of step with himself and with what is expected of him. One way to view Tom Jones, that healthy-minded, pleasant young man, is to see him trying to find out precisely what is expected of him, to note his attempts to fit into that image, to discover him missing at each phase, until at the end he succeeds.

None of this is cataclysmic. Change in characterization and attitudes is made up of small steps, not of sensational leaps. Nevertheless, change was occurring, attitudes were opening, views were being altered. Not the least as a parallel and anticipatory development with the novel was the growth of Methodism. Just as the novel both reflected and prodded its audience, demonstrated its sense of community and yet mocked its deceits, so Methodism provided a mirror for men's souls, indicating the degree to which they were receptive or antagonistic to Jesus Christ. Although Methodism, we recall, itself began without deviating appreciably from the Church of England, nevertheless its basic tenets suggested a growing openness of manner toward religious orthodoxy, the same kind of latitude that, apparently, characterized literary endeavors leading to the novel.

We are, here, in a gray area, but all sociological evidence appears to point to an obvious fact: traditional society, whether embodied in the Anglican Church, the landed aristocracy, or, negatively, the disenfranchisement of many populous boroughs, was giving way to a potentially larger electorate, a broader distribution of wealth, and a freer atmosphere. This human response helped make the novel possible, for in a society dominated by the Tory strictures of a Swift, Johnson, or Pope, a relatively open and potentially subversive form would not have had the opportunity to develop along its own lines.

More important, Methodism threw matters of faith back upon the individual. While the creed honored the Trinity, the person of Jesus Christ, and the Atonement, and while it basically accepted the Apostle's and Nicene Creeds, it also honored justification by faith and the authority of the word of God in the Scriptures—two elements that can exist apart from formal churchgoing. With a ministry, often ignorant and itinerant, composed of those who had sought and found God, Methodism suggested a form of conduct that ranged from low to high rather than from the traditional high to low. Further, by removing the Calvinist taint of predestined evil in all men, John Wesley "freed" his followers from a historical, impersonal act that predetermined personal behavior. Without undermining the doctrine of original sin, Wesley did not make it irrevocable. Through justification and sanctification, one might reach the peak of perfection which God made immanent in all men, although man's perfection, in an imperfect world, could never attain to God's.

Despite the fervor and excesses of Evangelical Methodism, it implied a degree of doctrinal tolerance. In this respect, also, it reflected the openness that was beginning to characterize English society. A novel bridging two eras illustrates how religious forms can abet a new social phenomenon. In George Eliot's *Adam Bede*, set in 1799, only eight years after John Wesley's death, the chief movement in Methodism centers on Dinah Morris, an itinerant preacher. As a woman in a male-oriented society, she moves freely among social classes, more freely perhaps than she could possibly do in any other profession, except that of a prostitute. Thus, one social phenomenon intimately connected with the development of the novel—the growing voice of women—is also a by-product of Methodism and the latitudinarianism it advocated. In still another way, paralleling the fortunes of female characters, Evangelical Methodism became a precursor of the "sentimentalist" movement in English fiction, which surfaced after 1750. Even before that, however, we can see in Richardson certain anticipatory elements—fervor transformed into hysteria, fainting, fluttering hearts, waves of heat, and exorbitant dreams.

Further, Methodism came to emphasize certain elements that also characterize the novel: the commonplaces of life, the fact of universal redemption, the individual's salvation through faith, the need for good works as evidence of one's authentic faith, the taking in of God's will through revelation. If we examine Wesley's famous *Journal*, we see that a primary consideration is his middle-class fear of wasting time. While Wesley honors the religious life, his sense of time is as profane as that of the merchant anxious about bills falling due. His entries for October 21, 1735, when he left for Georgia, indicate an almost pathological fear of waste. From four in the morning until bedtime, eighteen hours later, his day is filled with constant activity; all thought is group thought, all time is enterprise. To work back from this to Crusoe's intense compulsion to seize the moment is to see a common impulse at work. Fixity of purpose, the fervent belief in doing God's work, the faith that God is watching and judging each individual, the continuing need to justify oneself—so much is common to Methodism and to eighteenth–nineteenth-century fiction. Such elements of belief throw the individual back upon himself. He will be saved or damned by his own efforts. Implicit here are the beginnings of that sense of bewilderment and loneliness—so much an aspect of the novel—which are the concomitant of individual choice in matters of faith.

We have suggested, so far, that the novel is capable of moving flexibly in and out of eighteenth-century expectations, catering at one time to the profane experiences of the middle-class public, at another paralleling its religious experiences, and at a third assaulting its bourgeois assumptions.[4] It may be useful, here, to list the elements of eighteenth-century literary realism, that series of attitudes and developments which the emerging novel reflects:

1. Individual cut off from his cosmic beginnings and from cosmic experience
2. Use of clock time, actual time, finite time

[4] For a more precise definition of that "bourgeois audience," see pages 31–6.

3. Man in his true physical setting, man who must be fed, clothed, and sheltered
4. Use of denotative language aimed at communicating qualities that all men share—sense of touch, color, temperature, etc.—without regard for *how* they come to feel these sensations
5. Development of faith centered in the individual, without need for formal religious experience
6. Quest for improved status, a class or classes which refuses any fixed, permanent connection to society or cosmos and demands retribution and justice
7. The slow but steady emergence of the woman from under the veil, the important role of the female novelist in shaping experience, in reflecting it
8. Conflict between bourgeois values (money, advancement, justice) and the traditional values of the gentleman (manner, fashion, noblesse oblige)
9. Development of a new type of "gentleman"—born yesterday, but with innate virtues
10. Emergence of money in its new role as status; money tied to sex, marriage, and romance
11. Development of norms of social justice which replace privilege, waning away of noblesse oblige, chain of being, hierarchies based on bloodlines and tradition
12. Ridicule of the parent, growing independence of the young, disruption of the traditional family
13. Movement toward interiors—houses, ballrooms, music rooms, bedrooms, studies, and closets, etc.—despite the continuing outdoor picaresque conventions
14. Movement of society from tradition-directed to inner-directed, of individual from value-oriented to self-oriented
15. Easing of strict notions of good and evil, of vice and virtue, forging of new rules of conduct

Many of these elements of realism can be found in the development and growth of eighteenth-century picaresque. In one way or another, Defoe, Fielding, Smollett, and Sterne—to name only the more illustrious—utilized the picaresque form and its conception of the rogue as protagonist, even as hero.

Picaresque began, in the anonymous Spanish book *Life of Lazarillo de Tormes* (1554), as a realistic portrayal of sixteenth-century Spanish frontier life. Lazarillo fights an intermittently piratical battle of self-survival. Anxious to enter a society that rejects him, he rebels only when predatory masters block his ambitions. As a matter of survival, physical and psychological, he moves on. There is no end to the road until he can himself become a master. Indeed, when the outcast or rogue becomes respectable and independent, the comedy is finished. By the end of the book, the protagonist of *Lazarillo* has a decent government job, has married a young lady who is probably the former as well as the present mistress of the archpriest, and accepts his role. His belly full, his sexual needs gratified, his home well tended, his status assured, and his ego satisfied, Lazarillo has achieved the good life. Allowing for differences of time, place, and style, he is not unlike Tom Jones at the end of Fielding's novel, or Smollett's young men on the make.

Running parallel in English to *Lazarillo* is Thomas Nashe's *The Unfortunate Traveller, or The Life of Jack Wilton*, published in 1594, only eight years after the first English translation of *Lazarillo*.[5] Nashe's picaresque differs considerably, however. His Jack Wilton exists almost solely as a voice, to whom an aggregate of adventures is joined. Jack himself, apart from his gruesome episodes, usually associated with Elizabethan drama, is insubstantial, a narrator rather than one who experiences. The success of Nashe's work is not that it leads into the mainstream of the picaresque, although its more harrowing details foreshadow Smollett. Rather, it is in the attempt of his prose narrative, however tentatively, to delineate a society in which life, death, rape, murder, execution, disembowelment, treachery, the eliminatory functions, and sexual intercourse are all routinely intermixed, a society in which individuals live at high passion without regard for the future or for life after death.

This sense of the "now" gives Nashe's narrative its novelistic dimensions, somewhat counter to the prevailing literary practices which, in 1594, reflected an intensely devout as well as intensely profane society. Thus, Shakespeare combined high and low life and Donne wrote both religious and erotic poetry; Nashe, however, was wholly profane. In a line such as "I was at *Pontius Pilates* house and

[5] Within forty years, several other Spanish picaresque fictions were translated into English, among them: *El Español Gerardo* of Gonzales de Cespedes y Meneses, translated in 1622 as *Gerardo the Unfortunate Spaniard*; and, more importantly, Mateo Alemán's *Guzmán de Alfarache*, translated in 1623 as *The Rogue*. Somewhat later, in 1657, appeared the English translation of Francisco de Quevedo's very stylish *La Vida del Buscón*, as *The Swindler*.

pist against it," he juxtaposes the high with the bodily functions, the mighty with the jocular, and so presents a society far lower than any in Shakespeare.

Nashe's secularity, which he maintained against those who would call upon God's grace, is a breakthrough in prose narrative. There is little coherence, though Jack serves one master rather than the variety attended by Lazarillo. The lack of cohesion results from the extensive traveling Jack does, from the historical figures he encounters seriatim, from the profusion of burlesques, parodies, and rhetorical inflations which Nashe employs.[6] Despite all this dispersion and loss of focus, Nashe reflects the intense secularity of his age as much as Defoe was to reflect his; and the Elizabethan's descriptions of the Roman plague curiously forerun Defoe's own *Journal of the Plague Year.*

For people who believed that life was met most satisfactorily with common sense—and the English novelists of the eighteenth century did—picaresque fiction was a realistic, sober description of man's problems and compromises, with an admixture of muted idealism. Under such conditions, when a man turned disadvantage to advantage, he was fulfilling his own needs and, indirectly, society's dictates. Add up his benefits, multiply them by the benefits desired by all men, and one has a utilitarian product which can make all men happy. Thus the picaro, while still somewhat suspect, becomes a middle-class hero.

Early picaresque—whether *Lazarillo*, Lesage's *Gil Blas*, or Cervantes's *Don Quixote*—contained a built-in social criticism indigenous to the novel. In *The Literature of Roguery*, still the best study of the genre, Frank Wadleigh Chandler speaks of the rogue novel as possessing "two poles of interest,—one, the rogue and his tricks; the other, the manners he pillories." Such fiction was an apt reflector of the tough life of the roads when cities were still an anomaly; and when, later, people began to use roads chiefly as ways of getting to the city, picaresque adapted to urban values. The dust and poverty of the country lane become the filth of a city street. In many instances, the city was to become simply a busier and more highly populated form of the country. Formerly, the picaro bounced off people and

[6] Margaret Schlauch, in *Antecedents of the English Novel 1400–1600*, illustrates the numerous rhetorical devices, the use of the high style, epithets, similes, paradox, climax, anaphora, apostrophe, et al., so that Renaissance usage is intermixed with novelistic realism.

situations as he went from village to village or from master to master; now, in the city, he was to be cheated by people he barely knew or manipulated by institutions and ideas he could not fathom.

By the eighteenth century, the measure of the picaro was his ability to survive in the still-young, frontierlike city. Not that the city was the sole locale of picaresque fiction—by no means—but the city had become the measure of most things. A citizen graded his standing in society by urban values *even when* protesting against the city. What went on there, directly or indirectly, mysteriously or openly, affected all in a society based on competition. Yet, despite commercial pressure, city life, like that on the road, was so impersonal that the citizen had to fall back on himself. The individuality of Defoe's Moll Flanders, a city version of Robinson Crusoe, is the result of this fact: survival meant fending for herself.

In the city, everything was possible and everyone was predatory. In one of those curious transformations from one culture to another, the Spanish and English picaro became the American frontiersman. The transition was surprisingly easy to make. The rejection of official masters, virtually of institutions, was a pragmatic and decisive repudiation of society as such and the creation of the individual as a supreme being, wherever such a belief in oneself may lead. God himself had passed, mythically, into the frontier picaro.

The picaro is the ultimate competitor, because his very life often depends on his success. Like Crusoe, he must create an empire on his island, overcoming the elements as well as his own desire to capitulate. Huck Finn, the American Crusoe, uses the river as Crusoe uses his island: to ensure self-survival. Failure means loss of life to Crusoe, loss of freedom to Huck—similar things depending on different needs. For the picaro, all situations call for struggle; he can hardly relax. He must move on, feel out the terrain, look ahead for a new frontier, look behind for his enemies, look within for treachery, and compete anew. To the end, his spirit is undiminished, his energy unflagging. Eventually, only his arteries give way.

The picaro ideally depends on no one. He hopes, in fact, to make the system—usually vague, distant, and hostile—bend to himself. He may or may not be rebellious. While he is subversive, he is never directly politically oriented. To get what others seem to have (he can never be sure precisely what it is, because he has never had anything), he tries, although different, to adopt ways that have worked for them. Put another way: he attempts all methods he deems necessary in order to obtain the goods of this world, and he pursues his means wherever they take him, regardless of the consequences.

In this respect, the picaresque protagonist is always on the frontier. Obviously so, since he does not know exactly what the norm is, and he must fumble around on the perimeter making forays toward an ideal center. The center, of course, never holds still. Always in motion, like the hero, it remains out of reach. Each step, then, by the protagonist creates a new set of conditions. To ponder is unthinkable; he must act, move on, resolve nothing. He can rarely be certain where he is. The past, history itself, becomes expendable. History is worked out in society at large; he must survive as an individual. The question often is: Is he anywhere? If so, in what relationship, if any, with others and other things? What good, eventually, will it do him, whatever he does? His situation in some ways is absurd, without having the finality even of absurdity. He lacks an existential tone.

The picaresque hero—to establish his ambiguous heroism—must often resort to violence. Violence, in fact, becomes his sole resort in areas where talk and persuasion do not exist. Physical force is expected, and the youth who cannot respond endangers his life. The picaro seeks space wherever it may be. As he moves on horizontally, he hopes ultimately to move up. As assimilation eludes him, his horizontal energy is often directed toward a vertical goal. In the process, he fills space. Everything will be sacrificed to the inner need to move on.

The eighteenth-century picaro is alone. Even when he travels with a companion, the two diverge in interests and goals, like the prototypical Don and Sancho. Yet, at the same time, the picaro and his companion share a common anxiety: that the world has no place for them, that it rejects their view of reality. In either instance, they are thrown back on space and solitude.

The picaro treads a very thin line. For while he must pierce the façade of society's hypocrisy, at the same time he tries to become part of what he criticizes. He must not destroy completely what he desires to join; and the path he follows is not unlike that of the novelist himself, who must reflect reality without becoming too realistic. In a certain way, the early novelist is himself a kind of picaro, moving out onto new ground, trying out space, denying history.

Picaresque does not lend itself easily to love, and male-female relationships remain, on the whole, primitive. Since the picaro is involved in a rugged struggle to survive, he has little time for niceties; unlike Jane Austen's protagonists, he never gets close to a drawing room, rarely closer than the kitchen. He beds down in a barn and rolls in the hay with the local belle. It is an intensely male world, this world of the picaro, although woman is needed and is honored for her sexual and homemaking abilities. Paradoxically, the picaro allows more democracy to women than we find in more genteel fictions, where women are exalted so that men may be chivalrous. Since picaresque involves, almost, a warring society, women take on strong roles, as pioneer women always have; and while they remain somewhat mysterious and hooded beings, they do manifest human needs and desires. They are, however, allowed little consciousness.

Men dominate, without question. Courtship, engagements, and such are eliminated. The picaro often has a vision or ideal of womanhood, but in practice he takes whatever flesh is available. On the run, he pinches, unbuttons, and beds down. Women are, chiefly, bodies, yet it is all very good-humored. Neither male nor female is victimized by sex until Richardson. Woman is not yet Eve—once in the drawing room, she becomes Eve—she is still unencumbered flesh. Among serious novelists, Fielding caught the note that sex is fun for both men and women. Such a view of sex in the picaresque ranges outside of religion and church. We note no Calvinism here, no guilt, no victims, no damnation. This is a society secularized, desacramentalized, the ultimate in Eliade's view of the profane: "a radical secularization of death, marriage, and birth . . ." (p. 160)[7]

We cannot overestimate the importance for the eighteenth-century novel of the development of picaresque. That often unsubtle, rudimentary prose narrative provided a welter of detail of daily, ordinary life. As a social phenomenon, the picaro recognized that his brand of practical agnosticism is preferable to the moral anarchy that passes for order in the bourgeois world. As a political phenomenon, the picaro adjusted to society, for his personal anarchy and individualized democracy would threaten the state. And as a literary phenomenon, the picaro helped to identify appearances,

[7] Eliade goes on to say, however, that even within this secularization "there remain vague memories of abolished religious practices and even a nostalgia for them." We recall that elements of ritual remain in the picaresque, one of the most common being the rite of passage, or initiation, which tests the protagonist's ability to survive.

provide labels, and stress particulars, all of which mark the modern movement, as opposed to the emphasis on universals and generalizations which remained from classical and medieval practice. In this respect, as in so many others, then, the novel appeared to run counter to the established belle-lettristic practices and theories of the eighteenth century.

At this stage, we may indeed ask how the individualized realism of the novel fitted into a more generalized eighteenth-century aesthetic. How, in brief, did lowbred particulars fare in more elegant discourse about universals? For representatives of the established neoclassical order, I have selected Samuel Johnson, Edmund Burke, and Sir Joshua Reynolds. Yet even as we discuss their arguments, we may be surprised to see how the novel bored its way into the interstices of their aesthetics, although, admittedly, it entered as an alien and a provocateur.[8]

In some ways, the development of the novel ran parallel to aspects of a neoclassic aesthetic, while in others it produced a counterforce, although lacking a formalized aesthetic of its own. In this respect, the development of the novel demonstrated its peculiar dialectic, penetrating the fabric of the larger culture and at the same time creating adversary problems which that culture could not always contain.

We know the familiar ideas: that reason was the neoclassical way of probing the ideal or the universal and that reason could be supported only by rules which provided a clearly understood methodology. Thus, any innovations were themselves incorporated into the rules; or put another way, the rules were flexible enough to embrace innovation. The important point, however, was that a method was always based on rational processes, so that imagination

[8] Watt (*The Rise of the Novel*, pp. 15 ff.) provides a good summary of the eighteenth-century controversy over universals, citing, among others, Shaftesbury, Lord Kames, Sir Joshua Reynolds, and Mrs. Barbauld (Richardson's first biographer and editor of his letters). As the century developed, Lord Kames's argument, which emphasized particulars and directed attention away from universals, began to prevail. In more recent times, Mario Praz has raked over some of this concern with novelistic detail. In his *The Hero in Eclipse in Victorian Fiction*, Praz compares Victorian fiction (particularly Thackeray's work) to Dutch genre painting, in which a "picture" is preferable to a dramatic scene. Such stress on detail at the expense of imagination links Praz's comments to those of Reynolds. Praz, however, goes even further and asserts that fear of generalization makes the novelist a middle-class preacher devoted to pathos and a diluted Christian morality. Thus, particularity is debilitating, turning potential strength into mere common sense.

and vision were contained. This stress on method, at the expense of freer play, was part of the continuing reliance on the great chain of being, in which each individual and each species is part of a fixed order, predetermined by what it is.

This assumption both underlies a good deal of novel practice and is inimical to it. The great chain theory undeniably was a source of stability; at least theoretically, it outlawed the temptations of anarchy. It denied revolution in favor of status quo, another large concern in neoclassical theory. Later, we will see even such a "progressive" writer as William Godwin struggling in this web: of man, trapped by necessity and causation, who must yet change and change the society with him. Earlier, the picaresque novelists actively sought such stability, for their aims, inevitably, were to procure for their protagonists a quiet, convenient niche. Thus, the novel was sympathetic to the chain, for the latter was a socially based as well as political and religious conception.

Yet, at the same time, the novel could not hold completely to the chain hierarchy, for such a hierarchy has certain Calvinistic assumptions underlying it. After all, it assumes that man needs a predetermined role, without which he will revert to bestiality and chaos. The chain of being was indeed a chain predisposed to prisoners. Make man a link, convince him he is trapped by necessity, and he is, like Dostoevsky's Inquisitor, willing to accept his bonds. The novel, however, argued otherwise. It contended, especially in Fielding—its chief theoretician—that the individual, despite immoderation and occasional lapses, was essentially good. Fielding came very close to Rousseau's educational theories, although, in his resolution, he embraced the rational process. Nevertheless, Fielding certainly did not agree with the neoclassic stress upon reason. The chief point of *Tom Jones* is not to emphasize that a young man has gone astray through lack of reason but to show that a young man whose guiding force is *not* reason may be charming and capable and, finally, grow to maturity. It is surely not reason that makes Tom preferable to Blifil, who is the personification of perverted rationality; it is Tom's impetuosity and intemperance, his hell-bent desire for immediate gratification, that make him one of God's children. In this respect, a passionate nature ensures his innocence—and Samuel Johnson's condemnation.

Yet Johnson's distaste for Fielding does not indicate the full range of the doctor's aesthetic stance. Actually, in the conflict between realism and romance, particulars and universals, Johnson assumed a straddling position. While he usually aligned himself with neoclassical assumptions about the ideal and the universal, and more or less opposed the empirical drift of British philosophy, he was less vociferous about inflexible rules than we usually acknowledge. Johnson's various dicta are consistent if we see him as focusing more on probability, as against the marvelous, than upon rules. As Walter Jackson Bate illustrates (in *From Classic to Romantic: Premises of Taste in Eighteenth-Century England*), Johnson's attack upon the metaphysical poets was directed to their improbability, their movement toward exceptions and particulars, whereas "great thoughts are always general." We recall this well-known passage:

> What they [metaphysical poets] wanted however of the sublime they endeavoured to supply by hyperbole; their amplification had no limits; they left not only reason but fancy behind them; and produced combinations of confused magnificence, that not only could not be credited, but could not be imagined. [*Lives of the English Poets*, V. I, 12]

Accordingly, Johnson's seeming reliance on rules was aimed at promoting a certain decorum of plot and thought or certain consistencies of language and metaphor, not at imposing classical standards. In this way, Johnson's thought was moving inexorably closer to an acceptance of the novel form. His championing of Richardson is well known, while his attack upon Fielding may be construed as a condemnation of the latter's so-called loose morality and other excesses, rather than his lack of realism or inability to present the probabilities of experience.

We have entered a crucial area, this area of Johnson's own dilemma, for most novelists tended to continue along Fielding's line, making innocence and passion (within bounds) of equal importance. Richardson, of course, presents the conflict differently, but even *he* is more sympathetic to Lovelace than he is to Solmes, and he presents Clarissa's dilemma vis-à-vis Lovelace more favorably than her movement toward a hated marriage. The novel, in short, found disorder as compelling as order and denied Aristotle's decorum, with its stress on the ennoblement of the type and its basis in reason. Decorum, as Bate demonstrates, was never far from the neoclassical ideal, and decorum appears inimical to the development of fiction. With the latter's emphasis upon detail, its support of the goodness of human nature, its attack upon institutions, its vacillating defense of society, its stress upon individual choice, its democratic assumptions, its disregard for politics, its rejection of all hierarchies except those forged by contemporary man, its suggestion that anarchy and passion, not reason, intellect, or breeding, underlie human needs—with these motivations and stratagems, fiction was, clearly, the enemy, even while it beguiled with soft scenes of seeming compliance.

In a related area of values and tastes, we should cite Edmund Burke's *A Philosophical Enquiry into the Origin of Our Ideas of the Sublime and the Beautiful*, which derived from the same intellectual milieu as our mid-century novelists, Fielding, Richardson, and Smollett. Although Burke's analysis of sensations and passion in relationship to the sublime and the beautiful is not precisely empirical, nevertheless his examination moves toward realism. Rejecting preconceived ideas basic to the neoclassic mode, he insisted on an individual testing of effects. Less interested in traditional arguments of what the effect *should* be, Burke examined how the object discerned *actually* affects us. While impressionism dominates, there are also observation and direct experience, akin to an empirical method.

Burke's analysis of individual reactions based on emotions and sensations, with its corollary that terror is the foundation of the sublime, finds its parallel in several late-eighteenth-century developments, not the least of which is Gothic. At the same time, paradoxically, this reliance on emotion finds a complementary argument in the development of philosophical common sense, although we normally find feeling and common sense contradictory. Both Gothic (emotion) and the common-sense school (realism), however, were allied in a reciprocal attempt to break away from neoclassic precept; and it is here that Burke's *Enquiry* flirted with the relatively new position.[9]

One of the key passages in the *Enquiry* comes fairly early, in the conclusion to Part I. Here Burke is summing up the argument that

[9] Samuel H. Monk, in *The Sublime: A Study of Critical Theories in XVIII-Century England*, notes that Burke's *Enquiry* came at a crucial time, when there had been numerous attempts to question neoclassic theory. Monk mentions several other books which, at about the same time, were attempting "to explain the age to itself," among them Hogarth's *Analysis of Beauty* (1753) and Edward Young's *Conjectures on Original Composition* (1759). The student looking here for interaction between theory and practice should be aware that theory *followed* literary practice as an attempt to explain the mid-century rise of emotional art.

the sublime creates a far greater emotion than the beautiful and that this emotion is based on pain. In this manner, pain produces an aesthetic pleasure that is more physiological and psychological than philosophical. The traditional arguments of Longinus, Boileau, and others fall away. In the conclusion, Burke juggles both the neoclassic ideal and his own appeal, saying: "The elevation of the mind ought to be the principal end of all our studies, which if they do not in some measure effect, they are of very little service to us. But, besides this great purpose a consideration of the rationale of our passions seems to me very necessary for all who would affect them upon solid and sure principle." Burke balances "elevation," with its connection to the Creator, with "passions," very much an individually conceived notion.

Continuing, he says that the "true standard of the arts is in every man's power; and an easy observation of the most common, sometimes of the meanest things in nature, will give the truest lights, where the greatest sagacity and industry that slights such observation, must leave us in the dark . . ." Not only must the observer move beyond surfaces, but he must perform this act alone, clarifying both for himself and for others. Samuel H. Monk comments aptly on the radical literary potential of Burke's remarks:

> Theories and tastes which, during the Augustan Age, were well controlled and only latent, however much they may have worked to modify the opinions of individual writers, began in the fifth decade of the century to find positive and well-organized expression, and during the following decades they assumed a vitality that contrasts vividly with the moribund and decadent cult of neo-classical standards. If the first generation of romantics gave the *coup de grâce* to the outworn aesthetic and criticism of their literary ancestors, they were merely wielding weapons forged for them during the last half of the century. [p. 101]

As a new and changing genre, the novel stood to benefit from an atmosphere in which traditional modes were under attack. Rudimentary novel criticism cited above indicates how tentative were the early practitioners of the novel; and even Fielding's learned defense of the new in his introductory remarks in *Tom Jones* was more an act of bravura than one of certainty. In this respect, Burke's *Enquiry* and others like it helped survey the ground. Edward Young's plea for individual genius, for example, in his *Conjectures* and his concomitant attack upon imitation parallel Sterne's *Tristram Shandy*, itself a defense of eccentric genius. Young argues that rules can never produce sublimity in art, that freedom and originality are necessary for the highest art (as in Shakespeare), and that learning, while the source of pleasure, is insufficient for genius. Such remarks link up with Burke's assertion at the very end of the *Enquiry* that "poetry, taken in its most general sense, cannot with strict propriety be called an art of imitation." [10]

Sir Joshua Reynolds's *Discourses on Art* (from 1769 to 1790) indicate, however, how hardy traditional doctrines of universals and generalities continued to be. If anything, Reynolds's discourses toward the end of the century are more insistent on genius and imagination—that is, on generalizing—than those delivered in the 1770's. Surely, Lord Kames's *Elements of Criticism* was a prod to Reynolds's reassertion of his countering point with increasing insistence. In Discourse 11 (1782), for example, Reynolds says that genius consists in creating a general effect and the power of the whole, which can then take possession of the viewer's mind "and for a while suspend the consideration of the subordinate and particular beauties or defects." He cautions that while the painter, or any artist, must express particulars, it is also certain "that a nice discrimination of minute circumstances, and a punctilious delineation of them . . . never did confer on the Artist the character of Genius."

Reynolds's emphasis on imagination, on ideal beauty and ideal form, on Italian Renaissance painting (excluding the "decorative" Venetian school)—all of these are, evidently, variations on his theme of universals. While not eliminating the need for rules—those

[10] Ronald Paulson (in *Satire and the Novel in Eighteenth-Century England*) asserts a similar point but in different terms, arguing that the novel and satire are antithetical: "The novel, as the name implies, represents new values, and satire, usually a conservative genre, represents old. By the middle of the century the climate of opinion in England was Lockean, latitudinarian, Shaftesburyian, benevolist, even deist, reacting against exclusive and extreme systems like Puritanism and High Church Anglicanism." (p. 3) With these developments considered, Paulson charts the decline of satire, which has no role in a middle class interested in "real people in real-life situations." Such a bourgeoisie believes that man is basically good, an assumption at war with the satirist's opposite premises. This assumption, Paulson continues, demands that the individual grow and change. At the same time, Lockean empiricism struck at the abstract qualities of satire, at its reliance on general qualities like truth, hypocrisy, vice, virtue.

Paulson's argument appears to good advantage in the eighteenth century, when the novel was still somewhat rudimentary, but in a novelist like Jane Austen, satire is revisited as irony. Rather than working against the nature of fiction, satire in these terms becomes a strong element, indistinguishable from the novel—indeed, complementary to it.

particulars of line and method—Reynolds sees the real principles of art as having their basis in mind, not in rules (see especially Discourses 8 [1778] and 12 [1784]).

The persistence of universals was not restricted to painters like Reynolds. As a consequence, the novel, whatever its own particular moral assumptions, by its very conception of material was pitted against an ongoing antagonistic mode of thought. For the novel had to absorb the very particulars (warts, pimples, and lesions, waistcoats, boots, furniture, woods, and metals) that Reynolds found debilitating in art. It had, in its beginnings, no opportunity to move toward universal moral truths; for its morality had to depend on a composite of those details which were far from ideal.

There was little Platonic truth in the daughter of an innkeeper. Only Cervantes could make a peasant girl into a knight-errant's inamorata, and even the Don recognizes he has "created" his Dulcinea from base material, a medieval alchemist in his visionary power. Ideals and perfect forms disappear as the sacred did. *Don Quixote* is not only a farewell to knight-errantry and its medieval suppositions but also a farewell to the sacred in man. Part I assumes that illusions must be exposed; Part II, however, retreats from unmantling man's true self, draws back from a confrontation with reality, and sees in illusions a mythological-sacred view binding man to creation and the creator. When the eighteenth-century novelists adapted Cervantes's novel to their own needs, they eliminated the ideal forms that once provided a banquet and turned to breasts and buttocks as matter for their feast. It was among such base particulars that the battle of the novel was fought.

Time, Romance, the Audience

Nothing better illustrates the novel's retreat from the sacred than the use of time in eighteenth-century fiction. As we know from numerous studies, a given society's view of time is an index to many of its attitudes and assumptions. The Renaissance sense of time conveyed in Shakespeare's plays helps create what G. Wilson Knight calls Shakespeare's metaphysics. It would, for example, be impossible to read *King Lear* against a clock-and-calendar time sequence. Time there is, in effect, timeless, attached to season, moon, animal life, part of the sweep of the universe, close to magic and myth at the cosmogony. Time in the eighteenth-century novel is almost diametrically the opposite.

Time is, of course, connected to space, and as we see the secularization of spatial concepts away from the cosmogony toward bedroom and kitchen, so we note a similar pattern developing in our notions of time. When time was timeless, it persisted as part of a larger attitude, cosmic, universal, elemental. Eliade says that religious man lived in a temporal dualism: that sacred time which could be homologized to eternity, and the historical present, the time of daily activities. Thus, the seasonal changes were both sacred and secular, in one sense remaining part of that fixed world unchanged since the creation, in another producing certain crops according to variations of condition and climate.

Such temporal considerations are crucial for the eighteenth-century novel. In the chapter on Fielding, I will discuss how some of his introductory prefaces in *Tom Jones* deal with the question of time, while they are also an intermediary's remarks in the battle of the ancients and the moderns. In *Time and the Novel*, A. A. Mendilow points out that the eighteenth-century novel contains all the main types of representative time techniques. He demonstrates that in the fifty years between *Robinson Crusoe* and *Tristram Shandy*, we have the "unities of time, place, and action, strict sequence, selective causality, and associationist irregularity, intercalated, preliminary, and distributed exposition, continuity and selection, immediacy and the time-shift"—the entire paraphernalia of a conscious time technique. Even the mid-century stress on the epistolary form is an emphasis upon a time technique; an experiment, particularly in *Clarissa*, with the immediacy and contemporaneity of past time. In most studies of the technique, the epistolary form is viewed almost exclusively as a narrative—not a temporal—device, but it surely served a temporal purpose, too.

The concern of eighteenth-century novelists with time, Dr. Mendilow comments, is indicated in their critical prefaces and essays, in digressions in the body of the novels, in letters of intention, and in dedications. Sterne is the most obvious example of a novelist experimenting with time, and Sterne's forays are clearly a conscious movement toward a more complex kind of human reality through the breakup of normal time. Sterne, however, was by no means the first to recognize that a secular age required a secular sense of time.

One may argue cogently that Richardson's concern with time, whether conscious or not, is as indicative of a secularized age as Sterne's. It is possible to show that Richardson's shifting of time and narrators between past and present, foreground and background, near-present and past is an approximation of still more sophisticated versions yet to come in Bergson and Proust. If Bergson conceived of the world as a flux of interpenetrable elements unseizable, as it were, by the intellect, so did Richardson, in a somewhat cruder way, see all events as "one concentrated *now.*"

These novels are early attempts not only to rethink temporal elements in literature but to define an aesthetic for the new form that would later be called the novel. Experiments with time are part of a larger reshaping that would distinguish between romance and novel, between fable, legend, epic, history and the novel. Later in this introduction, I will describe more fully the history and development of longer fiction. It will suffice here to provide some elementary distinctions between romance (as well as epic and history) and novel.

Although Fielding is the most consistent theoretician of the genre, there is a rudimentary aesthetic for the novel that begins in the mid-seventeenth century and extends forward to Defoe, his contemporaries, and their successors. When we note as early as Defoe's preface to *Moll Flanders* (1722) that readers "will be more pleased with the moral than the fable, with the application than with the relation, and with the end of the writer than with the life of the person written of"—when we read these remarks, we can be certain there is already considerable background for Defoe's comments. Further, we see that Defoe's remarks are all broadly strategic, to fit his "novel" into something closer to sermon as a means of disguising his fiction.

Earlier in his preface, Defoe tried to make it clear that Moll's tale is true: ". . . particularly she is made to tell her own tale in modester words than she told it at first, the copy which came first to hand having been written in language more like one still in Newgate than one grown penitent and humble, as she afterwards pretends to be." This is a ploy to disguise the "debauchery and vice" of the tale by presenting it as an act of repentance, and to allay the reading public's fear that it was wasting its time on fiction by making it appear to be fact. In this instance, Defoe is blurring the line between matters for journalism and matters for fiction, a practice common to nearly all his novels. Even journalism, however, had to be toned down and presented as sermon, as something attractive to readers whose religion was close to that of Bunyan's Christian.

Still another motive behind Defoe's practice was his desire to furnish an alternative to the romance by means of a "fiction" based on verisimilitude. The romance was not, of course, muffled, and the conflict between romance and realism was not ended by Defoe. But the English novel as we know it takes its beginnings from the realistic mode, not from the romantic; and Defoe's insistence on verisimilitude helped create the audience for realism.

None of this means Defoe pioneered. Like the invention of the automobile, that of the novel belongs to many hands. On matters of realism and romance, Cervantes is surely our archetypal novelist, although what he wrote is, perhaps, not a novel but an intermediate form. Through the Don, Cervantes asks which is more real, the world of practicality and certainty or the conceptual world of fantasy and art. Cervantes returns us to the medieval mind, which viewed everything as symbol and emblem. Since, to him, the earthly object derives from the heavenly ideal, man's mind must move beyond the physical (common sense) to the spiritual. The Don, indeed, sees real things, but chooses to ignore them in favor of his conception of them.

The Don re-creates the world in his own image, making his adventures into poetic metaphors that upon analysis seem untruthful, even mad. The Don illustrates that he is concerned with more than social justice, although to seek justice is certainly part of his quest. His true vocation is to create a way of seeing, just as every novelist must transform reality into something both more and less than the original object. In his quest for this different kind of reality, the Don convinces nearly everyone, including the reader, that his vision is preferable to what he encounters and that individual interpretations are indistinguishable from the real. Early novel aesthetics (well before Defoe) was engaged with similar matters, especially in its concern with history and fiction, verisimilitude and romance, about which Congreve, in the preface to *Incognita* (1692), says that "Romances give wonder, Novels delight."

Like a poet, a revolutionary, a "sane madman," the Don forces a re-evaluation of one's assumptions, for his image-making mind is constantly re-forming events. Even if we claim that his vision is mad, his motives are good; while those around him, neither all good nor all bad, have the voice of the real, semicorrupt world. Under his tutelage, we recall, Sancho progresses from a pleasant but greedy hanger-on to a just and shrewd governor.

Yet Cervantes knew that the Don and his metaphors must not prevail, that reality (common sense) must triumph. The norm for Cervantes, as for most eighteenth-century novelists, is a God-driven universe in which man must make a final choice between illusion and reality, as the Don himself does. And when man makes his choice, he sorrowfully rejects poetry and imagination, or any form of ultimate beauty, and then dies.

What Cervantes asserts about the Don becomes a paradigm for the novel itself, what virtually every theoretician affirms in prefaces, letters, and forewords. No matter what metaphors the writer establishes—whether those of Earwicker's surrealistic dreams in *Finnegans Wake* or Robinson Crusoe's more tepid premonitions on his island—the ultimate effect heightens reality *without* rejecting it. In *Don Quixote*, the scene in the cave of Montesinos (Part II, chapter XXIII) is so significant because there the Don has to maintain his role as artist (novelist) at the same time that he is aware of the illusory nature of his experience below ground. As he later tells Sancho, he will protect the latter's illusions if Sancho will protect his. So the novelist temporarily makes a pact with the reader, who must suspend both his belief and disbelief, and allow himself to be transported into a world he knows logically is untrue.

As I mentioned above, Cervantes's modulation of his materials between illusory and realistic was not an isolated instance. In many comments which postdate *Don Quixote* but predate Defoe, we discover attempts to make distinctions among romance, fiction, and history. Frequently, the "truth" of history is played off against the fiction of "romance," although to little avail and without resolution. The important point, however, is that some movement toward a realistic mode is apparent. *This is not to say the novel had to be realistic,* but it had to be differentiated from existing modes, whatever shape the differentiation finally was to take, before a distinct form could exist. We can see in the short remarks of Roger Boyle (preface to *Parthenissa*, 1655), William Congreve (preface to the Reader of *Incognita*, 1692) and Mrs. Mary Delarivière Manley (remarks to the reader of *Queen Zarah*, 1705) how tortuous, uncertain, and wavering was the path to the eighteenth-century novel.

While not defining the novel, Boyle was careful to distinguish truth from fiction and to indicate that the kind of history he wrote was romance, not a factual narrative. Congreve touches upon the same point, but with more application to eighteenth-century realism, surely because his preface is so much closer to the period when the realistic mode came to prevail. "Novels," he writes, "are of a more familiar nature, come near us and represent to us intrigues in practice, delight us with accidents and odd events, but not such as are wholly unusual or unpresidented, such which not being so distant from our belief bring also the pleasure nearer us." Congreve then speaks of all literary traditions giving precedence to the drama, and toward that end he decided to imitate dramatic writing in his fiction, "namely, in the design, contexture, and result of the plot."

These remarks move us closer to practices we find in Defoe; and in Mrs. Manley's discussion of fiction, we note a clear foreshadowing of Defoe's journalistic method. As we remarked above, Mrs. Manley (1663?–1724) distinguished between those events which are probable and those improbable, recognizing throughout that certain truths are themselves improbable and therefore unsuitable for fiction. "He that writes a true History ought to place the accidents as they naturally happen" without sweetening them; but "he that composes a History to his fancy . . . places the accidents as he thinks fit . . ."

Her argument is evidently toward verisimilitude. She writes later that "the heroes in the ancient Romances have nothing in them that is natural . . . in short, they are not men." She believes that the heroes of modern romances are more ably characterized, with "passions, virtues or vices, which resemble humanity." She goes on to evaluate time and place, both in the natural progression of the narrative and in accidents that create suspense, asserting that the writer must achieve verisimilitude to gain the reader's esteem for the hero. She closes with a warning that "Moral reflections, maxims, and sentences are more proper in discourses for instructions [sermons] than in Historical Novels, whose chief end is to please." She understands that such moralizing must proceed from descriptive matter rather than from stated precept, an extremely sophisticated argument for someone writing only a quarter century after *Pilgrim's Progress.*

Any discussion of emerging romantic-realistic characteristics of the novel must take into account the related question of audience for the new form. There is, of course, no precise equation between an audience and the development of a literary form. There is little question that literacy among the middle class was a factor in the growing popularity of the novel, but there is a tendency to overestimate the numbers. The evidence is sketchy or misleading. For example, in 1779, Samuel Johnson—whose opinions are often to be relished rather than believed—asserted in the course of his remarks on Milton that "every house was supplied with a closet of knowledge," and that the nation was pervaded by literature, a comment that would appear to indicate almost universal literacy. More likely, however, Johnson's remark meant literacy only among the urban middle class, ignoring the illiterate millions of the agricultural and laboring classes. As we know from dozens of sources, wages were simply too mean and schooling too uncertain for any rapid development of a large reading public among the working classes. Richard Altick cites other commentators who exaggerated the literacy figures, out of either patriotism or miscalculation.

A brief review of annual incomes of working-class families in relation to the price of books will dissipate such overestimates of literacy.[11] Taking mid-century as the focal point, we can estimate that clerks earned one pound per week. That would work out to between twenty and twenty-five dollars in present-day purchasing power, and, by 1750, not a mean wage even for London. In the country, wages were lower; for craftsmen they might be half of that, about ten shillings. A rural school usher (an assistant teacher or a subordinate), Altick points out, might have earned four to eight shillings a week, plus board; and shopmen, once out of their apprenticeship, somewhat within the same range. These were relatively well-off groups for they involved teachers, craftsmen, and clerks—those who had achieved some degree of expertise in functions the society needed.

For perhaps half the population—servants, agricultural workers, general laborers, cotters or cottagers, those on charity—the weekly income may have been under three shillings per week, that is, under sixty cents, with a buying power of about three dollars. Such people, by the way, often found their position worsening later in the century, much as pensioners at present find their relatively fixed wages buying less in an inflationary spiral. Thus, half or more of the

[11] Sources for this particular information as well as for a general sense of the wage-cost situation are: Richard D. Altick, *The English Common Reader*; E. J. Hobsbawm, *Labouring Men: Studies in the History of Labour*; J. L. and Barbara Hammond, *The Town Labourer*; Ian Watt, *The Rise of the Novel.*

population were virtually impoverished, with their condition worsening. The middle-class shopkeeper, larger farmer, and administrator, those part of upward mobility, were the beneficiaries of the changes taking place. For half or more, however, mobility did not exist, and would not exist; their roles were defined for the next century.

The price of books was prohibitive for both groups, those who were to remain impoverished and those who were beginning to rise in the wage scale. Depending on size, whether folio, quarto, octavo, or small octavo, books ran from ten shillings down to two or three shillings, in most instances a week's wages for a single book. Even wrapped sheets could run to half a week's wages, or the price of several weeks' supply of staples. Similarly, a worker would have to sacrifice candles and other necessities for a month or more for a single volume of Pope or Addison and Steele. And toward the end of the century, book prices sometimes doubled, for publishers found it more profitable to issue their volumes in small editions at inflated prices, thus taking advantage of those who could afford higher prices and by-passing altogether those for whom books were a luxury.

With these figures in mind, we can see how idle it is to speak of large reading audiences.[12] We have cited wage-cost only for those who were fairly affluent in mid-eighteenth-century terms. For rural workers and farm laborers, books would have been unknown, even if literacy were widespread. And, as noted above, conditions were not improving for them. When Coleridge later countered Wordsworth's euphoria about the use of rustic diction in poetry, he noted that large areas of rural life were inimicable not only to poetry but to literacy as well.

We can, accordingly, speak only of those already urbanized as potential readers, and costs, clearly, put books outside their reach as well. Even if books had been given away, a large part of the population would have been unable to read them. As Watt points out, almost up to the end of the eighteenth century, "about a quarter of the parishes of England had no school at all, and nearly a half had no endowed schools." Where charity schools existed, their function was chiefly religious instruction and indoctrination in social obedience. Reading was a by-product. Additional factors discouraged

[12] See Altick, *op. cit.*, p. 49 ff., for statistics on sales of popular novels: *Pamela, Joseph Andrews, Amelia, Roderick Random, Clarissa* (2nd printing), *Sir Charles Grandison*, et al. The point is, as Altick notes, that an edition "seldom exceeded 4,000 copies," and this in a total population of six to seven million.

literacy: the fee, prohibitive to most, that elementary schools charged; the need for children to become wage earners; the long hours and arduousness of work itself. Thus, the reading public was small right through Jane Austen's time. Estimates are difficult to make, but we can say that between 2 and 5 percent of a population of six to seven million could be considered a reading public, and this is a generous accounting. Such a figure probably also includes a large group whose reading was limited to newspapers and pamphlets; the audience for books was possibly as low as 1 to 2 percent of the population, or around 75,000 readers.

While such figures are quite low for a relatively civilized country, we should not forget that reading was itself a subversive activity that would only make the poor take their minds off work and duty. The spirit of "patience with one's lot" prevailed, a condition encouraged by both church and government, which saw in widespread reading a possible political danger. And the figures are not so out of line with current estimates of a book-reading American public, which, despite 90 percent literacy, reportedly reads very few books indeed, and those often subliterary.

One other factor is significant, a sociological corollary of the above. That is that "reading" could not pretend to be a significant factor in a person's life until it became clear that reading and education were ways of changing his status. Reading, then, was subservient to a much larger process, one which, with its connection to a medieval hierarchy, assumed that a man or woman remained socially fixed, that his work was the labor passed down from father to son, that his expectations were set. Within such assumptions—and they persisted for most people throughout the century, despite the growth of industrialization—reading was a countercultural activity for a few, who only gradually became many. To read was to enter upon a long process of self-development and indicated dissatisfaction with one's place. Reading meant, also, the assimilation of dangerous ideas, for the novelists implied both a quasi-democratic criticism of a very undemocratic society and an equality of men dependent only upon achievement. Thus, the novelists were not necessarily full of high sentence. Rather, they were often pushy rascals, attacking hypocrisy in government and church, mocking traditional values, creating small crises of belief, advocating adversary values.

Despite innumerable hindrances to reading, there were counterforces. A middle-class society will, inevitably, find ways of advertising and selling a profitable product; and the novel, with its insistence on travel and adventure, its romantic narrative, its witty handling of minor figures, its common-sense approach to life, its fun at the expense of eccentrics, appeared even early in the century as something to be marketed, however such a procedure may come about when people were either illiterate or indifferent. Four factors were significant in the growth of the reading public, although some were indirect and not immediately perceptible:

The idea of circulating libraries, their major growth coming at about the middle of the century

The increase in book pirates, who published books at sharply reduced prices; added to this, the change in copyright law, by which the idea of perpetual copyright was ended and cheap editions of older works were made possible

The rise of the man of letters, who could make his fortune without patronage, a development that occurred not only in fiction but in poetry and journalism (Pope, Johnson, Goldsmith, as well as Fielding, Smollett, and others); with this, the growth of a small army of writers, including many women

The prevalence of men like James Lackington, who bought large numbers of books at auction and then resold them cheaply; dealers such as Lackington handled both new and secondhand books at cut-rate prices, forcing more competitive sales

Of these four developments, all occurring at different times and with varying intensity, the most significant for the growth of the novel was the rise of lending libraries. The plan involved an annual fee for the reader which allowed him borrowing privileges. Since most of the latest books were stocked, the reader had access to new fiction and non-fiction for a relatively small sum. It was soon apparent that, along with religious material, the novel was to be a profitable item, and libraries stocked hundreds of copies of the more popular ones. Watt speaks of such libraries existing in rudimentary form as early as 1725, but it is generally agreed that the decade between 1740 and 1750 saw their numbers rise.

While the annual fee to join these libraries would have been high for an agricultural worker or a house servant, it was not unduly exorbitant for a merchant or small businessman whose wife had leisure time and wished to fill it with reading. For such people, the ten-shilling to one-guinea subscription rate was within their means.[13] It would appear that the lower classes still could not afford books, even at this annual rate, but servants might have had access to books as a result of their mistress renting them. Also, books could be borrowed at a flat fee (as apart from subscription), which, of course, was much lower than a purchase price.

Available information does not reveal what effect libraries had upon literacy or precisely how much of the potential reading public they reached. It seems clear, however, that the growing availability of a new, exciting form of reading would encourage literacy. Add to this the other three factors—the establishment of respectable book pirates, the pressure of large numbers of authors each trying to make a living by the pen, and the bargain book rates offered by shrewd dealers like Lackington—and we can agree that an increasingly leisured bourgeoisie had more reason to read than ever before; and as it turned to books, its domestic servants, outside help, and other retainers would have greater access to books. With improved education not too far behind, a reading public was to develop, and it was, inevitably, to turn to fiction in this and the next century.

The eighteenth-century novelist may not have threatened Boodle or his political chums with public disclosure (although *Jonathan Wild* was not far off the mark), but he did at least judge public hypocrisy, unenlightened hierarchies, and privileged institutions. Through criticism, implied and direct, the novel was not least among the forces in the developing democratic process. In several ways we can see eighteenth-century fiction as a growing power for subversion of a particular kind, the subversion that leads to a different kind of social morality, not necessarily better or more stable, but one based on self-knowledge, self-evaluation, and self-assertion. All these were fresh attitudes for the majority of mid-century Englishmen, rather heady material for a society that still judged itself traditional and hierarchical.

Antecedents and Fulfillment

The most obvious question following any discussion of the developing audience is: where, specifically, did the novel come from?

[13] Such fees fluctuated, starting out near a guinea, falling after mid-century, and then rising near the end of the century when book prices rose. London fees were higher than those in the provinces. See Altick, *op. cit.*, p. 62, for further details.

To what extent did it evolve from previous materials? To what degree was it a spontaneous creation generated out of the psyches of Defoe, Richardson, and Fielding? What can we say of its antecedents that themselves stopped just short of being novels?

Discussion of the novel's background takes as many shapes as the novel itself. Without agreement on what the novel is, we cannot have a consensus on its antecedents, and therefore we must trace its genealogy through many centuries and many kinds of fiction. If we begin with Chaucer's *Troilus and Criseyde* and then move to *The Canterbury Tales*, we may ask why these are *not* examples of fiction, even though the latter approximate the short story and the former seems "novelistic."

The two questions we must ask in judging the extent to which older works influenced the development of the new form are: first, do the events and characters seem probable? and, second, does the language catch detail denotatively or is it chiefly poetic or decorative embellishment? Using these two guides, we see that *Troilus and Criseyde* is not precisely a forerunner of the novel, chiefly because it forsakes details of the characters' lives to make some anagogical point. That is, despite frequent realistic encounters, the Chaucer work is, basically, allegorical. While allegory and the novel crisscross throughout the history of fiction, nevertheless the allegorical process is inimical to the novel, for its main drift is toward generality and spirituality, away from the particulars of event, character, and language. These distinctions are somewhat arbitrary; but the novel has almost always been socially based, while allegory has been theological, moving toward Scriptural interpretation or toward a view of virtue and vice. In the novel, the final arbiter of justice, however disguised, is not God but a society somehow established by the author.

In a book cited earlier, Margaret Schlauch notes that *Troilus and Criseyde*'s approximation to modern social comedy and to the modern psychological novel should not be overstressed. Chaucer was portraying men who still believed, however cynically, in the chivalric code, so that he viewed fictional and psychological details within fixed conventions.[14] Miss Schlauch's remarks would appear to bear out my contention that the novel could develop only when it moved ahead of convention and fixed attitudes, or at least questioned them

[14] For further exploration of this point, see *Chaucer and the French Tradition* (1957) by Charles Muscatine and *Design in Chaucer's Troilus* (1959) by Sanford Meech.

seriously enough to threaten them. None of this, however, should make us underestimate the important place of *Troilus and Criseyde* in the later development of prose fiction, for we note Chaucer's use of detail, his criticism of conventional behavior, his reliance on social comedy, his use of the "apprenticeship" of a young man to the vicissitudes of life, his control of a narrative technique, his sense of setting, place, and dress.

Are the same cautions, however, applicable to *The Canterbury Tales*? Are not the *Tales* as unlike the allegory of *Troilus* as Defoe's fiction is unlike *Pilgrim's Progress*? When we read the familiar lines describing the Friar, "His typet was ay farsed ful of knyves / And pynnes, for to yeven faire wyves. / And certeinly he hadde a murye note:"—with these lines, we seem deep within the novel tradition, virtually in the camp of the naturalists and the Joyce of *Dubliners.* Ultimately, however, Chaucer's description serves another function, to suggest moral standards primarily and to present character secondarily. Detail leads ever upward toward an anagogic purpose; society's values are not established by society itself. The portrayals in the *Tales* are like the seventeenth-century character portraits of Joseph Hall, Sir Thomas Overbury, and John Earle. Such portraits were based on temperament or occupation, and they worked out a fixed view of society, rather than one that was in the process of changing.

There is no reason why fixed values, generated from universal ideas, could not have been part of the development of the novel. Under such conditions, the novel would have been a prose fiction of a sort, however different from what in the later eighteenth century acquired the name of novel. In that latter form, there are clear departures from earlier developments, although the eighteenth-century novelists utilized the conception of detailed character the portraitists afforded. Some of the distinction is clarified by Northrop Frye's classifications of modes: the hero of myth, the hero of romance, the hero of epic and tragedy (high mimetic), the hero of comedy and realistic fiction (low mimetic), the hero of the ironic mode.

Although Chaucer, Boccaccio, and Rabelais demonstrate clear identification with the "low mimetic," the fiction of comedy and realism, they have a sense of order and of priorities that maintains them closer to myth, epic, and tragedy, with singular departures to irony and realism. In the main, they reject the kind of anarchy implicit in a society always becoming. Rabelais, for one, introduces the spirit of Pan in the figure of Panurge, but to equalize his chaos, he offers the Abbey of Thélème, which is controlled anarchy.[15] The true concerns of these writers, despite their juggling of contrary notions, was the maintenance of a given society on its traditional lines so as to support personal fulfillment rather than frustrate it.

The background of the novel as we know it is possibly more tangled than the history of any other genre, for the novel has never had a clear-cut definition of form, much less of content. As a consequence, the novel has also been the most protean of forms. Frye isolates the particular quality of the novel as having its basis in a low-mimetic society, that is, in a realistically oriented society with democratic assumptions whose literary values center on domestic tragedy. In such a society, as reflected in its fiction, the stress is upon the individual, who is neither epical nor heroically flawed.

Frye was evidently very much influenced by the development of domestic tragedy in the eighteenth-century novel; one thinks, chiefly, of *Clarissa*, but also of Sophia and Tom's persecution in Fielding, of *Amelia*, of *Pamela*, and so on. There are sufficient examples on which to base a theory. But in stressing the trials of domesticity, in seeking symmetry in the development of a genre, Frye understressed the social basis of the new form. One need not be a Marxian critic to see that the novel fits more than a paradigm founded on Aristotelian categories.

Yet Frye's general position is well taken. The novel is an offshoot from an established society and literature; it protests against closed forms; and it proselytizes for a community based on dignity, acceptance, equality, and virtue through achievement, not birth. It is also socially oriented, not in the sense of having a social program, or even a social vision, but in presenting a view of society that is always in a state of flux or in suggesting a society in which almost infinite changes and variations are possible, and desirable. For this reason, we have called the early novel subversive, for it was nearly always testing out the received and the given, attacking hypocrisy, and demonstrating alternate ways of action and response.

[15] The motto *"Fais ce que voudras"* ("Do what thou wilt"), which served as the basic rule of the Order, assumed that an aristocratic court would maintain virtue and eschew vice, that every act would, in some way, help preserve and maintain the divine order of truth. The novel, on the other hand, while accepting partially this assumption, questions received truth, wears away the past, and establishes its own norms, which are often counter to or modifications of those of the larger society.

If Frye intends the above to fit into low-mimetic, then his category is sound. On the other hand, *any* category is suspect, no matter how brilliantly defined, and one finds Margaret Schlauch's approach on the whole more rewarding, albeit messier in terms of any final resolution. Her very point is that backgrounds to the novel are many and deceptive, that there is no categorizing the novel, and that one cannot speak of the eighteenth-century English novel as an entity. On the contrary, we must view it as a continuing variation on themes established in pieces and fragments from a myriad of sources, both prose and verse, both medieval and later, both realistic and romantic.[16]

While stressing the realism of the novel in its content, style, sense of detail, and dialogue, Miss Schlauch seeks in relatively minor forms those aspects which the eighteenth-century novelists brought together as a new type of prose fiction. If we consider one important point—the establishment and strengthening of female characters—we see that this element is not simply a literary device but is connected to the entire development of Western culture. The existence of any convention, especially one so essential to a genre as the strengthening of female characters in the novel, is socially based. Once we

[16] After praising the first chapter of Ian Watt's *The Rise of the Novel*, she indicates that closer attention to backgrounds—which was not Professor Watt's intention, in any event—would disclose that most aspects of the eighteenth-century novel had been anticipated by medieval and early Renaissance writers of prose fiction. (*Antecedents*, p. 136, n. 16) This point is part of Miss Schlauch's thesis that the derivation of the novel is as complicated as the structuring of society itself; that it follows no clear-cut pattern of development; and that while it may, as Watt says, parallel certain patterns in science and philosophy, it also follows a past literary pattern as checkered as its own later evolution.

A related issue is the so-called Englishness of the rise of the novel. English Showalter, Jr., in his excellent study *The Evolution of the French Novel 1641–1782*, asserts that we cannot "consider the novel as an entirely new phenomenon," or ignore the considerable cross-breeding between English and French fiction of the eighteenth century and before. Showalter cites several examples: "Lesage was extremely popular in England and was translated by Smollett; Fielding read widely in French fiction; Prévost's *Manon Lescaut* (1731) and Defoe's *Moll Flanders* (1722) are similar enough to have inspired a controversy over whether Prévost copied Defoe; the same is true of Marivaux's *La Vie de Marianne* (1731–45) and Richardson's *Pamela* (1740); Rousseau's *La Nouvelle Héloïse* (1761) was widely admired in England, although less than in France; Defoe's *Robinson Crusoe* (1719) became an immediate classic in France; Richardson was translated by Prévost and widely imitated in France; Fielding was also popular, although less than in England; and finally, Sterne was particularly appreciated and imitated by Diderot." (p. 69, n. 2) Showalter's book draws heavily on Georges May's *Le Dilemme du roman au XVIIIe siècle* (1963), which, while also refusing to accept either the Englishness of the novel or any explanation based on spontaneity, insists we can demonstrate no clear line between the romance and the early novel.

recognize this condition, it becomes simplistic to assume that the growth of a large female audience in the eighteenth century led more or less directly to the appearance of strong, centrally located female characters, although the nature of the audience is not to be discounted.

The feudal romance demonstrates that women even then had considerable freedom of choice, and the societal roles of such women bore out their increasing prominence. Perhaps surprisingly to us, they had in real life equality before English law in matters of land inheritance, in suits, in the making of wills and contracts. (Schlauch, p. 15, n. 6) Thus, the feudal romance, which is several centuries distant from the work of Richardson, parallels it in one important factor. What confuses any clear-cut line of development is that a particular literary form, like the romance, may in most qualities appear quite divergent from the novel—in its allegorical dimensions, in its lack of realism, in its reliance on traditional values—and yet contain one salient aspect that, once isolated from the rest, gives us a sense of direction toward the novel.

For example, we have discussed the conventions of pre-Renaissance romance in Chaucer's *Troilus and Criseyde.* Yet even as we assert that the poem belongs to a medieval tradition, we must note Chaucer's presentation of Criseyde, who balances the qualities of courtly love with a realistic evaluation of her own needs that anticipates Moll Flanders and Roxana. Further, in her situation, we observe glimmerings of Clarissa, although Criseyde is not a tragic character. We can carry the analogy to Chaucer's narrative further and see Richardson's novel as based on courtly love, noting that his characters' names are partially allegorical and that the elements of chivalric romance in the novel are as suitable for his middle-class audience as such elements in the poem were for Chaucer's more elevated audience.

Similarly, in types as "medieval" as the *fabliaux* and the *exempla,* we can find matters of detail, realism of characterization and setting, homeliness of point of view, functional use of atmosphere and environment. The *fabliaux,* in particular, eschew the allegorical and the marvelous. Of marked interest is that the locus of activity in most *fabliaux* is the interior of a house or castle, and, more specifically, the bedroom and kitchen—almost domestic comedy from the start. Thus, these types, which clearly are not novels in our later sense, contain aspects of the novel.

We can see this point in a still further shift, a kind of mutation that occurs almost imperceptibly. In the development of the Renaissance *novelle,* which many scholars feel are the true source of the novel, one finds once again this mixture of romance and anti-romance.[17] But the main force of the *novelle* (Boccaccio's *Decameron* is the most celebrated) is their accumulated detail even when the intent of the *novella* is romantic or rhetorical. Withal, the *novelle* are different in kind and degree from works such as the *Roman de la Rose* or Dante's *Commedia*, whose allegorical assumptions and basis in a conventional medieval philosophy make them typical anti-novels. Miss Schlauch considers the *novelle* as a definite "advance" on the *exempla* and the *fabliaux* in the development of the novel, basing her opinion on two points: that the *novelle* were in prose (unlike the verse *fabliaux*) and that they were not designed as homilies (unlike the sermonlike *exempla*). These two deviations, superficially slight, are significant, self-evident in the prose but less apparent in the homiletics, which in the novel become implied rather than explicit.

If we examine the well-known *fabliau* "Le Meunier et les Deux Clers" in the light of its adaptation by Boccaccio, in the sixth story of the ninth day, and by Chaucer in "The Reeve's Tale," we can see how the *novelle* move toward our idea of more advanced prose fiction. The *fabliau* is a piece of raw narrative in which every element helps move the story forward. There is little individualization of character or scene; the two clerics are interchangeable with their kind, as are the miller and his wife and daughter, as well as the mill. The homiletic nature of the material moves it inexorably toward the goal of reciprocal penalties. The miller steals and, in turn, sees the virtue of his wife and daughter "stolen" from him. In balance, no man wins over another.

In Boccaccio's variation, the moral element gives way to the trickery of a woman, the miller's wife, and the cleverness of her tongue in avoiding a calamitous confrontation. By playing on her husband's credulity, she is able to transform the homiletic quality of the original *fabliau* to a more fictionally oriented jest in which no one is injured. While Chaucer's version is still freer than Boccaccio's in its scenic and character development, it reverts to the *fabliau,* keeping

[17] *Modern Novels*, printed for Richard Bentley, 1692; *A Select Collection of Novels*, ed. by Samuel Croxall, 1722, 1729—a total of eighteen volumes of short novels, most of them translations from the French, Italian, and Spanish.

close to the original idea of the stolen grain, the misplaced cradle, the fornication with wife and daughter, and, also, to the homiletic quality of the *fabliau*, which Boccaccio had avoided. Chaucer ends his tale with: " 'Hym thar nat wene [expect] wel that yvel dooth'; / A gylour [beguiler] shall hymself bigyled be. / And God, that sitteth heighe in magestee, / Save al this compaignye, grete and smale!" Despite divergences, both Chaucer's and Boccaccio's versions represent movement toward the novel, although even the *fabliau* itself clearly foreshadows a fictional narrative line.

Thus, as we move toward the development of the pre-novel, we find ourselves in the seventeenth century, more than one hundred years before Defoe's fiction. We have reached this pre-novel through many romantic materials, and yet, in the work of Thomas Deloney, Robert Greene, Thomas Nashe (cited above), among others, we note an extrapolation of the realism in medieval and Renaissance verse fiction. The pre-novel becomes more recognizably the type of prose fiction we identify with the eighteenth-century mode.

In Deloney's *Jacke of Newberie* (1597), near the end of the first chapter, a passage recalls Chaucer's Wife of Bath, for it concerns the woman's sovereignty in marriage. Deloney writes:

> Husband (quoth shee) thinke that women are like starlings, that will burst their gall before they will yeeld to the Fowler: or like the Fish *Scolopendra*, that cannot be toucht without danger. Notwithstanding, as the hard steele doth yeeld to the hammers stroke, being used to his kinde, so will women to their husbands, where they are not too much crost. And seeing ye have sworne to give me my will, I vow likewise that my wilfulnesse shall not offend you. I tell you husband, the nobel nature of a woman is such, that for their loving friends they will not sticke (like the Pellican) to pierce their owne hearts to doe them good. And therefore forgiving each other all injuries past, having also tride one anothers patience, let us quench these burning coales of contention, with the sweete juyce of a faithfull kisse, and shaking hands, bequeath all our anger to the eating up of this Cawdle.[18]

While the sentiment is Chaucer's Wife's, the language of Deloney's shrew is virtually Defoe's Moll Flanders's. The prose has the same functional quality, a similar undertone of wit and common sense, a comparable directness about human feelings. Furthermore,

[18] The comparable passage in the Wife of Bath's prologue (lines 816 ff.) is as follows: "And made hym brenne his book anon right tho. / And whan that I hadde geten unto me, / By maistrie, al the soveraynetee, / . . . After that day we hadden never debaat. / God helpe me so, I was to hym as kynde / As any wyf from Denmark unto Ynde."

we have the recurring insistence of the woman on her rights, on her sovereignty in matters of marriage and home, on her strength of will when confronted by challenge. This is prose that establishes identity, as much as does Defoe's when it asserts point of view.[19]

Lest we get carried away by Deloney's prescience regarding the novel's development, we recall later scenes in *Jacke of Newberie* that are medieval in intent and execution. The description, for example, of the king's reception into a great hall, is pure romance: "All the floore where the King sate was covered with broad cloathes in stead of greene rushes: these were choice peeces of the finest wooll, of an Azure colour . . ." Yet the same passage gives the cost of this "finest wooll," a Defoe touch surely; and still later in the passage, Deloney says it would take him too long to describe the banquet itself and leaves off, a self-deprecating touch that reaches its climax when Jacke refuses a knighthood, asserting he wants to "live a poore Clothier, among my people, in whose maintenance I take more felicity, than in all the vaine titles of Gentillity." To lighten this democratic rebuff to his sovereign, Jacke adds that he and his kind labor for the glory of God and do service to their king. This passage anticipates the opening of *Robinson Crusoe*, in which Defoe chronicles the moral superiority of the middle class over any other. The rebuff itself foreshadows the snarl in Smollett's voice when his protagonists are confronted by privilege.

Further, Deloney, consciously or not, pointed up the subversive potential of the novel. For his Jacke, of lowly origin, becomes virtually the equal of his monarch, being certain enough of his own identity to reject a knighthood which, he fears, will remove him socially from his people. Later in the novel, Jacke moves at the same level as the aristocracy, is accepted as one of them, and becomes something of a judge and elder statesman. Although Jacke is a loyal subject, implicit in his attitudes is a Cromwellian revolt, or else the spirit of the Glorious Revolution, a "revolution," incidentally, whose assumptions anticipated the development of the novel in the

[19] Cf. Moll: "It is true she [a young lady living nearby] was pretty well besides, that is to say, she had about £1400 in money, which she gave him; and the other, after some time, she brought to light as a perquisite to herself, which he was to accept as a mighty favour, seeing though it was not to be his, it might ease him in the article of her particular expenses; and I must add, that by this conduct the gentleman himself became not only the more humble in his applications to her to obtain her, but also was much the more an obliging husband to her when he had her." (Riverside edition, ed. James Sutherland, p. 65)

eighteenth century.[20] His rejection of a knighthood foreruns the sharpening attitudes of the middle class in the eighteenth century as it confronted the landed aristocracy. Tradition, family, vast lands give way to new names, new money, newly built estates and town houses. All this is implicit in Jacke's gesture, the kind of gesture which the novel was to embody: a literary stance that disguised a socio-political act of some radical tendency.

Still another literary development was Robert Greene's pamphlets on cony catching, five of which appeared from 1591 to 1592. They are a curious mixture of rogue literature, romance, Newgate tales, and revelations about the London underworld—all qualities that are significant in the early novel tradition. While the central point—that the cony or sucker is cozened because of his own greed—appears to be in the moralistic tradition of the *exempla,* the main thrust of the pamphlets is sensationalism, the detailing of crooked practices as an end in itself. The relationship of Greene to Defoe is apparent, for both outline criminal activity with great relish while occasionally intruding with disclaimers and acts of piety. Clearly, the primary aim is to entertain, the secondary to teach, although the baseness of the material is excused on precisely opposite grounds. In Greene's prose, also, we note a rebellion against a euphuistic style in favor of a more realistic, unembellished language. The urban setting, with its persistent crime, is a clear anticipation in the pre-novel of one of the novel's dominant themes, the corruption of city life. Greene's cony, cozened because of greed, is presented as little different from one of Defoe's "innocent" merchants deceived by a thieving Moll.

We find no steady progression from late-sixteenth-century realism —Deloney, Nashe, Greene—through the seventeenth century and on to Defoe. On the contrary, romance remained powerful, almost dominant, in the seventeenth century, and surfaced in some characteristic prose narratives by Emanuel Ford, Richard Johnson, Thomas Gainsford, as well as continuing in the popular *Valentine and Orson, Amadis de Gaule*, and others in the tradition of the *chansons de geste.*

[20] The Revolution of 1688 strengthened the hands of the Whigs against the crown and gave increased power to Parliament, especially in areas involving economic matters. The strengthening of Parliament and commensurate weakening of the crown was part of the democratization of the country, although social attitudes remained well behind political developments. In any event, movement was toward that world the novel was soon to define, in which a seat in Parliament was potentially within reach of all and the idea of the crown was increasingly alien.

Ford's *The Most Pleasant History of Ornatus and Artesia* (1598?), for example, is closer to the reigning genres of the time—the romantic epic, the pastoral idyll—than to the materials of what was to coalesce as the novel. Ford's narrative also has overtones of Sidney's *Arcadia*, Spenser's *Faerie Queene*, and Rabelais's *Gargantua and Pantagruel*, all works that cannot be easily classified. This suggests that *Ornatus and Artesia* is a catchall, a prose narrative employing forms that are nearing a dead end. Epic, pastoral, romance—all of these merge with each other in Ford's work; while manners, morals, class, status, detail, realism of event are absent. What makes even this narrative noticeable as a precursor of the novel, however, is the use of certain devices—disguises, disappearances, among others—that turn up in prose fiction as frequently as they do in romance.

Cervantes's *Quixote* led the way to numerous parodies of chivalric romance. Very often, as in *Moriomachia* (1613) by Robert Anton, virtually all literary traditions—including pastoral, chivalric narrative, birth and development of the hero, fairies, supernatural events—are mocked; but these burlesqued elements are also the substance of the narrative and never coalesce into new forms or into alternate points of view. Such parodies and burlesques eventually lead toward a more realistic literary tradition, but that, too, is a later development, the result of other factors besides a literary transfiguration.

Anton's burlesques, as well as Samuel Holland's *Don Zara del Fogo* (1656) and Charles Sorel's *The Extravagant Shepherd* (1653) and *The Comical History of Francion* (1655), both translations from the French, combined into a potpourri of realistic and anti-realistic elements.[21] The latter persist in the following forms: pastoral, chivalric-romantic tradition, fantasies influenced in style by Lyly's *Euphues*, morality tales based on the *Gesta Romanorum*, utopian and travel literature.

It is necessary to stress these anti-realistic forms so that the student of the novel should not deceive himself about its development into the eighteenth-century form we know. The path to the novel is not well marked; false starts and intersections confuse the route. For example, the anonymous *Tinker of Turvey* (1590, redacted in 1630) is modeled on Chaucer's *Canterbury Tales*, supplying both the prologue descriptions and the tales themselves, six in all in the redaction. Coming two hundred years after Chaucer, the *Tinker* pieces, we

[21] Charles Mish's short introduction to the Anchor edition of *Short Fiction of the Seventeenth Century* provides a valuable survey of this almost forgotten material.

might expect, should show some development toward more "novelistic" techniques. The very opposite is true. If anything, the *Tinker* tales lack the fictional devices that characterize Chaucer's work and remain narratives of so-called merry tales without specificity of detail, particularization, or clear definition of either character or event.

Similarly, a series of thirty stories called *The Triumphs of God's Revenge* began to appear in the 1620's (in groups of five each) and would seem to be a continuation of the gory stories of late Elizabethan England. But these "Triumphs" by John Reynolds are moral tales that attack wickedness somewhat in the later cautionary style of Bunyan's *Pilgrim's Progress* (1678) or his *The Life and Death of Mr. Badman* (1680).[22] In one, "Don Juan and Marsillia" (1635), the elements of Jacobean drama and Gothic fiction are apparent: the evil passion of an older man, his machinations against his wife, conspiracies against children, use of poison, strangulation, dueling, presence of unbridled lust, surfacing of anarchic feelings that destroy all. These elements are accompanied at virtually every turn by a whiff of hell fire, so that puritanical judgment is present even while forbidden pleasures are indulged. As a consequence, the tale rarely leaves the level of sermon, even though the ingredients are themselves capable of fictional extension.

Throughout most of the seventeenth century, activity in prose fiction was abundant and varied; but there was, for several decades, no clearly marked "novelty" discernible to a contemporary eye. The first early, vague definitions of the developing genre came toward the end of the century, when the new form began to run against some of the more dominant traits of the culture. Those early commentators on the novel, Roger Boyle, William Congreve, Mrs. Mary Manley, among others, were chiefly concerned with distinguishing the novel from romance. But while one stressed the novel, another the romance, all were moving toward one unassailable point: that the new form, whatever shape it would take, would be psychologically realistic. To be psychologically realistic, a novel must relate to the

[22] Generally neglected in most discussions of the development of the novel, Bunyan's narratives are catchalls of later fictional ingredients: the picaresque of Defoe, the domestic middle-class life and homiletics of Richardson, and the raucous vignettes of Fielding. Of course, in any evaluation of the novel, Bunyan's work is closer to sermon than to fiction, although, once again, we find medieval and Renaissance forms opening up toward the novel, demonstrating parallel developments, without themselves becoming fiction.

undercurrents of feeling that individuals experience; and such feelings, in the late seventeenth and early eighteenth centuries, were secular, anarchic, iconoclastic—and could best be expressed in the activities of rapists, pirates, sensualists, criminals of every stripe. That is, the novel's self-definition is allied to its taking an adversary position to the age—sometimes muted, sometimes overtly—in matters pertaining to sex, the id, individual identity, the individual's relationship to his community, social justice, the growth of secularity, and ultimately to the more open life styles of both individuals and societies.

If we temporarily interrupt this line of argument to look at Mrs. Aphra Behn's *Oroonoko* (1688), we note her drive toward new ideas and new forms that can only be called startling. The content is a curious mixture of romance and realism. Oroonoko is a romantic (chivalric) figure caught in a realistic situation, i.e., the slave trade, and destroyed by those who would enslave him. At a time when Christianity was viewed as the highest religious form, Mrs. Behn offers Oroonoko's romantic paganism as closer to truth and decency than his masters' Christianity. The precepts of an accepted religion and morality are questioned, indeed undermined, by an attractive alternative. Thus, Mrs. Behn moved not only toward a plot structure and a narrative method but also toward a substantial point, that an alternate way of life may exist, with its own rules, its own morality, with minimal reference to the larger culture, which is corrupt, deceitful, and conspiratorial.

Most noteworthy, however, is not the content but the narrative method Mrs. Behn chose for the piece. Eschewing frills and embellishments, she relates Oroonoko's story in a straightforward narrative based on what she says the hero told her and what she claims to have seen herself. There are no intrusions or digressions. In one stroke, Mrs. Behn asserted the psychological realism and historicity of her material, two significant steps in the development of the genre.

We recall that while early-eighteenth-century novels were expected to attract a growing female audience, the dominant themes were criminal activity, including incest, rape, bigamy, child abuse, atheism, and sympathy for rogues, pirates, highwaymen, petty thieves, and pickpockets. Apparently, a definition of the novel as a middle-class genre must account for the middle class's attraction to the criminal, the insane, and the antisocial. It must account for a rather obvious fact: that such themes, persistently retold, could be attractive, not because of literary influences, but because both authors and audience sensed anarchy and criminality in themselves. Thus, each serious author was indeed interpreting his audience correctly, that the latter in its own secular life was or wished it were as close to criminal behavior as the pirates and thieves of the narratives.

In his extremely penetrating book, *Popular Fiction Before Richardson: Narrative Patterns 1700–1739*, John J. Richetti notes the paradox of a respectable audience gratifying its tastes with such material.

> On this level [of pirate literature and the self-destructiveness of its political assumptions] the conscious political prejudices common to most men of the time are satisfied: total democracy leads to total chaos. A workable society requires authority, but in the pirates' 'open' society that authority is tenuous, because it rests on force and compulsion rather than on traditional, sacred rights and duties of both governor and the governed . . . But at the same time on another and deeper or less explicit level, the ruthless and expansive self-seeking of the pirate in his open society fascinates because it mirrors many of the actual forms of life in an increasingly secular and competitive society. [p. 84]

In commenting on Defoe's *Of Captain Mission*, Richetti says that "Bellamy [a pirate captain] knows that he is honestly wicked in a world of hypocritical knaves and obsequious fools. He recognizes that his brand of practical atheism and amoral independence is a superior version of the moral anarchy that prevails in the world . . . in a world which is in fact given over to the swift and the strong, the pirate exemplifies strength and speed in heroic proportion." (pp. 74–5) Defoe clearly saw the connection between the anarchic criminal and the respectable, secular individualist. The apparent connection between Defoe's audience and, later, Richardson's is their common flirtation with criminal themes in fiction as reflectors of their own more subliminal longing for—or fear of—criminality.[23]

[23] If we refuse to simplify, we must note that there was an obverse side to the eighteenth-century concern with the rogue, the pirate, the highwayman, and the criminal as capitalist—a growing interest in the revival of medieval romance. The medieval revival, both in itself and as a precursor of Romantic themes, took many forms: interest in Chaucer and the Scottish Chaucerians; revival of Elizabethan and Jacobean drama; the codification of folk ballads; scholarship, false and otherwise, into Old Norse and Old Welsh; the movement into history, myth, peripheral literatures. These movements were not remarkable in themselves, but all are indicative of the

We can note this dual level of operation—an idealistic surface prescribing certain democratic assumptions about justice and a realistic subsurface deploying elements of anarchy—in nearly every thematic tension: in providential reward for hard work and an individualistic ruthlessness, in sexual exploitation and condemnation of promiscuous sexuality, in a character hopeful of moving toward respectability and yet repeatedly committing illegal acts. In Freudian terms, the conflict is between the mechanisms of the id, the "ruthless and expansive self-seeking" Richetti mentions, and the regulatory, conscience-stricken superego. The resolution is often tenuous, increasingly so in Victorian fiction, and often unconvincing, because the main thrust has been in opposing directions. Nevertheless, it is part of the social demand for order, justice, and moderation balanced against an equal fear that anarchy may become a political principle.

Once we move away from a total reliance on literary and sociological influences, we can see such psychological undercurrents as more and more significant. It is surely necessary to read *Clarissa* as the embodiment of the audience's psychological needs: its desire not only for salvation but also for temptation, adventure, marital infidelity, and, ultimately, rape by a slim, sworded (not sordid!) aristocrat. The illicit element in the novel, we must stress, is not for purposes of titillation. It is a very real part of the psychological anticipations of the audience, which found in the "criminal" themes of fiction the expression of its own desires and needs.

We must take issue with Dorothy Van Ghent's emphasis upon Clarissa as a hypocritical cultural heroine who cheats her audience even as she appears to nourish it. What must be remarked is Richardson's remarkable flirtation with forbidden themes and desires. That such exotic wishes should be resolved by Clarissa's martyrdom is not the salient point. Of much greater significance are the facts that Richardson should play upon repressed desires in his audience for nine tenths of the novel and that the man who embodies

---

counterforces operative in the period, forces which diminished in insistence only when the novel form dominated.

These new studies did not arise fortuitously. The renewed interest indicated that an almost limitless number of "challenges" were arising to the main culture, that the novel was one such challenge, and that, because of several related and seemingly unrelated factors, the novel predominated. For a variety of reasons, not all of them literary, the novel form touched the audience most strongly and thus came to be the most important challenge.

the inexpressible, Lovelace, should himself possess considerable insight into his own motives. Lovelace is not a stock villain. He apparently represents a sexual ethic that a bourgeois society must ultimately deny to itself. In reflecting such an ethic so attractively and compellingly, however, he personifies a subversive idea which is nothing if not destructive, the uncontrolled id attempting to destroy the unguarded ego.

Clearly, such counterdisplays are essential elements of the novelist's vision; and the novel gains its definition only when the larger culture itself comes under attack in the body of the novel, *regardless* of the resolutions fiction employs to demonstrate its loyalties. As the early critics and commentators of fiction suggested, the novel presented another view of the self: a self that demands to visit hell as readily as it seeks a safer course. These momentous conflicts, which are really psychologically irresolvable, are as clear a demonstration of character development as are those realistic details which place people among ordinary events and settings.[24]

In "The Shadow of the Divine Marquis" (*The Romantic Agony*), Mario Praz speaks of Richardson, as a result of the materialistic philosophy then dominant, as being "at bottom a supporter of the instinct against whose manifestations he preached in the name of a virtue which he estimated also by materialistic standards." (Meridian Books, p. 97) In the course of his comments, Praz touches upon the point we have been developing: that Richardson, whether consciously or not, sensed the anarchic impulses in his audience and in himself, and manipulated elements which created the greatest tensions and conflicts. According to this line of thought, Lovelace's materialistic philosophy allows him to pursue pleasure according to his needs and thus to evolve the embodied threat to spiritual values personified by Clarissa. Consequently, through the presentation of a strong countertheme, which becomes as significant as the central thrust of virtue and spirituality, Richardson could shape the novel. One thinks of Georg Lukács's distinction between epic and novel, in which the latter forces uncertainties and unknowns: "The novel is the epic of an age in which the extensive totality of life is no longer directly given, in which the immanence of meaning in life has become a problem, *yet which still thinks in terms of totality* [italics mine]." (*The Theory of the Novel*, p. 56)

[24] Many of these ideas are indirectly suggested in different contexts by William Empson in "The Beggar's Opera: Mock Pastoral as the Cult of Independence," chapter VI of *Some Versions of Pastoral* (1960).

In Lovelace and Clarissa, as in Faust and Gretchen, the author has epitomized the conflicting halves of his society, creating a dialectic between one force that pursues pleasure and another that denies it, between one that seeks release and another that dams up the unmentionable. Although the pleasure principle—whether embodied by Lovelace or Faust—is defeated by the integrity of the superegoistic female, the id-directed male, nevertheless, enjoys a Pyrrhic victory. While the carnage at the end of *Clarissa* is not quite comparable to that at the conclusion of *Hamlet*, still Richardson has established that the adversary force is as telling as the social values he ultimately upholds.[25]

Obviously, what Lovelace represented was not the view the age had of itself; on the contrary, it wrapped itself in the myths of common sense, practicality, self-help, progress, allegiance to God, king, and Parliament.[26] Fiction, clearly, was beginning to do what it has done in every subsequent age: that is, act as severe critic, a measuring device, along the way suggesting alternate modes of behavior, indicating conflicting goals, many of them dangerous. From the first, the novel acted out a fantasy world—wishes, dreams, hopes, fears; at the same time, it worked within acceptable modes. Consequently, we have the conflict between elements which test out, even condemn, a given society, and elements which insist on allegiance to that society.

In this respect, the novel presents paradoxes and poses irremediable dilemmas. Eighteenth- and nineteenth-century novelists recog-

[25] Lukács has an appropriate comment here, also, on how the novel's parts structurally can assume an independent nature of their own and, like Lovelace himself, take on their own meaning: "The structural difference in which this fundamentally conceptual pseudo-organic nature of the material of the novel finds expression is the difference between something that is homogeneously organic and stable [the epic] and something that is heterogeneously contingent and discrete. Because of this contingent nature, the relatively independent parts are more independent, more self-contained than those of the epic and must therefore, if they are not to destroy the whole, be inserted into it by means which transcend their mere presence." (p. 76)

[26] That the novel developed in a period that classified itself as "enlightened" and "Augustan" indicates the strong dualism of mind and emotion in the eighteenth century. In his introduction to *The Augustan Age*, Ian Watt speaks of the rearguard action taken by Pope and Swift, as well as their myrmidons, in order to hold back chaos; that Bolingbroke developed a style which "seems to sum up a whole ideal of personal character that came to dominate English life: a tradition that combines a relaxed indifference to emotional or imaginative experience with an equable, independent, and wide-eyed self-command." (p. 19) Such an elitist attitude is completely at odds with the nature and development of ideas in the novel, which would not even recognize a Bolingbroke, except, perhaps, as a figure for mockery.

nized both potential and real danger in their materials, and we can explain their hasty and sometimes contrived resolutions, often in the final few pages, not only as a way of maintaining suspense, but also as a means of evading the potential explosiveness of their materials. This is not to suggest that novelists were at heart anarchists—far from it—but such a view does affirm that through the arrangement of images, scenes, characters, and phraseology the novel could counter nearly every shared social opinion. Often we have only glimpses, as in Defoe; but, on other occasions, we have entire vistas, as in Richardson and Fielding.

In still another way, even though the novelists paid lip service to common sense and practicality, the novel itself argued against objective consciousness as a way of experiencing reality and urged, instead, a kind of emotional truth dependent on the individual, not on society. Objective reality was, indeed, treated as a myth, while subjective reality was handled as real, the thing-in-itself. In *Tom Jones*, Blifil is the perfect result of a commonsensical education, and yet Fielding presents him as perverted, as sexually deviant in some obscure way, as a force for death; much as in Dickens's *Hard Times*, Gradgrind's school and its chief product, Bitzer, are exponents of death.

The novel, however, strikes even deeper than this, for it exposes the terrible weaknesses of every community and demonstrates how societies through myths try to disguise their serious flaws. *Mansfield Park* is, in this respect, a resolution of certain ideas developing in the eighteenth-century novel, for Jane Austen draws the line very fine between sacred Fanny Price and profane Mary and Henry Crawford, much more finely than any novelist after her except James. It is her glory. Her novels could not have existed in this area, however, unless she had sensed that the novel offered dangerous alternatives, which, from her conservative point of view, had to be exposed and repulsed, however delicately. Her art, we can suggest, resulted from just this dialectic; that is, from her structuring a society in shaky balance only after she had examined the minute threats to its existence. In this way, she sums up the eighteenth-century proposition: that the forces of balance must be commensurate with the danger to the society.

Move back two centuries. *Don Quixote* (1605, 1615) explores the essential dialectic of the novel: the line based on stability, represented by the commonsensical Sancho, a peasant Leopold Bloom, and the alternate or adversary line based on the adventurer, dreamer, iconoclast, idealist, destroyer of stability and moderation, represented by the Don and in later fiction by picaro, pirate, criminal, libertine, and artist. Thus, *Don Quixote*, both novel and character, is archetypal, not only embodying the cultural myths of its own day but suggesting, in its variety and expansiveness, a vision of alternate lives and disruptive styles which, ultimately, must be rejected.

The alternate style is always terribly dangerous. When presented by an effective novelist, it goes beyond temptation; it may lead to choice and action. Yet the novelist, whether Cervantes, Richardson, or Tolstoy, rejects Blake's view of Milton's Satan and destroys the force or figure he has been flirting with, even as he has shown us that such forces may, temporarily at least, represent greater life, greater expansiveness, greater acceptance of fate than characters who offer balance. *Don Quixote* explores nearly all of these issues sympathetically and becomes, in the process, the single most important literary influence on the eighteenth-century novel.

I

Don Quixote as Archetypal Artist and Don Quixote *as Archetypal Novel*[1]

The Don explains to Sancho that what everyone thinks is a barber's basin is to him really Mambrino's helmet. When Sancho insists it is really a basin, not a helmet, the Don accepts that Sancho sees it for what it is—a basin. The reason the Don gives for Sancho's way of seeing is that enchanters and sages, recognizing the value of disguises, have made everyone except the Don see the helmet as a basin. Their wisdom is such that they "change and alter all our deeds, and transform them according to their pleasure and their desire either to favour us or injure us. So what seems to you to be a barber's basin appears to me to be Mambrino's helmet, and to another as something else." (Penguin edition, p. 204)

The Don is grateful to the enchanters, for they know that to reveal the object as it is would leave the Don open to all the world's thieves. "However, as they see that it is nothing more than a barber's basin,

[1] If this chapter were a full-scale study of the picaro and picaresque, we would include Alemán's *Guzmán de Alfarache* (1599, 1604), Scarron's *Le Romant comique* (1651), Lesage's *Gil Blas* (1715–35), and many other French and Spanish pre-novels. Except for Lesage's influence on Smollett, however, their significance for eighteenth-century English fiction was marginal, while that of *Don Quixote* was exceptional, in Fielding, Sterne, Charlotte Lennox, Smollett, and several others.

they do not trouble about it, as was evident in the case of the wretch who tried to destroy it and left it behind him on the ground; for I promise you that if he had recognized it he would never have left it there." (p. 204) As a knight-errant, the Don is protected by what appears to be a chimera; and, as madman, he is likewise shielded from those sanctions of judgment and attitude which are applied to the sane.

We must never lose sight of Cervantes's point in this famous scene; that is, his mockery of the chivalric romance and the figure of the knight-errant. Even as we recognize the purpose and accept the resolution of the incident, however, we must not judge it superficially. For beneath Cervantes's mockery and burlesque is an archetypal or mythical response that we all have to the lunatic—our awareness of him as the artist.

A corollary of this theme, as well as an intensification of it, occurs in the second part, in the puppet show (chapter XXVI). This scene, coming shortly after the ones involving the cave of Montesinos, with its distortions of time, warns us that the nature of the novel is turning toward a conflict between art and life, symbol and reality, what things seem and what they are. In that earlier scene, chapter XXIII, "The Knight's Vision," Cervantes makes a classic distinction between time in a work of art and time in real life. The Don, according to Sancho and the scholar, has been in the cave for about an hour; yet his memory of it, as though a Proustian moment, is of at least three days. ". . . for night fell there and morning rose, and three more nights and mornings; so that, by my reckoning, I must have stayed three days in those remote and secret regions." (p. 620)

At the same time that the Don dwells on the psychological duration of his speleological experience, he is also play-acting. For by now, we have sufficient insight into his role playing to recognize he is doing what is expected of him, that he is *willing* himself to be madman and performer. Wittgenstein says that "the will is an attitude of the subject to the world," that the "act of the will is not the cause of the action but is the action itself." (*Notebooks, 1914–1916,* 87e) Thus, we experience a peculiar kind of spiraling, in which our sense of reality and another's very different view of it are in almost constant rotation, comparable to what one experiences in any work of art that establishes its own rules of time and space.

The Don's vision in the cave, like his transmutation of the barber's basin and his transfiguration of Dulcinea and the players of the "waggon of death," is part of a metaphorical dimension of the Don's madness. This metaphorical sense, this analogy between mad visions and artistic distortions, all *consciously* conceived by the Don in the second part, becomes the archetypal experience of the novel.

By the time we reach the puppet show chapter, then, we have been prepared for several layers of subjective experience: the Don persists in opposing his ideals to the reality of others and does so consciously; he willingly allows others to think him a madman; the line is nevertheless often blurred for the Don himself between his play-acting and his real self; his visions are often artistic images, symbols, metaphors, allegorical flights of fancy. The puppet show, in this respect, is crucial, virtually the keystone of the second part, as the book moves from the mockery of chivalry toward a dualistic awareness of reality.

In the puppet show, we recall, Master Peter appears with an ape that is apparently something of a divine, although its powers are chiefly to recount the past. When asked for a fortune, Peter places the ape on his shoulder, listens to its chatterings, and then reproduces, miraculously, events and incidents from the person's past, with some small prophecy of the future. Among other things, Sancho presses the Don to ask if the events in the cave of Montesinos were imaginary or real. When the Don does ask, he receives an ambiguous answer: that part of his experience in the cave was false, part real. The Don immediately asserts that the ape speaks with the voice of the devil and that time will reveal all things, even the events in Montesinos's cave.

The divining powers of the ape, however, are only a preview of the real act, an involved and rather elaborate puppet show with a story line based on conflicts between a knight called Sir Gaiferos and the Moors, who hold his wife, Lady Melisendra. The events in the story call for a knight-errant's help. Accordingly, when Sir Gaiferos's position worsens and the Moors advance to capture him and the escaping Melisendra, the Don unsheathes his sword and destroys the puppets, beheading some, maiming others, along the way almost slicing off Master Peter's head.

While the Don acts out his knight-errantry and gallantly rescues Sir Gaiferos, Master Peter pleads that the puppets are only "pasteboard figures," that they represent his entire fortune. The Don only increases his attack, hacking both figures and fittings to pieces. When he calms himself, he says, " 'I should like to have before me at this moment all who do not believe, and do not wish to believe that knights errant are useful in the world. Consider what would have happened to the good Sir Gaiferos and the fair Melisendra if I had not been present here.' " (p. 642)

How can we explain the Don's behavior? At one level, of course, Cervantes is demonstrating how the Don, in his madness, can no longer distinguish between real and false, a typical form of schizoid behavior. At this level, evidently, Cervantes is consistent with his point established in the first part, that the Don's allegiance to books of chivalry has blurred his reason, screened out his logic, and made him irrational. That, however, is to read the novel literally. Any work presenting a blurring of real and false is, unless lacking in all dimensions and reverberations, testing out our assumptions of the real, forcing us to refocus upon or to question our own angle of vision. Such a work is opposing art's way of viewing phenomena to the logical way; or, conversely, it is suggesting that the logical way is, perhaps, illogical, relativistic, not fixed.[2]

Since the puppet show has presented itself as real, the Don has accepted its assumptions. The logical, objective mind, on the other hand, normally distinguishes between art and life, and rejects art even while approving the distortions art imposes, even when artistic reality may seem more intense, more real. The Don, on the contrary, insists that the value of art, i.e., the puppet show, has created a dimension beyond logic and reason, and that he must honor that new dimension. Traditionally, the person who fully accepts the reality of art, the reality of the ideal, or Plato's assumptions about perfect ideas and forms, is deemed insane, a man whose self, as R. D.

[2] Ortega y Gasset adds still another dimension to the dialectic. "Within, the puppet show encloses a fantastic world, articulated by the genius of the impossible. It is the world of adventure, of imagination, of myth. Without, there is a room in which several unsophisticated men are gathered, men like those we see every day, concerned with the daily struggle to live." Among them is a fool, a knight, the Don. We are involved in several layers of actuality and imagination. We may enter the room, he says, and touch those who are no different from us; but even as we do this, we enter not an ordinary room but a room in a book, which is, in its way, still another puppet show. Accordingly, emanations proceed from "along a conduit of simple-mindedness and dementia . . . from the puppet show to the room, from the room to the puppet show." In still another permutation, we have a book within a book, as Cervantes plays on his characters' knowledge of Part I of the *Don* and of Avellaneda's attempt at a sequel, which appears to have occurred when Cervantes was in his own chapter LVIX. None of this is simple or mechanical. Set-in pieces are themselves metaphorical devices, creating ways of seeing and, at the same time, bolstering the Don's own vision. (*Meditations on Quixote*, 1914, p. 134)

Laing says, is detached from his body; although this very detachment, he reminds us, can be utilized as a basic means of defense.

Such detachment or divorce may be a symptom of insanity, but just as reasonably it may be a sign of the artistic temperament. Under certain conditions, the man who can convey certain visions in poetry or painting is deemed an artist, although personally eccentric; the same man without the ability to turn visions into words or paint is judged certifiable. Paul Tillich has commented that the neurotic avoids non-being by avoiding being. In our terms, however, the neurotic and the artist, or the neurotic's and artist's way of viewing, are analogous; for the artist or the one fully committed to art does avoid "being" as most of us define it.

In the puppet show, the Don demonstrates why those who fully accept the artistic vision are so dangerous, for he not only assumes the reality of the show but he acts upon it. He uses art and the artistic vision, in other words, to try to bring about in both degree and kind a life different from our usual sense of objective reality. Implicit in the Don's use of force against the puppets is a criticism of life, an attack on many social assumptions, and a subversive view of history—all categories of every serious artistic vision.

Adding further dimensions to the scene is the fact that Master Peter, the puppeteer, is really Gines de Pasamonte, the criminal and thief, although this fact is unknown to the Don. If the puppets are not real, nevertheless they serve a very real function as disguise and income for Gines, and they seriously weaken our distinctions between being and non-being, or between what we consider true and false reality. Behind the crazy-quilt story which the puppets demonstrate is a crazy-quilt Gines, suspending his own being while he becomes Master Peter and using his information as he gleans it to put it into the prophetic sayings of the ape. Thus, Gines is making over his appearance to Master Peter and his information—his mind—to an ape. We assume *he* is not crazy because he has consciously taken these disguises. But is the Don any crazier for consciously trying to penetrate these disguises and to destroy Master Peter's illusions? We say Gines is sane because he is a normal man trying to make a living; yet we declare the Don insane because he takes on the assumptions of the artist without creating any tangible art. In "Pierre Menard, Author of Don Quixote," Borges tells of a modern writer, Menard, who wanted to write *the Don Quixote;* that is, to penetrate the reality of the work as if Cervantes had not written it.

At this point, we can, possibly, see the kind of burden the novel generically must assume. At one level, the novel must present probabilities in human affairs. The major distinction early prose writers made between what they were attempting and the historical romance, as we noted in the introduction, was that the novel came close to verisimilitude, whatever that concept meant at any given time. A desire for verisimilitude governed the practices of Defoe, Fielding, Richardson, Smollett, and, despite his devotion to associationism, Sterne.

Yet, at another level, the novel needed to establish its own metaphors, as much as had lyric poetry, the epic, and historical romance. And these metaphors had to upset the notions of verisimilitude upon which the novel depended. The course of long fiction was fraught with paradoxes. Consider: the novel's metaphors had to be grounded in the real world and yet be critical of that world and its affairs. Since the novel differed from other genres in length, narrative line, use of established characters and realistic social background, the novelist had to seek a middle path between an excess of verisimilitude and flights of fancy.

In this respect, *Don Quixote* is archetypal. For whatever other interpretations we place upon the Don, he is playing with the substantive existence of the novel. Testing out his magical powers, denying social reality, defying routine fact, the Don almost convinces us he can turn an iron age (the novel) into a golden one (epic, romance). Itself a poetic, metaphysical conception of reality—and valid only metaphorically and analogically—the Golden Age is an idea with only limited application to the novel. Implicitly, it is destructive of all existing societies, for it embodies an ideal that relates to history even as it transcends it.

What the Don suggests, then, is the dualism of the novel: imagination and chivalric knight-errantry reflect a radical distaste for an existing society confronted by the dull, plodding, routine character of that inescapable society. Once again, Wittgenstein has come close to finding a paradoxical place for Quixote in the world: "If the will has to have an object in the world, the object can be the intended action itself." (87e) Ortega y Gasset approximates this statement of the problem when he speaks directly of the Don: "But actually, if seeing is understood as a merely sensorial function, neither they [people] nor anyone else has ever seen an orange in their terms." (p. 63) We have here the paradox of Cervantes's point of view and the experience of novelists after him: *that no matter how imaginative, poetic, ideologically pure the novelist was in his intentions, the novel form would itself force him into social attitudes, into a confrontation with routine activities, even to the extent of making him assume an adversary position without his consciously knowing it.*

Near the end of Part I of *Don Quixote*, the Don responds to the priest's admonitions about his activities. He says that the priest suggests "there have never been knights errant in the world, that all books of chivalry are false, lying, hurtful" and denies the existence of "either Amadis of Gaul or of Greece, and of all those other knights of whom the writings are full." (p. 437) The priest agrees the Don has restated his position accurately. The Don then answers that the priest is blaspheming "against an institution so universally acknowledged and so authenticated, that anyone denying it, as you do, deserves the very punishment you say you inflict on certain books when you have read them and they displease you." Cervantes's play on the real and the metaphorical brings him to a crucial point. For in the same passage, the Don argues the reality of these books and the pleasure they give him *as if* he were discussing the Bible. The point is not lost. If belief is to be acknowledged, then the Don's faith is comparable to the priest's. All of society's values sway in the balance.

To question all values is a key part of the episodes in which the Don's madness appears to dominate. He is indeed mad, but virtually all of these episodes involve a valid criticism of society. In Part II, in a duplication of the earlier priest episode, the Don answers still another ecclesiast, an especially grave one attached to the Duke and Duchess. This priest sharply admonishes the Don, in effect warning him to cultivate his garden and "stop wandering around about the world, swallowing wine and making yourself a laughing-stock . . ." (p. 673) The Don responds, "I always direct my purposes to virtuous ends, and do good to all and ill to none." In brief, he is one of God's knights, or perhaps one of His fools, a lunatic or madman with his own particular wisdom, and therefore a danger to a normative society.

The Don's foolishness represents the kind of reality the priest is unable to see or understand, an inability which makes him kin to

Dostoevsky's Grand Inquisitor. In fact, all of Cervantes's priests, kindly though several are, are interested in the Church as a rational enterprise, as bread, not as a body of faith. The demand the Don makes involves far more than the Church as an administrative body and the ecclesiast as a mayor can give. In a brilliant image contrasting the real with a mirage, Ortega y Gasset captures the off-again, on-again dualism of the Don's function. In *Meditations on Quixote*, he writes of the sun pouring down with such heat and force that the point at which it touches the earth looks like a body of water. While the water is not real, its very "appearance" calls up its contrasting quality, the dried-out husk of the earth which is its source *because* of its dryness.

We can, Ortega y Gasset says, view this phenomenon in two ways: the first, simply, believing that the water is real; or, the second, metaphorically and ironically, seeing "through the coolness of water the dryness of the earth in disguise." The variegated image—whatever one's explanation—reflects on the novel genre itself. The novel, he states, views the image in the ironic and oblique way, because the novel needs the mirage to make us aware of both sun and earth, while the adventure story (or romance) can accept the mirage as actual. "So it is not only that *Quixote* was written against the books of chivalry, and as a result bears them within it, but that the novel as a literary genre consists essentially of such an absorption." (p. 139)

If we agree that a genre as realistic as the novel requires the presence of mirage, then we must accept that the novel is always in conflict against both the actual and the mirage. Put in Ortega y Gasset's terms, we can say the novel insists on asserting that the cool water does not exist, that it is a mirage created by contrast with the dryness of the earth, that the adventure story or romance distorts real things when it accepts the mirage as actual. Even while it takes this matter-of-fact stance, however, the novel sets up a dialectic between the actual and the ideal; even as it insists that the earth *is* baked, not cool and liquid, even then, the novel is defying those who think the matter is simple, or that the ideal has no place in a rational, logical universe. Put another way, the novel considers subjectivity seriously even when, finally, it comes down on the side of objective consciousness.

If we extend our angle of vision, the Don's activities not only provide alternate ways of confronting actuality but bring into focus a different way of seeing moral and social issues intrinsic to the development of the novel genre. In the final chapter of his *The Tragic Sense of Life*, called "Don Quixote To-day," Miguel de Unamuno views the conflict as that between science and faith, asserting that the process is a dialectic of interests and criticisms equivalent to energy, vitality, life itself. "No, Don Quixote does not resign himself either to the world, or to science or logic, or to art or aesthetics, or to morality or ethics." (Dover edition, p. 321)

When reason is king, the ridiculous is wisdom. The converted Don dies, but the immortal Don continues "to incite us to make ourselves ridiculous." The Don's insistence on his vision and on our sharing it is an attempt to regain for poetry a world moving rapidly toward the profane and the secular, that is, toward verisimilitude. The Don's adventure with the lion (Part II, chapter XVII) is an attempt either to make a natural object, the lion, into something sacred or to view him as part of both sacred and natural worlds. Eliade writes that, for religious man, "nature is never only 'natural'; it is always fraught with a religious value . . . coming from the hands of the gods, the world is impregnated with sacredness." The gods "*manifested the different modalities of the sacred in the very structure of the world and of cosmic phenomena.*" (*The Sacred and the Profane*, p. 116)

Like everyone else, the Don sees the real lion, but, unlike everyone else, he chooses to ignore what he sees as such. Like the medieval mind, his makes everything into symbol and emblem, so that the earthly object–whether lion here or peasant girl elsewhere–becomes part of the heavenly ideal. To rise "above," man's mind must vault phenomena or else transform them by giving them sacred powers. In the "Adventure of the Lions," the Don forces the keeper of the lions to open the cage of the fiercest of the animals. Instead of bounding out and attacking the crouching Don, however, the lion yawns, licks himself, and rests in the cage. The Don then orders the keeper to tease the lion until it emerges roaring and clawing. The keeper, however, convinces the Don that the latter has proven his courage, an argument that persuades the Don to desist and ask only that the keeper provide written proof of what occurred.

The literal explanation of the episode is that the Don, like the early Christian martyrs, had to experience the lion in order to test and prove his faith. If we follow this argument, the Don forced himself to undergo an ordeal that put him, as a knight-errant, in a direct line of descent from the Christian martyrs and from Jesus himself. If the Don survives, he has survived a Colosseum massacre or a crucifixion. The Don's logic, if we accept he is indeed a knight-errant, is that he is sacred and, therefore, according to superstition, protected against the lion's wrath.

This is only part of the explanation, however. More apparently, the Don is attempting to control nature itself. By defeating the lion, he himself becomes the "king of beasts." It is not merely pride, although that is present. The Don is also trying to identify with nature by making the lion, the most feared of beasts, lend itself to his brand of spirituality and idealism. Thus, if the lion succumbs to the Don's powers, all nature must be responsive to something *super*natural. The entire universe, then, is "fraught with a religious value"; even a lion is "impregnated with sacredness."

This desire to control nature, to make it respond to one's self, is attached to both godlike and demonic powers, which are not unlike the powers the creative artist exerts over his material. We are all familiar with the Faustian pact with the devil, which confers on a mortal great powers, artistic and otherwise, at the expense of his soul. Cervantes, of course, plays it from the other end, from the Don's assumption of godlike powers deriving from his enchanters, eschewing the devil and demonry. Whichever way it is presented, however, the Don's creative compulsion to control nature is competitive with God's Creation. It is also antagonistic to society, which normally bends with nature, accepting it as the ultimate reality and punishing those who attempt to alter its course.

Even here, the Don's artistic powers coerce nearly all around him to play his game, making them remark the curious combination of wisdom and foolishness the Don displays. Yet the wisdom exists, Cervantes comes to accept in the second part, because of the foolishness, not despite it. The so-called foolishness is innocence, a lyricism of spirit, a rejection of objective consciousness; and it is connected to the Don's self-imposed mission to throw old forms into new light and give us new ways of seeing.

In identifying with the Don's foolishness and ridiculousness, Unamuno writes:

> But the truth is that my work—I was going to say my mission—is to shatter the faith of men here, there, and everywhere, faith in affirmation, faith in negation, and faith in abstention from faith, and thus for the sake of faith in faith itself; it is to war against all those who submit, whether it be to Catholicism, or to rationalism, or to agnosticism; it is to make all men live the life of inquietude and passionate desire. [*The Tragic Sense of Life*, p. 322]

Thus, the Don is associated with will, determination, an existential vitality of self, and compulsion toward personal choice and direction; another way of saying that the Don has exerted control over nature. Still later, Unamuno touches on these vital questions from another point of vantage. He speaks of Quixoticism as comprising "a whole method, a whole epistemology, a whole esthetic, a whole logic, a whole ethic—above all, a whole religion—that is to say, a whole economy of things eternal and things divine, a whole hope in what is rationally absurd." (p. 325)

These are not final arguments for the Don's immortality. What they suggest is, instead, a metaphysical reading of the Don's metaphors. The Don himself suggests that his metaphors are alchemically based and that they have reference to poetry, beauty, and the powers of transformation.

> Poetry, my dear sir, in my opinion is like a tender, young and extremely beautiful maiden . . . But this maiden does not care to be handled or dragged through the streets . . . She is formed of an alchemy of such virtue that anyone who knows how to treat her will transform her into purest gold of inestimable price. Her possessor must keep her within bounds, not letting her run to base lampoons or impious sonnets. She must not let herself be handled by buffoons, nor by the ignorant vulgar, who are incapable of recognizing or appreciating her treasures . . . For art is not better than nature, but perfects her. So nature combined with art, and art with nature, will produce a most perfect poet. [pp. 568–9]

So the Don rambles on, touching all aspects of his quest, his ideals, his search for a spiritual life that negates, denies, scarifies the actual as others accept it.

Change poetry to prose fiction, change the Don's defense somewhat to fit the exigencies of prose fiction, and one has encapsulated the problems involved in the development of the novel. The chief image is of an art form running a gauntlet, as it were, of science, journalism, uneducated practitioners and readers, of those who would stress art at the expense of nature and those who would emphasize nature at the expense of art. The dividing line between advocates is very fine, and, as we shall see, the emergence of the novel as form and substance is also very fine, virtually an existential act in its precocity.

It may be instructive in this examination of the novel's beginnings in the images of *Don Quixote* to compare and contrast a contemporary picaresque, *The Swindler* (*La Vida del Buscón*) by Francisco de Quevedo, published in 1626, although written in about 1608. Quevedo was, of course, aware of Cervantes's novel and refers to it in several places. Yet, despite the author's apparent sophistication in nearly every aspect of the novel—in its conception of scene, in the witty comments, in the sharpness of detail—Quevedo relied entirely on the simplistic forms of picaresque.

This purer form of the picaresque, which Cervantes helped destroy as much as he helped ridicule the chivalric and historical romance, looks back to *Lazarillo de Tormes* for its narrative techniques and rarely questions the reality underlying its assumptions. For example, late in *The Swindler*, Pablos meets up with a traveling troupe of actors, much as the Don does in Part II, chapter XI, called "Of the strange Adventure which befell the valorous Don Quixote with the Car or Waggon of the Parliament of Death." To take the Cervantes novel first: the Don's actors are still in costume, and the first one he meets represents Death with a human face. Beside him stands an angel, on the other side an emperor with a crown, nearby Cupid at the feet of Death, and so on through the allegory of the "Parliament of Death," which the troupe will perform for Corpus Christi week.

The bizarre scene confirms the Don's belief that appearances are not to be credited and that the enchanters who have turned Dulcinea into a garlic-smelling peasant girl are busily operating to confuse us and distort our values. From this supposition, the Don moves to the illusory side of his kind of reality, in which he empathizes with the actors who mask reality and then penetrates their disguise by noting that all men, whether emperors or popes, come to an equal end—all of which provides an apt symbol for what both the Don and the novel stand for.

When Quevedo's Pablos meets a troupe of actors, in chapter 9, he comes upon flesh-and-blood people who are traveling the provinces to make a living. Pablos joins them, sleeps with the ballerina who acts the queen, and himself becomes temporarily an actor of note. There is no speculation about the kinds of reality an actor portrays, nor is there any questioning of the nature of life and its mirror image, death. The narrative line is uncluttered; acting is at the same level as gaming. Novelistic dualism and metaphysical dialectics are not at issue.

In other respects, as well, Quevedo stays within the picaresque form, providing scenes of great strength, of Zolaesque naturalism, in their portrayal of drunkenness, poverty, deceit. Food is swilled, drink is sucked in at the barrel, faces and bodies are seamed with knife slashes, chamber pots are overflowing with excrement, criminals are buggerers and sadists, the narrator's uncle is an executioner. There is no romantic give and take, not even in the narrator, who portrays himself as rightfully and normally brutish. The world is strikingly predatory, far more than anything in Cervantes or, later, in Defoe.

We can say, accordingly, that Quevedo concerned himself solely with the actual, while Cervantes, in his very shaping of material, brought into range the problems to which every serious novel must respond.

Although Cervantes's ridicule of the chivalric romance did not put an end to the romance, his *Don* did establish a line of utmost significance for the English novel. As we shall observe in subsequent chapters, *Don Quixote* was the archetypal novel for Fielding, Smollett, Sterne, and a host of lesser writers. They modeled their characters on the Don and imitated entire sequences. Even more compellingly, however, they were influenced by the Don's mystique, his mythical aura, his bearing as a Christian knight, and his sweet adversariness to bourgeois values. Indeed, having accepted the Don's countering, even subversive, arguments, they molded the novel into an alternate, adversary experience.

2

Daniel Defoe: The Politics of Necessity

At precisely the midpoint of *Robinson Crusoe*, the narrator sees the single naked footprint of a man on the shore, and this sight sends him into a panic bordering on hysteria. His initial fear is, obviously, for his safety, for he thinks of savages who will devour him or destroy his goods, causing him to perish amid the ruins. The fear is very real, connected to Crusoe's desire to survive along the contours of nature and to preserve his goods against predators. Robinson has visceral responses to possible loss, much as Sancho Panza feels possessive about his island until he comprehends that God's way is different from man's.

Although Robinson shares Sancho's desire for real goods which he can view, touch, and pile on shelves, he also belongs to a Christian world in which goods and property constitute only one segment. Robinson says that fear "banish'd all my religious hope; all that former confidence in God which was founded upon such wonderful experience as I had had of his goodness, now vanished . . ." (Riverside edition [based on first edition of 1719], p. 126) He then speculates on life, fortune, and experience, and arrives at conclusions somewhat different from Sancho's; in fact, conclusions comparable to many of the Don's own arguments about his enchanters. Crusoe says:

How strange a chequer work of providence is the life of man! and by what secret differing springs are the affections hurry'd about as differing circumstance present! To-day we love what to-morrow we hate; to-day we seek what to-morrow we shun; to-day we desire what to-morrow we fear; nay even tremble at the apprehensions of; this was exemplify'd in me at this time in the most lively manner imaginable; for I whose only affliction was, that I seem'd banished from human society, that I was alone, circumscrib'd by the boundless ocean, cut off from mankind, and condemn'd to what I call'd silent life; that I was as one who Heaven thought not worthy to be number'd among the living, or to appear among the rest of his creatures; that to have seen one of my own species would have seem'd to me a raising me from death to life, and the greatest blessing that Heaven it self, next to the supreme blessing of salvation, could bestow; I say, that I should now tremble at the very apprehensions of seeing a man, and was ready to sink into the ground at but the shadow or silent appearance of a man's having set his foot in the island. [pp. 126–7]

Crusoe then says that although he does not know God's purpose—although "as I could not foresee what the ends of divine wisdom might be in all this"—nevertheless he "cannot dispute his sovereignty." According to this view, since Crusoe was God's subject, God had an unquestioned right to rule and punish him as He thought fit, and Crusoe had no choice but "to submit to bear his indignation, because I had sinn'd against him." (p. 127)

The sense of this passage, and others similar to it, is extremely curious, for it discredits any interpretation that is one-sidedly capitalistic or religious. It indicates that Crusoe, and, we can assume, Defoe, was working within a dialectic of forces and conflicts, avid to push the limits of the possible, testing how much was man's and how much God's, before falling back upon the safe, the acceptable.

Crusoe's conclusion in this section of the novel is Pauline in its awareness of sin. It fits well into the pattern we normally relegate to the Middle Ages or the Age of Elizabeth. E. M. Tillyard, for one, writes: ". . . the part of Christianity that was paramount was not the life of Christ but the orthodox scheme of the revolt of the bad angels, the creation, the temptation and fall of man, the incarnation, the atonement, and regeneration through Christ." (*The Elizabethan World Picture*, 1943, p. 18) The scientific revolution of the seventeenth century may have disrupted this form of order, but as an idea bearing on God's presence, it exerted continued pressure into the next century. It is attached, we recognize, to the "*culpa felix*" in *Paradise Lost*, also to Milton's restatement of the concept of tested and untested virtue.

Crusoe's temporary loss of faith upon seeing the footprint is nothing less than a test of his faith. Crusoe says later that it was his duty to "resign my self absolutely and entirely to his will; and on the other hand, it was my duty also to hope in him, pray to him, and quietly to attend the dictates and directions of his daily providence." (p. 127) Redemption, if it is to come, will derive, then, from a God whose ways are not man's; from a God who demands obedience rather than a purely Christian life. This point has been at the basis of muscular Christianity since the Middle Ages and reaches its paradoxical climax in Dostoevsky's scene of the Grand Inquisitor. While Crusoe's agony of soul is not comparable to the greater agonies and passions of other historical or mythical figures, it demonstrates the central philosophical situation in Defoe's novels. Since this conflict is of such importance, it deserves lengthy consideration.

The conflict in Crusoe between what belongs to man and what to God is, in one sense, comparable to the conflict between the more expedient views of Sancho and the "other voices" of the Don in Cervantes's novel. If we assume the Don stands for conceptualization, idealism, romanticism, adventurousness, while Sancho and his earthy proverbs represent realism, practicality, natural functions, then we can see Robinson as fluctuating between both worlds. His disobedience of his father's command, as Maximillian E. Novak has reminded us, is a break with his middle-class heritage and vocation. Novak argues that "Crusoe does not disobey his parents in the name of free enterprise or economic freedom, but for a strangely adventurous, romantic, and unprofitable desire to see foreign lands . . . it is a conservative warning that Englishmen about to embark on the economic disaster of the South Sea Bubble should mind their callings and stick to the sure road of trade." (*Economics and the Fiction of Daniel Defoe*, p. 48)

Any economic system, however, carries with it psychological pressures. A desire to be released from mercantilism, which is based on a society with fixed values, fixed degrees of wealth and position, in which the individual's wealth was meant for king and court—any such desire for release is tantamount to revolt against king, country, father, even God. Crusoe could not quite accept that his destiny was to fit into a middle-class niche, even though his values may have been middle-class in themselves; and his rejection of father, as the rejection of mercantilism, was an attempt to throw off external pressures that at the time he felt might have buried him. Young Robinson's rebellion leads him into a different life, at the outward margins of the middle class, distant indeed from the salvation God affords the bourgeoisie. At this outer margin, life is full of real dangers, both physical and spiritual, and it places terrible pressure on the individual. The Crusoe myth, as we shall see, is more complicated than we generally grant.

Robinson is a young man who feels he must both respect his father's ideas and break with them. While he appears to accept his father's definition of middle-class moderation and balance, nevertheless he must break loose; and, at nineteen, while "casually" at Hull, he curses both the ship and himself and sails out. This is clearly a voyage into the vicissitudes of life, that theme which was to dominate English fiction as the *Bildungsroman*.

Robinson's voyage places him in disharmony with one part of himself, that part which is traditional, bourgeois, safe. It fulfills, however, the other part, which seeks danger, which needs to test the new even at the expense of life itself. Crusoe, like Jonah, with whom Defoe compares him,[1] is probing other areas of himself, even if they prove counterproductive. By this break with safety, he works out a scenario of maturity and identity. Erik Erikson, writing of Gandhi, says he tried to compete with his memory of his father by wielding power in a new way. He notes that the uncommon man feels filial conflict with such intensity because he senses his originality, which "seems to point beyond competition with the personal father." Accordingly, the young man "grows up almost with an obligation beset with guilt, to surpass and to create at all cost." (*Gandhi's Truth*, 1969, p. 132) In his intense search for his own center, the son may prolong identity confusion as he seeks the one way, the one time, the one medium in which to create his future or to express himself.

The conflict of values and, ultimately, of destinies between Crusoe and his father has far-reaching consequences for that novel, as does the conflict between Moll and her mother in *Moll Flanders*, although

[1] Jehovah's order to Jonah is clear: Go to Nineveh and "cry against it"; but Jonah tries to flee from Jehovah's command and presence by going down to Joppa and boarding a ship headed for Tarshish. His action puts a curse upon the ship, much as Crusoe's disobedience of his Jehovah-Father leads to gigantic waves which "would have swallowed us up." Unlike Jonah, however, Robinson does not learn his lesson. In the eighteenth century, Defoe is not solely interested in having his protagonist work out his divine destiny; he must also work out his own destiny.

there the struggle assumes as many distinct guises as Moll herself does. In *Crusoe*, however, the nature of the conflict deserves considerable stress, and perhaps it should receive more attention in every novel of apprenticeship where sufficient information allows us to observe the son's moving outward as a reaction to values held by father and family. For the father who can restrain his son from seeking his own center—for whatever reasons—retains family and social power. To allow the son to defy him is to permit a shift of power, to allow the son to displace him, a form of emasculation through emancipation. Thus, most of the interaction in the Crusoe family is between father and son; the mother has virtually no role, except as intermediary, a marginal role women played not only socially but psychologically in the distribution of power.

Our sense of parental involvement thickens when we reconstruct Crusoe's career on his island in terms of his need to find his own center. If Crusoe's guilt stems from his defiance, then it is surely justice that Crusoe should be forced to abstain sexually for twenty-eight years, as if by his enforced abstention he were dropping out of all other competition with his father. Accordingly, Defoe's choice of the island interlude was not fortuitous, but was attached to a novelistic sense of how guilt feelings operate, how they are attached unconsciously to the father, to sexual roles, to furtive competition for the mother. By positioning Crusoe on an uninhabited island, Defoe has objectified the Oedipal myth in familial and religious terms, so that Crusoe comes to accept that only by abstinence can he do penance for his disobedience against family and God.

Further, this long interlude, in which penance, the working off of guilt, as well as physical survival and psychological well-being, are significant, involves Crusoe's becoming a kind of mother. In a sense, he becomes his own mother: taking care of his needs, nursing himself when ill, nourishing himself, tending his garden, doing a housewife's job of cooking, baking, cleaning, aligning himself with Mother Earth, Mother Nature, placating these mothers by pleading with God for mercy. Once established, he makes an excellent housewife, even forgoing the male hunter's role of shooting game in order to keep a herd of goats, milking them, and so on, womanly in every seventeenth–eighteenth-century regard and surely satisfying what he assumes his father desires in steadfastness, industry, and application.

Crusoe's rebellion, we recognize, could have involved any number of alternatives besides a voyage to foreign lands. To name one: separating oneself from father and family, as Robinson does, could have resulted in political activity, movement into the great world to accumulate power, both symbolic and actual, as counter to the father's power. Thus, Defoe might have moved Crusoe on to an inhabited island, as Cervantes moved Sancho on to his, and then drawn the lines in political or social terms. Defoe avoided this kind of settlement of an identity problem, however, and it is clear that the myth he created involves a psychological dimension as much as it does considerations of economics and adventure.

A psychological view of Crusoe by no means vitiates Ian Watt's stress in *The Rise of the Novel* on economic individualism. Watt writes that the "hypostasis of the economic motive logically entails a devaluation of other modes of thought, feeling and action: the various forms of traditional group relationship, the family, the guild, the village . . ." (p. 64) He points out that while Defoe's heroes either have no family or leave it at an early age, "in *Robinson Crusoe* at least, the hero has a home and family, and leaves them for the classic reason of *homo economicus*—that it is necessary to better his economic condition." (p. 65) From this, Watt argues that "Crusoe's 'original sin' is really the dynamic tendency of capitalism itself, whose aim is never merely to maintain the *status quo*, but to transform it incessantly." (p. 65)

The weakness of Watt's formulation comes with his relegation to secondary importance of Crusoe's divided self, his motivation often by fear, and his desire not to move out fully into the territory that his choices appear to have defined for him. That is, Watt sees Crusoe too strongly as conquering new territory, transforming the past, striking out bravely for autonomy and self-identity, and helping to establish a new order based on "the rising tide of individualism."

A psychological interpretation *includes* the economic order, finding in the growth of capitalism a revolt against the established order, not dissimilar to the "revolt" that occurs when the son or daughter (say, Clarissa) tries to compete with the parent's success or compensate for the parent's failure. Economic individualism involves a dialectic of forces, chiefly the revolt of capitalism against a mercantilist system that demanded citizen obedience to state and crown. Even though individuals were surely motivated by self-interest under mercantilism, the ultimate figurehead was the state, embodied in king and court. Change was suspect, the *status quo* was assumed: state and crown were the political, social, economic equivalent of the omniscient, omnipotent father in the home.

Economic and political changes are accompanied by the psychological reorientation of those involved in the change. The question of which force is greater or which comes first—whether the individual initiates the shift or whether he is caught up by forces already in play—is psychologically immaterial. Essential for our understanding of the apprentice hero or heroine is the sense of a dialectic involving the individual himself and the element or person he is striving to master. In that area of conflict, the gray, ambiguous area of sublimation and repression, we can situate Crusoe and those who succeeded him.

Such psychological considerations are significant in the entire genre of growing-up novels, and our stress here on *Robinson Crusoe* can be extended to *Moll Flanders, Joseph Andrews, Tom Jones,* the novels of Smollett, and so on through the eighteenth century into the next. Following Erikson, we can say part of the suspense we feel in every apprenticeship novel is really attached to our ambiguous feelings of whether or not the protagonist will come through the stages which we expect him to pass through to achieve mastery. In this way, suspense is a corollary of psychological expectation, and in many instances we may, subconsciously, desire failure as well as success.

Thus, to return to our initial problem, the naked footprint: Crusoe's terrible fear when he sees the foot has expansive psychological implications, as well as the economic and religious ones usually cited. According to the traditional view, Crusoe's terror is attached to his possible loss of property, his need to husband what he has, and his own sense of danger. In the economic-religious interpretation of the footprint, Crusoe must double his defenses and plead for God's mercy. His paranoia here, as if part of a cold war, is attached to what he has acquired: he must retain what he has so obsessively stocked.

Yet, as readers, we find it curious that Crusoe after fifteen years alone on the island does not see the foot as possible companionship. Perhaps, we speculate, it may be a woman's foot; or even if a man's, Crusoe might not by this time be sexually discriminating. And yet it is fear, *not* desire, *not* sexual interest, *not* physical relief, which drives him to thought and action. Possibly, Robinson's masturbatory fantasies have been sufficient satisfaction, so much so that Defoe could eliminate the sexual question. Possibly, all such feeling has died from disuse, but then we would have to assert the same for the first as well as the fifteenth year. Whatever the reason, by eliminating all question of a sexual life, Defoe paradoxically raised several parallel issues, only some of which we have already examined.

We know now that *Robinson Crusoe* did not derive solely from the early-eighteenth-century interest in travel literature; that the four-and-a-half-year (from 1704 to 1709) adventure of Alexander Selkirk isolated on an island west of Chile was, as James Sutherland notes, "useful to him [Defoe] more as an analogue than as a source." (Riverside edition, p. x) There is little question that Selkirk's adventure was important in Defoe's thinking, and it may, of course, have been that episode which gave impetus to his own version of Crusoe. But Selkirk had returned to England in 1712, and the material that went into Defoe's novel was many years in the making.

It is fair to say that every mythical story or episode grows out of something deeper than the writer's conscious desire to create this or that character or adventure. We see by the second part of *Don Quixote* that Cervantes has given himself over to the Don's attempt to remake the world to fit his readings and illusions, even though that development ran against authorial intention. In every mythical conception, there is a strong dualism. For Cervantes, it was the illusory world of the Don, which he first denies, then explores sympathetically, and finally closes off as subversive. For Defoe, it was, possibly, the expiation of internalized sins or the working out of an alternate mode of existence. Defoe's first serious attempt at fiction is based on the solitude of a man who keeps a journal, which becomes the substance of the novel; and, thus, we have the alternate, isolated experience of the writer tried out by Defoe after a life of busyness, of buying and selling both goods and himself. Seen this way, Robinson Crusoe's solitude is a viable alternative and *his* work as a writer is comfortably close to Defoe's own temporary change of style from public to private.

This signifies that any work drawing on a dualism of experience—whether Defoe's or far greater work—cannot easily be attributed to sources. In his "external biography" of Defoe (*Daniel Defoe: Citizen of the Modern World*) John Robert Moore speaks of other forces at work, chiefly the trade wars between Spain and England, the earlier movement of Sir Walter Ralegh against Spain near the mouth of the Orinoco (Crusoe's island), the presence of pirates and mutineers, the slave trade—all of which turn up in the novel. Further, Moore charts events and occupations from Defoe's earlier years, in travel, camping out, in making utensils and building boats, and demonstrates further that Crusoe's two shipwrecks draw upon Defoe's own book about the Great Storm of 1703. Along these lines, Defoe had as a classmate at Morton's Academy one Timothy Cruso, and his reading in Shakespeare's *Tempest* suggested, perhaps, the characters of Crusoe and Friday based on Prospero and Ariel. In Defoe's *The Family Instructor* (1715), Moore points out, a "white boy attempts to instruct the Negro slave Toby in religion" and Toby speaks like Friday; also, other writings and interests of Defoe long before 1719 turn up in the further adventures of Robinson Crusoe, especially in the second part.[2]

[2] A run-through of recent Defoe criticism indicates there is no end to possible references for *Robinson Crusoe*, once we note that sources can be "life sources" as well as literary and biographical ones. J. Paul Hunter (in *The Reluctant Pilgrim: Defoe's Emblematic Method and Quest for Form in Robinson Crusoe*) traces the novel to Defoe's interest in didactic treatises, to works in the guide tradition. "Factual accounts in both providence and travel literature reflect events which recur again and again in an age of increasing maritime exploration and colonization, but, unlike the travel tradition, the providence tradition focuses upon the strange and surprising aspects of these events and interprets them within a religious and philosophical framework which invests them with important meaning." (p. 73)

G. A. Starr (in *Defoe and Spiritual Autobiography*) tries to demonstrate that Defoe drew upon an entire lifetime of reading and experience for *Robinson Crusoe*, rather than on a simple list of readings or on immediate contemporary events and narratives. Analyzing *Robinson Crusoe* against the anonymously published *An Account of Some Remarkable Passages in the Life of a Private Gentleman* . . . , a work sometimes attributed to Defoe, Starr shows that elements of spiritual autobiography carried over significantly into Defoe's novel. "The same basic structure is to be found in *Robinson Crusoe*: the hero's vicissitudes, highly individual and complex as they appear to be, actually follow a conventional and regular pattern of spiritual evolution." (p. 72) Of course, spiritual autobiography and the novel differ in significant ways, in matters of interpretation and narrative, and in stress upon spiritual meaning.

Although his emphasis differs, Maximillian E. Novak, perhaps the most influential contemporary Defoe scholar, sees Crusoe's derivation and career as a complex of events attached to fear and a sense of sin. In Novak's view, Crusoe does not, like Ian Watt's isolato, work out an emerging economic doctrine of laissez-faire. On the contrary, for Novak, Crusoe reflects Defoe's own shifts from Whiggish opposition to free trade to Tory support for it, depending on who was in power. In the final balance, Novak believes Defoe was a mercantilist because of his fear of overproduction and the disruption of the circulation of goods. "He was more interested in short-term projects that would buttress an old and collapsing system than in new ideas that might bring change." (*Economics and the Fiction of Daniel Defoe*, p. 31) Thus, rather than being adventurous supporters of free-enterprise capitalism, Defoe and his Crusoe feared capitalist ideas as possibly disruptive of the normal processes of circulation of goods,

Robinson Crusoe presents not a straight line, not a linear development, but a series of resolved and semiresolved conflicts. The novel is ordinarily viewed as a working out of the Puritan myth of industry, fulfilling labor, the correct combination of faith and good works, and celibacy. Such content provides the myth of Crusoe. The axis of this myth rests on Defoe's creation of a relatively "low" individual who rises economically against the background of a somewhat traditional landscape. Writing of this mythical Crusoe, Ian Watt observes:

> *Robinson Crusoe* falls most naturally into place, not with other novels, but with the great myths of Western civilisation, with *Faust, Don Juan* and *Don Quixote.* All these have as their basic plots, their enduring images, a single-minded pursuit by the protagonist of one of the characteristic desires of Western man. Each of their heroes embodies an *arete* and a *hubris*, an exceptional prowess and a vitiating excess . . . [Crusoe] too has an exceptional prowess; he can manage quite on his own. And he has an excess: his inordinate egocentricity condemns him to isolation wherever he is. [*The Rise of the Novel*, pp. 85–6]

Let us now probe more deeply into the myth and at the same time see if the myth provides sufficient explanation of the novel and its main character.

The Crusoe myth involves a frontier. This creates a near-existential situation, for the frontiersman is isolated, without visible props, and confronted by a generally hostile or indifferent nature. He may suffer and die alone and unnoticed. Further, confronted by possible death, he must not only save himself but extend his empire. He must make, create, hang on for personal salvation. Not unnaturally, this aspect of the Crusoe myth has appealed to American readers, who (overhastily) see their own historical and literary heroes in the same pioneer tradition. The myth itself passes into nostalgia for a golden age, in which Crusoe, isolated for twenty-eight years, undergoes a purifying experience, tests out human ingenuity and endurance, and succeeds.

Such is the substance of the myth. The sense of it is that of an individual defying some social order or at odds with whatever forces are attempting to influence him. Mythical figures, whether Greek, Roman, Germanic, or American, are those who could not adapt,

---

fixed values, fixed degrees of wealth and position. From an eighteenth-century point of view, this Crusoe is conservative, even reactionary. Like all mythical figures, Crusoe straddles a broad ground and can become whatever each age, indeed each generation, wants him to become.

those who hunted while others spun; or else those identified with the forces of life and death, part of the rhythmic sway of seasons and seasonal changes, of regret, memory, hope. If we follow this reasoning, then Crusoe, despite his somewhat smaller scale, gains stature from his association with life, death, nature, the sea. As an individual broken off from the rest of mankind, tested by his God and redeemer, Crusoe must appear to stand for something special—the individual who embodies the quest of an entire society undergoing severe change. Thus, in the myth of Crusoe, we find in his experience on the island an entire eighteenth-century view, focusing on the transformation of a traditional culture into a secular, capitalistic, profane society.

That is the private-enterprise myth, and it has its moments of grandeur. Occasionally, it almost touches upon tragedy. It is, however, a somewhat deceptive reading of the novel. It forgoes all the pain, fear, hesitation Crusoe feels and expresses; it tends to make a socio-political point at the expense of a personal, human reaction.

Let us review some of the problems we cited at the beginning of this chapter and carry them further into the novel. Robinson has seen the single footprint, and his sense of inner security has been completely shaken. From a man certain of his economic and military advantage, he becomes paranoiac in his need for further, more intense security. The footprint, we may argue, has triggered the kind of crisis which involves the individual's revaluation of his orientation. In the lives of great men or historical figures, such a crisis usually arrives when their period of waiting—what Erikson calls their moratorium—is over, and they must move from one period in their life to one that will, finally, define them and their aims.

In the life of a literary creation like Crusoe, such a movement may take many forms, usually not toward great achievement, but toward philosophical reflection, theological doubt, psychological dread and anxiety. In Crusoe's instance, the response is a testing of faith and a revaluation of self; that is, in a meeting of philosophical and psychological themes.

Events, clearly, are beyond Crusoe's control; and, therefore, this man, usually seen as the embodiment of economic man, of the individual, of the new humanist, throws himself completely into God's hands. He is not here individualistic, or even profane. He is, on the contrary, taking up a sacred view of man and the cosmos to find protection against human fears. As a Dissenter, and a Calvinist of sorts, Defoe here moves in and out of a religious vision, in which he seriously questions, through Crusoe, his entire philosophy of self-interest. Novak writes that Defoe's "Nature" and, we may add, even his God, is a "hodge-podge of traditional Puritanism . . ." (*Defoe and the Nature of Man*, p. 7) Accordingly, whenever any of his "fictional characters fall into difficulties, Defoe will present a variety of natural causes to explain the situation, but the final cause is God . . . Success is the test of all action for Defoe, for it reveals God's will." (p. 7) From these comments, we can see that Defoe never strayed far from the Puritan notion of original sin as the reason for man's depravity.

As J. Paul Hunter has pointed out, the Puritans observed things and events in the created world as "emblems of spiritual matters," and man's task was to discover God's meaning and purpose in all phenomena. Hunter concludes that this emblematic way of perceiving life was transformed by Bunyan and Defoe into an artistic method "as art began to masquerade as life." (*The Reluctant Pilgrim*, p. 208) Thus, the Puritan artist, whether Bunyan, Defoe, or Richardson, described detail in "order to suggest fully the larger meanings which informed all things and events in a world of total divine control." (p. 208) The footprint, we may say, served this emblematic, Puritan purpose, for its presence created in Crusoe a sense of his own helplessness before God.[3]

The economic view of the footprint is limiting. It is, surely, more meaningful to view the episode and the image as elements in Robinson's own conflict, as part of the tension resulting from his

[3] Defoe's functional prose is also an indication of his closeness to the Puritan style in rhetoric and ornamentation. Hunter points out that Puritan thought had a fondness for metaphor, but metaphor, we should add, that was functional, not simply grafted on as it often is in symbolical and allegorical works. Charles Feidelson, Jr., in *Symbolism and American Literature*, observes that the Puritans relied heavily on the philosophy of Peter Ramus, a sixteenth-century logician and rhetorician. Feidelson says: "Whereas Scholastic philosophy had given rhetoric virtually an equal status with logic in the scheme of things, thus providing a sanction for symbolism as a form of knowledge, Ramus treated rhetoric as decoration added to and presupposing a logical framework." (p. 85)

Hunter, then, is correct in connecting the early novel with Puritan ideas about language and rhetoric, although he should, as well, have stressed additional factors besides Puritanism that were equally important in the development of a sparer, more functional prose style: the influence of the Royal Society in particular and the growth of science and technology in general; the development of journalism; the increasing secularity of society, with the gradual disappearance of superstition; urbanization; and so on.

secular rebellion against his father's wishes and the sacred, traditional elements that remain as guilt and superego. In psychological terms, this and comparable episodes involve Crusoe in the kind of "balancing out" that is the lot of every man who tests his potential. The law of compensation is as much psychological as economic. One major difference between the psychology of the novel and the rudimentary psychology of the romance lies here. In the novel, anxiety and dread are real and necessary for the sense of conflict. In the romance, the dread is never integral; it is stylized, allegorical, present as emblem, not as feeling. In this respect, Defoe was reaching toward some definition of the novel.

Hunter points out further that, while Milton and Bunyan are usually considered to present the "poetry and prose epitomes of the Puritan view of life." *Robinson Crusoe* embodies the "Puritan view of man on a most profound level; it also portrays, through the struggles of one man, the rebellion and punishment, repentance and deliverance, of all men, as they sojourn in a hostile world." (p. 126) He asserts that Crusoe's thoughts on the island transform the novel "from a story about punishment to a story about deliverance, from a story about God's judgment to a story about God's mercy." (p. 147) Within this pattern of rebellion against the father-Father and deliverance through God's mercy, Crusoe travels the path of Everyman, comparable to Bunyan's Christian. Like Jonah's voyage, Crusoe's own trip is through the turbulent seas of disobedience toward reconciliation and peace, all within a more modern psychological framework than Christian's.[4]

To see Crusoe's situation whole, however, it is necessary to back up and note his early career, up to the point of the footprint, when he reconciles his severe crisis through renewed faith in God's all-encompassing power. Up to that footprint and that critical decision to embrace God, Crusoe has fluctuated and faltered, sure neither of himself nor of his control of events.

[4] We could argue, following the Biblical parallels of Jonah and the Prodigal Son, that on his island Crusoe experiences the comparable burdens of Job. Despite his travail, he must retain faith in God. At the end of his twenty-eight-year penance, God rewards him with all his goods fattened and multiplied.

This view of Defoe's prose narrative illustrates how close the novel at this stage was to allegory. While Crusoe is not a personification, he is apparently close to Everyman, at least to an English Everyman. Crusoe's stay on the island finds several levels, many of them overlapping with elements of allegory: man with God, man with other men, man with nature, man with himself, man filled with uncertainty, dread, doubt.

Defoe is very novelistic in the first few pages of *Robinson Crusoe*: that is, he is careful of details that define the novel, matters of place and date of birth, names and destinies of the protagonist's siblings, family ancestry, changes of name, economic and social status. These are the particulars of the novel, not of romances or histories. They help establish Robinson Crusoe for the kind of audience that sought both immediate identification with its heroes (and heroines) and a sympathetic relationship to their tastes, attitudes, and careers. As such, Defoe presents Robinson's father as wise, not tyrannical, and his advice as sensible; Robinson suitably fears and respects his father.

In addition, the father's definition of the Crusoes as middle-class, as in "the upper station of *low life*," was a kind of wish-fulfillment fantasy for most early-eighteenth-century readers, only a relatively few of whom were so fortunate. What is most attractive about the middle is its moderation, and when Robinson rejects his father's moderate counsel, he is evidently seeking the adversary element in himself that is wild, extravagant, and eccentric. In his rejection, he heads directly into storms—the book's imagery is based heavily on winds, waves, torrential downpours—directly into those extremes which his father had warned him against.

Clearly, there are other forces in Crusoe besides those which are emblematic of a Puritan economic tradition. Robinson goes out to seek his fortune, even though he "was under no necessity of seeking . . . [his] bread." (p. 7) His transgression leads him and his crew close to death in a storm reminiscent of both Jonah's journey and the flood of Noah. Even after this near-fatal adventure, Robinson does not return home, although common sense has already warned him that happiness lies in homecoming. Whatever is wild in him has not been satisfied, and he must play out his destiny, saving himself for his great moment, which is not the moment his father has designed for him.

We can speculate that Robinson has conceived for himself several roles, all vaguely defined, but all involving a break with home. Of course, once on his island, he performs traditional homemaking roles, but he does so under the threat of extinction, not in the relative safety of civilization. Protean in his skills, Robinson identifies in some way with the Proteus who lives in the sea,[5] which is so much a

[5] While various protean roles are suggested in *Robinson Crusoe*, in *Moll Flanders* they are essential, for Moll almost from the start plays roles, is involved in masquerades, masks, costumes, different faces and appearances, and, in fact, saves her life because of

part of his own experience, since it is the sea that almost claims him at the same time that it is the sea that washes him up to new experiences. Through the sea, he can voyage through his own fantasies, work out his own destiny, although he eventually is reconciled to middle-class life.

The sea, indeed, takes on both a threatening aspect (the father) and a quieting aspect (the mother); it plays on Robinson's duality. In his own family, as we saw above, the mother plays almost no role. She acts as an intermediary, while the father makes the decisions, defines the terms, and plans the future. This is, apparently, as it would be in Defoe's time; as we see later in eighteenth-century fiction, the mother is rarely present, or if present, not important. There are few mothers indeed in Fielding—merely mother surrogates and often not at all motherly; in Richardson, Clarissa must deal almost entirely with father figures—father himself, uncle, brother—while the mother's voice is virtually stilled.

Accordingly, when Robinson is washed up on his island near the mouth of the Orinoco, it is the ship and the accompanying sea which mediate between the real harshness of his experience and a potentially harsher fate. The ship and the sea, then, are metaphorically the mother who comes to his assistance just when the father's dire predictions would appear to be fulfilled. The ship entombed in the canyons of the sea is itself a gigantic cavern with endless supplies, and Robinson roaming around within has become a fetus seeking out sustenance, rowing back and forth to his island, as though still attached to the umbilicus, holding on, and drawing out every possible nourishment before the supply ends. Thus, he regains, at least symbolically, the mother who fled into the background when the father spoke.

We should not forget the psycho-sexual side of Robinson's homelike, economic acquisitiveness. In his desire to pen things in, whether goats or goods, in his penchant for storing in caves, or hiding himself in ships, like Jonah "in the innermost parts of the ship," he is displaying the character traits of the anal personality. In "Character and Anal Eroticism" (1908), Freud spoke of "anal persons" as being "exceptionally *orderly, parsimonious,* and *obstinate.*" By "orderliness," he meant "reliability and conscientiousness in the performance of petty duties"; by "parsimony," he indicated a quality close to avarice; and

---

her ability to change shapes and to avoid the truth, a semblance of Proteus and perhaps of Eve as well.

by "obstinacy," he signaled defiance. Robinson's—and Defoe's—cult of money, gold, coins, and treasure fits well into this union of excrement and value. Robinson hoards. And perhaps the lack of sexual satisfaction so notable in the novel is attached to his enjoyment of compensatory gratification. The point of such remarks is not, of course, to define Crusoe as anal, oral, or otherwise, but to suggest that, psychologically, there may be more consistency in the portrayal than Defoe is usually granted.

We remarked above that sexual matters become significant by virtue of their absence. Yet we can never dismiss Crusoe as sexually neuter or uninterested. We must seek alternatives. Direct sexual fulfillment may have become psychologically impossible because of (1) Crusoe's penitential posture; (2) the Puritan injunctions against fornication and their concomitant application to the economic state of man, in which industry and fear of God produce material goods, while sex produces only the specter of the devil. Indirect gratification, however, comes in his acquisitiveness. Of course, Robinson marries, fathers two sons and a daughter, and experiences his wife's death—but all in less than one short paragraph, after he is old and his fortune is made. No Tannhäuser lured by Venus, no Samson entranced by Delilah, Crusoe shows exemplary devotion to business.

Before his shipwreck and hoarding—which form the gist of the "myth of Crusoe"—Robinson has another adventure on the sea, trying to make his fortune as a "Guiney trader." We note that his fortunes do appear to increase, but he continues constantly ill and seasick when on board ship, as if the law of compensation were already operative. For every financial gain, he must suffer, if not neurotically, then physically.

As a consequence of this adventure, he is captured and held as a slave for two years before he escapes. From this, he moves into a further business deal, involving tobacco, cloths, slaves—people and goods mixed together as simply a money valuation—and he is now ready, he says, "for all the happy things to have yet befallen me for which my father so earnestly recommended a quiet retired life . . ." (p. 33) However, he senses in himself a "wilful agent" which forces him to wander, that is, to seek the devil that is driving him on. Amid all this prosperity and acquisition of goods is a self-destructiveness; so that if we wish to speak of the acquisitive nature of laissez-faire capitalism, we must also speak of its counterpart, the death instinct, which is as powerful as its life component.

When as a still-young man Robinson abandons prosperity, he is very much aware of sinning against the natural order.[6] It is, after all, the elements, the forces of wind and wave, which negate his wild self-determination. In a sense, nature is a limiting force, or at least a mitigating force, against Crusoe's self-love and self-aggrandizement. In a further sense, in order to survive, he must win over nature, embodied as primitivism, *even when nature appears benevolent.* We see this reaction to nature when Friday appears, described racially as a well-set-up Englishman recently down from Oxford or Cambridge, "his nose small, not flat like the Negroes; a very good mouth, thin lips, and his fine teeth well set, and white as ivory." It becomes clear that Friday is a Noble Savage, Montaigne's and (later) Rousseau's natural, noble man. Yet Crusoe must alter even this aspect of benevolent, perfect nature to suit the civilized man's view of nature and life. Friday, like the island itself, must be bent to serve Crusoe's needs.

Friday is gradually transformed into Crusoe's conception of the civilized Englishman, capable of being saved as a Christian, whereas earlier Friday was doomed by his worship of Benamuckee to reside with the devil. Thus, Defoe takes a position that is anti-nature. Novak says that for Defoe, as for Crusoe, "true freedom is not to be found in the state of nature but rather under law and government." (*Defoe and the Nature of Man*, p. 18) Although not a strict Hobbesian, in that he granted more individual freedom than Hobbes did, Defoe believed in a strong, hierarchical state, a point that is immediately apparent in Crusoe's structuring of his island once a society is constituted. He insists on a ruler, a government, a contract. "First of all, the whole country was my own meer property; so that I had an undoubted right of dominion; 2dly, my people were perfectly subjected: I was absolute lord and lawgiver." (p. 194) Within this structure, Friday is clearly destined to be a servant, despite his embodiment of nature's most noble features.

We now measure the full dimensions of Robinson's Crusoe's rebellion, for he finds himself opposing not only father and family but nature and God. Of course, he is not truly existential, for he

[6] In *Defoe and the Nature of Man*, Novak points out that Defoe's belief in necessity made him urge that certain forces were operative that went beyond individual will; and therefore we can say Crusoe was caught up by events and desires that were outside personal choice. (p. 88 and passim)

neither expects nor receives the droppings of an absurd universe. On the contrary, he remains optimistic that if nothing else helps, prayer will provide salvation. God *is* a comfort, and man in solitude is never completely alone. Ultimately, all roads lead to and away from God. If we speak of Crusoe's self-destructive impulses—his desire to probe the forbidden and flirt with death—we must also see them as part of a psychological and religious process. Such destructive impulses are not truly co-equal with the life-giving libido. They are, after all, temporary, and life is permanent. Crusoe is much closer to Benthamism than to any twentieth-century "ism" which flirts with self-destruction. His rebellion runs its course, not toward any alteration of society, which would be contrary to Defoe's beliefs, but rather toward reconciliation with the values that Crusoe's father asserted were the best part of the middle class.

Moore speaks of Crusoe finding his life shattered by the appearance of the savages, but that very shattering reveals salvation. Fear and trembling must always precede self-discovery. Crusoe differs considerably from Moll Flanders in that he is very aware of a superego, that social and parental gift of a sense of right and wrong. Moll lacks this quality, since her background is crime, but Robinson rarely deviates to her extent to trafficking so openly with pure id.

We can measure the true mythical quality of Robinson Crusoe in his movement toward the periphery of what his society permitted. Like Defoe himself, he is caught between worlds: between mercantilism and an emerging laissez-faire economy; between social and economic man; between the status quo and economic and political individualism; between king, state-oriented Toryism, and trade-oriented Whiggism; between Hobbesian allegiance to the contractual terms of the state and rebellious commitment to personal tastes and goals; between traditional parental advice and the desire to seek dangerous new experiences; between Puritan religious traditions with their sense of sin, salvation, predestination, delayed gratification, emblematic symbolism, divine purpose, and a more atomic approach to the cosmos in which spiritual matters were merely part of the mixture.

Under such tensions, it is not unusual that Crusoe should suffer a conflict of conscience, that he should suffer the guilt of social breakdown. Although his society did not itself collapse, it was divided enough to preclude certainty and security. For persons caught in such divisions and near-breakdowns of tradition, Robert

Jay Lifton has coined the phrase "protean man," used to denote an emerging type that can assume various roles seemingly without pangs of conscience or any great psychological transformation. Like Proteus, such a "new person" plays his roles as if they were all the same; unlike the mythical figure, however, the new man suffers "often without awareness of what is causing his suffering."

His guilt—and here we have parallels with Crusoe's—is a "vague but persistent kind of self-condemnation" related to his inability to identify consistently with anything outside of himself. Only midway through the novel can Crusoe pinpoint what he calls his "original sin," the source of his sense of guilt, unworthiness, and anomie. And he can only pinpoint a reason for his feelings *because* his society is sufficiently structured. In a society that absorbed all ideas as co-equal, in which virtually no differentiation of values occurred, Crusoe would have moved much more unsurely, perhaps never defining his uncertainties.

Popular use of the Crusoe myth is curious. We tend to discount the uncertainties; surely this is not a myth of apprehension or failure. It is, we feel, pre-eminently the myth of achievement. And, characteristically, we have stripped away the religious element, stressing only the makings and doings—which are, of course, the most compelling parts of the novel. There is little question that the religious passages seem tedious now, that Crusoe's dreams and anxieties are seemingly digressions, that the working out of an island society in the latter third of the novel indicates a decline in power and interest; so that the making-and-doing elements do predominate in our reading experience. The real sense of the novel, however, is not that myth; no more than the myth of natural man defines Rousseau or Thoreau. Defoe, we can speculate, may have thought in the wake of the enormous popularity of *Robinson Crusoe* that the public wanted pure adventure, but the lackluster sequel (published just four months later) indicates he misjudged either the public or his own powers.

In his next considerable novel, *Moll Flanders*,[7] Defoe shifted from a sea and island adventure story to a city background, although the

[7] The full title: *The Fortunes and Misfortunes of the Famous Moll Flanders*, & C / Who was Born in Newgate, and during a Life of continu'd Variety for Three-score Years besides her Childhood was Twelve Year a Whore, five times a Wife (whereof once to her own Brother) Twelve Year a Thief, Eight Year a Transported Felon in Virginia, at last grew Rich, liv'd Honest, and died a Penitent. Written from her own Memorandums. (The novel was published in January 1722.)

making-and-doing, survival part of the myth remains strong. Moll is truly a protean woman. Situated as a "poor desolate girl without friends, without cloaths, without help or helper . . ." (Riverside edition, p. 10), she should rightfully hope for nothing more than domestic service. When she is but eight years old, she decides very certainly that she will not serve: "I had a thorough aversion to going to service . . . and I told my nurse that I believ'd I could get my living without going to service . . ." (p. 11) Moll prefers a marginal, dangerous existence. By taking her stand, she has set herself against the social expectations of someone of her low birth. By adamantly rejecting anything less than the status of a gentlewoman, she reveals some of the rebelliousness we saw in Crusoe.

Her desire to rise, despite danger, anxiety, dread, flirtation with the hangman, is her "original sin." Although she is not set against the wishes of her parents, she is set against her lower-class status. She defies birth; she defies her name. She asserts her basic democratic rights, which at this time was still revolutionary. As much as Crusoe sets dangerous ideas into motion with his rebellion, so Moll tempts the God who worried Jonah and Job. Her assumption of so many protean roles, then, is connected to her desire to be something she is not.

For a woman like Moll who is not born into something definitive or identifiable, the various roles are all attempts at identity and definition. Thus, she lives out almost her entire career wearing masks, costumes, makeup. Moll is the perpetrator and often the victim of her own farces. Yet she is driven to creating new roles and identities. The narrative is a loose series of episodes in the picaresque mode, held together by a picara of sorts;[8] held together, specifically, by Moll's sense of roles and shapes which enable her to survive within her notion of what a gentlewoman should be. Although she is no idealist, Moll recalls Don Quixote as a character who will reshape and revise reality to accommodate her own view of it. When we read Cervantes, we try to disentangle what others see from the way the Don sees; when we read *Moll Flanders*, our task is evidently

[8] Ian Watt argues correctly, I believe, that Moll and the picara or picaro are not completely similar. The essential difference is that the picaro's experiences are part of a "literary convention for the presentation of a variety of satiric observations and comic episodes," while Moll and those like her are "ordinary people who are normal products of their environment, victims of circumstances which anyone might have experienced and which provoke exactly the same moral conflicts between ends and means as those faced by other members of society." (*The Rise of the Novel*, p. 94)

easier, but we must, nevertheless, probe beneath masks and disguises to find the "real" Moll.

A good place to begin is Defoe's, and Moll's, sense of the city. While Defoe's vision of London is not quite comparable to Dickens's sense of the city as a world, we must not ignore Defoe's presentation of its streets and activities as part of the precarious balance of life and death. Our pursuit of disguises should start in the city, which masks its innumerable paths to death with a surface of life, bustle, activity, riches, cloths, foodstuffs, material well-being. Even as Moll moves upon the streets, herself a figure of great energy and vitality, we are aware of the several traps which await her, and all of them point toward Newgate prison and execution.

At the time Defoe wrote, more than one hundred different crimes were called felonies, punishable by death; and at the earlier time Moll roamed London's streets, the kinds of felonies punishable by death numbered at least fifty. Thus, if one were poor, expedient, predatory, or simply interested in survival, the gallows was an ever-present danger. And the definition of a felony was often as fickle as life itself. A felony might be stealing five shillings' worth of material from a shop, or breaking a windowpane, pickpocketing more than twelve pence (about one dollar in current value); while a misdemeanor, for which the punishment was less—usually transportation to a colony for a set term of years—often involved violence and crimes of much greater intensity, such as assault and arson. If one were to live by crime, he was attempting to survive within a crazy pattern of punishments administered by a crazy patchwork of judges and juries; bribery and perjury were as much the rule as the exception.

Death, then, was always at one's elbow, and it was disguised only thinly. Newgate prison, the ultimate death symbol, lay waiting, as ferocious and vicious as anything in Christian literature, described as a veritable hell:

> . . . the justice upon that point committed me [Moll], and I was carried to Newgate; that horrid place! my very blood chills at the mention of its name; the place where so many of my comrades had been lock'd up, and from whence they went to the fatal tree [the gallows]; the place where my mother suffered so deeply, where I was brought into the world, and from whence I expected no redemption but by an infamous death. To conclude, the place that had so long expected me, and which with so much art and success I had so long avoided. [p. 238]

The last sentence is important: Newgate was waiting for Moll as surely as the island awaited Robinson Crusoe. In Defoe's terms, there is a necessity that acts beyond individual will, not as crushingly as in Hardy, or as malevolently, but it nevertheless exists, and it restricts those who hope to move unopposed against the world. Newgate, then, is necessary as part of Moll's experience; she must see that life is only a thin shield against death, that what she has always feared is always ready to limit her acquisitiveness. By noting that punishment—swift, harsh, and fickle—awaited all endeavor, whether in crime or in trade, Defoe created psychological tension; whereas his contemporaries, who wrote romance or history, failed to see that necessity blocked man's drive for power.

For our purposes, however, the element of death is the significant factor. For if death is hidden in the streets of the city, then the character—Moll—must also assume the mantle and shape of different creatures in order to throw off death's pursuit. Seen this way, the disguises and masks, the assumption of different roles, different accents, and even the form of the opposite sex, are all attempts to survive the ever-present, ever-ready, insistent death threat. We normally do not interpret Defoe as a tragic novelist, saving that epithet for Richardson, but the tragic element in *Moll Flanders* is surely the shadow of the gallows which is present in every poor man's life; as much as a crushing iceberg awaits every unsuspecting ship in Hardy's great poem "The Convergence of the Twain." London, then, is not merely "life" or "energy" but a place in which lives are intensely reduced because of the specter of doom.

In his *Journal of the Plague Year*,[9] Defoe presented a comparable London, a city of death, a necropolis, in which those who wanted to dupe themselves maintained a thin disguise. Eventually, however, disaster poked through every seam, until death reigned amid life, rather than life amid death. Even the description there of life-and-death, the way one is coiled within the other, recalls how London gulled the living to their graves. Defoe writes:

> For example, many persons in the time of this visitation never perceived that they were infected till they found, to their unspeakable surprise, the tokens come out upon them; after which they seldom lived six hours, for

[9] According to William McBurney's *A Check List of English Prose Fiction 1700–1739, Moll Flanders* (despite 1721 on the title page of the first edition) and *A Journal of the Plague Year* were published in the same year, 1722, a point of some interest when we examine the London of both pieces.

> those spots they called the tokens were really gangrene spots, or mortified flesh in small knobs as broad as a little silver penny, and hard as a piece of callus or horn; so that, when the disease was come up to that length, there was nothing could follow but certain death, and yet, as I said, they knew nothing of their being infected, nor found themselves so much as out of order, till those mortal marks were upon them. But everybody must allow that they were infected in a high degree before, and must have been so some time, and consequently their breath, their sweat, their very clothes, were contagious for many days before. [Doubleday edition, p. 313]

If London is a snare, morality is unfixed and life must take varied shapes. In several ways, Moll embodies what Lifton has called "self-process," which conveys the idea of flow. This "self-process" or unfolding replaces the notion of identity for Moll, and it may have application to any number of eighteenth-century protagonists, male and female, who assume various shapes and roles during their careers until, at the end, they gain some fixed identity. We should note that this theme begins to appear in literature for the first time in something other than romance or comedy, where it had always flourished. Mistaken identity, disguised identity, men in drag, women in men's clothes, all of these are traditional in Terence, Plautus, Shakespeare, but in *comic situations.* In the novel, they appear in the intermediate stage Frye calls the "low mimetic," which is not quite comic and usually not tragic: what we may call "bourgeois serious." In this sense, Moll is the first of our bourgeois heroines, whose route to the top is somewhat bizarre since it consists of inflation and deflation, of constant reshaping. To fit is all.

The need to assume and to penetrate disguise was surely significant for Defoe, who cyclically and cynically moved in and out of political positions, who argued for both sides, who hid behind one ministry after another, who was a Tory when Tories were in power, a Whig when Whigs were, who moved as spy, at times seemingly for either side, who alternated between bankruptcy and solvency, who dipped in and out of professions. A jack-of-all-trades, like Figaro, is a man in a masquerade, disguised as this or that, now here, now there, his center nowhere or everywhere. Two years after *Moll*, Defoe published *Roxana*, in which the protean self is even more apparent. At one time or another, Roxana disguises herself as a Quaker, a Turkish woman, a lady of quality, a countess, a wife (while still a mistress), and a French lady (when she is English to her fingertips). While hidden within the folds of her disguises, she piles up gains, whether clothes, titles, or marriages. All gain, evidently, must be paid for with loss of identity; one literally gives oneself away in order to be rewarded with money and property. Since the shape or form of the object is never the object itself, the individual learns that "seeming" is more rewarding than "being."

If we agree that disguise and mask are keys to Moll, as well as to her literary progeny, then we can see that in the eighteenth century the novel caught the "psychobiological potential of individual behavior," to use Lifton's phrase, long before the idea became established. We can now discuss the contours of Moll's career. Defoe's narrative technique reinforces the idea of layers and clothes both literally and symbolically hiding the true self, or the true sense of things. The narrative of the novel is related by Moll and is really the narrative of a creature named Betty, born in Newgate to a woman who escaped hanging by pleading her belly. Moll Flanders is a name Betty acquires, although Defoe never states her real name. "These were they," he writes, "that gave me the name of *Moll Flanders*: for it was no more of affinity with my real name, or with any of the names I had ever gone by, than black is of kin to white, except that once, as before, I call'd my self Mrs. Flanders, when I sheltered my self in the Mint . . ." (p. 186) Thus, the form of the novel, narrated by a character living under an assumed name, has its own ambiguities; for the realities of the experience are subject to Moll-Betty's way of seeing them and, therefore, to whatever coloring she puts upon these experiences.

In his preface to *Moll Flanders*, Defoe compounds the disguised nature of the narrative by saying that "the original of this story is put into new words, and the stile of the famous lady we here speak of is a little alter'd, particularly she is made to tell her own tale in modester words than she told it at first . . ." Defoe points out that the original tale was written "in language more like one still in Newgate than one grown penitent and humble . . ." (p. 3) He mentions he has taken all possible care to prune out all lewd ideas and the worst profanities. Of interest is that another hand has worked over the inset narrative, so Defoe asserts, and we find ourselves approaching a modernist's narrative technique, such as Conrad's in *Heart of Darkness*; there, the novelist controls an "I" narrator, who introduces Marlow, who tells us a tale of Kurtz. While Defoe is less sophisticated and less artful, there is sufficient evidence to note that at every level, from narrative method to subject matter, his idea was to reveal concealed layers.

Moll's failure to achieve anything close to passion or emotional commitment to men or children may perhaps be ascribed to the method of narration. Since she relates these experiences when she is at least seventy, all that remains in her memory is the fact of a long-ago and faraway relationship. The emotional coloring has faded with time. In a way, Defoe has found the perfect vehicle for his own unsentimental approach, and a perfect means for an age that said it valued the reasonable over the passionate man. From her vantage point of years, Moll can retell her history as if it were the history of *all* women caught in need and trying to rise above their station. What appears to us mechanical may be merely a chronicling, not an emotional release.

In another sense, of course, the narrative form of *Moll Flanders* is strikingly close to the picaresque. Moore points out that at least two of the sources of the novel are rogues' biographies. In one, Defoe, as early as July 1720, "had written a letter from 'Moll of Rag-Fair,' an expert pickpocket"; and in the other, Defoe wrote a news story for Mist's *Weekly-Journal* which told of one Moll King, "a most notorious offender, famous for stealing Gold Watches from the Ladies' Sides in the Churches, for which she has been several times convicted, being lately return'd from Transportation, has been taken, and is committed to Newgate." (*Daniel Defoe: Citizen of the Modern World*, pp. 242, 243) Although this story was not published until almost eight months after *Moll Flanders*, it would appear that Defoe drew on common material for the two pieces.

Once we see how closely *Moll Flanders* is connected to the picaresque—whether or not she is a picara—we note that the picaresque form allows for the shaping and reshaping of man or woman in the process of becoming. Moll comes into our view with that peculiar combination of tough realism intermixed with a good deal of ambiguity because of her lack of center: the same qualities that recur in most picaresque novels. What disturbs us as we read her narrative, with our expectations that the novel will somehow resemble life, is how unrealistic her sense of herself is, even as her adventures and reactions are quite realistic. There is a connection we feel Defoe has not closed, so that our doubts dribble through, and much as we want to accept Moll for herself, something disallows such knowledge.

As I have suggested, all true picaresque contains the same failing. Despite its energy and vitality, it lacks a real center located in moral principle. (*Don Quixote*, with its solid metaphysical basis, falls outside the genre. It is a romantic anti-romance, what Frye calls "intellectualized satire.") What Moll lacks is reaction to an "other," whatever we ascribe to that quality. An "other" differs for each individual, but it involves what we measure ourselves against, our way of coming to terms with our personal lives against the larger sense of life.

For Moll, the "other" is simply the shadow of the gallows which falls over all her activities. She has little sense of herself as an individual in a certain time and place; survival pre-empts virtually all. Moll could not be deflected by an idea, a need, a vision not directly related to survival and salvation. There is no poetry in Moll, and it is not enough to say that her desperate economic condition precludes poetry. The economic condition aside, there would still be small chance for poetry, for there is no speculation, little symbolical existence (despite all the clothes), less metaphor.

When we say she lacks a center, we mean more than that she lacks a passionate life. She lacks, as well, any sense of restriction, of frailty, of human limitation, of love. She never slides toward tragedy. She shows no interest in London beyond what its goods offer, beyond its inhabitants as shills and gulls. Her self-centeredness precludes introspection; despite her will to survive, she lacks that other side of "will" which connects one to the larger world. Her marvelous vitality cuts her off from introspection; and it is, of course, introspection which gives identity. Moll lacks all the dreads of civilization—a sense of sin, guilt, anxiety, foreboding about final things besides the gallows. We could obviously counter this argument by reaffirming that Moll's purpose in life *is* set by her unfortunate beginnings; that she has focused all her energies upon raising herself from the situation in which her mother left her; and that, like Crusoe, she has eliminated from her mind and actions those introspective elements which could hobble or shackle her. According to this view, Moll is so "inner-directed" that all other phenomena exist only to further her own purposes.

Even as we say this, however, and perhaps grant its validity, we recognize that what may be necessary for Moll's own sense of her life is insufficient for the sense of fiction. Even while we grant that Moll and Crusoe, as well as Roxana, Colonel Jack, and Captain Singleton, have found how to deal with their lives by eliminating waste—passion, sexual love, emotional depth—even while we grant this, we must return to these elements as necessary for the fictional development of character. Admittedly, in real life there are people who are without such commitments, without identity, and they are not necessarily freaks; nevertheless, the probabilities of fiction always return us to those generalizing qualities which we assume and expect in all people.

Moll's lack of center leads to several suggestive points. Since she is not clearly identified by her psycho-emotional life, she is virtually interchangeable with a man. That is to say, Moll may appear to be a "liberated woman," and she is, evidently, liberated. The liberation, however, is of a *person, not a woman.* Clarissa, perhaps ironically, in the light of her destructive career, is really the first liberated woman; for she refuses the roles cut out for her when actual survival is not at stake. She insists on her psychological survival, the point that deceives those around her.

Moll is too willing to assume any shape, including that of a man. She would be a man if she had the opportunity, while Clarissa insists on her rights as a woman. Thus, Moll is psychologically indistinguishable from Defoe's other male-female characters. In her attitude toward her children, for example, parental love is not a significant factor; nor is, except with Jemy, her attitude toward the opposite sex. One poke is as good or as bad as another. Her reaction to sex is undifferentiated, useful when it makes her money, unmissed when she reaches menopause. Her ideas about life and about herself are in a middle ground, neither defined by her situation as a woman nor delineated by her historical role. She could as willingly be a male as a female whore, a male as a female thief. She insists upon nothing, while Clarissa insists upon all.

In still another respect, Defoe's prose style is a direct factor in the lack of center in Moll and in his other protagonists. His factual, thing-filled, objectified language is of great importance in the development of fictional prose, but in Defoe's hands it is incapable of expressing a great range of subtle feelings. Following Locke and his imitators, such a language stresses primary qualities: matter, solidity, motion, extension. Ian Watt draws attention to the connection between Defoe's prose and the "new values of the scientific and rational outlook of the late seventeenth century." (*The Rise of the Novel*, p. 102) Watt mentions the desire of the Royal Society (chartered in 1662) to further a more factual prose, an influence that would extend throughout society; and the growing tendency for sermons to become less pedantic, less "rhetorical," in which "plainness [was the] supreme aim." None of this suggests that Defoe was himself influenced by one particular force or style, but it does indicate his normal, usual style was itself part of a late-seventeenth-century development. Defoe's prose does not demonstrate much abstraction, or qualities such as taste, color, and sound. It has no aestheticism—no awesome sunsets or sunrises, no interest in nature aside from its life-sustaining qualities, no concern with involved metaphor.

Richard Altick observes that the people who "devoured *Robinson Crusoe*" were "small shopkeepers, artisans, and domestic servants—people who had gone to school for only two or three years." (*The English Common Reader*, p. 63) The success of such books, as well as the fact of their very existence, is connected to a plain prose style; and certainly if the new prose fiction found such success with Defoe's work, the tendency would be to repeat a workable formula. Altick continues: "Then when the writing and sale of fiction became the occupation of hacks and booksellers who cultivated a shrewd awareness of the special interests and limitations of their semi-educated audience, the novel became the favorite fare of the common reader . . ." (p. 63)

This reliance on successful formulae hobbled Defoe as a novelist. He provides little linguistic equivalent of what we assume should be profound experiences. Moll's sharp reaction to her fraternal incest is realistically healthy, but her language cannot express the psychic blow such transgression of a social taboo would normally carry: ". . . and tho' I was not much touched with the crime of it, yet the action had something in it shocking to nature, and made my husband even nauseous to me . . . and thus I liv'd with the greatest pressure imaginable for three years more." (p. 79) When she finally informs her brother-husband of the true state of affairs, his look is wild, but her command to the servant is for a "little glass of rum." The taboo relationship is itself part of Moll's role, and our quarrel is not with that aspect of it but with the failure of language to distinguish between feelings which should be everyday and those which should be extraordinary.

In some ways, Defoe's inglorious prose style was his glory; it could do certain things essential for the establishment of a new form. Yet, at the same time, it could not provide sufficient differentiation among various states of feeling. And even if the point is that passions must be tamped down in favor of survival, nevertheless that point is itself outside the fictional values involved. If language cannot distinguish among states of feeling, character must remain one-dimensional.

In another instance, when the moral values of the novel demand we understand Moll's extreme horror and desolation at facing, finally, the gallows, the novelist is unable to convey that sensibility at the moment it is to be extinguished forever. This moment is extremely important, for throughout the novel we have been drawn closer and closer to the gallows as the ultimate arbiter. If all roads lead to the gallows for the poor and the poorly born, then Moll's experience with her just fate must be hers and Everyman's. Yet her reflection upon *this* world (of sordid trifles) and *that* world (of eternal felicity) is little different from Crusoe's bland instruction to Friday. Moll speaks of "severe reproaches for my wretched behaviour in my past life; that I had forfeited all hope of happiness in the eternity that I was just going to enter into . . ." (p. 250) Later, when after confession she feels the illumination of God's grace, she finds her name on the death warrant, and "indeed my heart sunk within me, and I swoon'd away twice, one after another, but spoke not a word." (p. 252)

The language is little different from that used to describe a theft, or the casual birth of a child, or an arrangement for room and board, and yet it is here involved in confronting death on the most sordid terms, without any sense of grandeur or sacrifice or value. Because the prose remains homogeneous, the important point of the content, which is Moll's conversion under the shadow of the gallows, goes the way of all other elements. Death, which had been the monstrous enemy, becomes matter-of-fact. Further, there can be no extension into a larger world of values, no measurement of self against general selves, no opposition or reconciliation between individual and metaphorical elements.

Such shortcomings in the prose and in the vision flatten out Moll and other Defoe characters to more typical picaresque figures and help account for our sense of their centerlessness. Yet even as we apply strictures, we are driven back to Defoe's major point: that a person like Moll has to experience indignities without buckling under, that survival is a matter of necessity, that any kind of experience is bearable if survival is at stake, that the wise man or woman does not quibble about ends and means when his life may run out. Even as we may be appalled by such amorality, and it is Crusoe's philosophy as well, we find anyone admirable who can constantly seek new shapes for new situations. Unlike Dickens, Defoe supports upward mobility; it is not yet, as the Victorians were to see it, exploitative.

We admire, further, Defoe's attitude toward women. His egalitarianism in regard to the sexes does not stress "feminity" or "feminine grace" as a means for attacking women. Novak reminds us that in his *Essay Upon Projects* Defoe criticized the lack of educational facilities for women in England and asserted that women were more worthy and fearless than the men who directed them. We recall, in this respect, that Moll makes all the arrangements in the New World, while Jemy, the gentleman, hunts. Further, while Moll's husband-brother is "half-dead," she is all bustle and energy, stocking her plantation as Crusoe stocked his island.

Necessity is all, men are predatory animals who must be given their rights, and women, no less than men, are caught in the traffic for survival. Any means are justifiable, even, under certain conditions, murder. What also impresses us through the amorality of this is the simplicity and purity of motive; crime does not harden Moll, no more than isolation maddens Crusoe. People are capable of adjusting without changing internally. They remain precisely what they have started out to be, even though twenty-eight or fifty years of experiences run strikingly counter to their original state of being. Their psychological condition is keyed in to what they want, not to frustrations or failures.

We can only marvel at the purity of such lines, and all this in a realistic frame of reference. Man's function is to apprehend the world, find ways to grapple with it, hang on while events frustrate him, defy society if it runs counter to his own needs, stand firm as his body grows flabby and his hair grays; and, eventually, he comes through, while those around him may waste away. Defoe is interested only in the successes, and even God and fate cannot prevent the persistent individual from coming through. It is a marvelous myth, which, like many myths, does not warrant too much close examination. For later English novelists, such as Dickens, life begins where Defoe leaves off.

Yet Defoe established enough material for the development of the novel, enough for us to say that the novel as we know it was created within the thirty-year period following the publication of *Robinson Crusoe.* By 1749, with the major work of both Fielding and Richardson behind them, the genre had been defined and practiced; except for variations of form and content, the novel was fixed until the last quarter of the nineteenth century. Defoe imposed form on the picaresque, turned it somewhat from its episodic nature, transformed the picaro into character, gave substance to female aspirations, provided a realistic temporal and spatial frame of reference for characters and events, assimilated his society and its ethic into his fiction while giving play to those who rebelled against the social ethic, and, finally, established a prose style that was sufficiently denotative and yet flexible enough to differ from journalistic prose. *Robinson* and *Moll* made possible a Defoe world, a Defoe style, even a Defoe myth.

3

Samuel Richardson and Clarissa

Following Samuel Johnson's remark (contrasting Fielding as a novelist of nature with Richardson as a novelist of manners), most commentators have identified Richardson as the genius of plot. Richardson was also the genius of interiors, the first to note that the English talent in its novels, unlike its poetry, was to be indoors, not in the streets or countryside. Exceptions abound—Eliot, Meredith, and some of Dickens are not to be held within any formula; but the major development of the English novel from Richardson and Austen has been along time-oriented, interior-oriented lines.

The drawing room, normally with two, often at most four, participants, has provided drama; the technique has been epistolary or a self-conscious first- or third-person narrative, and the tone usually has been comic. Even Fielding, who pursued a space-oriented picaresque form in *Joseph Andrews* and *Tom Jones,* helped to define, however inchoately, a style and mode that would blunt the outdoor quality of picaresque and position its rakish characters and their activities within. We can suggest, then, that the major movement of English fiction starting with Richardson has been away from picaresque episodes toward the two-person, interior scene using elements of irony, concealment, wit, hypocrisy, affectation, vanity, and innocence.

Seen as the first major interior novel, Richardson's *Pamela, or Virtue Rewarded* loses some of its banality and becomes a cultural landmark. Although most of this chapter will be devoted to *Clarissa*, the greatest fictional achievement of the eighteenth century, it is not always the greater work which is the more significant cultural guide. For, in its way, *Pamela* became an "event," comparable to Dickens's fictional debut with *Pickwick Papers* or, differently, and more importantly, Flaubert's with *Madame Bovary*. *Pamela* established certain ideas about the art of the novel which are comparable in their relative importance to the ideas established later by Flaubert, as well as by James, Conrad, and their epigoni.

As the epic was exhausted in the triviality of the mock-epic, so the romance was finally to expire and re-emerge realistically in the "triviality" of the domestic novel. In some extended generic sense, *Pamela* (called the "Cinderella archetype" by Northrop Frye) is mock-epic, what *The Rape of the Lock* is to the rape of Helen by Paris, a tone Fielding missed in his burlesque *Shamela*. For the career of Pamela is the apotheosis of the mock- or petit-epic housewife; she is a de-heroinized heroine, the chief character in a work of fiction that in virtually all categories is anti-fiction. Her novel works within a realism that defies realism and outfarces farce, with a narrative whose sentimentality challenges logical extension.

Richardson advanced over Defoe in his heroine's ability to say no, and no again, not in thunder against God, but in defiance of a lesser god, the male, and to say it until the novelist has plumbed all possible situations based on "no"—temptation, seduction, danger. When "no" finally prevails, an existential moment of self-assertion, Richardson moves to "yes, with marriage," and he is set for the later parts of the novel and the sequel to it. In saying no, Pamela achieves a status denied Moll Flanders and most of the previous amatory heroines (from the novels of Mrs. Davys, Mrs. Haywood, and Mrs. Manley), whose trials proved far simpler to resolve. For Pamela, whether in innocence or in full knowledge of how to trap Mr. B., achieves the qualities normally associated with a goddess. One may scorn her as a hypocritical love goddess, one who frustrates the male in order to make him subservient, but whatever the intent or the nature of the resolution, her qualities deify her and make the novel a landmark.

What, then, in her dull, petit-bourgeois way, does Pamela demonstrate? Physically charming as Pamela undoubtedly is, her personal qualities demonstrate an even greater beauty, a Platonic ideal of goodness, honesty, and honor. Indeed, her vaunted virtue, which is all a servant girl has to bargain with, is an ideal virtue,

Richardson repeats, that replaces the high birth, dowry, and other accouterments of the upper-class young lady. Such virtue is the backbone of the sentimental novel. Even more than Clarissa, Pamela lives a Christian life, and her journey toward marriage—whether one takes it seriously or with raised eyebrows—is the Christian's pilgrimage toward the holy place. To attain Mr. B. in marriage is, in a petit-bourgeois way, the equivalent in a more heroic culture of the attainment of the Holy Grail by a questing knight besieged by incessant temptations. Of course, in the domestic or sentimental comedy, a rake's bedroom has replaced Venus's bower; the action has gone indoors.[1]

[1] Marivaux's Marianne (*La Vie de Marianne*) experiences many of the trials which Pamela also undergoes. Several of the similarities are so remarkable that scholars have expended much energy trying to trace a direct influence of the French writer upon Richardson. Apparently, Richardson knew little or no French—or so he said—although it was possible for him to have read the early parts in translation four years before the November 1740 publication of *Pamela*. Yet despite the similarities (comparably humble heroines, first-person narratives, temptations and seductions of innocent beings, certain congruences of psychological detail), there seems to be no proof of influence, or even of awareness. A good summary of the evidence is provided by William H. McBurney and Michael F. Shugrue in their edition of *Marianne* (Southern Illinois University Press), pp. xxiii–xxxv.

More significant than the matter of influence is the coming together of certain cultural phenomena—attitudes toward women, toward parents, toward relationships between the sexes, toward the rights and integrity of the individual, toward questions of choice, dignity, and honor. Such matters made it possible for an entire literature to develop, both on the Continent and in England, involving women, written by women, assessing human relationships of different hues and colors. The writing tends to show a gradual isolation of the individual from the social pact and the body politic, an extremely slow process in which the individual's "aloneness" by degrees begins to define the person.

In two letters, the first to Aaron Hill (late January 1741) and the second to Johannes Stinstra (June 2, 1753), Richardson explained the derivation of *Pamela* in terms that ignore the possible influence of French fiction. In the letter to Hill (*Selected Letters of Samuel Richardson*, ed. John Carroll, pp. 39–40), he wrote that his idea for a servant girl marrying her upper-class master came from a friend's story about a Mr. B., a gentleman whose wife had entered his house at twelve, in his mother's service. When the mother died and the girl continued to develop in beauty and manner, Mr. B. attempted to seduce her. At last, however, "her noble resistance, watchfulness, and excellent qualities, subdued him, and he thought fit to make her his wife. That she behaved herself with so much dignity, sweetness, and humility, that she made herself beloved of every body, and even by his relations, who, at first despised her; and now had the blessings both of rich and poor, and the love of her husband." (p. 40)

In the second letter, a very important autobiographical letter to Stinstra, his Dutch translator, Richardson explains that two bookseller friends had asked him to compile a "little Volume of Letters, in a common Style, on such Subjects as might be of Use to those Country Readers who were unable to indite for themselves." Richardson agreed to the project, including in it his plans to "instruct them how they should think & act in common Cases, as well as indite." In the process of writing the letters, he included two or three, he says, which would instruct "handsome Girls, who were obliged to go

While it is difficult from the vantage point of the twentieth century to avoid mocking the events, we must try to accept the seriousness of the eighteenth-century heroine's personal and social problems. There is no doubt that the view we have of Pamela is a man's, Richardson's. Her role is shaped by her social destiny, which is to be a wife. Her values are in perfect accord with those established for women by society. More than that, she has to become perfect of her kind in order to attract and hold a seemingly unattainable man. Her "flaw" is low birth, lack of family and fortune; but she can overcome it by overcompensating with virtue, a commodity that defines her. Thus, we could argue that Pamela has very little room in which to maneuver, that her destiny is that of every woman in society, and that Richardson sees her only as wife, keeper of the house, belonging like a chattel to the male.

There is, however, another ingredient in Richardson's formulation of Pamela—her insistence on her own values despite considerable pressure, uncertainty, and fear. Within the orbit of her desires, she brings the male to his knees; she does so, of course, in order to capitulate to him. But *on her terms*—she insists upon certain conditions; and while this may not be the liberation of the female—is, indeed, far from it—it is, nevertheless, a movement toward female identity. In the long run, we recognize what Pamela is doing, and for what purposes, but we must not lose sight of the process itself, which does contain elements of limited self-assertion.[2] Religion (her awareness of God's grace) and economic individualism come together to create in Pamela a sense of individual rights and, through

---

out to Service . . . how to avoid the Snares that might be laid against their Virtue." (p. 232) Richardson says he put together his friend's anecdote with the instructive letters and "hence sprung Pamela." Incidentally, Richardson published the book of instructive letters in 1741, the year after *Pamela.*

[2] Like many ideas attributed to Richardson, the self-assertiveness of women in fiction preceded the author of *Pamela.* To mention only one example, Mrs. Mary Davys, in *The Accomplished Rake or Modern Fine Gentleman* (1727), discusses female passions as co-equal with man's and shows at least one female, Belinda, who demands an equal voice in marriage: ". . . a single vote can never do in a matrimonial affair. There must be a joint consent or we shall make a sad botch of what would otherwise be very clever." (*Four Before Richardson: Selected English Novels, 1720–1727*, ed. W. H. McBurney, p. 343) Of course, Richardson did pioneer by making his self-asserting Pamela a servant, unlike the well-born ladies of Mrs. Davys.

Similarly, Hazel Mews (*Frail Vessels: Woman's Role in Women's Novels from Fanny Burney to George Eliot*) points out that we can explain the spate of female novelists later in the eighteenth century by seeing that "underneath it all was women's growing need to explore their own new position in society." (p. 25) Such an exploration of new positions was evidently not only in the author but also in her heroine.

that, a sense of a woman's rights. Clearly, these values remain whether Pamela is herself or Fielding's parody of her.

Connected to these qualities of self-respect and self-assertion is Pamela's display of humility. Whether "insincere" or not, her humility, especially when she appears in "humble garb," is an act of democratic spirit. She seeks to gain respect for herself, even if she intends to trap Mr. B. by such devices. Similarly, her "blood wholesome" is the result of healthy middle- and lower-middle-class stock, lauded in much the same spirit as Robinson Crusoe's father praises the middle state. If we carry the democratic spirit further, we can see that Richardson considers Pamela's self-education—she is said to be a great reader—the equal of the more formal education of the upper classes and superior to it in teaching common sense. Implicit in everything Pamela represents—her self-education, her low but respectable birth, her discretion and common sense—is her equality to those more advantageously born and bred. Democratic qualities connected to the Christian virtues create a cultural heroine far more aggressive and defined than the ambiguous, uncertain Clarissa.

Despite her democratic feelings, Pamela retains respect for the aristocracy and asserts her dutifulness as long as they recognize her rights. She is, clearly, no social revolutionary. On the contrary, she embodies the resolution of conflicting social values. One of the weaknesses of *Pamela*, in fact, is its lack of a rich inner life, and that failure is attached to Pamela's (and Richardson's) attempts to resolve all differences within the bourgeois comforts of a hypergamous marriage. In *Clarissa*, on the contrary, the varied inner life of that novel helps to contradict the external, conscious decisions, and the ensuing conflict between conscious act and unconscious need provides a richly textured dialectic that *Pamela* does not begin to achieve.[3]

[3] Even here, we must be circumspect. A. M. Kearney ("Richardson's *Pamela*: The Aesthetic Case," *REL*, pp. 78–90) attempts to present a more ambiguous and, therefore, a more complex *Pamela*. He argues, among other things, that the reader does not always know the "correspondence between what is written down, and what actually happened." Two kinds of experience operate in the novel, Pamela's own as well as Richardson's; and these two voices or commentaries create complexities and ambiguities, for the Richardsonian voice is continually trying to control the raw materials of Pamela's experiences. There is, accordingly, a rich dialectic between the subjective flow of experience and the more objective authorial commentary. This conflict releases tensions at the same time it attempts to control them, and Kearney praises Richardson for his efforts at reconciling "the internal and external narrative

The narrative line of *Pamela* is singularly simple, almost a model first novel in that the author moves gradually from his interest in "familiar letters" to the letters themselves as narrative. This grouping of letters, their progression toward a predetermined end, the concomitant working out of a central situation, whose incidents and characters are related to the overall structure, is a rudimentary imposition of the letter form itself on the material to create plot. This use of a rudimentary plot structure is attached to a further point, which Ian Watt has shrewdly established: that novels came into being when the "code of romantic love began to accommodate itself to religious, social and psychological reality, notably to marriage and the family." (*The Rise of the Novel*, p. 136) In the romance, Watt asserts, courtly love was a peripheral element, while the main thrust of the narrative concerned a knight's exploits in the field. When this peripheral element moved toward the center, as in Richardson's hands, it usurped all other elements. With Richardson, this accumulation of letters with an established focus, in which marriage is the base, was just such a phasing out of romantic courtly love and the installation of a sense of plot, which is essentially a psychologically-socially realistic element.

In his letters to Sophia Westcomb in 1746, Richardson touches upon his use of the epistolary style as a means of creating a fictional plot. While he does not refer directly to plot, he does speak of the pleasures of letter writing, cites *Clarissa*, the first parts of which were ready in manuscript, and demonstrates that he views letters as a way of imposing order and shape on experience. When the individual sits in her study to write uninterruptedly, "she can assert and vindicate her Claim to Sense and Meaning." (*Letters*, ed. Carroll, p. 68) Letters are preferable to conversation because they are "more pure, yet more ardent, and less broken in upon." (p. 65) They were, evidently, part of Richardson's compulsive desire for order, the professional printer justifying each line, evening out type, seeking the exact character for the available space, careful of detail, proofreading for errors. This professional neatness in Richardson the printer is consistent with the

viewpoint." While we may grant this argument, we must still question the effectiveness of Pamela's commentary, the limitations placed on ideas emanating from a fifteen-year-old, and the restrictions that result from her beliefs. In these areas, Richardson is bounded by the nature of the speaker, regardless of the quality of his own commentary.

detailing of experience in the letters of *Pamela* and *Clarissa*; and, inevitably, just as individual letters are attempts to make sense of disordered events, so the accumulation of letters provides a plot or kind of total order.

None of this suggests Richardson "discovered" plot as one discovers gold or oil.[4] In fact, Mrs. Mary Davys, in her 1725 preface

[4] Nor did he "discover" the epistolary technique. In *Told in Letters*, Robert Day charts the long history of the epistolary technique prior to Richardson: "We may very roughly estimate that a thousand works of fiction, new or revived, appeared in something like forty-five hundred editions or issues between the Restoration and 1740. Of these, over two hundred works in five hundred editions or issues were letter fiction. This proportion compares very favorably with that for the years 1740–1800, when the English epistolary novel was in its heyday." (p. 2)

As Day points out, however, the mere use of letters does not in itself constitute an epistolary technique. The latter involves more fully letters which "tell us much about the emotions and reactions of the sender," and which make essential contributions to plot or narrative. In this respect, Day writes: "before Richardson's emergence as a writer all the elements of the genre which he brought to maturity were present in English fiction and had already been developed to a degree which he certainly reached but did not often surpass. What the earlier epistolary novels lacked was the simultaneous presence of all these elements combined into an organic whole and sustained through a long narrative of significance and depth." (pp. 190–1)

For an analysis of the epistolary technique *after* Richardson, see Frank Gees Black's *The Epistolary Novel in the Late Eighteenth Century*, which is concerned primarily with the period from 1781 to 1800. Black asserts that eight hundred epistolary novels appeared in the century after *Pamela*, and that in the thirty years beginning in 1760, epistolary novels and their type accounted for one third of all novels published, although Richardson's ingenuity left "comparatively little for his followers beyond tame imitation." (p. 1)

Black lists some of the later variations of the epistolary method: the suppression of return letters; the use of improbably long, even one-hundred-page letters; letters headed with the hour as well as the date; letters inserted within other letters; letters used to modify the narrative line; use of secondary commentators to vary the angle of vision; use of auditors to comment on passages; use of a character who writes *different* things to three or more people (the opposite of Smollett's technique of having different people focus on the same experience). Many of these variations and developments, of course, appear in more important writers, such as Smollett and Burney, as well as in Richardson's minor imitators.

In a somewhat different approach to the development of the epistolary technique, Charles Kany in *The Beginnings of the Epistolary Novel in France, Italy, and Spain* asserts that both the eighteenth-century use of letters and Richardson's method owe much to earlier letter forms in Romance languages. By citing earlier forms on the Continent, Kany tries to deny Godfrey F. Singer's argument (in *The Epistolary Novel*) that the method achieved maturity only in England. Kany, however, does not distinguish between the simple use of letters and the epistolary form. Thus, he includes as Continental variants episodes involving "rifled postbags, letters of travel, friendly correspondence, the correspondence of lovers," and other such relatively isolated devices. As for the novel form itself, Kany considers anything a novel which contains elements of verisimilitude. This attitude takes him as far back as Machaut's *Livre du voir-dit* (ca. 1363), which is a combination of "poetic correspondence with a story based on reality," but hardly our current view of a novel.

to her *Works*, declared she had "in every novel proposed one entire scheme or plot, and the other adventures are only incidental or collateral to it, which is the great rule prescribed by the critics, not only in tragedy and other heroic poems but in comedy too." While this comment is familiar as part of the classical notion of unities, it does look ahead to the sense of plot demanded by the novel, and Mrs. Davys tried to keep within her declared terms. *The Accomplished Rake* is a realistic portrayal of a "Hamletic" rake, a forerunner of Lovelace—even to his rape of the drugged heroine—whose career, however, is dealt with in "plain fact."

Mrs. Davys is only one of numerous writers who came upon plot well before Richardson. What Richardson did, however, was to pare away excesses, so that the outline was sharp; and, at the same time, he intensified each character's relevance to the central problem. The way Richardson could exclude, focus, and intensify was through letters, which allow no interruption of thought or feeling and are directly related to the experience of the writer. This is, surely, an appropriate place to examine some of the ways in which the epistolary method was a perfect expression of Richardson's individual and novelistic needs. We recall, incidentally, that the age was itself one of great letters and great letter writers, among them Horace Walpole, Lady Mary Wortley Montagu, Swift, Pope, Cowper, and Gray.

One significant aspect of the Richardsonian method, and that which so outraged Fielding's sense of propriety, was the former's self-indulgence. The epistolary method springs from and plays to exhibitionism and voyeurism. Richardson speaks of correspondence as an opportunity for "displaying the force of friendship," for showing the "pleasures that flow from social love," for recalling to "sweet remembrance all the delights of presence," of having the individual "before me in person"; indeed, he writes, "I see you, I sit with you, I talk with you, I read to you, I stop to hear your sentiments . . . your smiling obligingness, your polite and easy expression . . . are all in my eye and my ear as I read." (To Sophia

---

Like most literary topics, the epistolary technique has divided its chroniclers. While Helen S. Hughes's "English Epistolary Fiction Before *Pamela*," which appeared in 1923 in *The Manley Anniversary Studies in Language and Literature*, appears to be the pioneering study, Robert Day's book in 1966 is the most sensible and best balanced. Perhaps his most important contribution is that he speaks of the epistolary technique in its relationship to the *novel*, as distinguished from a "fiction" or "romance" which simply utilizes a letter or letters.

Westcomb, *Letters*, ed. Carroll, pp. 64–6) The tone is self-indulgent, the manner sentimental. Letters are clearly an insistent expression of individuality, and their repeated use in fiction is a movement toward sentimentality and romanticism, away from classical rules and external order, toward an internalism based on the individual psyche. Through letters, Richardson could become Pamela, Clarissa, Lovelace, Miss Howe, and so on.

In this respect, we should cite the title essay in Richard Poirier's *The Performing Self*, which discusses literature wherein the authors treat "any occasion as a 'scene' or a stage for dramatizing the self as a performer." Poirier adds: "I can't imagine a scene of whatever terror or pathos in which they would not at every step in their account of it be watching and measuring their moment by moment participation." He speaks of the importance of the "rendition" of the scene, the performance by the authors, since the event "doesn't exist except in the shape they give it."

Poirier is assessing a development in the Romantic movement that is not quite as new as he makes it appear, but is actually already implicit in the self-oriented epistolary method.[5] Poirier's authors are varied: Frost, Mailer, James, Byron, Yeats, Lawrence, even Marvell and Thoreau, all of whom are, in differing ways, more concerned with performance than with the event itself. Poirier's terms of definition very aptly fit the self-indulgent correspondents in a Richardson novel. Nothing is more "performance-oriented" than the letter written "to the moment," as George Sherburn calls it. Richardson employed "a technique that transcribed emotional tensions instantly as they arose and not (to use a later phrase) when they were recollected in tranquillity."[6]

[5] From reading still another Poirier essay in *The Performing Self*, "The Politics of Self-Parody," we can see how the novel is always changing into some further image of itself, how its head is always seeking and finding its tail. Poirier's aim is to find a point of vantage for understanding the fictions of Borges, Nabokov, Barth, Beckett, and Burroughs; but along the way, he speaks of authors who overindulge "in mostly formal displays where little more is accomplished than a repetitive exposure of some blatantly obtuse formal arrangement." While Richardson's work seeks after plot in a way denied by Borges and Nabokov, nevertheless the sense of Poirier's point is present. The epistolary method assumes repetition, views the same material from various angles of vision, and negates objective reality except insofar as it is screened by an individual intelligence. Curiously, objective reality meets subjective consciousness both in the "new novel" and in Richardson's use of correspondence.

[6] " 'Writing to the Moment': One Aspect," *Restoration and Eighteenth Century Literature: Essays in Honor of Alan Dugald McKillop*, ed. Carroll, p. 201.

"small details show that in his mind he actually *saw* the episodes that he depicted." We could, as easily, emphasize that each character is a performer dramatized. Numerous commentators have remarked the influence of the drama on Richardson. Further, we see each performer caught in his role, a condition that becomes especially true in *Clarissa*, where each character insists on his or her own psychological fix even if it proves self-destructive. Each letter, therefore, in a very modern sense is an expression of the character's self confronting the role he has been picked to play; he seeks himself in a mirror image, holding himself up to scrutiny and searching for the "real" person in the reflection.

The further we probe into the epistolary technique, the closer we must come to *Clarissa* and the further we move from the more rudimentary *Pamela.* One of the major weaknesses of the epistolary style, in fact, becomes apparent in *Pamela*: that is, for purposes of verisimilitude the words must fit the speaker, and, accordingly, any limitations in the speaker as to age and education must, realistically, result in limitations in her words and thoughts. This is surely one of the liabilities of having most of the novel reported in the letters of a fifteen-year-old, although Richardson attempted to mitigate such limitations with asides concerning her unusual intelligence, maturity, and reading habits. In *Clarissa*, we find no comparable problem. Clarissa herself convinces us of her intellectual resilience, and Lovelace is clearly a man of considerable subtlety. So, too, with Belford and Miss Howe. Modulations of every kind are possible, and Richardson allows himself the indulgence of roles and styles that goes with the method.

In a very astute essay on rhetoric in Richardson, called "The Style and the Action in *Clarissa*," William J. Farrell argues that Richardson often fell back on traditional rhetorical devices and language from the stage and from the various *Academies of Compliments*, handbooks that supplied inarticulate lovers with stock phrases and hackneyed references. Of particular interest in Farrell's analysis are Richardson's borrowings from the weeping women of the so-called she-tragedy, a melodramatic theater based on supplicating, moaning women. Farrell demonstrates how Clarissa's pleas and turns of phrase are borrowed from the melancholy pleadings of such heroines; while Lovelace's language ranges from the old rhetorical models, the language of "high style," to newer modes of prose that avoid posing and posturing.

Farrell indicates that verbal style is often a clue to action: "Lovelace's shift from the plain to the flamboyant style—or from the flamboyant to the plain—reflects a parallel change in his relationship to Clarissa . . . By associating his villain with a well-known stylistic tradition, then, the author is able to distinguish the 'real' Lovelace from any of his poses." Similarly, with Clarissa's declamations, Richardson "continually and explicitly calls attention to their higher-than-life qualities. If such a passage is not simply labeled as a 'tragedy-speech,' some comment will usually be made about its stage-like delivery." [7] Thus, performance, stage rhetoric, and dramatic effect are rarely far from *Clarissa*, whether as matter or manner.

Once we have noted these dramatic and rhetorical points, we can proceed with our assessment of the epistolary style, recognizing it works best when characters are mature, when they can indulge their own sense of performance, whether it is to play the woman-hating rapist or the man-hating, death-seeking nun. It is performance we seek in the method, that sense of acting out which the novel has exploited since *Don Quixote.*

In several ways, the stream of comments in letters is comparable to the stream of consciousness in the modern novel, whether Joyce's particular kind of "stream," which involves free association, or the more traditional kind of interior monologue we find in Virginia Woolf. In both the epistolary method and "stream" novels, the characters' comments or thoughts *are* the novel. That is, whatever control the novelist has—and he obviously retains a considerable amount—is siphoned through the characters. The character makes the book—in the same sense that an actor "makes" the play.

Further, the characters can always throw into question the visual ability of the other characters, by themselves displaying alternate modes of seeing, feeling, thinking, which are subjectively just as valid. Part of what distracts Lovelace is Clarissa's way of communicating her completely different reaction to similar phenomena. Lovelace has assumed that his way, the male way, of seeing and judging is valid; but Clarissa's views, which her letters reveal, and which are intercepted by Lovelace, reveal to him that all his truths

[7] Farrell's essay was originally published in *Studies in English Literature, 1500–1900*, pp. 365–75; but may be more accessible to the student in *Samuel Richardson: A Collection of Critical Essays*, ed. John Carroll. Quotations are from this edition, pp. 97 and 101.

are problematical. *Thus, Clarissa is shaping the reality that is to include her even as she is reacting to the reality she has helped to shape.* Lovelace must react not only to her as a person seen by his own intelligence but to her reordering of a reality he has never before questioned. In these respects, the letters and the later "stream" both insist on a "way of knowing" and a "way of seeing," and both, therefore, insist on a constantly shifting order of experience, often a contradictory dialectic between outer, objective action and inner, subjective thought.

There are evident differences between letters and stream of consciousness, chiefly in the subject matter. A conservative writer like Richardson is a "closed" author, one seeking to hide even while he pretends to reveal all. As such, his letters screen out anything too revealing. If we wish to see further, we must do so through image clusters, metaphors, inadvertent revelations, the subsurface matter where deposits of meaning accumulate unknown to the letter writer. There is, accordingly, certain to be less breadth and sense of movement in Richardson's stream of letters than in the later stream of consciousness; subjects are taboo, language is restricted, passions are bounded. We sense this in the possibilities Richardson affords Lovelace, in particular. We will observe him later as a character of immense range and potential, but Richardson explores only certain aspects, not out of inability—he does suggest great depths—but because of limitations of propriety to which later writers were not subject. The consequences are immense and are not simply the result of a conflict between a restricted writer and an "open" one. Such consequences involve limitations on the epistolary style, which purports to be revelatory and yet cannot be, for every letter writer weighs his words.

On the face of it, there would appear to be a contradiction between the "flow" of the epistolary method and our sense of it as dramatic. The epistolary technique, however, has within it ironies we normally find in dramatic presentations: the irony resulting from characters seeing in different ways, the irony consequent upon the audience reacting to one set of experiences while the actors react to another, the irony implicit in the ambiguities of actor and role, of real and "performing" person. When we see the letter writers as performers, we see them in double roles: uncertain if their letter will arrive, unsure if it will arrive in time, fearful it will be contradicted by an arriving letter, uncertain whether contact is actually being made and whether the issue is even the same as they stated in their most recent letter.

In Richardson's novel, further, the actor, through his letters, has involved himself in a process which his own role is going to change, and that change will lead to more complications, and so on through potentially almost unlimited variations. The twists of narration are always the result of ironies coming to bear upon certainties, certainties giving way to uncertainties. When this process involves characters such as Lovelace, who has assumed he can control all, and Clarissa, who is used to her own way, the irony is intensified. Although Richardson's view of man is by no means comparable to Hardy's, there is much of what Hardy called the Immanent Will operative in *Clarissa.* The Immanent Will—the sense that man's individual designs are secondary to universal forces akin to chance—blunts Clarissa's desire to honor her own feelings, denies Lovelace's tremendous drive for power through sexual conquest. Thus, the epistolary technique, with its role playing, its lack of clear resolutions, is suitable accommodation for Richardson's half-conscious, half-unconscious mix of self and society.

The dramatic qualities of multiple points of view are of extraordinary psychological interest, for the method posits a reality as *seen* diversely, not as something constant. It stresses the individual mind, which screens and sifts, and by diversifying the objective world, it creates a relativistic one based on subjective data. The multiple point of view works only when it is really multiple, when the reality it questions is unsettled, and when the issues of that reality are intense and momentous.

One of the limiting factors in a novel such as Smollett's *Humphry Clinker* is that multiplicity, although shrewdly conceived, adds very little to what we already know of any given place or event. Matthew Bramble may see Bath as one thing, the younger people see it as another, but what both observe is neither intense nor mysterious, nor, we may add, very complex. Richardson, however, rises to the occasion in *Clarissa*, for the multiple point of view engages itself with profound issues indeed, involving individual and society, class structure, class and sex, parent and child, individual will and chance, the limits of individual behavior, the quest for power, the nature of sexuality as Eros and Thanatos, and other matters. When a novel acts like a prism, showing any given issue in all its colors, then we have justification of method by matter.[8]

As a corollary of questions involving technique, we should note that many of Richardson's letters to Aaron Hill affirm his extended strategical problems in *Clarissa.* The following letters are especially significant: for January 20, 1745/6; for October 29, 1746; for January 5, 1746/7; for January 26, 1746/7. In the last of these, Richardson writes: "I must still say, that I would not have Clarissa in Love, at setting out: And that I intended the [Flame] Passion should be inspired and grow, unknown to herself, and be more obvious, for a good while, to every-body than to herself." (*Letters*, ed. Carroll, p. 81) The concern here and elsewhere with strategic problems is in one major aspect a concern with multiplicity: the need to *authenticate* the individual's vision and not to impose an external viewpoint (the authorial "I") upon the materials of the novel. While these letters are, of course, somewhat crude from the vantage point of later novel criticism, they are nevertheless an early version of the Jamesian concern with narrative technique, what the latter in his *Notebooks* called finding "the real magic of the *right* things." Washed along by his million words of insistent text, Richardson would surely have agreed with James's final comment about *The Ambassadors*: "that the Novel remains still, under the right persuasion, the most independent, most elastic, most prodigious of literary forms."

In a related matter, the epistolary technique satisfied the eighteenth-century novelist's desire to create a sense of history in his fiction, a motif found in Cervantes and continuing through Defoe and Fielding. At the same time, the method allowed fictional elements to enter and distinguish the novel from history. In a non-epistolary form—*Moll Flanders*, for example—it is possible to believe that the entire narrative is true. Moll may be a historical

[8] Alan D. McKillop points out that most of what we know of events in *Clarissa* comes from secondary correspondents, not from primary sources. In fact, as he says, "no protracted correspondence ever takes place between Lovelace and Clarissa." Further, McKillop asserts, Richardson probably suppressed letters that duplicated things we already know, and otherwise abridged or summarized matters we are familiar with. These comments help us to understand why multiplicity of viewpoint does work here. McKillop's final observation is that Richardson's "use of the letter form led him in one direction toward a specific analysis of enmeshing complexities of life, and in another direction toward a heightened awareness of the discontinuities and blockages, the frustrations and loose ends, that seem to make up the plight of man." ("Epistolary Technique in Richardson's Novels," *Rice Institute Pamphlet*, pp. 36–54)

character. Richardson's technique circumvents this problem. The epistolary technique keeps the "living" character before us—writing, thinking of writing, fending for materials, devising schemes for delivery, making deals with servants, seeking hiding places, conspiring, deceiving, revealing—as distinct from the historical element every novel presents, of something lived and past. "Being" replaces the historical past.

All this suggests that the epistolary method is a period convention, and like all conventions, it both contains and creates illusions.[9] While for the Elizabethan dramatist the soliloquy was a "mental process," verbalized to create the illusion of depth and complexity, for Richardson the use of correspondence serves a comparable illusion, one of instant reaction: passion, thought, depth of response. Both the letter writing and the soliloquy are artificial. The audience knows that people do not normally speak out their thoughts in blank verse, and the reader recognizes that young men and women do not spend their days writing eight-page letters. In this respect, the techniques are conventional and illusory: factitious devices we have come to accept for the light they cast, for the intensity with which they carry the burden of matter. At certain points in *Clarissa*, we wonder *if letter writing is not the norm;* much as Proust makes involuntary memory into a way of thinking and Joyce makes the subjective stream seem the whole of experience. When used intensely, the convention and its corresponding illusions become for us the way a certain kind of reality is borne along, a central form of communication.

Primarily, a convention conveys the passion and intensity of the moment. It brings us inside the mind, however crudely, and provides for us, at the same time, the routine affairs of the characters. The latter is a particularly important point because, as a consequence of the convention and the illusion it creates, the observer participates in the minute routines of each character; and this "time sense" is a quality we have already discussed as so significant in the development of fiction.

[9] I use the word "convention" in its primary meaning of a device employed for solving certain technical problems. Such devices differ for each medium and each age. Once they are widely accepted, we call them conventions, and an author or playwright may use them with full assurance the audience will not question this way of presenting reality. The second sense of the word—which does not concern us here—involves elements like stock characters, turns of phrase, conceits, et al., in effect, elements of subject matter, character, plot development.

Such are the advantages of the method, and they clearly outweigh the disadvantages, just as *any* convention that successfully carries the burden of its kind of reality takes on a life of its own. In reading *Clarissa*, we accept that letters *are* reality. Manner *is* matter. Nevertheless, the method has obvious faults, which should not go unnoted. First, there is the limitation we indicated above: that the letter writer, if the matter is to be realistic, must be true to his age and his education, and a limited character must pen a limited letter. This is more a problem in *Pamela* than in *Clarissa*, although Clarissa's letters may be tedious because of her restricted outlook and education. Second, there is likely to be a good deal of repetition, only some of which can be abridged. Repetition is double-edged, for while it may create resonance, it may simply be dull. Replies, especially, involve a duplication of existing material, and, frequently, the additional point of view is inadequate compensation for the review of material. Third, the availability of time, desk, privacy, and writing materials is not always apparent, and on too many occasions the author must work hard to make his method plausible. That is, frequently, method abuses content. The method, accordingly, may call attention to itself, when technique should be chiefly vehicle.

Such limitations become distasteful only in inferior Richardson.[10]

[10] *Sir Charles Grandison*, in seven volumes, two thousand pages, and over 500,000 words, is precisely this kind of inferior Richardson. Richardson wrote *Grandison* in 1753–4, shortly after he extensively emended the third edition of *Clarissa*, and both novel and revisions appear to have derived from similar intentions. The glory of his use of the epistolary technique had been its tunneling effect, and it is precisely that quality which is missing from his revisions and, also, from *Grandison*.

Grandison maintains the method without the dramatic quality demanded by it. This endless novel is, in effect, a badly disguised episodic narrative, and the epistolary method serves not as a way of delving but as a linear device familiar to us from the picaresque narrative. Linear and epistolary, however, are contradictory, since one functions primarily in space and the other, principally, in time. Accordingly, whenever Richardson used epistolary techniques in order to recapitulate past history, as he did frequently in *Grandison*, he was utilizing a method that works at cross purposes to his intentions. More exactly, he was confusing literary means with moral ends. He wrote the novel as a way of presenting a "good man," an imitation of Bunyan's Christian and a forerunner of Goldsmith's vicar; such a presentation, without the dialectic of opposing values and forces within the character himself, was evidently antithetical to Richardson's artistic intentions, with technique too much for the material and the material too lacking in dramatic cogency for the technique.

Further, the novel is much too long. *Clarissa*, while it has arid stretches, is worthy of its great length because the burrowing process makes us live within Clarissa's hothouse, enclosed milieu. The endlessness of *Grandison* is not maintained by any such intensity, but by side issues that consume hundreds of pages. One short example will demonstrate how Richardson has forsaken dramatic intensity for moral fervor.

Early in the novel, toward the end of Volume I (Letter XXXVIII, Harriet Byron to Miss Selby), method and content appear to work together. Richardson is describing a

In his major effort, we accept the epistolary style as the method of a man's vision, both as a psychological and dramatic device. Just as a poem should be explicated only by another, comparable poem, so, too, possibly *Clarissa* should be analyzed in a medium that involves slow revelations, deceit, disguised intentions, mixed motives—that is, in an epistolary style.

Clarissa

By 1748, Richardson had completed the publication of the most ambitious novel of the eighteenth century, in seven volumes, a work of nearly one million words. Published anonymously by the "Editor of *Pamela*," *Clarissa* had appeared, with Volumes I and II on December 1, 1747; III and IV on April 28, 1748; V, VI, and VII on December 6, 1748. For a second edition, in 1749, Richardson printed only the first four volumes. For the third edition, in 1751, however, he added about two hundred pages and published the novel in eight volumes. A fourth edition of seven volumes followed in the same year, and still another edition within Richardson's lifetime appeared in 1759, in eight volumes.

T. C. Duncan Eaves and Ben D. Kimpel, drawing on work by Richardson scholars McKillop, Sale, and Hilles, as well as their own researches, have shown that Richardson had probably completed most, if not all, of a first version of *Clarissa* by mid-1744. The establishment of this early date gives us considerable insight into Richardson's way of working. For it indicates that the first edition was itself a revision—indeed, an abridgment—of an earlier draft; that he rejected Aaron Hill's advice to soften Lovelace's character, although he did make the duel appear to be forced on the rake; that many Clarissa-Lovelace letters were probably abridged or cut out entirely. More importantly, the revisions Richardson made even prior to the first edition demonstrate how he viewed *Clarissa* as a

---

scene reminiscent of *Clarissa*, in that Harriet fears Sir Hargrave will challenge Sir Charles to a duel unless she accepts the attentions of the former, whom she detests. A possible dramatic situation quite novelistic in scope becomes apparent. The use of the epistolary technique could have served effectively, with letters from several sources—Harriet, Sir Charles, Sir Hargrave, et al.—functioning to explore her dilemma and her suitors' conflict. Richardson, however, lost the opportunity—his last opportunity, incidentally, in the entire novel. Instead, Sir Charles magnanimously withdraws from violence, the conflict evaporates, and the plot turns into predictable episodes. At this point, less than one seventh through, Richardson has fallen into the very narrative traps he avoided so skillfully in *Clarissa*, and the novel sinks into bathos.

continuing process. Through rewriting, abridgment, revision, Richardson created several *Clarissas*, so that the novel in its variously shaped and reshaped versions dominated the world of fiction for more than a decade after its publication.

Most of the controversy over the various editions of the novel focuses on the third (1751), for here Richardson did considerable rewriting in order to stress Clarissa's delicacy and to de-emphasize what his readers thought was her prudery. Modern editions of the novel reprint, basically, the 1751 edition. Each version has its own differences and variations; there is no accepted edition of the novel, nor can one be foreseen, since the faulty Everyman edition, based on the 1751 version, is more or less established, even while attacked. In a detailed article on the various editions, "*Clarissa* Restored?", M. Kinkead-Weekes shows that even by the second edition, in 1749, Richardson was stressing Lovelace's duplicity; that is, emphasizing his deceit in leading Clarissa on toward marriage, while making the condition of marriage itself impossible. By this time, Richardson evidently felt *Clarissa* was being misread and Clarissa misunderstood. He wanted to stress his heroine's delicacy, which allows a girl to judge a suitor only by his behavior, and to deny that her rejection of Lovelace resulted from prudery or frigidity.

By the third edition, in 1751, which determined all future editions during his lifetime, Richardson was prepared to make certain his 1749 meaning was understood. Adding more than fifty thousand words of new material, notes, and interwoven comments, he underlined the homiletic quality of the novel, turning Clarissa into an even more angelic figure than before. Reacting almost directly to his audience and especially to female readers, Richardson stressed the didactic elements and denied any weakness in Clarissa herself. The possibility of such flaws had implied a tragic irony in the first edition. Thus, as Kinkead-Weekes points out, the second and, especially, third editions are much cruder dramatically, considerably more diagrammatic. In the 1759 edition, the last within Richardson's lifetime, the author's preface stressed the moral bias of the material, along with a denial of Clarissa's perfection, an emphasis which is not borne out by the much-revised text.[11]

[11] The 1759 preface makes the point that Clarissa is imperfect so that "Divine Grace and a Purified State" have something left to do, that is, to carry her from woman to angel. Later in the preface, Richardson speaks of his aims: "To warn the Inconsiderate and Thoughtless of the one Sex, against the base arts and designs of

Most readers will not read all of *Clarissa* and, therefore, will not be much concerned with editions. They should keep in mind, however, that the various abridgments available are based on the 1751 edition, possibly with some collation from others, so that the student may expect somewhat more stress on Clarissa's perfection and Lovelace's perfidy than would have fallen had earlier editions been taken as bases. By 1759, Richardson was more concerned with homiletics than drama. Nevertheless, we need not take Richardson on his own declared terms, for that would blind us to the fact that *Clarissa* has assumed a life of its own apart from the author's tampering with it.

A novel of one million words allows the reader many starting points. If we begin with the title, we note that editions of the novel during Richardson's lifetime did not mention the heroine's last name, the novel being titled: *Clarissa, or, The History of a Young Lady*; although the opening page of the text refers to "The History of Clarissa Harlowe." [12] In a sense, the slight shift in emphasis between the two headings demonstrates Richardson's own divided aims: between a young lady and her fortunes *and* a more complete history of the young lady in her family setting.

The opening-page addition of the Harlowe name moves us from the general to the particular, from "a" character to the specific struggle she engages in with her family.[13] Throughout the long novel, Richardson reminds us of the Harlowes and keeps them before us

specious Contrivers of the other— To caution Parents against the undue exercise of their natural authority over their Children in the great article of Marriage— To warn Children against preferring a Man of Pleasure to a Man of Probity, upon that dangerous but too commonly-received notion, *That a reformed Rake makes the best Husband*— But above all, To investigate the highest and most important Doctrines not only of Morality, but of Christianity, by shewing them thrown into action in the conduct of the *worthy* characters; while the *unworthy,* who set those doctrines at defiance, are condignly, and, as may be said, consequentially, punished."

[12] One title Richardson rejected: "The Lady's Legacy: or, the whole gay and serious Compass of the Human Heart laid open, for the Service of Both Sexes. In the History of the Life and Ruin of a lately celebrated Beauty, Miss Clarissa Harlowe. Including great variety of other lives and characters, occasionally interested in the moving story. Detecting and exposing the most secret arts and subtlest practices, of that endangering species of triumphant rakes called Women's Men, assisted by corrupt and vicious engines of the sex they plot against. Published in compliance with a lady's order on her death-bed, as a warning to unguarded, vain, or credulous innocence." (*Letters*, p. 77, n. 64)

[13] The student with any edition at hand, whether abridged or full, can follow all page references by date and day (and hour, if necessary). In addition, I have given the letter number and page for the four-volume Everyman edition, which is accessible in most libraries.

even though the middle thousand pages concern Clarissa and Lovelace. The Harlowes are part of the intense struggle:

1. As setting for the generation gap reflected in Clarissa and her family, Miss Howe and her mother, Lovelace and his uncle, and in numerous other subsidiary relationships. This is a point Richardson stressed, as part of the continuing title in the first edition: "Comprehending the most Important Concerns of Private Life And particularly shewing The Distress that may attend the Misconduct Both of Parents and Children, In Relation to Marriage"
2. As particular upper-middle-class representatives in the first half of the eighteenth century, a class defined by business interests and property rather than by heredity; in the potential marriage of a Harlowe with a Lovelace, the latter would be very much aware of his titled family, while the former would bring only money and property
3. As a group of individuals, almost incestuous in some of its attitudes; note the conflicts within the family itself, the role of the women within it, the struggle for power between father and son, between male and female, the role of aunts and uncles in decision-making; the conflict, not only generational, but among siblings
4. As a social unit defining and demanding duty, raising questions of the nature of obedience
5. As a group in relationship to outsiders; its dispensing of power in the form of moneys and properties; e.g., the family as part of a capitalistic society

Unfortunately, many discussions of the novel give relatively short shrift to the family, while Clarissa and Lovelace are brought to center stage. The tensions in the novel, however, are many, rather than few, and we must recognize a kind of slow ballet in which three elements, Clarissa, Lovelace, and the Harlowes, dance attendance on each other. If we recognize this, we see Clarissa torn among her desires in the matter, which is to be left to her own choice of a marriage partner, when and if she is ready to make that choice; the wish of her family that she marry Solmes, ostensibly as a way of consolidating family properties; the wishes of Lovelace, a compounding of several elements of pride, egomania, revenge, delicate feeling, need for and yet hatred of women, self-destruction, will to power.

The minor characters floating in orbit around the protagonists, Clarissa's Miss Howe, Lovelace's Belford, are themselves not directly involved in any conclusive action or in any compelling decisions. They are, as it were, accessories or accomplices after the fact. Clarissa never heeds Miss Howe's advice, nor does she accept her offer of aid, even when such aid could have saved her life. Likewise, Lovelace ignores Belford's cautions, even while he half-recognizes the validity of his friend's warnings. They and the other subsidiary figures act out what the major figures dictate, and so we can rightfully move the novel back to the three basic units: Clarissa, the Harlowe family, and Lovelace.[14]

Since the plot idea is often ambiguous to the modern reader, it may be helpful to clarify that aspect before proceeding further. Much of the uncertainty concerns Clarissa's role: specifically, what avenue of choice was open to her? Put another way, is there any manner or means in which Richardson saw Clarissa's free will leading to her salvation rather than to her destruction? Clarissa is trapped between the Harlowes and Lovelace. To bow to the Harlowes means acceptance of Solmes, whom she detests; to defy her family means eloping with Lovelace, whom she does not want to marry at this point. In either instance, her own wishes are negated. There is, potentially, a third area of choice, which would involve escaping to Miss Howe's, but Clarissa's delicacy prevents her from drawing another into her own problems, though it is, evidently, the only reasonable choice.

Consequently, she is thrown into option one or two, both of which thwart conscious free choice. Once she opposes her family's wishes, she is doomed; and yet she must oppose them. Like a bourgeois Antigone, she must seek what will destroy her. This is precisely Richardson's conception, for what Clarissa is doing is sacrificing earthly satisfaction in favor of everlasting happiness.

[14] The novel takes place in an eleven-month cycle from January 10 to December 18, some time after 1720 and possibly as late as 1732. Eaves and Kimpel (*Samuel Richardson*, p. 239) demonstrate that Richardson evidently did not wish to stipulate a particular year, and his use of Wednesday, March 1, as one of the datings indicates 1721, 1727, 1732 on the perpetual calendar. As for sources: there are no clear-cut sources for the novel, although scholars have mentioned various possible references. For Clarissa and her situation, there are several parallels in dramatic works; for the character of Lovelace and some of the plot elements, we might cite Nicholas Rowe's *The Fair Penitent* and Charles Johnson's *Caelia.* For a more thorough discussion of Richardson's use of dramatic sources, see Ira Konigsberg's "The Dramatic Background of Richardson's Plots and Characters," *PMLA*, LXXXIII, 42–53.

We note, in the intention, a kind of "fortunate fall" in her career, in the following terms: a mythical dimension of the novel suggests the expulsion of Adam and Eve from Eden. Before her expulsion from the Harlowe hearth, Clarissa's family life is, by Richardson's description, idyllic, paradisiacal. Much to the chagrin and jealousy of her siblings, Arabella and James, she is the favorite child in the family and the darling of her uncles. (See, especially, the letter from Belford to Lovelace, Friday noon, July 21; Letter CXX, v. III, 506.) Part of the intense sibling rivalry in the family lies here. All recognize she is bright, sweet, talented, a perfect lady. She is, seemingly, the epitome of acquiescent eighteenth-century womanhood, not unlike our own pre-Faulknerian Southern novelists' ideal of the Southern lady. It is very important we recognize how favorable Clarissa's situation was, and how much she reveled in her role as the "perfect" young woman. When Morden returns to avenge Clarissa, his memory is of a twelve-year-old who was already "perfection itself."

Clarissa's existence, then, was truly prelapsarian in its blissfulness. Her own needs ostensibly were in perfect balance with what society and her family demanded of her; her ego and society's expectations were identical. Then, with the advent of Lovelace, the serpent of the myth, Clarissa becomes a lonely Eve, driven out of her blissful state by her awareness of a new type of knowledge. Any experience of Lovelace is, obviously, forbidden to young ladies who are doted upon by their families. As a rake and libertine, he is a destructive force; not a man to trifle with and not a man to marry, except under special conditions. If her adoring family represents Eden, Lovelace and what he represents are her temptation.

In his restructuring of the myth, however, Richardson understood that the real Clarissa had not yet emerged. Beneath, and untested, was the dynamic Clarissa. In a way reminiscent of Milton's idea of virtue, Richardson tries Clarissa—to see if her virtue is innate or emerges only under testing. In this respect, Richardson rakes over the Miltonic-Bunyanesque material while focusing upon the Eden myth as a method for Clarissa's "trying-out." For it is in the nature of things that Clarissa's prelapsarian experience was inadequate as a way of defining her capabilities. She is considerably more complicated than what her family has observed; but her complexities can only emerge under conditions other than those within the normal family situation.

Clarissa, like the mythical, classical heroes, must make her journey through the perils of various temptations and threats to find her real self. Like a Grail quester, she must preserve her virtue intact, even when guile and deception are employed against her. Opposed to Clarissa's innocence and virtue (superego?), Richardson pits Lovelace and his world (id?)—a world whose wild, feral, savage images strikingly contrast with the soft images of her bourgeois life. Repeatedly, Lovelace is defined by animal images representative of the rake and libertine.[15] His disregard of others is the law of the jungle, and he is the recognized lion, the supreme predator. He applies the spider-and-fly image to himself and Clarissa, but his view of his victim is more than savagely physical; it involves revenge. Desperately fearful of marriage, he intends to make her stand his test, and then to offer her something neither wants. Dancing beyond his outstretched claws, Clarissa is made aware of her frailty, her terrible solitude. She must pursue her destiny unaided. She has been cast out, and she refuses to draw in innocent people. She becomes isolated and doomed, a Christian lamb thrown to the beasts.

Once she finds herself in this situation, a domesticated animal amid lions, Clarissa's real life begins. Potential becomes reality. In

[15] Richardson's imagery describing Lovelace is particularly colorful, picturing him alternately as predator and sadist. Writing to Belford, Lovelace says: "We begin, when boys, with birds, and, when grown up, go on to women; and both, perhaps, in turn, experience our sportive cruelty." Lovelace follows with a graphic description of the struggling bird-woman victim: "How, at first, refusing all sustenance, it beats and bruises itself against its wires, till it makes its gay plumage fly about, and overspread its well-secured cage. Now it gets out its head; sticking only at its beautiful shoulders: then, with difficulty, drawing back its head, it gasps for breath, and, erectly perched, with meditating eyes, first surveys, and then attempts, its wired canopy. As it gets breath, with renewed rage it beats and bruises again its pretty head and sides, bites the wires, and pecks at the fingers of its delighted tamer. Till at last, finding its efforts ineffectual, quite tired and breathless, it lays itself down and pants at the bottom of the cage, seeming to bemoan its cruel fate and forfeited liberty. And after a few days, its struggles to escape still diminishing as it finds it to no purpose to attempt it, its new habitation becomes familiar; and it hops about from perch to perch, resumes its wonted cheerfulness, and every day sings a song to amuse itself, and reward its keeper." (Wednesday, May 3; Letter LXXI, v. II, 245–6)

Clarissa herself describes Lovelace as animalistic: "Never saw I his abominable eyes look as then they looked—triumph in them!—fierce and wild . . . and at times, such a leering, mischief-boding cast!" (n.d.; Letter LXXXVI, v. III, 370) She sees him as a "beast of prey," while Lovelace speaks of flaying a horse until it became a "mess of dog's meat." Later, Mr. Mowbray says he has taken a "pailful of black bull's blood" from Lovelace. Of course, one of the key images is that of the spider and fly, which I take up later. Blood, rage, animal drives, entrapment, bull-like masculinity—such images capture the Lovelace behind the social graces; much as images of flight help define the other, rebellious Clarissa beneath the acquiescent manner.

Richardson's moral frame of reference, the only reality is full of pitfalls and potential disasters. Clarissa now lives intensely. She must be on guard against guile and deception, whether from lies, drugs, or forged letters. She lives, in a sense, existentially, without support from family or friends, her only lifeline the thin thread of letters from Miss Howe. With her own resources she must resist Lovelace, retain her dignity, preserve the virtue of her sex. If she succeeds, she becomes a culture heroine who can nullify Lovelace's profligacy and annihilate his potency.

For Clarissa sex becomes hellish, rotting, and corruptive; sexual activity is illicit, nasty, dirty. Eaves and Kimpel, in their massive biography of Richardson, are naïve to state that "*Clarissa* is not a novel *about* seduction and sex." (p. 269) Seduction and sex are surely not the sole subjects, but the novel is saturated with sexual images *in key parts* of the narrative. Let us run through a representative group: Clarissa's dream of a graveyard rape, both feared and possibly a fantasy wish; her sexual hysteria when Solmes's weight eases onto a chair; the swordplay between James and Lovelace for sexual supremacy, ultimately for Clarissa; Lovelace's obsession with his sexuality, so that sword and sex are inseparable; the "maleness" of Arabella in family matters and especially the masculinity of Betty Barnes; the stress Clarissa places upon chastity, a sexual weapon; the great spider-and-fly image, in which the two insects move in a sexual ballet; the scene between Clarissa and Lovelace at the wall, in which sword, hand, scabbard, sheath, door, and key become symbolic of their sexual fate.

Involved in Clarissa's sexual transgression is also a subconscious social transgression in which she flirts with values that offer alternate and often subversive choices. That is, we can see transgression against chastity—whether by choice or forced—as disastrous, but as a *chosen* disaster, a refusal to accept social propriety at the expense of the self, even when catastrophe awaits the transgressor.

Thus, sexual, and indirectly social, transgression is a descent into a personal hell, complete with inferno images; but it is also the opportunity—often the sole one—for Clarissa to live intensely, the chance she has to project her hidden desires even while martyring herself to a social vision of chastity. Whether or not Clarissa was conscious of the implications of her actions, her decision to run off with Lovelace is a projection of a sexuality and adventurousness which could have no socially sanctioned outlet. Though worlds may separate Defoe's Moll from Richardson's Clarissa, both women are thrown out into the storm, both are forced to seek inner strength, and both must work within male worlds, to succeed or succumb. Ultimately, they will triumph over adversity, in this life for Defoe, for Richardson in the hereafter.

We can now understand Richardson's use of the Eden myth. For Clarissa truly regains the favor she has lost once she has settled on her death course. When she runs off with Lovelace, she moves from the paradise of her early Harlowe years into the hell of her own activities; and, later, when through her virtue she triumphs over those around her and becomes impregnable (though, possibly, pregnant) in her resolutions, she returns to the state of inner grace. Clarissa never really falls, although outsiders assume she has. She can, however, only fully realize what paradise is by losing it. And she can only regain it by searching deeply within herself. She must heed the instruction of the angel Michael to Milton's fallen Adam: "then wilt thou not be loth / To leave this Paradise, but shalt possess / A Paradise within thee, happier far."

Clarissa's intention is always to find meaning, plan, and design in her life, even when chaos seems to direct it. Her resort to letter writing is one means of controlling her destiny; but her own will is the master instrument. Often, modern readers become caught up in the religious nature of Clarissa's quest and, unfortunately, think she is a stereotypical eighteenth-century melting type. Nothing is further from the truth. She is adamant itself. Although she is not predatory—unlike Moll, she has no need to be—she has the willfulness of the predator and the stubbornness of the egoistic. In this respect, she is an excellent foil for Lovelace, for if she makes herself unconquerable, he is the male who must always conquer. She is truly the immovable object, while he is only seemingly the irresistible force.

Lovelace is an extremely complex male figure—the most complex in fiction up to this time and, possibly, in all of English fiction for the next hundred years. Certainly nothing in Defoe or early Fielding prepares us for a Lovelace, and we could well argue that nothing in the roll call of later novelists—the mature Fielding, Smollett, Sterne, the sentimentalists, Burney, Austen—provides as many insights into the male as does Lovelace. Not until the Brontës do we find maleness exemplified in so many of its complications, of warmth and power, sensuality and revenge, charm and self-destructiveness, need for a woman and intense hatred of women, fierce masculinity mixed with sharp doubt. In the Brontës' Heathcliff, Rochester, and Monsieur Paul (*Villette*), we find some of these contrary qualities, and then we must wait another span of years, to Hardy, Lawrence, and Conrad, for someone comparable.

The modern reader's view of Lovelace tends to come from the 1751 edition of *Clarissa* and therefore reflects the changes Richardson made for that edition. The Lovelace there is considerably more obsessed and villainous than earlier, and Clarissa is considerably more "delicate." In the earlier versions, however, Lovelace as a suitor appeared somewhat more possible, and Clarissa's more accentuated prudery seemed to prevent the match. Of course, the point in the earlier version was the same: that Clarissa's virtue would triumph over Lovelace's profligacy. Nevertheless, the psychodramatic possibilities were more evident, for the distance between the two combatants was closer. If we keep this in mind, we become more aware of Richardson's triumphant presentation of such a complicated male character, especially when he had virtually no precedent *in fiction*.

Lovelace (pronounced "love-less") is a Caesar of love, a Napoleon of the bedroom. Lovelace identifies with all the rebels of the past as well as those of the future. He is really interested not in women but in conquest. For Lovelace, the Nietzschean will to power is all, and existentially, he is prepared to die unless his will can control everything external to him. This is a very important point: he must be complete master of his environment, even though, within, he is a personage of uncertain qualities and ambiguous aims.

The complexities intensify. For Lovelace is, essentially, an anarchist, in the modern sense, and yet his mask involves a complete mastery of surface detail. There are really at least two Lovelaces—the man and his double, or the self and anti-self—and neither understands the other. There is the Lovelace who can survive only by defiance, who sees in bourgeois compliance the death of the spirit, and who must always deny in himself any tendency toward acquiescence. This Lovelace must have whatever is within his reach, even at the expense of destroying it. This is the anarchistic suitor for Clarissa's hand, who must transform his life and endeavors into the gaining of an end.

Then there is the other Lovelace, who is the opposite of chaotic, the man who feels he can manipulate destiny in order to gain his ends. This is the man who can work superbly with people and within society in order to shape and reshape reality. This is the spider calmly spinning his web, preparing intricate circles of deception, waiting patiently for his victim. In continuation of a letter dated April 11, 12 (VII, v. II, 22–3), Lovelace tells Belford that man is a spider and his victim, ultimately, is a girl. Lovelace's utilization of the image, however, is not *merely* spider and fly, or man and girl. The image, after all, is a common one, and we would not need to elaborate except that Richardson has given it a broad, symbolic significance.

In his elaboration, Lovelace speaks of the "infectious spider," which is comparable to those tame spirits held "within the skirts of the law by political considerations." This spider, a coward and hypocrite, "will run into his hole the moment one of his threads is touched by a finger that can crush him, leaving all his toils defenseless, and to be brushed down at the will of the potent invader." Yet this same spider—what Lovelace calls a "self-circumscribed tyrant"—as soon as a buzzing fly gives notice, will come out to cover his victim with "his bowel-spun toils." Then, when the victim is fully secured, this once-cowardly spider "gloats over it at a distance; and, sometimes advancing, sometimes retiring, preys at leisure upon its vitals."

At this stage, having established an image of cannibalism, Lovelace extends the metaphor and applies the spider analogy to "us brave fellows," who are not even self-circumscribed and, therefore, have fourfold the potential of the spider. "Begin with *spiders,* with *flies,* with what we will, girl is the centre of gravity, and we all naturally tend to it." He concludes by stating that "tame spirits" stand a "poor chance in a fairly offensive war with such of us mad fellows as are above all law . . ."

For several reasons, the description is extraordinary. It establishes:

1. That at the imagistic and symbolic level Richardson was moving well beyond his stated purpose in the novel, to demonstrate that virtue triumphs over vice
2. That Lovelace has potentially all crimes within him; that he is Milton's Satan at his core
3. That sadism is often indistinguishable from an intense attachment or need
4. That Lovelace is as much connected to the animal and insect world as he is to the human

5. That man believes he can create his own destiny, that there are no bounds to his powers
6. That the other side of gentleness and charm is an animalistic instinct to trap and kill one's enemies
7. That the siege of a young lady is comparable to an assault in an offensive war, that success, no matter what the means, is the goal
8. That most women must become victims to a force or fate that goes beyond male-female relationships
9. That weakness creates victims, power creates conquerors
10. That all life is made up of seeming and appearing, that "reality" can only rarely be perceived

We should not conclude that Richardson accepted all these premises; but the above points, among others, do indicate that we cannot turn the novel into a simplistic exercise. Always awaiting us in *Clarissa* is the "other," the contrary experience, the anti-self of every self, the mask or persona of an entire society.

We should stress still another aspect of Lovelace, and that is the man who can move with charm, poise, and learning through the highest levels of gentle society. Repeatedly, we are made to admit Lovelace's deftness. Colonel Morden, his enemy, recognizes the accomplishments of his rival, and even Clarissa, at the nadir of her fortunes, speaks with sorrow of Lovelace's wasted talents.

There are, then, at least these three facets: the social Lovelace, all charm, poise, presence; the power-mad Lovelace, who must manipulate all, the man almost puritanical in his busy drive to control everything external to him; the self-destructive, anarchic Lovelace, full of wild stabs, animalistic urges, potential and actual violence. At least two of these three Lovelaces are contemptuous of human life and reduce others, as well as self, to objects. Lovelace's "crime" in relation to other people—both his female victims and his male admirers—is his use of them, as if they were mere extensions of his own will; and part of that reifying of others is what Clarissa resists, as she had resisted it within her own family. What she tried to escape in them—their refusal to admit her own subjective self—is precisely what she discovers in Lovelace: his fear of letting others live and choose freely, his need to turn all into flies over which he, the machinelike spider, can gloat.

Clarissa and Lovelace are opposites of the same color, complements of each other's unrest. Clarissa's need to identify herself with

Lovelace's rebellion, although subconscious and inadmissible, is as intense as his unspoken need to identify with her purity. Each is incomplete, for each possesses the potential of the other. Psychologically, they are analogous to the diagram of Yin and Yang, in which the shading of each enters into the other, in which lights and darks are intermingled in such a way as to show their dependence upon each other. Yin and Yang stand for two contrary principles: one negative, dark, and feminine; the other positive, bright, and masculine. Their interaction creates the destiny of things.[16]

Richardson disturbs the usual sexual attribution, so that for him feminine is not destructive, nor is masculine positive. However, he retains the principle of reciprocation. In her rebellion against her family's wishes, Clarissa wears Lovelace's mask, and in his attitude toward her purity, he wears hers. Each is the persona of the other. As we have indicated above, this point is somewhat clearer in the early edition of the novel, before Richardson more consciously stressed Lovelace's sadism and Clarissa's purity.

These opposites complement each other in the matter of sexuality. Clarissa believes in conservation, Lovelace in spending. Since "spending" is more interesting than "saving," Lovelace's attitude seems more active and individualized, while Clarissa's appears more passive. Dorothy Van Ghent views Clarissa's tragedy as the tragedy of her (Puritan) class, for whom sexual transgression was equated to self-destruction unless within marriage and for purposes of childbearing. John Richetti points out that the "inescapable end of any sort of illicit sex act by a woman, whether slyly seduced, raped, or the aggressor herself, is to rot to death in a whorehouse." (p. 40)

In *The Other Victorians* (1966), Steven Marcus argues a similar point, in connection with the anonymously written *My Secret Life*, which, after several curious twists and turns, has affinities with *Clarissa.* Marcus comments that in the Age of Victoria the degree to which a young lady could repress her sexuality—make it "inaccessible to herself"—to that degree "she might have the chance of extending her humanity in other directions." (pp. 148–9) We must add that while Richardson did not directly question this aspect of his culture, his novel dramatized the issue. What on the surface appears to be acquiescence toward certain stated cultural norms becomes

16 Clarissa's own name is evidently such a combination of contrary elements: Harlowe ("harlot," as Lovelace plays with it) or whore combined with Clarissa or very clear, very pure. Further, place a "harlot" next to a "loveless" and one needs several reversals of roles to achieve a consummation. (Only Miss Howe "knows" how.)

subsurface the subject of dramatic tensions in his main character.

Clarissa must survive by repressing; but this kind of repression, which was a curious enough life even for an eighteenth-century woman, would be death for Lovelace. Her fear is of misuse, his of non-use. Her fear is that usage will lead to vaginal rot and decay; his is that rot and decay will attack his penis unless he keeps it busy. In this way, then, they are terrible, complementary enemies, for she denies him what he considers to be life, while he is forcing upon her what she considers to be death. Nevertheless, they cannot exist without each other, for their very attraction depends on the fact that their destinies are intertwined, like Yin and Yang, and that the kind of destruction each offers the other is precisely what each subconsciously desires to embrace.

Once again, this is not what Richardson is consciously telling us; but the novel comes with such intensity of purpose that conscious behavior frequently acts as a screen or filter for other human needs. Lovelace recognizes this "wild" streak in Clarissa, commenting (Friday, June 30; Letter LXVI, v. III, 315 ff.) to Belford that ". . . what a devil had she [Clarissa] to do, to let her fancy run a gadding after a rake? one of whom she *knew* to be a rake?" He then makes a telling point: "Oh! but truly she hoped to have the merit of reclaiming him. She had formed pretty notions how charmingly it would look to have a penitent of her own making dangling at her side to church . . ." (p. 316) Lovelace's remarks evidently turn on his own needs, his desire for justification for his lies and deceptions; and his comments do not align with Clarissa's own professed aims. Once we cut through all conscious motivation, however, we see that Lovelace has touched on a secret spring in Clarissa which *seeks* her opposite. The chaste angel seeks the satanic rapist, in the sense that her counterforce educes the "rape situation," not of course in the sense that she consciously wishes to be raped. There is a core of rebellion in her fervent desire for identity, so intense that she must force what will destroy her as long as it destroys those who would thwart her.

Lovelace's comments to Belford cited above complement Clarissa's own insights into their relationship, in which she recognizes their unsuitability and their dislike. "O Mr. Lovelace [as Lovelace reports her words to Belford], we have been long enough together to be tired of each other's humours and ways; ways and humours so different that perhaps you ought to dislike *me*, as much as I do *you*." Lovelace further quotes Clarissa: "You have given me an ill opinion of all mankind; of yourself in particular: and withal so bad a one of myself, that I shall never be able to look up, having utterly and for ever lost all that self-complacency, and conscious pride, which are so necessary to carry a woman through this life with tolerable satisfaction to herself." (Monday evening, May 22; Letter CII, v. II, 389)

Clarissa's insight is tremendous. Despite her inexperience with the world, she has somehow recognized that intense love can mask a basic dislike and that a compulsion to destroy can underlie the normal social graces. She has thought, and thought profoundly, about her role as a woman. With sure divination, she touches upon the wellspring of her relationship with Lovelace: his dislike, even hatred, of any woman who resists, ultimately of all women; on her part, a revulsion toward any male who puts her on the defensive, whether James Harlowe, Roger Solmes, or Robert Lovelace.

In the earlier edition, Clarissa's diatribes about men seemed to derive from a basic prudery, a dislike of the male sex for its wanton ways and free manners, its lack of discipline and offensive assumptions. As a virgin princess, a faerie queene, Clarissa has refused offers from several suitors before Solmes is put forth, is himself rejected, followed by Lovelace. In a real sense, she shared Miss Howe's antagonism for all men. At one point, Miss Howe offers Hickman to Clarissa, as if the man either married were interchangeable with all men. Thus, when Clarissa turns to Lovelace and finds him seriously wanting, it appears that *any* man in her terms would be wanting.

In Lovelace's view, since he much prefers the company of Belford and his fellow rakes, any woman will likewise be wanting. With marriage something he distinctly shuns, Lovelace uses women as foils both for gaining power and for disguising whatever it is he fears to face in himself.[17] His constant testing, as he tests Clarissa, is a way of

[17] Eaves and Kimpel shrewdly comment on Lovelace's fright at a sustaining relationship with a woman: "Her [Clarissa's] demand for respect aids Lovelace in his effort to avoid marriage, but even without it he could have succeeded. Clarissa, at the beginning of the novel, explains how Lovelace had proposed to her sister in a way which even the insensitive Bella could not accept: he has worked up a quarrel and at the height of it mentioned marriage and urged it in a way which made it impossible for her immediately to accept—and he had given her no time to cool down. He now does the same thing with Clarissa herself . . . Lovelace provokes her into resentful remarks and then mentions marriage in such a way as almost forces her to do half the proposing." (pp. 272–3)

Unfortunately, in their excellent biography, Eaves and Kimpel shun nearly all

proving to himself that all women will eventually fall if the siege is long and clever. Lovelace *needs to* prove that to himself; he must demonstrate that no woman can resist the complete male (himself) and that, therefore, no woman is worthy of him.

Comparably, no man, Clarissa's friends say, is worthy of her. Only Miss Howe is worthy of Clarissa, possibly because she poses no threat to the latter's virtue. The overtones of their "marriage" are more ominously sexual in our day than they would be to an eighteenth-century reader, to whom such a relationship could be seen as friendly and not Sapphic. Even if we suspect Sapphic overtones, however, Richardson is careful not to let Clarissa be dominated. She never falls in with Miss Howe's schemes. Still early in the game, Miss Howe offers Clarissa an escape from her dilemma: "If you allow of it, I protest I will go off privately with you, and we will live and die together. Think of it. Improve upon my hint, and command me." (Thursday Morning, April 9; Letter LXXXI, v. I, 416)

Defying the socially accepted role of the young lady, Miss Howe is almost a liberated woman, and she sees women, like men, creating their own destinies. She refuses the mild tyranny of her own home and refuses the repeated offer of the good Hickman until she feels ready. Actually, her suggestion to Clarissa is well-advised, and had the latter run off with her friend, she could have escaped her fate. Clarissa's world becomes "absurd" only when she cuts herself off from her friend while she is herself being cut off. The more immediate point, however, is that despite Miss Howe's intentions, Clarissa will not be dominated or directed.

---

psychological interpretation. Yet surely connected to Richardson's treatment of Lovelace and the latter's attitude toward women is Richardson's own persistent hypochondria—bouts of illness, fear of illness, recurring patterns of attacks, cures, and depression. Eaves and Kimpel say Richardson attributed his physical ailments to mental shocks (death of friends, disappointments, "nerves"); but the critical matter may have run far deeper. Initially, we must cite Richardson's identification with his female characters, Pamela and Clarissa, even Miss Howe; his presentation of men as the "enemy," as threat, as hateful of women even as they pursue them. Second, while we may assert that such views are culturally based on male-female relationships in the eighteenth century, nevertheless the fervor of Richardson's obsession with female purity and male guile needs further explanation. Third, we are not speaking of Richardson as homosexual, latent or otherwise—that explains nothing—but of critical identity crises in the man himself which became translated into the ambivalences of the novels. Fourth, we may argue further that the epistolary style, based as it is on secrecy, secret messages, deceptions, is itself the outward manifestation of a man in hiding, whose real aim is not to present but to disguise. The study of Richardson incorporating these possible points of interpretation yet remains to be written.

Before going further into the Clarissa-Lovelace relationship, we should note Richardson's triumph in his creation of Miss Howe. At first, she may appear to be a foil for Clarissa, as Belford is for Lovelace. Belford, however, is dominated, even humiliated, by his friend, who permits no opposition to his domination. Miss Howe's relationship with Clarissa is quite different. She is very much her own person and full of excellent insights into the nature of things. In a letter to Clarissa, after her elopement with Lovelace, Miss Howe "reads" both Lovelace and the Harlowes, along the way commenting on woman's place in life. She sees Lovelace "From his cradle . . . as an *only child,* and a *boy,* humoursome, spoiled, mischievous; the governor of his governors. A libertine in his riper years, hardly regardful of appearances; and despising the sex in general for the faults of particulars of it who made themselves too cheap to him." (Sat., April 22; Letter XLIII, v. II, 155) Advocating marriage with him, Miss Howe ironically adds: "*That we must love them* [men], however presumptuous and unworthy, *because they love us.*" (p. 155)

In a follow-up letter (Tuesday, April 25; Letter XLIX, v. II, 171 ff.), Miss Howe demonstrates her understanding of the Harlowes. She perceives all their comments, whether from sister, brother, or uncle, as self-justifications, not as suitable familial advice. "But do not mind their after-pretences, my dear—all of them serve but for tacit confessions of their vile usage of you." She views the Harlowes as unrelenting, although anxious to defend their actions toward an undutiful daughter. She understands that their cruelty is unthinking, and, therefore, doubly cruel for thoughtful persons. She recognizes that they have so completely accepted society's definition of a daughter that they will sacrifice their daughter to society. She observes that in their desire to do "right" and be well thought of, they will turn their child or niece or sister into a piece of clay, to be molded at will. She knows how legalisms can be made to justify any course of action.

Because Miss Howe is not a member of any power group (whether family or rakes), she is independent of presuppositions and social roles. She is able to see all around, and she questions not only the Harlowes and Lovelace but Clarissa and her intention to remain the dutiful daughter. In her, Richardson created a distinct female character; she does not really turn up again in fiction until Jane Austen, whose witty Elizabeth Bennet owes far more to Clarissa's friend than to Clarissa. But even in Jane Austen, where does one find a comment as grimly ironic as Miss Howe's suggestion that Clarissa should take Lovelace, not as reward, but as punishment, to remind her of the world's imperfection?

In a novel of this immense size and scope, one must choose amid riches. For the rest of this chapter, I will take up sequentially several points of controversy or simply areas of interest, most bearing on the Clarissa-Lovelace relationship. If I stress psychological aspects, it is because Richardson comes closer than any other pre-modern writer of fiction to giving us the raw materials of the psychoanalytic process. The social, familial, and economic material has far-reaching psychological implications. It is not enough to accept that the Harlowes want Clarissa to be dutiful and marry property. It is not enough to accept that Clarissa throws herself on providence—that is, reason and revelation. It is not enough to accept that Lovelace understands his own motivations, or is even in control of himself.

1. We should question Richardson's tacit explanation of the Harlowes' persecution of Clarissa. Richardson makes the motivation social and economic; the child must bow to the wishes of the parents. The family, he implies, desires merely what any family desires, but it pursues its object beyond reason and should have desisted in deference to Clarissa's clear wishes to the contrary. If each side had compromised, tragedy could have been averted.

Must we accept this? It is possible to see the Harlowes as restless and bored. By using Clarissa as bait, they can break the routine of rural life. As we learn from innumerable studies of English life, rural life is insufferably monotonous; the least break provides endless conversation. Parlor games are insufficient. The Harlowes decide, although of course not consciously, to "sacrifice" Clarissa to their boredom. Clarissa comments on this possibility in a letter to Miss Howe (Thursday Night, March 23; Letter LII, v. I, 265) in which she encloses a recent missive from her brother James. She remarks: "For here in this my particular case, my relations cannot be happy, though they make me unhappy! Except my brother and sister, indeed—and *they seem to take delight in and enjoy the mischief they make.*"

2. In addition to the obvious sadistic overtones of Clarissa's relationships with James, Arabella, and Mr. Harlowe are the lines of

incest. We could argue that James's insistence that Clarissa marry Solmes is more than family-oriented. It goes deeply into his own feelings about Clarissa. Solmes is no sexual threat; in manner and appearance, he is virtually asexual. At one point, he even agrees not to consummate the marriage until Clarissa decides she is ready, as long as the wedding itself takes place. While assuming that Clarissa is sexually skittish, Solmes himself seems sexually vague.

From James's point of view, however, Solmes is perfect; the marriage will not be a sensual affair, and Clarissa will not be possessed by any other man. In this sense, she will still belong to James and to the other Harlowe males. What is true for James fits as well with uncles and father. In a kind of Ur-Sadean drama, Clarissa is surrounded by father figures who loom as sexual threats. To complete the scene: Clarissa's Uncle Antony has a house with moat, drawbridge, and chapel—a Gothic, Sadean setting made for real or imagined debauchery. Clarissa speaks of James—in an image foreshadowing her relationship to Lovelace—as having "got me into his snares; and I, like a poor silly bird, the more I struggle am the more entangled." (Sunday Morning, March 5; Letter XXII, v. I, 112)

The male world represented by James, the uncles, Mr. Harlowe, Solmes is all solidity, heavy, moving bulkily. Solmes is himself described as a fleshy animal ("sitting asquat," "bent and broad-shouldered creature," "stalks towards a chair," "squatting in it with his ugly weight"). Lacking grace or wit or charm, they are antagonistic, non-romantic figures. They have the heaviness of the society they represent, of the threat they pose. Clarissa's sister, Arabella, is of their world—in league with James and the other men against her own sex. They must crush Clarissa's sexuality before it can relate *outside* the home. If she marries someone like Solmes, her feeling is channeled within; if she marries a Lovelace, she is lost to them.

3. The entire novel can be viewed as a "dialectic"—of forces, opposites, contraries, of the accepted and the forbidden, the romantic and the sadistic, the innocent and the destructive. In de Sade, evil or vice is in conformity to nature. While Richardson rejects this view, he flirts with its every possibility, pre-dating de Sade in an examination of nature's potential, taking everything, and nothing,

for granted. Mario Praz writes that the "Marquis de Sade empties his world of all psychological content except the pleasures of destruction and transgression, and moves in an opaque atmosphere of mere matter, in which his characters are degraded to the status of instruments for provoking the so-called divine ecstasy of destruction." (*The Romantic Agony*, p. 104) This is an excellent description of Lovelace, thirty years before de Sade. Richardson supported instinct and the "emotional life" against the materialism of the bourgeoisie, as Praz suggests, but he was forced, inevitably, to deny the values he supported and support the values he denied. What his imitators used as a way of heightening sensuality, he used as a way of questioning respectability, the bourgeoisie, family life itself. He never came to grips with the forbidden half, but he offered it with intense, morbid interest.

4. The line between normality and abnormality is inconclusive. One need not read the novel psychologically, to the exclusion of other meanings, to see Richardson stretching the natural, even nature. Within the Harlowe family, Lovelace finds his counterpart in James. Mr. Harlowe has lost the struggle within his own family and has given way to his son. The son is "father" figure to Clarissa, as well as wicked stepfather, brother, uncle. As a respectable surrogate for Lovelace, he is as disdainful of women, as arrogant in all sexual matters. He is contemptuous of sexual equality, unable to find emotional correspondence in himself.

Clarissa recognizes she is the prize in a rivalry between James and Lovelace. The novel, we recall, opens with a duel between James and Lovelace over one sister, Arabella, then the duel continues over the other. Having lost his manhood in the duel with Lovelace—whose sword proves more effective—James can win it back by keeping Clarissa to himself. The novel ends, incidentally, with a duel in which Colonel Morden, Clarissa's cousin, stands in, as it were, for James. The violence in James, insistent and sadistic, is the Harlowe version of Lovelace's impetuosity, which Clarissa so much fears. Clarissa describes to Miss Howe her interview with Solmes, with James present, both men alternating in acts of threat; James's face glows, Solmes ravishes her "struggling hand" with "his odious mouth." James, ever the voyeur, looks on. The scene is near-rape. Paradoxically, the Harlowes form the "normal" world, while the abnormal is Lovelace's. Clarissa is sought by both worlds.

5. The theological ideology of the novel is ambiguous. Clarissa gives herself over to providence, this after the rape by Lovelace. The providence theme gains importance when she feels forsaken by all except Miss Howe. Earlier, she appeared to be mistress of her own destiny. Does Richardson suggest that providence, which seems to be all, matters only when one is in need?

Lovelace, who denies providence, believes in a more pagan form of fate. In his involvement with the insect-animal world, he appears to accept instinct as implacable. Yet instinct is antithetical to Lovelace's sense of command, antithetical to his professed belief that he is born to rule through reason and charm. Is he Oedipus forced to come to terms with the limitations of mortality? Is he Faust trying out godlike powers, only to surrender everything when his time comes? We must not go too far here, or else we run the same risk of distortion by which Blake saw Satan as hero of *Paradise Lost*. The rape could be a dream's fulfillment. Perhaps Richardson's indecisiveness here is the uncertainty of his point of view: the attractiveness of Lovelace's rebellion, which must be blunted; the attractiveness of Clarissa's victimization, which must be transcended.

6. Are both Pamela and Clarissa comparable to Gretchen in the Faust story—that is, potential and actual victims of a male seeking power? Writing to Belford (Sunday, August 20; Letter LIV, v. IV, 123), Lovelace shows tremendous insight into both his and Morden's character: ". . . Colonel Morden has had his girls as well as you and I. And indeed, either openly or secretly, who has not? *The devil always baits with a pretty wench* when he angles for man, be his age, rank, or degree what it will." (my italics) The Faust theme lies there. Pamela, of course, resists her fate, which is to be seduced, then cast out; but *Pamela* was only a trying-out. Clarissa accepts her fate, which is providential, Richardson tells us, and that is, like Gretchen, to be victimized by men.

Yet the theme is not Faustian. The struggle is not over a man's soul but a woman's virtue. Lovelace may be more interesting, but Clarissa is the mote in Richardson's eye. Despite Reynaud's comparison of Clarissa to Margarete (Gretchen) in his *Le Romantisme, Ses Origines Anglo-Germaniques* (pp. 172–3), the Faust theme is blunted. Lovelace may be damned, and even know it (see letter of Wednesday Morning, May 17; No. LXXXVIII, v. II, 315, in which Lovelace wants Clarissa "although damnation were to be the purchase"), and

Clarissa may be the victim of men's desire for total power; but the focus is not Lovelace's struggle, it is hers. De Sade is closer than Goethe.

If Lovelace's soul were to become the focus of the novel, then we would be close to Lewis's Monk, Maturin's Melmoth, tortured figures who sell their souls for lust and power; *they* are the center, they are the interest, and the novels circle around their fortunes.

7. Is it possible to see Clarissa's course of action as, subconsciously, one vast scheme for revenge? That is, the kind of revenge a suicide takes upon those who will "feel sorry" or, in Clarissa's words, "rue past actions or decisions"? Is her course childish willfulness? We do not normally think along these lines until a long letter from Clarissa to Miss Howe (Sunday, July 30; Letter XVIII, v. IV, 59), five weeks before Clarissa's death, when she speculates on how her death will affect the Harlowes. She writes: "They indeed deserve to be pitied. They are, and no doubt will long be, happy." More telling are her comments on how she sees them: her mother trying to "suppress her sorrow at her table . . . her virtue made to suffer for faults she could not be guilty of"; her father beset by "pangs that tear in pieces the stronger heart" of a man whom tears cannot relieve; her brother full of "overboiling tumults," and so on. Clarissa glories in her downfall. Not only will it unman and destroy Lovelace, it will unsettle her complacent family. Whereas once the Harlowes took her for granted—she was a conventionally talented and dutiful daughter—her behavior has forced them to rethink who and what she is; and her planned death makes them recognize her presence in a way not realized before. Thus, her course of action reveals not only superego but ego. Death now completes what life provided only partially. Her "revenge," in this interpretation, makes them live with her as long as they live. Whereas they had thwarted her in life, in death she thwarts them.

8. The epistolary method has overtones of voyeurism; Lovelace's voyeurism, in particular, might be seen as indistinguishable from his sexual life. In a long, complicated letter to Belford (CXXVIII, v. II, 517), begun Thursday morning, June 8, and continuing through the day and night, Lovelace connects the perusal of others' letters to his sexual exploits: ". . . then will I recollect all her [Clarissa's] perverseness; then will I reperuse Miss Howe's letters, and the

transcripts from others of them; give way to my aversion to the life of shackles; and then shall she be mine in my own way." If we say that the writing of letters is itself a form of "spending," a vicarious sexual outlet, then the opening, copying, forging of others' letters is a comparable sexual activity. In the same letter to Belford, Lovelace foreshadows the rape: "Oh, that I had given her greater reason for a resentment so violent!"

In and around this date, June 8—within a week of the rape—Lovelace runs rampant, peering into letters, building resentment and excitement by what he sees and hears secretly, forging letters from Clarissa (another form of voyeurism) to Miss Howe, from Miss Howe to Clarissa. His love life up to and including the rape is all deceit; the rape itself is carried out while Clarissa is drugged. Thus, Lovelace can "look on" during the act itself, since there can be no response, no sharing, no resistance. Voyeurism is a form of necrophilia, since one admires or ravishes something motionless and silent. Reified, senseless, Clarissa is deflowered, and Lovelace's sexual conquest recalls Ozymandias's acquisition of riches, a hostage to his quest for power. Lovelace's voyeurism is surely attached to his fear of impotence; and for all, to some degree, the intense epistolary apparatus is a repressed sexual activity, but particularly frantic for Lovelace and Clarissa.

Necrophilia appears very much part of the Puritan ethic. Not only does Lovelace become a necrophiliac in embracing the drugged Clarissa, everyone associated with her plays the "death game." Miss Howe (in Morden's letter to Belford, Sept. 11, Monday Afternoon; CXLI, v. IV, 402) "makes love" to the dead Clarissa, "kissing her lips at every tender appellation . . . Let my warm lips animate thy cold ones." Clarissa herself toys with death, plays house in her coffin, forces death images upon everyone near her, enjoys her forthcoming death as much as others enjoy life. After her death, letters arrive that she will never read, rendered more meaningful by the fact that unknowingly they are addressed to the dead; and her own letters are sent posthumously to the Harlowes, made doubly poignant by the fact that they are, literally, letters from the cemetery. Added to the above is the family guilt, Clarissa's blessings upon them, their knowledge of acts they will carry to their own graves. Read this way, the novel shows Puritan society triumphant, not in life, but in death. Further, all those involved in sexual "play"—especially Lovelace and the Harlowes—are dead or damned; while those "untainted" by sex, or reformed in time, live on happily. As Dorothy Van Ghent pointed out, sex *is* death in Richardson's ideology.

9. Richardson uses dreams, not allegorically, not symbolically, but in a very modern way of interpreting displaced fears, wishes, hopes. Both Clarissa and Lovelace dream, and both experience final things in their dreams. Clarissa's dream, related to Miss Howe (Friday Morning, Seven o'clock, April 7; Letter LXXXIV, v. I, 433), comes just after she has set her terms for departing with Lovelace, terms intended to remove her from a coming marriage to Solmes and, at the same time, protect her from Lovelace's advances. Yet the dream asserts fear of doom, even as she plans to escape. Release and doom come together, not in her waking consciousness, but in the dream, in which an enraged Lovelace, fearing a plot, carries a distraught Clarissa into a churchyard. There, despite her tears and pleas of innocence, he "stabbed me to the heart, and then tumbled me into a deep grave ready dug, among two or three half-dissolved carcasses; throwing in the dirt and earth upon me with his hands, and trampling it down with his feet."

The "stabbing" is an apt symbol, involving several activities circumscribing Clarissa's life: the duel at the beginning, the rape itself (a bloody "stab wound," which leads to her death), the sword thrust at the end killing Lovelace. The "dirt and earth" part of the dream attaches itself to the necrophilia mentioned above. Added to this is Clarissa's constant fear of violence, which the dream reveals; a fear which makes her go along with Lovelace whenever he threatens violence or when she fears her family will be threatened. Her fear of violence is revealed in the escape scene when Lovelace plays upon her dread of bloodshed to persuade her to elope with him. Shrewdly, he offers his sword to her, his breast to her brother's sword, all the while stooping for the key to put to the lock. The images of escape—sword, lock, blood—embody the sexuality she has equated in her dream to death.

Richardson repeats these images. Dream material suggests sex, violence, death. Later on, during the fire scene, the sword image is repeated in Clarissa's threat to kill herself with a "pair of sharp-pointed scissors"—not a dream scene, but one close to it in its disarrangement of reality. Lovelace has his own "sword" dream, related to Belford (Tuesday, Aug. 22; Letter LVI, v. IV, 135). In the dream, through the joint intercession of his relatives, Lovelace finds reconciliation between himself and Clarissa. Grateful for the possibility of relief, Lovelace is on his knees, sword in hand, "offering either to put it up in the scabbard, or to thrust it into my heart, as she should command the one or the other"—clearly a repeat of the escape scene in which sword and scabbard play significant roles. At that moment of mixed contrition, threat of violence, suppressed arrogance, Lovelace is suprised by the entry of Morden, sword drawn, crying, "Die, Lovelace . . . this instant die, and be damned . . ." At this point, Clarissa intercedes and begs Morden not to kill Lovelace, but as the latter prepares to embrace her, Clarissa rises into heaven and Lovelace is himself dropped into a bottomless black hole. The imagery of the dream is comparable in some details to Clarissa's, with her churchyard grave becoming his bottomless hole. Once again, sex *is* death.

In an earlier dream, also related to Belford (June 19–20; Letter XLIII, v. III, 248 ff.), shortly after the rape of Clarissa, Lovelace has a shifting and turning experience, in which Clarissa escapes from him, is involved in further plots, is then transformed into the mother of a smiling boy. Catching the violence of Lovelace's ever-changing world, the dream is a mélange of previous and forthcoming incidents run together in a kaleidoscope of riotous images, changing shapes, new roles and new names, even shifting sexes.

Belford himself has a dream of death (related to Lovelace, Friday Morn., Sept. 1; Letter XC, v. IV, 256 ff.): ". . . and when I dozed, I dreamt of nothing but of flying hour-glasses, death's-heads, spades, mattocks, and eternity . . ." The immediate cause of the dream is the "devices" Clarissa has arranged around her coming death, the principal one being a crowned serpent with its tail in its mouth on a field of white metal and, in the circle of mouth and tail, an inscription announcing Clarissa's death at nineteen.

Thus, the dreams—and there are other minor ones—cohere in demonstrating the sex-death orientation, indeed the necrophilia, of a society which considered itself life-oriented.[18]

[18] Eaves and Kimpel (p. 108) discuss a striking dream scene which Richardson omitted from his final revision of *Pamela*, but which was published posthumously in 1801. In her dream, Pamela gives vent to her repressed, murderous feelings: ". . . that I broke his Head in Revenge, and stabb'd one of my Coach-horses. And all the Comfort I had when it was done, methought, was, that I had not exposed myself before Company; and there were no Sufferers, but guilty *Robin*, and one innocent Coach-horse; for when my Hand was in, I might as reasonably have kill'd the other three."

10. Ovid's *Metamorphoses* is paradigmatic for the eighteenth century; rightly so, since this was the first era of real mobility or of the sense that mobility was possible. The novel involves constant "seeming" and "becoming," so that everyone and everything except, perhaps, the older Harlowes are involved in an unfolding process. Lovelace is continually disguised, Clarissa disguises herself to escape; letters may be forged. Life appears to be a game for some, earnest for others, rarely "even" or balanced, for the terms of life and death are ever changing. With her usual insight into the illogical, Miss Howe writes Clarissa:

> I never had any faith in the stories that go current among country girls, of spectres, familiars, and demons; yet I see not any other way to account for this wretch's successful villainy, and for his means of working up his specious delusions, but by supposing (if he be not the devil himself) that he has a familiar constantly at his elbow. Sometimes it seems to me that this familiar assumes the shape of that solemn villain Tomlinson: sometimes that of the execrable Sinclair, as he calls her: sometimes it is permitted to take that of Lady Betty Lawrance—but, when it would assume the angelic shape and mien of my beloved friend, see what a bloated figure it made! [Sunday, July 9; Letter LXXXVIII, v. III, 376]

We could well argue that changing shapes, disguises, lies, deceptions, all the reflection of Proteus—devices made to order for magic, for puppet shows, for theater—are intrinsic to the epistolary method. The letter permits, indeed encourages, acting, since the act of writing is comparable in a sense to performing for another without worrying about the spontaneity of reply. One can plan his answer, cross out, shape and reshape—all the qualities of metamorphosis. It is easier to become another person, or seem like one, in a letter than face to face; or, put another way, the letter complements, or reinforces, one's mask or anti-self.

Early in the novel, when Lovelace is only warming to his task, letters indicate that various lines of deception are gradually being established; that to make Clarissa absolutely dependent upon him, Lovelace warns Miss Howe that Clarissa should escape to the Howes' protection, at the same time he is turning both the Harlowes and Mrs. Howe against her. To stress the details of Lovelace's stratagems lest his readers miss the lines of the ever-shifting terms, Richardson added an explanatory footnote to the 1751 edition. Scenically, the role-playing is equally intense when Lovelace must pass as Clarissa's husband in front of the others, even as she rejects him. Both theatricality and falsity meet here—symbolic of the entire novel.

In another usage of the epistolary method to create a changing reality, letters reach more than one correspondent. In a letter to Lovelace (Tuesday Night, July 18), Belford indicates he is showing Clarissa Lovelace's letter to him; so that the letter conveys at least two impressions, a primary and a secondary effect. Likewise, Lovelace discovers scraps and pieces of letters Clarissa never sent, letters thrown away incomplete (to Belford, Friday, June 16), all of which provide a commentary on letters she does send and, at the same time, act as witness to feelings she does not intend to display to others. The significance of all this is that it demonstrates a "counter" line of development which serves as commentary on the major one, a "seeming," as we noted above.

11. Is Clarissa pregnant? [19] Lovelace thinks so: ". . . I am encouraged to hope . . . that the dear creature is in the way to be a mama." (to Belford, Friday, July 28, continuation; Letter X, v. IV, 38). On Monday, August 7, John Harlowe asks Clarissa directly: "Your mother can't ask, and your sister knows not in modesty *how* to ask; and so *I* ask you, If you have any reason to think yourself with child by this villain?" (Letter XLI, v. IV, 100) To this direct question, and to an equally direct one from her other uncle, Antony Harlowe (August 12), Clarissa gives an evasive answer: "This then be my answer: 'A *little* time, a much less time than is imagined, will afford a more satisfactory answer to my whole family, and even to my *brother* and *sister,* than I can give in words.' " (Sunday, August 13; Letter XLVI, v. IV, 106)

This is barely two months after the rape, and no one really knows. Also, Lovelace's "certainty" may be his way of viewing Clarissa's dependence upon him, since, if pregnant, she *must* marry now. Discounting his certainty, we can say that (1) the suggestion of the pregnancy is a good indication it exists; or (2), by suggesting it, Richardson *is making it a consideration* for the reader. If anything, Clarissa's "pregnancy" supports her decision not to marry Lovelace under any conditions, even while her family calls her a whore. Her possible condition, furthermore, places her mode of reasoning

[19] The abridged editions of Clarissa give only fleeting glimpses of this matter, so that those interested in exploring it must refer to complete editions.

completely outside the understanding of a Lovelace, who, with typical male chauvinism, assumes a pregnant girl will have to marry her seducer.

We can never be certain. If we assume a pregnancy, however, we can better comprehend Richardson's point about Clarissa's resolution to be her own person, to seek death rather than live with a remembrance of her shame. As we have noted, Lovelace cannot understand this.

12. Perhaps Richardson is parodying his material, his society, his characters; is not himself part of the death orientation he shows all around him; is, possibly, critical of the equation of sex and death, escape and damnation; is a kind of pre-Lawrencian critic of a repressed, doomed ethic. The novel always seems close to parody—Clarissa is too virginal, too much the oppressed, repressed maiden; Lovelace is a melodramatic, theatrical villain; the Harlowes are heavy, parental figures, and so on through the devoted friends of one "type" or another.

When Richardson foreruns the "novel of sentiment," parody comes closest. "O my dear cruel father! said she [Clarissa] in a violent fit of grief . . . thy heavy curse is completed upon thy devoted daughter! I am *punished,* dreadfully punished . . ." (Lovelace's long narrative letter to Belford, Fri. Night, June 9; Letter VII, v. III, 71) Or when Richardson foreshadows the full force of Gothic terror—here, too, he seems close to parody. However, the eighteenth century experienced an ecstasy of such excessive emotionalism, and parody for a later age is conventional for an earlier. Part of Richardson's purpose, we realize, was to exploit deep emotionalism as a counter to passionless reason, to exploit instinct at the expense of logic; then to withdraw from both as excessive, to move toward moderation and balance. Parody lies elsewhere.

13. Is *Clarissa* more a morality drama or an allegory than a realistic novel? Elements of a morality play abound. The parallel story of the rake Belton and his ill fortunes is a *danse macabre,* a Bosch-like picture of hell. (See Belford's letter to Lovelace, Thursday, July 20; CXVI, v. III, 480 ff.) Four days later, Belford comments in Bunyan-like terms on the materialistic assumptions of fellow rakes which disallow weakness: "Our friendships and intimacies, Lovelace, are only calculated for strong life and health. When sickness comes, we look round us, and upon one another, like frighted birds at the sight of a

kite ready to souse upon them. Then, with all our bravery, what miserable wretches are we!" (Monday, July 24; Letter III, v. IV, 5)

Still later, the reader gets a whiff of the inferno in which rakes live when Belford, with Hogarthian caustic, tells Lovelace of Mrs. Sinclair and her horrible death, as compared with the peaceful bliss of Clarissa's end. (Undated, following Sunday, Sept. 10; Letter CXXXVIII, v. IV, 380 ff.)

The Belton and Mrs. Sinclair motif runs through the final five or six hundred pages of the full version—paralleling Clarissa's transcendental experience—so that the elements of a morality drama lie heavily, for neither character is at all necessary to the novel's main development. Perhaps Richardson's need to suggest allegorical *exempla* explains the periodical weakening of the novel. Precisely those elements which Richardson stressed for the moral edification of his audience make us lose sight of the real matter, the psychological drama.

Some Dilemmas

To what extent can men and women exist sexually in Richardson's novel? Does not every sexual situation lead to frustration, abound in ironies and paradoxes? Solmes agrees to forgo sexual relations with Clarissa after the marriage until she signals her readiness. The Harlowes unman Solmes at every turn. Miss Howe puts off Hickman, ridicules him, makes him dance in attendance and pay for Lovelace's treatment of Clarissa. Clarissa offers to remain single, while permitting Lovelace to pursue his interests. Clarissa offers Solmes to her sister, Arabella; Miss Howe offers Hickman to Clarissa; Lovelace is himself Arabella's leavings. Thus, the men in the novel are manipulated by the women as casually as if they were pieces on a checkerboard. The contrary is also true: all the men, except Mr. Hickman, see women as objects, for rape, seduction, or other victimization and manipulation.

Following from the above, is there any place for passion, for feeling? Lovelace speaks of his three passions: love, revenge, ambition (or a desire for conquest). All are destructive.

Is the novel perhaps more naturalistic or fatalistic than is usually granted? Is fate or individual doom the dominant motif? Is not everyone out of step with everyone else? When Lovelace is happy at being near Clarissa, she is miserable at the escape; and when

Clarissa has become adamant about accepting Lovelace, he pursues her with grim intensity: the cross purposes of naturalistic fiction. Perhaps the novel is about the individual's alienation, his isolation from all positions of safety and assurance.

What is Richardson saying about class? The merchant middle and upper idle are hostile to each other, and one would destroy the other. Yet Richardson accepts both, while relishing their mutual hatred. Can the novel be read as irreconcilable forces setting out to destroy each other? Can only divine transcendence, a Clarissa, save the sides from mutual destruction at the expense, martyrlike, of her own life?

Does Clarissa experience something akin to the existential absurd when she ventures outside the limited protection of the Harlowe home? Can her safety be guaranteed only by acquiescence? If she thrusts herself into the blind will of the world, must she perish? Is such a reading psychologically viable, running, as it does, against the grain of the story's surface?

If *Clarissa*, in its final sense, advocates reason over passion—a fully acceptable mid-eighteenth-century attitude—is not Richardson denying most of the movement of the novel? Is not the novel less concerned with reason than with finding suitable outlets for irrational passions, however destructive they may prove? Is the "rakes' rule of law" (Friday, June 16; Letter XXXIII, v. III, 214, 216) Richardson's own flirtation with ultimate anarchy, his equivalent of the id running free? Surely, it is the testing of limits for a rational, quasi-democratic society.

Can Lovelace's schemes and stratagems be explained as his terrible fear of being considered common? Must he seek his destruction in order to evade an even more unacceptable fate, that is, realization of his ordinariness? Lovelace admits as much to Belford in a burst of candor (Monday Morn., 11 o'clock, June 19; Letter XXXVI, v. III, 229) Can he be believed even here, as he foresees his own demise? ("What to do with her, or without her, I know not.") Is he, then, a man seeking to locate his center, part of a long line of egoists who destroy themselves in an attempt to find themselves?

Is Belford's admitted adoration of Clarissa a way of forming an even closer tie to Lovelace, a more avowed homoerotic attraction than anything else in the novel, achieved through a common mistress? If so, once again Clarissa is the locus of all desires, homoerotic between Lovelace and Belford, sadistic within the family, disruptive between Miss Howe and Hickman.

Even during her physical decline, does Clarissa need to flirt with opposites? After having experienced Lovelace's perfidy, she puts herself in the hands of still another rake when she turns to Belford for aid. Lovelace recognizes the irony: that Belford can move freely in her presence while he himself is banished, and yet both are rakes with rakes' ethics.

Is Clarissa's ultimate plan to transform all desires and all hopes into an overwhelming death force? Is she doom itself, a fate who is fated? Late in the novel, when her coffin becomes her house and her marriage is to God and death, her funereal movement drags down all life. Ironically, Lovelace is not oriented toward wife and sons. Does morality function only in the shadow of the grave?

At one point, Lovelace questions all of Belford's assumptions, saying that the latter should have freed Clarissa when he recognized Lovelace's designs upon her. Why did he, Belford, let the sport continue unless he were himself excited by it? By universalizing his desires, Lovelace suggests all people share in his sense of opposites, that all wish destruction even while they value life. Truth lies somewhere deep within human desires, which are normally contradictory. If we accept this view, then we see that Richardson plastered over what he could not publicly reveal. When everyone at the end "pays" with some sense of loss, he or she has participated in Lovelace's sport; the rape of Clarissa is what everyone has desired. Perhaps Richardson was saying this all along.

4

Henry Fielding: The Novel, the Epic, and the Comic Sense of Life

Tom Jones is the first of a small number of novels that helped to establish the genre at critical points in its development, or else prevented the genre from deteriorating when existing energies had slowed or were dissipated. Among eighteenth-century novels, *Tom Jones* takes somewhat the same relative position as Joyce's *Ulysses* does among twentieth-century novels. By the 1740's, the pre-Richardsonian novel was still inchoate, with Defoe's novels by no means shutting off the continued outpouring of romances (historical and chivalric), borrowings from French romances, imitations of *Robinson Crusoe* and *Gulliver's Travels*, adaptations of French and Spanish picaresque, as well as further imitations of picaresque, translations of Italian *novelle*, and so on.[1] With Richardson's *Pamela* and Fielding's response with *Shamela* and *Joseph Andrews*, we note virtually the first attempts to turn prose fiction into new shapes, and with *Tom Jones*, we find Fielding establishing finally his conception of Homeric epic or history transformed into social comedy.

[1] William H. McBurney omits "verse fictions" in his *A Check List of English Prose Fiction 1700–1739* and, with that, a considerable carryover of the medieval, chivalric forms.

In his reshaping of narrative, character, plot, theme, and language, Fielding turned prose fiction away from romance and epic in much the same way Joyce was to turn the novel from late-Victorian and Edwardian naturalism and realism. Virtually all attempts at breakthrough in a literary genre take the shape of innovations in language. The real breakthroughs, however, are made by those who also find themselves at a particular point in the development of a genre, when existing language, forms, themes are insufficient to carry the freight of the age; or at the stage when existing forms have dissipated their yield.

Such points are relatively easy to find. At the beginning of Book IV of *Tom Jones*, just after the introductory comments which form an attack upon "idle romances," Fielding introduces us to Sophia Western. The first paragraph of this description is illustrative of Fielding's method, for his use of a kind of prose here marks *not* the continued use of such a style but its death. The paragraph follows:

> II. A Short Hint of What We Can Do in the Sublime, and a Description of Miss Sophia Western
>
> Hushed be every ruder breath. May the heathen ruler of the winds confine in iron chains the boisterous limbs of noisy Boreas, and the sharp-pointed nose of bitter-biting Eurus. Do thou, sweet Zephyrus, rising from thy fragrant bed, mount the western sky, and lead on those delicious gales, the charms of which call forth the lovely Flora from her chamber, perfumed with pearly dews, when on the 1st of June, her birthday, the blooming maid, in loose attire, gently trips it over the verdant mead, where every flower rises to do her homage, till the whole field becomes enamelled, and colours contend with sweets which shall ravish her most.[2]

Clearly, Fielding's language establishes several points. As I suggested above, it marks the end of the serious use of romantic prose to describe a fictional heroine. More than that, it lends respectability to Fielding's own endeavors, even as it serves to end an entire tradition. Reference to the "Sublime" in the chapter heading is, of course, an ironic comment on the controversy raging about the relative merits and moral values of the sublime and the beautiful. Classical allusions further establish Fielding's mastery of a tradition which he has chosen to terminate; and the mock-heroic tone demonstrates that no matter how dazzling Sophia is, she is mortal,

[2] Modern Library edition, p. 107; with neither the Riverside nor Oxford-Wesleyan editions as yet ready, there is no acceptable text of *Tom Jones*. (As this study goes to the printer, I note the Norton Critical Edition, edited by Sheridan Baker, 1973.)

not an allegorical spirit of spring. The display of learning, the poetic imagery, the repetition of well-worn images and references—all underlie a comic intention.

Fielding has sensed that language itself must serve the new muse of fiction, a recognition that, despite his greater psychological intuition, we rarely find in Richardson.[3] Richardson's prose can be extremely supple, almost Shakespearean in its conciseness. But it is not the language of a man playing with language itself; rather, it is the verbal play of a man grasping whatever language resources have come to him from the past, albeit using such resources with imagination and often wit.

Having brought Fielding's role thus far in the development of a fictional language, we need the other part of our analogy, which is a passage from Joyce's *Ulysses.* As that novel begins to wind down toward its points of reconciliation and departure, we find Bloom and Stephen heading into 7 Eccles Street, where the mysteries of a father-son relationship take place amid a typical Joycean mockery of sentimentality and romantic attachment. The method for the section (Part III, chapter 2) is impersonal catechism, that is, a series of seemingly inconsequential questions followed by very solemn answers; questions such as "What in water did Bloom, waterlover [opposite of Stephen, an established waterhater], drawer of water, watercarrier returning to the range, admire?" The response to what he admires takes almost one and a half pages of tight, virtually

[3] Robert Alter (*Fielding and the Nature of the Novel*) argues that Fielding "through the fine control of tone, rhythm, imagery, syntax, by the shrewd play with and against the received meanings of words, achieves the qualities of precision of reference, complexity of statement, aesthetically pleasing form, that are traditionally associated with the language of poetry." (p. 32) Alter asserts that Fielding's novels "were written to be read ideally in the way we have been reading the so-called art novel since the time of Conrad and James." (p. 24) This, however, solemnizes Fielding and makes him sound grim and severe, as though his every word were oracular.

By 1968, the time of Alter's study, Fielding hardly needed this kind of defense. The opposite is rather more true, that Fielding should be protected against those who feel his prose style, which is playful and loaded with mockery—anything but the solemn prose of the "so-called art novel"—must be made to seem fraught with intangibles and weighted by imponderables. Virtually everything in Fielding argues against a prose style that is "associated with the language of poetry" or a manner that calls up James and Conrad. Fielding may write playful, non-arty, rather loose prose and still compete successfully with and survive Richardson. Even if we put aside Cervantes, Fielding learned from Marivaux (from both *Le Paysan parvenu*, 1735–6, and *Pharsamon, ou les Folies romanesques*, 1737) the nature of witty intrusions and an ironic narrative manner, a playfulness that mitigates any comparison with the tone of the art novel or the intensity of the art novelist.

unintelligible prose. Lists of groceries, tabulations of relative ages, an examination of shaving, a narration of gestures and movements as if they were epical postures—all of these are established to mock a prose style employed by the realistic and naturalistic writers. The form of the mockery is, as in Fielding, a prose style which excludes the very style that is being utilized.

By employing a style that was not life-giving according to *his* vision, Joyce created a context in which the serious use of that style henceforth was impossible; much as Fielding had used language as a way of establishing a comic vision which, first, had to deny the romantic, the historical, and the epic. We leave aside the more formal similarities between *Tom Jones* and *Ulysses*—their both belonging to the *Bildungsroman,* their mutual reliance on a solitudinous protagonist, their common rejection of the typically romantic hero, their self-conscious association with epic—to stress how each employs language as a way of establishing a particular vision, and how this emphasis is crucial in each one's development of the genre at particular historical eras.[4]

Joseph Andrews

Henry Fielding wrote fiction for only ten years, from 1740–1 with *Jonathan Wild* and *Shamela* (1741) to 1751, with *Amelia.* If we discount the two early works as more burlesque than fiction,[5] then the career

[4] Although the aim here is not to suggest or illustrate a theory of language—but simply to indicate the development of a genre—we can cite Roland Barthes's *Writing Degree Zero* (1953; English translation, 1968) as grappling with personal language (*écriture*) as a means of defining the writer's intention. The following passage is appropriate to our study: "History, then, confronts the writer with a necessary option between several moral attitudes connected with language; it forces him to signify Literature in terms of possibilities outside his control. We shall see, for example, that the ideological unity of the bourgeoisie gave rise to a single mode of writing, and that in the bourgeois periods (classical and romantic), literary form could not be divided because consciousness was not; whereas, as soon as the writer ceased to be a witness to the universal, to become the incarnation of a tragic awareness (around 1850), his first gesture was to choose the commitment of his form, either by adopting or rejecting the writing of his past. Classical writing therefore disintegrated, and the whole of Literature, from Flaubert to the present day, became the problematics of language." (p. 3) In the English novel, such disintegration was becoming apparent by 1750, the time of *Tom Jones.*

[5] Any full examination of Fielding's burlesque of *Pamela*, in *Shamela*, and the controversy surrounding it falls outside the province of this study. The best survey of the material is Bernard Kreissman's *Pamela-Shamela: A Study of the Criticisms, Burlesques, Parodies, and Adaptations of Richardson's "Pamela."*

shortens even further, from *Joseph Andrews* (1742). And if we consider *Amelia* as evidence of decline or miscalculation, we can see Fielding's entire novelistic career as running from 1742 through 1749, with the publication of *Tom Jones.* The brevity of the career is of some significance, since Fielding really demonstrated only one kind of development, from burlesque through picaresque. Of great interest, however, is the way Fielding turned from burlesque, which led nowhere in fiction, to picaresque satire, which led into the mainstream of novel writing. The development behind the shift in emphasis is, of course, Fielding's theory of the comic epic in prose. Later, I will discuss whether Fielding really held to that conception in portions of *Tom Jones* and especially in *Amelia.*

While it is difficult to pinpoint when Fielding turned from the burlesque features of Lady Booby's infatuation with Joseph, a significant shift for Fielding and for the development of prose fiction, we can say Fielding's change came when technical matters became secondary to dogma. The beginning of *Joseph Andrews* is all technical matters. The first chapter opens full of typical eighteenth-century mockery, of Mrs. Pamela Andrews and the fatuous Colley Cibber. Rhetorically, it is neoclassical, beginning with a general point and then gradually moving to the particular. The initial chapter is in every way an extension of the author's preface, and the lead in to Joseph Andrews, the character, is by way of his sister's virtue: "since it will appear that it was by keeping the excellent Pattern of his Sister's Virtues before his Eyes, that Mr. *Joseph Andrews* was chiefly enabled to preserve his Purity in the midst of such great Temptations." (Wesleyan edition, p. 20)

Chapter II is described in mock-heroic, mock-epic terms concerning birth, parentage, education, and "great endowments," which has a genital as well as epical meaning. We approach the "birth of a hero," described in psychological-mythical terms by Otto Rank and Lord Raglan, but, of course, to mock, not praise, our hero. Technique, not content, remains uppermost; as it turns out, our hero has no genealogy extending beyond his great-grandfather. The mythical, epical, heroic terms continue, although applied to a boy and young man who waits, respectively, on birds, dogs, horses, and, finally, Lady Booby. Joseph is, like the later Humphry Clinker, rather bare to the world, a mock-mythical hero of unknown parentage found in a field.

All this is, however, by way of bravura, the apprentice novelist kicking his rhetorical heels, demonstrating his skill. These early pages, in fact, demonstrate how Fielding could have taken prose fiction down a cul-de-sac. So much apparatus this early in the development of a new genre might have stifled its growth, or made it secondary to other, already-established genres: the mock-epic in verse, the theater of burlesque, social comedy, or romance. Even chapter III, with its introduction of Parson Adams and Mrs. Slipslop, is not a move outward; for the elements here are imitative either of *Don Quixote* or post-Restoration comedy. There is still nothing distinctive. Fielding is clearly uncertain of direction and, even more apparently, devoted to his sources and his contemporaries. The explanation under the title of the book, "Written in Imitation of The Manner of Cervantes Author of *Don Quixote*," lies very heavily, as do the mock-heroic rhetorical devices. Chapter VII closes with a Virgilian simile beginning "As when a hungry tigress . . ." that lasts almost the entire paragraph. In its knowing way, with mythical creatures and devices used mockingly, this pyrotechnic display is self-defeating. All mock-heroic, or mock-epic, is an act of diminution. The juxtaposition of Hesperus, Phoebe, Phidias, Praxiteles, and others with Joseph's fortunes relating to Lady Booby are all ways of reducing Joseph, *even while* Fielding is attempting to justify Joseph's virtues in the reader's eyes.

A curious form of development has begun to take place. For comic purposes (the "comic" of the prose epic, the ridiculous, the sense of affectation), it was necessary to reduce, to create a scale of values which puffed gods while miniaturizing man. Such disproportioning is a necessary comic element in puncturing vanity and hypocrisy, which are the true sources of affectation. Thus, diminution was absolutely necessary, or else, instead of a comic epic, Fielding would have produced a heroic adventure.

Here, then, is the paradox. For the novel depends to some degree on the development of characters with choices, will, and a sense of themselves. This is a point Fielding himself recognized in many of his interpolated tales, which are stories of identity and the establishment of the self. They often parallel the major action. And yet the reductive process of the comic elements inhibits character growth. Miniaturization keeps the novelist hovering over every act of the protagonist in order to reduce him, deny his intentions, keep him bounded within the small world of the ridiculous. Technique, we observe, can work *against* matter. It is, incidentally, a paradox that

Fielding never cleared up, and Samuel Johnson's condescension toward Fielding's work can be partially explained by this: Fielding, by virtue of his verbal and technical displays, rarely appeared fully serious or committed to the lives of his characters.

This debilitating confrontation between technical and human needs, while never fully resolved, is mitigated by Fielding's need to promulgate the terms on which social justice is possible. Fielding is one of the most moralistic of writers, a fact often forgotten or lost when he is compared with Richardson, whose moral values are more verbally detailed. So we can say: *The novel in Fielding's hands began to develop at the point that technical matters became secondary to matters of dogma.*[6] In other words, when Fielding's need turned to moralizing, his fiction turned closer to the novel. Even here, however, an implicit paradox is never resolved, because excessive moralizing also helps to destroy choice and decision, making puppets of characters and moving back toward allegory. All is a matter of degree, and the degree of moralizing must be less debilitating than the bombardment of compulsive mock-epic verbal displays.

Fielding's system depended on reason, goodness, and the application of "moral prudence." He believed that since human nature inclined toward natural goodness, it was possible for the individual to reason his way out of unruly passions. Fielding, in fact, often distinguishes between characters in this way. Winfield H. Rogers carries this distinction to a point of technique: "The difference between the humourous character and the serious character in much of eighteenth century literature may well lie in this: when corrigible the character might be satirized, when incorrigible he must be held up as an object of detestation." [7]

[6] The dogma lies everywhere. Martin Battestin places it historically: "The modified Pelagian doctrine of such latitudinarian churchmen as Isaac Barrow, John Tillotson, Samuel Clarke, and Benjamin Hoadly—all of whom Fielding read with sympathy and admiration—is essential background for a right interpretation of his ethics in general and of the meaning of *Joseph Andrews* in particular. In the sermons of these divines and others who shared their belief in a pragmatic, common-sense Christianity, he found ready-made a congenial philosophy of morals and religion. It was an optimistic philosophy stressing the perfectibility, if not the perfection, of the human soul, and one directed toward the amelioration of society . . . We may look here for the sources of Fielding's didacticism, for the rationale behind the ethic of good nature and good works that distinguishes his writing from *The Champion* to the end of his career." (*The Moral Basis of Fielding's Art: A Study of Joseph Andrews*, p. 14)

[7] "Fielding's Early Aesthetic and Technique," *Studies in Philology*, XL (1943), 529–551; more readily available in *Fielding: A Collection of Critical Essays*, ed. Paulson, 1962, p. 32. The entire essay is extremely valuable for the student interested in farce, burlesque, the comic epic, and matters of diction.

One of the turning points in Fielding's development into a novelist, from his earlier stance as a maker of farces, comes rather innocuously in chapter XIII. If we recall, an injured Joseph is brought to the Dragon Inn, where a surgeon—one of Fielding's usual assassins—tells the young man that he should settle his worldly affairs. A clergyman is sent for, and Mr. Barnabas—the name associated with the Levite missionary, companion of St. Paul—turns up. His advice is prayer, faith, giving oneself over to the divine will. Barnabas counsels salvation through God's grace, the sole way in which man may "divest himself of all human passions, and fix his heart above." (p. 49)

In this rather casual scene, still well within the comic mode of farce and satire, within which the reader has no fear for Joseph's ultimate recovery, Fielding has begun to settle into his major mode of development, perhaps without even being aware of the shift in direction. His satire, directed toward a preconceived point of view, turns the novel into a dialectic of forces—between those whose somewhat unruly passions can be tamed by reason and those whose affectations place them outside the pale of conversion. He becomes openly moralistic.

Shortly after, we see Parson Adams in action. Fielding contrasts his good deeds with Barnabas's assertions of prayer and faith. The dialectic is established, although timidly and pallidly. The change that occurs in the tone of the novel is comparable to the tonal change that occurs in *Don Quixote* when Cervantes moves from a satirical portrait of the Don to a more realistic presentation of what he is really attempting to do. In neither Fielding nor Cervantes is it fully possible to pinpoint such change; but it is certain that the development of the novel form in Fielding begins when the terms of the dialectic become clearer, when unruly passions—which are basically good and decent—are juxtaposed to incorrigible characteristics.

The "incorrigibles" in Fielding, and especially in *Joseph Andrews*, take many forms; they may be doctors, clergymen, mistresses of the manor, servants, Methodists, innkeepers, or false lovers. The democratic system in Fielding results from his ranging high and low. Likewise, his "corrigibles" may come from any strata, although they tend to be from the lower classes, at least until the conclusion of the novel, when they suddenly appear better born than we were led to believe. These latter devices, however, are merely resolutions implicit in the tradition of romance, while the matter that leads up to them is part of the major development. When we come to Joseph's higher birth, as, later, when we note Tom Jones's, we have already lived with Joseph as a servant and with Tom as a bastard of unknown origin; and our experience of these characters is essentially what we have been led to expect, not the resolution which re-creates their origins.[8]

In working out the dialectic of forces between corrigible and incorrigible, between those who can be saved and those who cannot, between low and high, Fielding integrated class conflict into the main line of the novel's development, like Richardson, who brought conflict between the bourgeoisie and the aristocracy to *Clarissa*. We can see that Fielding's mode in *Joseph Andrews* is a significant one, for his sense of "comic romance," or the "comic epic in prose," makes of class warfare a comic, not a tragic thing.[9] The line of demarcation between later English and French fiction on class matters is clear. For the English, class distinction, even in a melodramatic tragedian like Dickens, remains part of a comic mode, by which we mean both humor and a happy resolution.

Joseph is virtuous, while the upper classes are bored and on the make; Sophia is a virgin, while Lady Bellaston buys young men for herself. Fielding utilizes these divergent matters not only for the comic working out of the narrative line but also as a basis for class comment. Kettle says that Parson Adams "raises Fielding's anti-romantic criticism far above a mere common-sense repudiation of Richardson's moral pornography." Although this comment endows Fielding while demeaning Richardson, the point is that Adams creates a class foundation for criticism of his betters that is irreproachable. As a Quixote, he tilts against injustice in the name of values usually associated with the lower or working classes. His

[8] Arnold Kettle comes to a similar conclusion, although his is founded on a Marxist approach to the novel: ". . . it is interesting that the unkind are invariably the great and fashionable . . . while the kind are the humble people." (*An Introduction to the English Novel*, I, 1951, p.75)

[9] Fielding's preface to his sister Sarah's novel, *The Adventures of David Simple* (1744), repeats many of the same points he made in his preface to *Joseph Andrews*. At one point, he argues for the form of the picaresque, "where the Fable consists of a Series of separate Adventures detached from, and independent of each other, yet all tending to one great End; so that those who should object want of Unity of Action here, may, if they please, or if they dare, fly back with their Objection, in the face even of the *Odyssey* itself." (Oxford English Novels edition, p. 6) Following this, Fielding notes that three ingredients are necessary to works of this kind: ". . . that the main End or Scope be at once amiable, ridiculous and natural." (p. 7)

proclivities and activities are directed toward making life simpler, not more elegant or complicated. The English novelist has normally associated simplicity with the lower classes, affectation with the middle, vanity with the upper.

If the theme of *Joseph Andrews* is anti-romantic (what Fielding, among other things, inherited from Cervantes and Marivaux), then the bearer of the anti-romantic message—indeed the tribune of the people—is Parson Adams. Although he is not interesting as a person in the modern sense of having depth or charm, he is, nevertheless, compelling in the eighteenth-century manner as embodying common sense, basic decency, and personal eccentricity. He is the good man burlesqued in the drama because his innocence always puts him in a disadvantageous position; but he is also triumphant, because innocence is ultimately a better weapon than cunning. Only in the comic mode, however, could such a creature survive. In comedy, his isolation is mainly verbal and, if situational, temporary. The author's arrangement to "save" Adams, when it comes, derives not from the strengths of his character but from circumstances beyond his control; and the same elements which resolve the main line of the narrative happily also resolve all other problems in their wake, including those of Adams.

What is curious is Fielding's blending of a Don Quixote with an Adam. As a Quixote, Adams is idealistic, high-minded, a chivalric knight in his religious functions, naïve and innocent (or unmindful of realistic problems), the fool of his own imagination, a student of the past (Aeschylus, not Amadis of Gaul), the champion of the weak and the unfortunate, a stanch believer in deeds, not simply faith, but also a believer in faith when it does not preclude deeds. But this Quixote is also Adam. Adams's innocence may be the innocence of the prelapsarian Adam; and perhaps Adams's unwavering belief in mankind, despite all evidence to the contrary, is the faith of Adam before his corruption.[10]

[10] We recall William Hazlitt's remark (in *Lectures on the English Comic Writers*): "Perhaps, after all, Parson Adams is his [Fielding's] finest character. It is equally true to nature, and more ideal than any of the others. Its unsuspecting simplicity makes it not only more amiable, but doubly amusing, by gratifying the sense of superior sagacity in the reader." (Dolphin edition, p. 65) Hazlitt's comment suggests another aspect of Fielding's comic method, which was to make the reader feel superior to the very characters he accepts. Hazlitt notes that our laughter at Adams does not lessen our respect for him.

These remarks, published in 1819, are later completely contradicted by Thackeray, whose "Victorian" reading of Fielding's novels sees Jones as irredeemable and

For Fielding, Adams's dualism exists not to state something about nature or about "natural man" but to establish working coordinates for both man in general and the class structure. Another way by which Fielding sets up reference points is through the two interpolated stories, that of Leonora and that of Mr. Wilson. Unlike the interpolated stories of pure picaresque, or of *Don Quixote*, which only tortuous reasoning can integrate with the main development, these interpolations *are* related to the narrative line, are examples of elements at the core of the novel. In their way, they buttress whatever we may say of Parson Adams and Joseph.

The tale of the "unfortunate Leonora" recounts a life that relies heavily on vanity and hypocrisy. The simpering Frenchman, Bellarmine, and the inconstant Leonora are both villains of the piece. Bellarmine's villainy is his lack of moral prudence, which lets him tamper whimsically with others' affections; but Leonora's villainy, in eighteenth-century terms, is potentially worse, because she is not innately foolish or whimsical. Though she has a full knowledge of things, she is nevertheless won over by the serpent.

In the other interpolated tale, Wilson also has a full sense of things and yet chooses a life of leisure, an anti-life based on vanity. The deeper he delves into moral degradation, the further he moves from the simple life that brings salvation. And yet he ultimately discovers what Adams has known all along: that certain values remain constant, that a man must find his identity, that temptation comes from within, and that to resist temptation is to be true to one's best self.

The stories of Leonora and Wilson fulfill one major aspect of Fielding's method, which is to present a vast troupe of characters whose adventures and misadventures show the reader their diverse reactions to fortune. This is a point Aurélien Digeon, in *The Novels of Fielding*, establishes in reference to the twist of plot that makes us believe Fanny is Joseph's sister, a turn that tilts the action and redirects, temporarily, the feelings of the principals. The idea behind

questions Fielding's comic resolution of such a scapegrace to the good and kind Sophia. "I can't say but that I think Fielding's evident liking and admiration for Mr. Jones shows that the great humourist's moral sense was blunted by his life, and that here, in Art and Ethics, there is a great error." (*The English Humourists of the Eighteenth Century*, Everyman edition, p. 215) There could be some truth in Thackeray's view if Fielding had not already established his comic method, which permits a rapid turn of fortune in Tom's opportunities. Thackeray's own moral preoccupations, or else the demands of the Age, evidently blinded him to Fielding's ironic play.

these seemingly fortuitous happenings is always the idea behind comedy—that only one more twist is necessary to bring things right; while in tragedy, each change of fortune always seems to be final, the one conveying personal doom. In still another way, the novel becomes in Fielding's hands something like the numerous facets of a diamond; each facet reflects a slightly different light. The aim of the diamond cutter is to provide small differences, where the resultant patterns are somehow representative or symbolic of a kind of life. In a similar manner, Fielding's comic method is a way of representing the hard pragmatism of his philosophy. Early in the novel, he speaks of the scene opening "itself by small degrees." We could argue, further, that the abrupt shifts, say, from mockery of *Pamela* to concentration on Joseph, Fanny, and Adams are part of this "facet" theory: Fielding, as a means of creating manageable scenes of real life, simply kept turning the material to reflect new light whenever one facet had served its function; as Digeon suggests, when one idea lost its forward thrust, Fielding moved to another. The flexibility of his comic method permitted precisely this kind of alteration of purpose.[11]

Any discussion of *Joseph Andrews* must come to terms with Fielding's intentions as he described them in his preface, in numerous remarks throughout the novel, and as he continued to redefine his fictional aims in the introductions to each book of *Tom Jones*. We can organize Fielding's intentions in the following way: *He was trying to approach, without intending to reach, realism in the novel,* and *he was attempting, concomitantly, to harmonize new forms with traditional ones.* In this attraction both to the new and to the pull from the past, we can discern the dialectic of forces in Fielding and the pervasive influences of Cervantes. In respect to Fielding's movement toward realism, Ronald Paulson, in his closely reasoned *Satire and the Novel in Eighteenth-Century England*, writes:

Fielding's analogy between his novel and the works of Hogarth makes his point clear. Hogarth's prints, which had become enormously popular after

[11] Fielding provides clues as to how to read him in his valuable preface to his sister's novel, cited above, written about the time of *Joseph Andrews*: "For as the Merit of this Work consists in a vast Penetration into human Nature, a deep and profound Discernment of all the Mazes, Windings and Labyrinths, which perplex the Heart of Man to such a degree, that he is himself often incapable of seeing through them; and as this is the greatest, noblest, and rarest of all the Talents which constitute a Genius; so a much larger Share of this Talent is necessary, even to recognize these Discoveries, when they are laid before us, than falls to the share of a common Reader." (Oxford English Novels edition, p. 5)

the publication of *A Harlot's Progress* in 1732, offered the best example of what Fielding himself wished to do: replace the fantasy of traditional, emblematic, and Augustan satire with a more restrained delineation, close to experience, and reliant on "character" rather than "caricature," on the variety rather than the exaggeration of expression. [p. 108]

Paulson draws the analogy even tighter, asserting that Hogarth tried to secure his place within traditional forms by steering "a course between the flatulent history painting of his time and the popular forms of satire and burlesque"; so Fielding "sought to establish a genre between the romance he discerned in Richardson's *Pamela* and the grotesquerie of travesty." (p. 108) Thus, we can speak of Fielding's theory of comedy as a way of defining his own brand of "external" realism, "external" in its lack of psychological detail, its narrative openness, its spatiality of plot, all of which must be contrasted with Richardson's internalizing of effects.

Thus, Fielding searched for the middle ground between romance and burlesque or farce. When he says that "no two species of writing can differ more widely than the comic and the burlesque," we are somewhat puzzled, for in loose modern usage of the terms, "burlesque" and "comic" are almost interchangeable, although we recognize that "comic" is a more inclusive term. For Fielding, however, the distinction is crucial. Burlesque, what he practiced in *Shamela*, was comparable to unrestrained farce, and to continue that was to move theatrical forms into fiction, blocking the latter and simply duplicating the former. Stress upon burlesque, further, keeps the writer uncomfortably close to romance, for burlesque "is ever the exhibition of what is monstrous and unnatural," and our delight in it arises from "surprising absurdity," as our delight, when it exists, in reading romance derives from its improbability. The comic, however, was for Fielding a movement toward realism, for the comic confines itself "strictly to nature, from the just imitation of which will flow all the pleasure we can this way convey to a sensible reader." The comic writer, Fielding warns, should not deviate from nature, which is another way of saying realism is an antidote to romance.

These points are corollaries of Fielding's earlier definition of terms, in which he said that a "comic romance is a comic epic-poem in prose," a phrase that critics have doted upon. In Fielding, it is followed by his distinction between comic romance and comedy, much as one distinguishes between epic and tragedy. He asserts that the comic romance is more comprehensive than comedy, by which he means that it should accommodate the picaresque variety of plot, character, and setting in a way Molière's type of comedy cannot. So, too, the comic romance is different from romance itself in the former's reliance on the ridiculous, in its introduction of "persons of inferior rank," in its diction, which limns the ludicrous rather than the sublime.

These distinctions point toward what we may call a *dignified picaresque*. Fielding rejects the outrageous (*caricatura*—whose aim "is to exhibit monsters, not men"), which in literary terms is equivalent to burlesque. Both *caricatura* and burlesque recall romance and must be rejected. Fielding says he will pursue his sense of the ridiculous, which has its source in affectation, vanity, and hypocrisy. Affectation is not only a falsification of reality, it is a lying to oneself, what the egoist does when he distorts the outside world. The crime of the egoist is lack of self-knowledge, or inadequate knowledge, or knowledge put to wrong ends. Fielding's terms suggest to us the age-old view of comedy as a social weapon devised to expose egoism, here adapted to the novel.

The egoist may become the subject of either tragedy or comedy, depending on the emphasis and the ultimate end. Tragedy is basically an extreme position: the protagonist himself lives at the social extreme, he commits extreme acts, he suffers extreme punishment. Comedy is, essentially, a sweetener, unless satire is its chief vehicle. Fielding's basic conservatism in the novel appeared when he tempered the savage satire of his stage works with the comic apparatus of his fiction. The struggle in Fielding between irony and sentiment (even sentimentality) is apparent in his early career, with the former dominating *Shamela*, the early or first version of *Jonathan Wild*, the opening chapters of *Joseph Andrews*, continuing through *Tom Jones*, and becoming paramount in *Amelia*. We will speak later of the substance of *Tom Jones* as structured upon contrasts intrinsic to Fielding's way of thinking; we are speaking now of such contrasts as existing in technique. In a more personal sense, the tensions created by irony and sentiment in Fielding's work are possibly manifestations of opposing drives within the man himself; much as in Richardson, the piety of Clarissa does not disguise his attraction to the destructiveness of Lovelace.

To carry the point still further: the Age required Fielding, and others, to adapt new measures to old practices, and always to explain a departure in terms of a tradition. Even as Addison, Pope, Johnson, and Swift voiced certain ideals based on tradition, status quo, and discipline—and their edicts ruled supreme in serious cultural matters—there was developing a counterorder, in itself a disguised threat to neoclassical precepts. The counterorder was the development of sentiment (a Parsons Adams, a Joseph Andrews, a Fanny Andrews), an entire array of low- or middle-born creatures whose rules and principles were quite different from the hierarchical and aristocratic assumptions of the essayists and poets. Even when democratic ideas appeared in the latter group, these ideas were usually concessions, not directives.

There is little question that the work of Fielding and Richardson reflects changing eighteenth-century attitudes. Despite their lip service to convention and tradition, they are part of the psychological shifting of the age, from reason to sentiment, to common sense intermixed with feeling. Accordingly, while Fielding's techniques recall old modes, whether epic, heroic, satiric, ironic, his content presages a more romantically oriented age. With all his apparatus, with all his notes and prefaces, with all his defenses of the past, Fielding is part of the development of an era, "marked by a general growth of the sentimental forces about to regenerate England." (Digeon, p. 229) Fielding's own growth, the intermingling of sentiment and common sense, the growth of a new psychological attitude—all of these are found also in the development of Methodism. We must view the mix of common sense and emotionalism in Methodism, not as an aberration, but as part of a change in sensibility; and although Fielding poured contempt upon the Methodists, especially upon Whitefield's Calvinistic faction, for its stress upon faith at the expense of good works, nevertheless he was himself caught up in the general evangelical fervor, manifest in the sentimental Adams, the benevolent Allworthy, the faulted Christian hero Jones, the knightly Andrews, the saintly Amelia.

As we noted above, Martin Battestin speaks of the influence of the latitudinarian divines on the movement toward sentiment. Men like Barrow, Tillotson, Clarke, and Hoadly, he says, turned Christianity from the cynicism of a Hobbes or a Mandeville to a moral system based on the innate virtue of man. In this moral system, innocence and passion become positive values, now as much respected as before they had been satirized and reviled. In addition, the third Earl of Shaftesbury's ideas about virtue generated certain impulses which surfaced, in literature, in the sentimental novel, in a more feeling type of poetry, in the emotional excesses of Gothic, finding adherents as disparate as Fielding, Sterne, Walpole, Thomson.[12]

Fielding's conception of comedy ("comic romance," the "comic epic-poem in prose") can itself be viewed as part of this sentimental turn, even though he tries to justify his theory in pseudo-classical terms. The comic, which intends to expose human folly and by so doing provide a corrective, is keyed to the idea that people are either innately or potentially good, or at least capable of demonstrating virtue. The "comic epic" de-emphasizes solemnity, stresses humanizing rather than heroic values, moves away from an aristocratic conception of a society's ideals or needs toward the life-size qualities of an ordinary human being subject to needs and wants.

The heroic stresses overcoming; the comic stresses not being overcome. The distinction is crucial, for it is a difference between neoclassical precept and the growing sentimental-romantic attitude. At a certain stage, we leave behind even the mock-heroic and the mock-epic, which are parodies at the same time they indicate a yearning for the bygone past. With *Joseph Andrews*, Fielding's longings for traditional forms at the beginning of the novel give way to a different set of coordinates. When these latter take over, standing as they do for common sense, sentiment, sensibility, democratic concepts, the age itself is in the middle of a literary convulsion.

The History of Tom Jones: A Foundling

Everything about *Tom Jones* is based on a dialectic of forces, whether those of prose style, ironic method, plot structure, characterization, thematic materials, tonal variety, or dramatic intent. While the pull of opposites enters into every aspect of the novel, rarely does it occur in a straightforward, diagrammatic manner. Fielding often works by excluding; that is, by his very use of a convention or style, he excludes that style as possible for the "novelty" he is creating.

Although many critics have viewed Fielding's conservative vision

[12] The ideas of Shaftesbury (1671–1713) helped form Augustan taste and indirectly found their way into the developing novel. With his belief in man's innate goodness and his insistence on the natural, he struck a blow for the kind of egalitarianism that would characterize aspects of the novel. Further, his emphasis on individual responsibility and his strong criticism of revealed religion did much to mold that profane world which was so supportive of mid-century fiction.

as blocking all excesses, in actuality he juggles counterdoctrines, adversary ideas, and received wisdom. He obviously resolved all seemingly irreconcilable elements with symmetrical endings; at the conclusion of *Tom Jones*, for example, we have numerous instances of warring parents and children coming together in mutual understanding, an apt image of Fielding's kind of justice. The important point, however, is not the resolution that ends all struggles but the struggles themselves. Neither the eighteenth- nor nineteenth-century novel is at its strongest in what it *finally* tells us. Its wisdom resides in what it can suggest in human and social possibilities *before* it comes to a conclusion. We must, therefore, read Fielding for glimpses of the "other" he affords us through style, characterization, and theme.

In his introduction to Book II of *Tom Jones*, Fielding must work out some theoretical problems involved in the massive "feast" that he is cooking up for the reader. In effect, he must discuss the menu. Since he has called the book *The History of Tom Jones*, he assumes that we will take his work as a history. Yet he fears that if we expect history, we will also expect the details of events that have no significant place in the story. He must explain and justify the selectivity undertaken by the creative writer, although he is still trapped by the categories of history, romance, journalism, et al. So he says that *his* type of history will *not* be the kind that fills up empty pages, for that type recalls a newspaper which "consists of just the same number of words, whether there be any news in it or not." His historical method will be based on selection: of events, of time sequences, of types of development.[13] It will skip, and its time sequences will not necessarily be ordered.

This theory, presented so early, at the beginning of Book II, has within it the contraries that will infuse every aspect of the novel. Neither history, neither journalism, neither this nor that—in so many ways the novel in Fielding's hands begins as the thing it is not. We cited above the prose passage describing Sophia Western in which

[13] Hazlitt picks up Fielding's own argument that the professional historian provides only dates and names, while he, the novelist, gives the truth: "I should be at a loss where to find in any authentic document of the same period so satisfactory an account of the general state of society, and of moral, political, and religious feeling in the reign of George II as we meet with in the Adventures of Joseph Andrews and his friend Mr. Abraham Adams . . . the painter of manners gives the facts of human nature, and leaves us to draw the inference: if we are not able to do this, or do it ill, at least it is our own fault." (*Lectures on the English Comic Writers*, VI, pp. 153, 155)

Fielding's use of a particular prose style excluded such a style; by making it ornamentation, by utilizing it as mock-rhetoric, he informs us it is no longer viable for the novel. By using its "sublime" aspects to limn Sophia, he is suggesting the opposite about her and her behavior. That is, while her face and body may be sublimely lovely, her appetites, her choices, and her actions are earthy, practical, and temporal. Sublimity suggests immortality, and the well-endowed Sophia is very mortal indeed.

In another way, Tom is representative of a dialectic of conflicting elements, and Fielding's presentation of his protagonist is full of such dissenting qualities, once again involving the inflated rhetoric of mockery. As part of the eighteenth century's concern with epic—whether as mock or as the new fiction—Fielding presents a hero not unlike the one Otto Rank describes in the myth of the birth and growth of the hero. Of unknown origin, Tom, like Humphry Clinker later, falls into what Frye has called the "birth-mystery plot." Cast out from Eden (from Squire Allworthy's Paradise Hall), where the ruling body is a forgiving but somewhat foolish goodman, Tom seems to be a typical displaced hero. He moves from country bliss (Paradise Hall) on to his travels, which center on Upton, and then he descends into the hellish city, where his journey is like that of Odysseus and Dante through the Inferno. He does not have the consolation of a family name, and he must win his identity through his own feats. He treads the thin line between disastrous defeat and potential retrieval from his self-made hell. He is alone, isolated, forced to re-create himself from his own ashes.

Several components of the mythical hero are missing, however. The hostile relationship with the father is, of course, not present, because no confrontation is ever contemplated. Instead of making war, Tom makes love. His journey involves one trial after another, nearly all of which he fails to meet successfully. All tragic trappings are also removed, because Tom's trials all turn out to be illusory.[14] Because the outcome is to be comic, not tragic, the "hero" differs in many personal characteristics from the mythical hero, whose doom and salvation are intertwined. After all, Tom's fate is to bed down with Sophia, not to found kingdoms, destroy his enemies, kill his father, or dispel plagues. Instead of being vain, he is generous of spirit; instead of knowing exactly how things work, he is innocent of

[14] For a parallel argument, see Frye's *Anatomy of Criticism*, the section called "The Mythos of Spring: Comedy," especially pages 164 and 180.

how anything except sex works; instead of holding himself in strict discipline, poised for his great moment, he dissipates all his moments and revels in unsystematic behavior; instead of holding off the forces of destruction even as they edge up on him, he denies that evil exists by comporting himself as if all men were basically good; instead of being worn down, eventually, by adversity, corroded by the acidity of his own struggle, he transforms the bitter of adversity into the sweet of reconciliation. Our point is that even as Tom appears to fit into the role of a tragic displaced hero, Fielding's counterpoint works to undermine that image and eliminate its viability for the novel.[15]

The major dialectic, under which all other conflicts are in some way subsumed, is order versus disorder. It is a familiar theme, a carry-over from the medieval and Renaissance preoccupation with man's place in both world and universe, a compelling theme in the eighteenth century, when industry, commerce, urbanization, mechanization were challenging the old ideas of order. The theme appears in every major novelist, poet, and essayist of the time. It was, of course, central to Defoe as well as to Fielding's great contemporary Richardson. It became the butt of Sterne's wit in *Tristram Shandy*, in which, like an eighteenth-century Panurge, he flails at outmoded theories of order.

Order and disorder are the bounds of the novel, and they are interfused with "plot" as R. S. Crane has used the term to mean character, thought, narrative.[16] Yet, such is Fielding's irony that we

[15] Complementing Tom as a mock "displaced hero" is the more traditional way of seeing him as a *Bildungsroman* protagonist. As such, he is part of an episodic, rambling form whose chief cementing force is the young, inexperienced protagonist himself. The looseness of the form permits the young man to make numerous mistakes of judgment and choice; he is given several chances to right himself, even when conditions look bleakest. The "several chances" are, in fact, part of his education, his apprenticeship to life; and the chances, missed or otherwise, are as much part of the plot as the character's final decisions.

Further, the attractiveness of the *Bildungsroman* to a bourgeois society was the plasticity of the genre, as protean as the audience it supposedly catered to. We can derive from the *Bildungsroman* the styles of any given society, its philosophical and theological concerns, its divisions and schisms, its obsessions and compulsions, its psychological conditioning. This is, of course, far less true of the "displaced hero" myth, where fixity of purpose, predetermined conditions and states of feeling, and rigidity of expectation and performance are the rule rather than the exception.

[16] After reading Crane's essay, "The Concept of Plot and the Plot of *Tom Jones*" (in *Critics and Criticism*, ed. R. S. Crane, reprinted from *The Journal of General Education*, IV, 112–30), it is impossible to divide *Tom Jones*, or any novel, into exclusive elements of plot, character, action, thought. Crane writes: "We may say that the plot of any novel

can never take any statement at face value. Like Moll clothed in her disguises, the entire novel is wrapped in a mantle of seeming and becoming. Narrative elements are rarely what they appear to be; people are not what they say they are; decisions are infrequently made for the reasons given. The comic movement of the narrative is toward the divulgence of elements that hitherto had remained clouded. There is little change, if any, in the characters; what does occur is revelation of what the character has really been. Eyes are opened, minds are cleared, suspicions dissipated. All of this is part of the ironic method, central to any work based on a dialectic of forces.

One of the important conflicts in the novel is between Tom and Blifil, although the evident differences are masked by their having been brought up together as brothers, by their being in fact half brothers, by their seeming identity of interests, with Blifil enjoying a real mother in Bridget and Tom enjoying a surrogate father in Squire Allworthy; or, conversely, while Blifil lacks a father from an early age, Tom lacks a mother from birth. Thus, the novel's major ideological and thematic opposites are presented *en famille,* so that the differences are hidden beneath social and familial amenities. Thus, we must always seek beneath appearances to obtain a view of the real character and real identity. And since the Shaftesburian Allworthy does believe in a benevolent universe, with justice, goodness, and fairness as its attributes, it is no wonder he fails to understand subsurface behavior or to place worth in malevolent intentions. Shaftesburyism, like later Benthamism, kept to surfaces.

Once this is clear, we can proceed to Tom and Blifil and find in their opposing values a whole range of Fielding's beliefs about man and society. Tom, seemingly disordered, untidy, often in disarray, represents normality; while Blifil, tidy, ordered, sanitary, represents abnormality.[17] The conception extends to the sexual tastes and preferences of each. Tom is able to give of himself as well as receive, and his sexual preferences are based on both giving and receiving

---

or drama is the particular temporal synthesis effected by the writer of the elements of action, character, and thought that constitute the matter of his invention. It is impossible, therefore, to state adequately what any plot is unless we include in our formula all three of the elements or causes of which the plot is the synthesis; and it follows also that plots will differ in structure according as one or another of three causal ingredients is employed as the synthesizing principle. There are, thus, plots of action, plots of character, and plots of thought." (p. 66)

[17] Superficially, the half brothers recall Jacob and Esau, and there is sufficient commentary about favorites and birthrights to suggest Fielding had the Biblical brothers in mind.

pleasure. Blifil, however, retentive, repressed, and capable only of receiving, relates to no other person on any terms even vaguely sexual or passionate. While Tom fornicates, Blifil masturbates, or at least seeks no reciprocation. Although we cannot insist that he must be tantalized by Sophia in particular, he is apparently moved by no one and by nothing except self-gain.[18]

Blifil is the classic anal type, holding on to everything for fear of loss, disorder, anarchy. His orientation, as the type implies, is toward money, property, goods. Tangibility is all; emotion, passion, attachments mean little or nothing. His type, of course, fills many Victorian novels, but it is surely to Fielding's great credit that he could create such an important type for the novel so early in the development of the genre. Richardson's Solmes, in comparison, is also sexually revolting, unfeeling, and wooden, but not seen in depth. The psychological tension derives from Clarissa's sexual detestation of him, and through him, seemingly, of any man who intends to ease himself onto her body. Blifil, however, exists in his own right, without any necessity of our accepting him on another's terms. Fielding reveals him fully, and Samuel Johnson's depreciation of Fielding's psychological powers was never less appropriate.

Fielding prepares us for young Blifil by his meticulous creation of the father, Captain Blifil. The captain is cold, calculating, and overbearing. His hatred of women is apparent: "He looked on a woman as on an animal of domestic use . . . and yet so tender was his pride, that it felt the contempt which his wife now began to express towards him; and this . . . created in him a degree of disgust and abhorrence perhaps hardly to be exceeded." (Book II, chapter 7, p. 65) From this mutual hatred springs young Blifil, the product of his father's calculating nature and the domestic coolness of Paradise Hall, the consequence of nature and nurture. Further, Fielding also

[18] Fielding writes about Blifil: "Though Mr. Blifil was not of the complexion of Jones, nor ready to eat every woman he saw, yet he was far from being destitute of that appetite which is said to be the common property of all animals. With this, he had likewise that distinguishing taste, which serves to direct men in their choice of the object or food of their several appetites; and this taught him to consider Sophia as a most delicious morsel, indeed to regard her with the same desires which an ortolan inspires into the soul of an epicure. Now the agonies which affected the mind of Sophia rather augmented than impaired her beauty; for her tears added brightness to her eyes, and her breasts rose higher with her sighs. Indeed, no one hath seen beauty in its highest lustre who hath never seen it in distress. Blifil therefore looked on this human ortolan with greater desire than when he viewed her last; nor was his desire at all lessened by the aversion which he discovered in her to himself." (pp. 276–7)

makes clear that Bridget Allworthy prefers Tom to her son by Captain Blifil, and toward compensating for that, Squire Allworthy extends consideration to young Blifil that he does not feel.

The terms, accordingly, are set: Blifil is part of the business, commercial world in which planning, legalism, calculation—Robinson Crusoe's virtues—are needed for survival; while Tom, living on love, affection, camaraderie, is anti-business, loses the money given to him, is an expression of orality, emotional generosity. In this sense, too, he is a child of nature, for his background is anything but calculating, and his birth was itself the consequence of a love relationship that never tarnished.

Viewed this way, Fielding's use of these two contraries moves us out into almost limitless possibilities of theme. Through Tom, we sense the aspect of marriage which creates healthy children and an open society; through Blifil, we sense relationships that poison growth and sour temperaments. Through Tom, we sense the rejection of city values which in Defoe made the fortunes of Crusoe, Moll, and Roxana; we sense, further, a rejection of any plan that excludes man's openness. Through Blifil, we note that retentiveness, whether of money or affection, leads to repression, which in turn lends itself to perversity of temperament and poverty of spirit.

Not surprisingly, Blifil has the other "perverse" characters, Square and Thwackum, in his corner. Fielding was the first of the English novelists to see that systems, whether based on man's good or evil, are impositions upon free human nature. Like Meredith and Dickens after him, Fielding associated systems and systematic thought with repression. His attacks upon Square and Thwackum, in the rhetorical idiom of ironic sallies, are not only for their respective ideas of deism and Calvinism but for their doglike defense of *any* system.

When we contrast Tom and the younger Blifil, we run into a philosophical problem that Fielding posed but never resolved. For if Blifil represents calculation at its worst and Tom represents profligacy virtually at its worst, how can Fielding favor Tom and yet argue that moral prudence is necessary for a balanced, healthy society? [19] This unresolved dichotomy in Fielding's view of individ-

[19] In a long article on *Tom Jones*, William Empson tries, among other things, to unravel Fielding's ethical and moral beliefs, writing: "Fielding might well protest that he deserved to escape this reproach [of Dr. Johnson and Sir John Hawkins that "morality is of no use"]; he had twice stepped out of his frame in the novel to explain

ual and society becomes part of the dialectic that characterizes his work. Those, like Robert Alter, who see Fielding as a synthesizer of opposing parts enforce a conservative resolution on his every impulse. It may be preferable to view Fielding in somewhat the same terms as Richardson: that is, as a man morally based on the idea of prudence, balance, moderation, who as a novelist is able to confront the "other," which is imprudent, amoral, unbalanced, immoderate, even antisocial and countering. Such conflicting forces we now note as commonplaces in the equally conservative Victorian novelists, and we surely have reason to believe that in a less repressed period like the eighteenth century an even greater creative urgency to "break out," to take an adversary position to society, was present. Both the novel of sentiment and the Gothic novel illustrate such impulses.

None of this argues that Fielding was radical or even unduly progressive. It does suggest, however, that he recognized that individual experience runs counter, frequently, to the social experience; that the individual experience is, ultimately, more significant and is not to be resolved, say, as Blifil's own mind and character are resolved. Loose ends and rough edges are necessary; and while irony, wit, and classical allusions are all present, they resolve nothing of the irresolvable. Fielding, like Dickens, suggested many of the elements he could not accept, and these elements became far more interesting novelistically than the parts reconciled for social purposes. Again, this is not to make Fielding more daring or adventurous than he was, but to grant him in his novels up to *Amelia* a trying out of several styles that ran counter to his sense of moral prudence.

A comparison with the American novelist Herman Melville may seem outlandish but is instructive. In many of his major novels, novellas, and tales, Melville tested out the possibilities of the forbidden, the destructive, the antisocial. In *Bartleby the Scrivener*, for instance, he rejected the death instinct of his main character and yet, simultaneously, made it seem purer, more moral than anything the world could offer. Melville sensed the contradictions in man and the need to move against death in the name of life. While self-destructive

that he was not recommending Tom's imprudence, and that he did not mean to imply that religion and philosophy are bad because bad men can interpret them wrongly. But he seems to have started from this idea in his first revolt against the *ethos* of Richardson which made him write *Shamela* and *Joseph Andrews* . . ." (*"Tom Jones," Kenyon Review*, pp. 217–49; revised and reprinted in *Fielding: A Collection of Critical Essays*, ed. Paulson, p. 128)

tendencies can derive from pure motives, they must be blunted in favor of social balance or a larger truth. In the process, the heroes are slain, the pure of purpose are hanged or impaled.

Recognizably, Fielding is a very different writer, working as intensely in the comic vein as Melville in the tragic. Yet there is a comparable attempt to capture the dualism of man *without* destroying the sense of the individual as superior to whatever social order ultimately prevails. One point of Melville's work is that stress on order at the expense of the individual is a melancholy notion, not to be applauded because it constitutes authority and order. As a comic novelist who provides the reader with security at every turn, Fielding need not emphasize the stifling, almost tragic quality of order. But it is apparent that when order predominates, as in Amelia, Squire Allworthy, or Joseph Andrews, at these times Fielding is weakest. Virtue has never lent itself easily to fiction, and Fielding's bouts with moral prudence are no exception.

His fiction is most effective when it suggests and presents disorder—the paradox of every writer whose personal conservatism is equivalent to a social ideology. It is the disorder of Tom, whether fornicating, eating, or fighting, which creates the sense of a young man growing up naturally, squandering his long-term assets in immediate gratification; his recklessness is part of his generosity, and these qualities, as we have noted, separate him from the characters in the novel who are unable to give. In stressing Tom's squandering, Fielding is foreshadowing Rousseau's "natural man," if we understand Rousseau's primitivism is not necessarily idyllic. Nevertheless, as Arthur Lovejoy notes, primitive man "is . . . happier than his civilized successors." Living for the moment, he is "untroubled either by regrets or by fears of coming evil." [20] Tom is, in a sense, much more the "wild boy" of the woods than Black George, who lives in and watches over the grounds. George is already urbanized: his values are commercial, and his tastes run not to replenishing nature but to taking from it what he can. While he is financially impoverished, it is also clear he is emotionally and psychologically impoverished as well.

Thus, if we are to speak of "nature" or "natural man," then we must refer such terms to Tom and Tom to them. The contrast between Tom and Blifil, comparable to all disorder and order

[20] "The Supposed Primitivism of Rousseau," *Essays in the History of Ideas*, p. 20; the entire essay bears indirectly on Fielding.

contrasts running thematically through the novel, is that between primitive and civilized. Fielding describes Blifil as "sober, discreet, and pious beyond his age"—the very qualities that a puritanical society admires. Tom's primitivism challenges these qualities. When Fielding, at the beginning of Book III, chapter II, brings "forth our hero, at about fourteen years of age," he is revealed as a friend of the gamekeeper and as someone involved in the secret disposition of apples, partridges, and a duck. Such incidents and images immediately "create" Tom as the "wild boy," whose natural habitat is the forest and whose early conquests, romantic and otherwise, are woodsy affairs.

Without making Tom into a nature myth, we can associate many such myths and mythical creatures with Fielding's portrait. Certainly in the contrast between primitive and civilized, Tom is Dionysiac without being Dionysus, while young Blifil is a caricature of the neoclassical Apollonian figure. There are numerous other mythic variations: the Venus and Tannhäuser theme; or the story of Adonis, the young man whose death is the death of nature and whose annual revival is the rebirth of life; or Tom as a male Persephone seasonally surfacing and disappearing. While none of these is stressed—evidently not—all of them are suggested. When Tom goes to London and moves among Lady Bellaston's circle, Tannhäuser is enticed by Venus, Faust has sold himself to Mephistopheles, and Adonis is beloved by Aphrodite—all in small measure and for comic purposes. It is perhaps not coincidental that Tom is befriended by Squire Western, whose Dionysiac turn is much firmer than Tom's own, a man devoted only to disruption, disorder, and drink. The mythopoeic element here and elsewhere, however, never overwhelms, never takes over the narrative, never displaces a normalizing society; but it is there in a way that foreshadows novelists as distant as Dickens and D. H. Lawrence.

Since Tom's subsequent development once he leaves the woods is not antithetical to these early scenes, we can say that Fielding's Shaftesburian predilections turned him to the primitive (naturalness, disorder, innate virtue), although he recognized that a civilized resolution (social balance, some individual order) was needed. From this, as we shall see, we can read the novel and virtually every element in it. We can view Fielding's introductions to each book of *Tom Jones* as a way of providing rules for the narrative without binding it; and we can certainly interpret his "comic prose epic," as defined in *Joseph Andrews*, as part of this same commitment to variety and otherness within the necessary establishment of rules. Fielding was sufficiently a man of his times to accept the need for regulation, but his interpretation of that fiat allowed divergence, flexibility, and counterthrust. As he himself remarked:

> And here we shall of necessity be led to open a new vein of knowledge, which if it hath been discovered, hath not, to our remembrance, been wrought on by any ancient or modern writer. *This vein is no other than that of contrast,* which runs through all the works of the creation, and may probably have a large share in constituting in us the idea of all beauty, as well natural as artificial: for what demonstrates the beauty and excellence of anything but its reverse? Thus the beauty of day, and that of summer, is set off by the horrors of night and winter. And, I believe, if it was possible for a man to have seen only the two former, he would have a very imperfect idea of their beauty. [Introduction to Book V of *Tom Jones*, p. 157; my italics]

We may, as follows, line up the contrasts or conflicts within *Tom Jones*, keeping in mind that the major dialectical element under which all else is subsumed is that between primitive "disorder" and civilized "order":

1. As noted, the conflict between Tom and young Blifil—the most significant subcategory
2. Normal vs. abnormal—as stated above, a key to Tom and young Blifil, but extending to every category throughout the novel. Love as rational vs. the irrationality of much other behavior. (Those who are anti-love are abnormal)
3. Further character contrasts: Sophia–Molly Seagrim; Sophia–Mrs. Western (the Squire's sister); Bridget–Squire Allworthy (another sibling relationship); Western–Mrs. Western; Squire Western–Squire Allworthy
4. Parents and children: Tom–Allworthy, Tom–Bridget Allworthy, Tom–Mrs. Walters (Jenny); Blifil–Allworthy, Blifil–Bridget; Sophia–Squire Western; Nightingale–Mr. Nightingale; the Hamlet theme (pp. 737 ff.)
5. A clash of philosophies: Tom–Square, Tom–Thwackum, Square–Thwackum
6. The society: in human terms, a closed vs. an open society, manifest in systems vs. Tom, parental obedience vs. Sophia, etc.
7. A political contrast: the emotional, virtually irrational Catholic rebellion of 1745 and the established Protestant king, church, and Parliament

8. Criticism vs. creation: the headnotes and prefaces vs. the body of the novel; the tension between revised neoclassical theory and the new genre and its demands
9. Social and political guidelines: values based on a "system," which is neo-Hobbesian in intent, and those based on "natural goodness," a neo-Shaftesburian development
10. Country vs. city, nature vs. urbanization, woods vs. "high society"—and all the personal, social, and political ramifications
11. Love marriage vs. arranged marriage, a personal and social category with religious and political implications that Fielding resolves only on the personal-social level
12. Reason vs. emotion, seen mythically as Apollonian vs. Dionysian, as well as personally and socially
13. Good vs. evil: in humanistic rather than theological terms. (Since *Tom Jones* is a comedy, it lacks any sense of final things, of final good or evil)
14. Duty vs. passion—the Sophia–Squire Western plot as analogous to Clarissa and the Harlowes
15. True virtue vs. seeming virtue: the verities as against the surfaces
16. Realism vs. romance: plot development and resolution played off against theoretical aspects
17. Form (outward, discursive sense of the novel) vs. feeling (inward sense)
18. Illusion vs. reality: the Cervantes formula, but in Fielding as attached to character and plot development, not to philosophy as such

If we picked up each of these contrasts, conflicts, dichotomies, our discussion could be as long as the novel. Several, however, as we saw, can be subsumed under major categories. We should note that these conflicts or contraries are interwoven of thematic, plot, character, and narrative developments. That is, they are, in a major sense, *the novel*, not parts or elements of it. Coleridge's statement that *Tom Jones* had one of the three most nearly perfect literary plots is attached to this organic wedding of content with procedure; every element of technical development or narrative is also a category of meaning.

The sense of seeming as against the sense of sharp, detailed reality in the novel is Fielding's approximation of the illusion-reality dichotomy in *Don Quixote*. While the Don may speak of enchanters changing what he sees, Fielding speaks of one set of values when actually he means another. In another way, enchanters change the way people see Tom, for they rarely view him as he is. Throughout his development, he is one thing for the reader (because Fielding, as it were, breaks through the enchanters to reveal the real Tom) and another thing for the other characters; a figure whose wildness and thoughtfulness mark him as Cain for the Squares and Thwackums, while giving him substance for the reader.

The comic method demands reverses, as much as the tragic method requires a change in fortunes. Much recent Fielding criticism has focused on his certainty of identity and order, making it appear that his characters are static, without fluctuation. Perhaps unintentionally, such remarks severely limit Fielding. An author's hesitations, reversals, and "seemings" reveal the opposite of certainty; a method based on changes of fortune demonstrates an author's experimentation with alternate modes. The author may, of course, finally arrive at resolutions and achieve certainties, but order so reached displays as much disorder as it does order. Fielding may have desired moderation, but he argues against it in the name of spontaneity; while Richardson in his penchant for order becomes a master of illogic and the irrational. To argue that either is certain about his characters is to forsake the conflict of forces operating in both writers.

Fielding was too much a man of the stage to accept certainties. The theater demands both seeming and not seeming, role-playing, distance between audience and actor, between actor and actor, between actor and role. Every performance is different; every inflection of word, every gesture involves new turns of meaning. This was Fielding's apprenticeship, and it would be shortsighted to lose the perspective of those early years. One may read the introductory notes to each book of *Tom Jones* as stage directions. Fielding, the dramatist, is always moving among us, indicating this or that, pointing out directions, telling us how to read and see, and, ultimately, how to feel about things.[21] And he is not at all sure of

[21] In commenting upon Fielding's "interventions" in *Joseph Andrews* and elsewhere, Irvin Ehrenpreis shows how a knowledge of Fielding's dramatic background is essential to a reading of his fiction: "But in several of his own plays Fielding had employed a 'rehearsal' pattern which has the same effect. *Pasquin* and *The Historical Register* are two examples. Here the scene is supposed to be behind stage at a theater where a new play is being rehearsed. While some of the characters act out the play-within-a-play, the rest of the cast discuss its value as drama and its connection with politics or morality. The 'frame' characters can thus deliver precisely the mixture

himself, for the contrariness of his characters and their attitudes is often the embodiment of his own doubts.

Squire Western, who is possibly the most vital character in *Tom Jones*, typifies some of this contradictory material, as well as embodying many of our other categories. Western's personal tastes are well documented, and his attitudes are not presented favorably. He has driven his wife to an early grave, having done so by crude treatment, by standing on prerogatives that allowed no dissent. Likewise, despite his evident affection for his daughter, he is willing to entrap Sophia. Western is fixed in our minds as an implacable force of powerful likes and dislikes, of potential and actual violence, of selfish disregard for other people's values, as a man of vicious, drink-befogged impulses. And yet this raucous individual, when he bursts in on Lord Fellamar and calls him a son of a bitch, expresses a country healthiness at the expense of city corruption. He is, despite all, a force for life; and when he sees Fellamar's sword, he offers fists. He is *the* country squire personified—anti-royalist, deeply conservative, suspicious of the city—representing something far closer to life than Fellamar with his ornate mannerisms, his deceptive language, his sense of position. Although Fellamar turns out to be more decent than we suspected, it is Western who seems the savior of virtue, unlikely though the role. Even in this simple matter, then, Fielding plays a double game. Western's burst of passion reveals an openness and naturalness not previously associated with the bossy squire.

We have already examined similar turns of seeming and not-seeming in Tom Jones, whose fortunes depend entirely on his standing apart in actuality from what he seems. *His* character portrayal results from Fielding's modulation of materials, much as the dramatist conveys to the audience how we should observe a certain character seen differently by the other actors. The perspective is achieved through tone, gesture, verbal irony, movement, expression. Through such handling, Fielding achieves, in part, what was later to be called "aesthetic distance."

Irvin Ehrenpreis speaks of *Joseph Andrews* as progressing by shuttling. "For, instead of an organic or cumulative plot of suspense,

---

of literary criticism and general reflection which the narrator provides in the digressive passages of *Joseph Andrews*. By moving from the theater to the novel, Fielding was giving scope to a multiple viewpoint for which dramatic technique seems repressive." ("Fielding's Use of Fiction: The Autonomy of *Joseph Andrews*," in *Twelve Original Essays on Great English Novels*, ed. Charles Shapiro, p. 37) the structure of this story depends upon small oscillations of emotion which gather, as the large design, into massive waves of reversal." ("Fielding's Use of Fiction," p. 23) He later writes of "ironies, unmaskings, conflicts, and reversals" as standing behind "the full pattern of the book." (p. 25) And he speaks of the kind of interruption which informs the novel: "This is a story in which many people set out but few reach their destination, and those get the farthest who have nowhere to go."

Such a play upon coincidence, reversal of fortune, and fortuitous events is also crucial to *Tom Jones*. These elements inform every aspect of Fielding, for they are integral to his belief in providence, which is there at every turn even when chance seems to rule. Further, these reversals and happenstances, interwoven into providential action, reveal a deep-seated lack of identity in Fielding. While there appears to be a good deal of surface control and surety, nevertheless the tentativeness of most actions, the unmasking of virtually all behavior, the play upon turns of fortune, the inability of characters to get to their destinations, the turning back, the aimless roaming—all reveal uncertainty, groping, sliding away: a comic method which is seeking its own psychological reality.[22]

If we comprehend the tentativeness of Fielding's method, then we can better understand the prefaces to the individual books of *Tom Jones*. For these prefaces are valiant efforts at definition. Whereas, in the other parts of the novel, identity involved character and role, here identity involves the much broader issue of the form itself, the development of the novel genre, and the place that the novel will have among previous genres. Fielding's remarks are attempts to fix prose fiction within certain limitations of time and probability and to distinguish the novel from romance on the one hand, history on the other. In these remarks, Fielding must fit the new into the period's sense of the old, and he must justify experimentation in traditional ways.

Accordingly, he begins conventionally, with the idea of the novel

[22] Professor Ehrenpreis traces many of Fielding's uncertainties to his family background, which was full of contradictory elements, unclear lines of responsibility, and involved relationships. Ehrenpreis even sees some connection to Freud's conception of the "family romance," in which the child creates fantasy familial relationships and reorders his line of legitimacy. Thus, even the elements of incest Fielding used for comic suspense can be explained by his female-oriented childhood—"five sisters, three mothers, and only a fraction of a father," as Ehrenpreis puts it. ("Fielding's Use of Fiction," p. 33)

as a banquet. Bacon spoke of books to be chewed, swallowed, and digested; and Dante, in the *Convivio*, presented a feast to be devoured by the reader. The author Fielding is a good cook, a maker of sauces, a fine tailor, and what is consumed and/or dressed is human nature. The important element, however, is not the subject matter, but the author's skill in "dressing it up," the chef's and tailor's method of disguising poor materials. In this respect, Fielding would agree with James that "humanity is immense, and reality has a myriad forms" and the writer must be someone "upon whom nothing is lost."

Even though his prefaces to *Tom Jones* may superficially resemble James's introductions to his New York edition, Fielding had to be considerably more circumspect than James. The former wished to define the *novel*, while James wanted to define *his* novels. In this respect the preface to Book II is crucial. Although he is writing a history (*The History of Tom Jones: A Foundling*), Fielding must distinguish his kind of history from that which mimics journalism. That latter type of history—really pseudo-history—is severely limiting, for it assumes *all* time must be accounted for, while Fielding's "history" presupposes different time sequences: "but if whole years should pass without producing anything worthy his notice, we shall not be afraid of a chasm in our history . . ." Some chapters, he says, may contain the time of only a single day, others an entire year or more: "for as I am, in reality, the founder of a new province of writing, so I am at liberty to make what laws I please therein."

Not unusually, the first "law" Fielding sets down involves the use of time, for a time scheme—different from that in history and romance—is crucial to the developing novel. Time is not the restricted twenty-four hours of the classical unities, nor is it the chronological sequences of the historian. Fielding returns to time in Book III and, indirectly, again in Book V, where he attacks the "nice unity of time or place." Fielding saw that theories of time had to become part of theories of probability, which was essential for distinguishing prose fiction from dramatic poetry or from romance and epic. In Book IV, Fielding says that "truth distinguishes our writings from those idle romances, which are filled with monsters," and from "that kind of history which a celebrated poet [Pope, *Dunciad*] seems to think is no less calculated for the emolument of the brewer . . ." Fielding's kind of truth, evidently connected to a time scheme, prepares us for his introductory remarks to Book V, where he speaks of "prosai-comi-epic writing" and attacks the critics for insisting upon artificial distinctions between genres.

Books VIII, IX, X—the center of the novel—contain the major arguments. In Book VIII, in particular, Fielding defines the possibilities of the novel by cautioning every writer to remember "that what it is not possible for man to perform . . . is scarce possible for man to believe he did perform"—thus removing prose fiction from myth, epic, and romance. At the same time, he lays the groundwork for realism: if fiction feeds off probability, then a single improbable instance does not undermine truth. Fielding agreed with Pope's definition in his "Bathos," a travesty of Longinus's *On the Sublime*, that the "great art of all poetry is to mix truth with fiction, in order to join the credible with the surprising." Fielding writes:

> . . . the actions should be such as may not only be within the compass of human agency, and which human agents may probably be supposed to do; but they should be likely for the very actors and characters themselves to have performed; for what may be only wonderful and surprising in one man, may become improbable, or indeed impossible when related of another. [Book VIII]

Fielding's argument here is very closely reasoned, as it must be. He almost immediately sees that a stress upon probability can lead the author into mundane triviality. Thus, he insists that ". . . though every good author will confine himself within the bounds of probability, it is by no means necessary that his characters, or his incidents, should be trite, common, or vulgar . . . Nor must he be inhibited from showing many persons and things, which may possibly have never fallen within the knowledge of great part of his readers." (Book VIII) Clearly, he is working within the eighteenth-century conception of elevation, at the same time insisting on an involvement with human nature in human terms.

Book IX picks up the argument with a different stress. Here Fielding speaks of the author as a historian of feelings, as distinct from orthodox historians, who "draw their materials from records." His type of author must possess judgment, invention, learning, and an ear for dialogue. The last brings the writer to distinctions of class, manner, and sincerity, allowing for variety within sameness. If the reader notes here a countermovement or alternative to Augustan classicism, he is responding to Fielding correctly; for the matters under observation are feeling, plainness, and natural virtue, qualities usually associated with romanticism. In Book IX, Fielding has moved into areas he is not likely to embrace, even though his tentative reaching out has helped to suggest the new.

In Book X, Fielding takes up then-current issues: critics, ancients and moderns, and learning. "First, then, we warn thee not too hastily to condemn any of the incidents in this our history as impertinent and foreign to our main design, because thou dost not immediately conceive in what manner such incident may conduce to that design." This warning prepares the reader for critical attacks, from "a little reptile of a critic." Although Fielding was answering his numerous critics, who were indeed venomous, he was also, here and in Book XI, clearing the ground for the novel. He speaks of the writer, and reader, as capable of finding differences in sameness: ". . . to mark the nice distinction between two persons actuated by the same vice or folly . . ." These seemingly innocent remarks assume an empirical judgment of detail in keeping with the common-sense school of philosophy, leading away from traditional and conventional ways of seeing and placing. The comments are, once again, an example of Fielding's grappling with the new, even while grasping the old.

The preface to Book XI continues the attack on critics, but also embodies a new point, which indirectly distinguishes between novel and romance. Like Coleridge Fielding insisted that the whole is more significant than the parts. Coleridge defined poetry as creating "such delight from the *whole,* as is compatible with a distinct gratification from each component part"; while Fielding's point is that the author should not be condemned "because some particular chapter, or perhaps chapters, may be obnoxious to very just and sensible objections." The salient element is his insistence on the primacy of the art object, especially when it is a long work and cannot be evenly sustained at every moment. He is, at the same time, trying to upgrade literary criticism from its concern with trivialities and its trading upon personalities, although we may rightly question Fielding's motives for so doing.

All his remarks tend toward a new kind of realism in method and substance. Subsequent prefaces in *Tom Jones* deal with contemporary critical problems, especially those of the moderns and ancients, as well as the issue involving learning itself—whether useful, of what kind, its effects upon the imagination. Fielding argues that learning must be varied and must be relevant to all areas of knowledge, so that the writer's picture is after nature; imitation is not enough. Fielding tries to redefine realism when he argues that virtue is no sure way to happiness (a point with which Clarissa would have agreed), nor is vice to misery. Of course, even while saying this, Fielding means it very guardedly; virtue and vice are suitably rewarded, but with enough difference for Fielding to maintain his point.

The comments end with a sharp distinction between novel and epic, which Fielding does not himself honor. He asserts that the novelist may not extricate his hero by way of a deus ex machina, as could the ancients: "we will lend him [our hero] none of that supernatural assistance." The ancients had a great advantage, Fielding says, because their belief in mythology was firmer than any religious hold now upon the vulgar. The point is important: homogeneity of belief in one era called for a particular literary practice; with the heterogeneity of the present, the critic and reader must accept the new. This is, of course, a familiar argument for the avant-garde. In a sense like Wordsworth in his famous Preface, Fielding is preparing his audience as well as defining his own terms. "To natural means alone we are confined," he writes; and by "natural" he means within probability.

Further, he means to show us how to read him, not by the rules of the past, although they should be honored; not by the wisdom of the ancients, although it should be listened to; not by the practices of contemporary reptilian critics, although they must be paid homage; but by a reliance on human nature at its best and worst. Tom Jones is not a new savior; on the contrary, he demonstrates that in the novel there are no real saviors, only flawed individuals who trust to providence.

A Note on Amelia

Fielding's third and last novel, *Amelia*, has often been considered problematic. In *Fielding and the Nature of the Novel*, Alter calls his chapter on *Amelia* "Fielding's Problem Novel," although the chapter has the tone of someone who has solved the problem. The author sees Fielding as "moving toward a new kind of integration of narrative and thematic materials, a first anticipation of the masterful interlocking of separate lives through shared situations that gives *Middlemarch* such remarkable structural coherence." (p. 151) The import of this comment is that the novel, once it has removed itself from the expansiveness and breadth of the epic, moves back toward epic proportions in that "integration of narrative and thematic materials" with the lives of the characters.

While this may have been part of Fielding's sense of his material, such integration cannot be supported by a careful reading of the novel. Once the epic became novel, the reader's assumptions about character changed. In the epic, character could have para-realistic dimensions, symbolic or allegorical. Ultimately, character in the epic was being manipulated by the author for reasons that went well beyond the character's experiential role. When the epical dimension gave way to the more realistic mode of the novel, our expectations of character altered, as Fielding himself recognized in the prefaces to *Tom Jones.* And in the massive novel, in *Middlemarch* as in *Clarissa, Bleak House, War and Peace, Remembrance of Things Past, Ulysses*, the reality of the novel depends on the grounding of each character in human qualities, in will, choice, self-determination.

Fielding's Amelia fails as a character in all the ways that Eliot's Dorothea Brooke triumphs. Fielding's novel remains an unsolved problem precisely because he could *not* interlock "separate lives through shared situations." Such interlocking depends on quite a different view of women or men from Fielding's devotional attitude toward Amelia. Amelia tells us nothing we don't already know from the type. She shapes or reshapes no aspect of our experience; surrendering herself, she acquiesces to her husband with wifely devotion. She has obviously defined little for herself. In terms of dramatic action, her behavior is meaningless, for all decisions are made for her, not by her. The very point about Dorothea Brooke is her wrongheadedness, the irony Eliot can generate between our knowledge of the facts and Dorothea's reading of them. There is ironic distance between her and the reader, as well as between her and the other characters. Dorothea lives as a character *because* she so foolishly allies herself with Mr. Casaubon, not despite it.

Vanity Fair is another example, although somewhat diminished, of the massive novel in which individual lives become part of the social fabric. *Vanity Fair* is a particularly good example with which to juxtapose *Amelia*, in fact: the subject of both is "seeming," a vanity fair for one, a masquerade for the other; the thematic material is the world of appearance, snobbery, affectation; both are social novels of high and low, individuals unsettled or acting, out for money or position, or self-indulgent without regard for propriety. The emphases are, of course, different for each novel, but Fielding's Booth has something of the foppish George Osborne, Amelia is herself a slightly less pallid Amelia Sedley, Sergeant Atkinson is at times Dobbin, and Miss Matthews is an upstaged Becky Sharp.

Yet even as we note cross-references between the two works and observe Thackeray's indebtedness to the eighteenth-century conception of the novel, we can see that Thackeray succeeds precisely where Fielding failed. Even though both attempted to immortalize their wives (Thackeray's was now mad, Fielding's dead) in their respective Amelias, Thackeray saw clearly that distance and irony are necessary for fiction. Fielding's Amelia is Chaucer's Dame Custance ("The Man of Law's Tale") and as such is more suitable for parable, allegory, the fairy tale. Her goodness and constancy are beyond belief; her devotion shatters credibility. She is a throwback to medieval courtly-love heroines, unsuited to the realistic demands of the novel.

What makes Amelia incredible is her lack of sense of self. Near the end of the novel (Book XI, chapter V), Amelia makes one of her characteristic replies when Booth wishes to prosecute the maid Betty for a petty theft. Amelia defers to his excessively cruel argument by saying, " 'I shall always submit to your superior judgment, and I know you too well to think that you will ever do anything cruel.' " (Everyman edition, II, 248) Amelia submits when Booth deserves a severe rebuke. Several critics have called attention to Fielding's use of Vergil's Dido, in the *Aeneid*, as a model for Amelia, citing Fielding's own reference to the relationship, in the *Covent-Garden Journal* for January 28, 1752. If we accept the rather loose parallelism, then we can assume that Amelia, like Dido, should be viewed as a sacrifice; or, put another way, her role is secondary to that of the male, whose power, judgments, and will must remain supreme. This epic attitude—Aeneas must not dally too long with Dido, love is secondary to duty—dissipates in Amelia the very energies which she needs for identity and loses, as well, any real definition for the novel.[23]

[23] For a full discussion of parallels with the *Aeneid*, see the following: George Sherburn, "Fielding's *Amelia*: An Interpretation," *ELH*, III, 3–4; L. H. Powers, "The Influence of the *Aeneid* on Fielding's *Amelia*," *MLN*, 71 (1956), 330–6; Maurice Johnson, *Fielding's Art of Fiction* (1961), pp. 139–56; also Alter's chapter 5, "Fielding's Problem Novel," pp. 142–6.

Many critics have observed, but not stressed, that *Amelia* is caught between parable-allegory and the demands of the novel. Realism there is aplenty, from the gaming scenes in prison to the tawdry domestic vignettes of Colonel James and his wife, the kind of realistic presentation of domestic strife that looks ahead to Becky Sharp and Rawdon in *Vanity Fair.* The realism of scene, event, and even character, however, does not relieve the sense of fortune or the metadimensions of the fiction. The realism is of detail, but the overall plan is closer to *Pilgrim's Progress* and works of that quasi-utopian kind than to the development either of the novel or of Fielding's powers as a realist. While Thackeray was completely loyal to the demands of the novel—his use of a vanity fair is never maintained on a purely symbolic or allegorical plane—Fielding's "vanity fair" partakes of both the allegorical vanity fair of Ecclesiastes and the social affectation which was the butt of his comic prose epic.

Along the way, Fielding lost the dialectic of his most mature novel, *Tom Jones.* In *Amelia*, there is no sense of an attractive "other" or adversary; those opposed to Booth and Amelia lead grubby, seedy lives of desperate passions purchased with extravagant sums. In *Tom Jones*, Fielding could make the life of freedom, excess, passionate exuberance an attractive alternative to bourgeois comforts. Booth, on the other hand, sneaks around, is bought and sold, and has no center in the novel except in Amelia's heart. The thematic structure of *Amelia* is linear, singular, constricted; and these qualities added to the motif of the Christian gentleman and the Christian life flatten out the novel to a paradigm of how the good life is to be lived. *Amelia*, then, is neither "integrative" nor "anticipatory," but is better read as one of the numerous devotional tracts current in the eighteenth century or as a precursor of sentimental fiction than as a novel in Fielding's line of development.

5

Smollett's Humphry Clinker: *The Choleric Temper*

The years 1748–9 were extraordinary for the eighteenth-century novel, somewhat comparable to 1915–16 for the modern English novel. Those early years saw the meeting of three major careers, Richardson, with *Clarissa* (1746–8); Smollett, with *Roderick Random* (1748); and Fielding, with *Tom Jones* (1749); much as the later years saw an even more extraordinary junction of Joyce, with *A Portrait of the Artist as a Young Man*; Conrad, with *Victory*; Ford, with *The Good Soldier*; Lawrence, with *The Rainbow*; and Woolf, with *The Voyage Out.* For the reader seeking another *annus mirabilis* in fiction, one could cite, also, 1847–8, for the meeting of Dickens (*Dombey and Son*), Thackeray (*Vanity Fair*), Charlotte Brontë (*Jane Eyre*), Emily Brontë (*Wuthering Heights*), and lesser fiction by Disraeli, Mrs. Gaskell, John Henry Newman, and Trollope.

Analogies, however, end in confusion: each period is unique in its origins and development. Even as we cite the comparison, we note flaws in the grouping of Fielding, Richardson, and Smollett. While Richardson and Fielding had for years been seeking new forms in the genre, in the process learning from themselves and from each other, Smollett was an apprentice novelist after a checkered early career as a medical man and dramatist.[1] While Fielding's and

[1] Smollett's views of Richardson and Fielding were radically dissimilar. He evidently admired Richardson, although it is difficult to know if he felt privately what he expressed publicly. Writing to Richardson, on August 10, 1756, he showed concern that a reviewer in his *Critical Review* (April 1756, p. 261) had disparaged Richardson's

Richardson's novels in differing ways expand the form of the genre, Smollett's return to an earlier form that had already been drained, to the Spanish picaresque or rogue-hero type.

All three would agree, however, that the novel somehow had to integrate changing mores with the status quo, so that the latter, as

---

prolixity. Smollett assures Richardson that he was not responsible for the remarks, that, on the contrary,

> I never once mentioned Mr. Richardson's name with disrespect, nor ever reflected upon him or his writings by the most distant hint or allusion; and that it is impossible I should ever mention him either as a writer or a man without Expressions of admiration and applause. I am not much addicted to Compliment; but I think such an Acknowledgement is no more than a piece of Justice due to that amiable Benevolence, sublime morality and surprizing Intimacy with the human Heart, which must be the objects of Veneration among People of good Sense and Integrity. [*The Letters of Tobias Smollett*, ed. Lewis M. Knapp, p. 48]

In his *Continuation of the Complete History of England* (IV, 128), Smollett wrote:

> The laudable aim of enlisting the passions on the side of virtue, was successfully pursued by Richardson, in his Pamela, Clarissa, and Grandison; a species of writing equally new and extraordinary, where, mingled with much superfluity and impertinence [i.e., irrelevance] we find a sublime system of ethics, an amazing knowledge, and command of the human nature.

Toward Fielding (whom he read but never met) Smollett's antipathy was overwhelming and unrelenting, perhaps because he sensed in Fielding a literary rival. The two careers were sufficiently alike to cause friction—both were failed dramatists, both had professional backgrounds and a fund of classical knowledge, both attempted to capitalize on the new literary styles. In these areas, Richardson was no rival; what he could do, Smollett could not do, or wish to do. Fielding, however, fell across Smollett's path.

The antipathy is apparent from remarks left by Smollett. In a letter to Alexander Carlyle, a friend who apparently had criticized *Tom Jones*, Smollett responded that he had to agree; that "the same observations occurred to me which you have communicated, and are indeed obvious to every reader of discernment, even the Author's most sanguine Adherents confess that there is an Evident Difference between that part of his Book which he wrote for the Town, and that which was composed for the Benefit of his Bookseller." (*Letters*, ed. Knapp, p. 11)

Smollett made his dislike public in *Peregrine Pickle*, in the fourth volume, where Fielding is ridiculed as Mr. Spondy. More telling is the controversy over *Habbakkuk Hilding*, which Smollett may have written, although its authorship is still uncertain. It violently accuses Fielding of having plagiarized the idea of Partridge (in *Tom Jones*) and Miss Mathews (in *Amelia*) from Smollett's Strap and Miss Williams (both in *Roderick Random*). Knapp argues that Smollett may have been reacting to Fielding's own ridicule of him, in *Amelia* and in his *Covent-Garden Journal* (for January 7, 1752). *Habbakkuk Hilding* appeared a week later.

Subsequently, Smollett relented sufficiently to write that Fielding was a faithful follower of Cervantes, whose novels "painted the characters, and ridiculed the follies of life with equal strength, humour and propriety." (*Continuation of the Complete History of England*, Volume IV, p. 127; in Knapp, *Tobias Smollett*, p. 133) He wrote these remarks six years after Fielding's death. With Fielding and Richardson dead by 1761, Smollett may have felt the field was now left to him; even if Sterne's popularity threatened, Smollett's own area of work was free of rivals. He could afford to be generous.

reflected in fiction, would not be appreciably disturbed. All three were on the surface intensely bourgeois, but with the ability to recognize the rifts in family and political life and the desire to make such rifts part of the literary experience. Consequently, their convergence is a curious one involving two focal points: alternate, subversive movements that suggest the real social and economic changes in England intermixed with traditional values that embody order and decency.

For Fielding and Smollett, such ideas were basic to the picaresque novel; and all three novelists set the mixture of tradition and dissent in the changing family scene. In the latter situation, the family, the nuclear unit of order and sanity, had to be held together—by mutual consent, not by tyrannical measures. Ronald Paulson, in his essay on "The Pilgrimage and the Family: Structures in the Novels of Fielding and Smollett" (in *Tobias Smollett: Bicentennial Essays Presented to Lewis M. Knapp*, ed. Rousseau & Boucé), has detected the broken family relationships in the novels of Smollett, Fielding, and Richardson, seeing their culmination in *Tristram Shandy.* The point we should stress, however, is that such broken relationships are always hidden within a supposedly functioning family. As Paulson says, our three novelists are unable to admit that the family structure is intrinsically weak when individual independence is at stake. They demonstrate the weakness, but then retreat and shore up the walls.

In *Humphry Clinker*, we can see how Smollett played this game of incipient revolt and traditional consolidation. For most of the novel, after Humphry appears, he seems socially to be an alternative to Bramble, who represents traditional values, the "golden past," such as Dickens later incorporated in his Pickwickians. Humphry represents the new spirit of the age, the youthful element moving outside the traditional family structure, coming, literally, naked into the world. An itinerant Methodist preacher, standing apart from the nuclear family represented by the Bramble party of brother-sister, nephew-niece, and various maids and retainers, Humphry pursues his own values. There is a real dichotomy here, although a gentle one. Smollett, however, like Fielding and Richardson, could not let Humphry float free of the family, for whatever purpose, and, thus, we have the familiar eighteenth-century device of the undiscovered son returning to the fold. The diffident, corrosive Bramble, it turns out, has sowed some wild oats as a youth, just as has the tepid Bridget Allworthy, and all divisions are resolved.

When we go from Fielding and Richardson to Smollett, we feel a reduction or decline. The reason is, I think, easy to pinpoint. In both of the earlier novelists, we found controlling ideas, a conceptualization of their material, so that matter and manner informed each other at most turns. Different elements fed into each other, creating paradox and irony and a sense of contraries interacting. The result was texture, perhaps more in Richardson than in Fielding, but in both, a play or dialectic between individual and social forms, between conflicting elements in the character himself, between the character's individualizing will and the author's traditional need.

In Smollett, that conceptualization is missing. In his preface to his first novel, Smollett says he has modeled *Roderick Random* on the plan of *Gil Blas*, although he has changed some of the latter's extravagant situations to the more compassionate and probable ones of his own hero. The plan, nevertheless, is for a loose narrative device of strung-out episodes, which precludes a sustained conception. What is observed by the author and by his characters is what any reasonably alert person would observe. Particulars remain particulars, not part of an author's way of seeing or arranging. What Smollett lacks is a "philosophy" of people, things, and life that is more than the sum of realistic detail.

By "philosophy" we do not mean any consistent idealization of matter, or a metaphysical process that attempts to probe the very roots of existence. Philosophy in a novelist is a tentative notion, meaning not consistency or comprehensiveness—what we mean in a professional or technical philosopher—but a tendency to lead the reader into a vision; really a way of expanding or intensifying both the seer and the seen. Even Defoe transcended his intense sense of detail and imposed a kind of coherence upon his material; by so doing he infused particulars with the sense of general things. Thus, fictional philosophy, as such, is the imposition of a view, and the writer may work as much as he wishes with particulars and singularities as long as he can make these cohere into a vision.

It is precisely here that Smollett fails us. More realistic than any previous English novelist, Smollett leaves us with the sense of scenes observed, not conceived. In fact, to find an equal for his realism, we must return to Defoe's *Journal of the Plague Year*. The march of disease and dance of death of Bramble's friends in *Humphry Clinker* recalls the afflicted and diseased during the height of the plague. In his novels, however, Defoe neglected this type of realism, tempering it, even in Newgate, where the horrors were far in excess of what he describes. Smollett does not spare the reader. One has the impression that, like de Sade, he rather revels in exploiting human misery or, perhaps, finds the equivalent of his own aggression and rage in the meaningless suffering of his characters. Whatever the reasons, psychological or otherwise, Smollett stresses disease, incapacity, sadistic tortures, painful moments (and lives), acts of gratuitous brutality. His type of realism approaches a much later kind, developed in France by Maupassant and Zola.

Yet, despite his intense observation of visual objects, Smollett lacks the view of them that would turn them from detail to meaning. Zola's scenes of brutality and cruelty cohere, finally, in his sense of a doom-filled universe in which decay and dissolution await all who step falsely. Accidents destroy; chance leads to disintegration. None of this informs Smollett, and perhaps we cannot expect it, for Zola's naturalism was a development co-existent with man's new ways of seeing himself.

We can, however, fault Smollett for failing to make something of what he observes. For example, in *Humphry Clinker*, the party has arrived at Bath (April 28 entry), where Bramble takes the waters. After an examination of the pump and the cistern, he concludes that drinkers are quaffing not fresh but bath water, that rotting, diseased bodies are being steeped in water that passes on to those who drink it for its curative powers. At another spring, Bramble discovers that the water passes amid the decaying bodies in a burial ground. Smollett presents the images of decay vividly, but then shunts the reader to a young letter writer, Jery Melford, whose view of Bath is one of wonderment at its variety and entertainments. He even sees the mingling of classes as a blessing, since the lower classes will in time polish their manners by aping their betters; while Bramble sees in the free mixing of classes a breakdown of all order, noting that such a breakdown will lead to arrogance on the part of the lower classes and to vulgarization of the upper.

Yet once Smollett has established, here and elsewhere, the fact that Bramble's generation observes one way and Jery's another, he does nothing to make what is observed cohere in a general way. No causative factors interfere with fact or detail. The omniscient observer does not himself, through suggestion, irony, or paradox, add to what is observed. He merely records what he sees. He is not an artist whose lies and distortions lead to greater truth and clarity; the truth is the fact itself.

All this is another way of saying Smollett's characters lack psychological depth. We could argue that since Smollett retained the features of the episodic narrative—perhaps more than any other English novelist of stature—we should not expect the kind of depth, psychological or otherwise, so alien to the picaresque mode. Yet, in *Humphry Clinker*, his final novel, Smollett by the use of multiple narrators was evidently trying to move beyond picaresque surfaces. This technique is an excellent way to create psychological depth through comparison and contrast of various points of view; that is, the novelist can suggest depth by means of an external device, an especially important development in Smollett since his previous methods precluded probing. We can infer that Smollett himself recognized the limitations of picaresque in *Roderick Random* and *Peregrine Pickle*, and attempted to compensate technically for surface thinness.

A device such as multiple narration works, however, only if it creates tensions that would be missing with a more conventional narrative. If multiplicity leads only to repetition, it is simply the picaresque method thinly disguised. If the latter, it causes not tension but a proliferation of episodes with slight variations, and it encompasses the same strung-out quality of most picaresque. It has ingenuity, not depth.

Unfortunately, Smollett's attempt to gain the kind of texture denied to the episodic narrative is not fully successful in *Humphry Clinker.* Despite a firmness of prose and manner indicating literary maturity, he could not use the new methodology to do something he was apparently incapable of doing: that is, to achieve a true novelistic sense of movement and countermovement, what his two rivals accomplished through plot. Although we may applaud Smollett's technical development, we should add that he was, nevertheless, a novelist in the mode of *Gil Blas*. While we may argue that multiple points of view enabled Smollett to achieve economy, we must always ask whether economy is necessarily a strengthening force.[2] In the eighteenth century, greatness in fiction was achieved,

[2] Byron Gassman, in "The Economy of *Humphry Clinker*" (*Bicentennial Essays*, pp. 155–68), argues that the multiplicity of point of view gave Smollett a tool for economy. He sees Jery's objective commentary as allowing for narrative efficiency, as against the

more frequently than not, by messy writers, overwriters, who were extravagant in their use of words and methods: Fielding, Sterne, Richardson.

One could, in fact, cite in Smollett instances of messiness that are his best work. Such subjectivity occurs most often in his characterizations, based as they are on humors or traits: Hawser Trunnion, Hatchway, and Pipes (in *Peregrine Pickle*), who inspired, in turn, Sterne's Uncle Toby and Corporal Trim; Bramble and Lismahago (in *Humphry Clinker*); to some extent Strap (in *Roderick Random*), who, with Random, becomes another ancestor of the Toby-Trim axis. Citing these second-rank characters as examples of Smollett's talent at its most effective, however, only points up his failings. For his major or titular characters—Random, Pickle, Fathom, Greaves, Clinker—fail to achieve the notoriety sufficient to carry their respective novels. Their lives and attendant narratives carry the didactic function of their novels; but the real life of the book appears elsewhere, in secondary characters and subsidiary plots.

Thus, we have to argue that Smollett's best is messiness; his least effective, attempts at objectivity. In effect, he remained a picaresque novelist *even* when he tried a cohesive narrative. Dickens, whose indebtedness to Smollett is well documented, could work in a somewhat similar manner—major characters carrying the didactic element, minor characters reflecting the multiplicity and messiness of life—with far greater success because of the socio-political underpinning of his long novels. Like Smollett, Dickens worked the picaresque vein, but by diversifying his efforts, he anchored himself firmly to elements that went beyond his characters.

Smollett conceived of the novel differently, and unfortunately his conception could not balance out his weaknesses. In his dedication to *Ferdinand Count Fathom* (1753), he stressed character, not event:

A Novel is a large diffused picture, comprehending the characters of life, disposed in different groupes, and exhibited in various attitudes, for the purpose of a uniform plan, and general occurrence, to which every individual figure is subservient. But this plan cannot be executed with propriety, probability or success, without a principal personage to attract the

more subjective and didactic reactions of the other characters. Gassman fails to ask whether or not such economy is necessarily an asset. Employing a similar argument, one could say *Clarissa* would have benefited from severe cutting, so that the narrative took on greater objectivity. The point of that novel, however, is not economy but the nature of the thing achieved, and that quality is gained through overlapping, messiness, duplication, thoroughgoing subjectivity.

attention, unite the incidents, unwind the clue of the labyrinth, and at last close the scene by virtue of his own importance. [Oxford edition, pp. 2–3]

For coherence, Smollett clearly relied on a principal character—his objective point of departure. As he further defined his intentions in the *Fathom* dedication, Smollett saw this central character as embodying the didactic function of the novel. "I declare my purpose is to set him up as a beacon for the benefit of the unexperienced and unwary, who from the perusal of these memoirs, may learn to avoid the manifold snares with which they are continually surrounded in the paths of life . . ." (p. 3)

What this suggests is that the moral intention of the novel serves as a point of coherence amid narrative formlessness and digressions. We are here on the margins of Fielding, whereby an ultimate didactic function, a fervent belief in "innate goodness," can inform the narrative even when it seemingly strays into byways. But Fielding, unlike Smollett, did not rely solely on a didactic mission. Fielding moved on several fronts: using ancient examples for modern points, contrasting past and present, employing a wide range of comic devices, varying his sequences, playing off scenes against each other. Amid didacticism, Fielding provided variety and abundance. Smollett tends to present a homogeneous kind of episode, generally based on the strong moving against the weak, the working out of considerable sadism and cruelty, a gradual withdrawal, and then a replay of the same episode renamed.

We note, consequently, that Smollett's conception of the novel is threefold:[3]

1. A loose, flexible narrative structure
2. A central or principal character who remains the focal point of the episodes; to whom all other characters are subsidiary
3. A persistent didactic theme, as embodied in the principal character

Only in *Humphry Clinker* (1771) did Smollett try to follow his three-part formula, and there is some reason to believe that had he not died at fifty, he might have taken the novel along a somewhat different road from that of his predecessors. Unfortunately, the body

[3] Smollett spoke of the novel as a form or genre in only three places: in the dedication to *Fathom* and in the preface to *Roderick Random*, both of which have been cited; and in incidental remarks in the *Critical Review* (January 1763) during a review of *Peregrination of Jeremiah Grant Esquire, The West Indian.*

of his major work in fiction, with the exception of *Clinker*, came when he was in his twenties and early thirties. Only *The Adventures of Sir Launcelot Greaves* (1760–2) appeared in his later career, and that novel surely cannot be numbered among his serious works. Based unimaginatively on *Don Quixote*, it is flat, without sufficient ideas to carry its length, and with an array of tedious characters. Thus, when we speak of Smollett's work in the novel, we are really discussing the three early novels (*Random, Pickle, Fathom*), all of which fell between 1748 and 1753, and *Clinker*, which was published three months before his death.

Once we have recognized that Smollett was not a novelist in the way we call Fielding or Richardson novelists, we can see *Clinker* as something of a departure; or, at least, as an attempt on the author's part to impress himself on the novel. Unfortunately, we lack any reference in Smollett's letters to the place or date of the writing of *The Expedition of Humphry Clinker*. According to George C. Kahrl, Smollett began the work in the winter of 1765–6, while in Bath or London. Knapp accepts that possibly the first two volumes, including perhaps part of Volume III, were written at London and Bath from 1765 to 1768. He concludes that the final form of the novel, with the rest of Volume III, probably took shape in Italy in 1770.[4] None of this is too important except to demonstrate that Smollett spread out the writing of the book and took more than usual care in his prose.

The immediate sources of the novel are several. Richardson's epistolary works are clearly in the background. In the foreground, Martz, Kahrl, and Knapp agree, was Christopher Anstey's *New Bath Guide*, a series of poetical epistles by a family, written from Bath. Published in 1766, with a fifth edition by the next year, Anstey's *Guide* gave Smollett the idea for a variety of viewpoints and also suggested certain scenes and characters, including Lydia and Tabitha. Anstey's *Guide*, however, had still another function, serving as a burlesque of neoclassical poetry, whereas Smollett eschewed such literary side effects in order to give a detailed, realistic presentation of life on the road. In the foreground of sources is

[4] See George C. Kahrl, *Tobias Smollett: Traveler–Novelist*, p. 121; Lewis Mansfield Knapp, *Tobias Smollett: Doctor of Men and Manners*, p. 289. Louis L. Martz, in *The Later Career of Tobias Smollett*, pp. 124–35, discusses the genesis of *Humphry Clinker* without altering any of the above basic facts.

Smollett's own very successful book *Travels Through France and Italy* (published May 1766). This book, in fact, was itself part of the upsurge of public interest in travel and in distant places. As Martz writes:

> Supporting this particular motivation [Smollett's use of travel letters] lay the contemporary demand for travels of all kinds, and the vogue for relating these travels in the epistolary form already familiar to Smollett from his work upon his own and Drummond's *Travels*. [p. 132]

Ever-present and integrated with Smollett's thought is *Don Quixote*, even in *Clinker*, which attempts to break with picaresque, romance, and anti-romance. Lismahago has the general build of the Don, while Humphry himself moves in and out of Sancho's image. Smollett's attitude toward Methodism has in it some of Cervantes's ambivalence toward the romances he was attacking; and the travel format is close to episodic narrative. Bramble also moves in and out of the Don's image, without the latter's ideals but with his desire to preserve the best of the old world. Bramble's attacks on the modern and new can be related, although not firmly, to the Don's desire for a static golden age. Even the perceptible mellowing that occurs in Smollett in the later part of this novel finds its analogy in the mellowing of Cervantes's attitude toward the Don in the second part of his book.

The chief influence of *Don Quixote*, however, is reflected in Smollett's way of creating a dialectic. While Smollett could not hope to achieve the Spanish writer's texture, his conception is immersed in the "Don" idea. That is, he uses Bramble—who reflects many, if not most, of his own attitudes—as a way of moderating a series of socially threatening plot developments. If we range through Smollett's way of thinking, we note two forces side by side: first, a recognition that man is capable of the worst, that there is an innate desire to destroy as well as preserve, that violence is never far below the surface of behavior; and, second, a realization that societal moderation must ever be ready to balance out anarchy. Smollett, in the destructive violence of his characters, in the obvious relish with which he describes acts of vengeance, in his savage attacks upon other authors, surely recognized this aspect of himself.

Although by the time of *Clinker* much of the violence and cruelty has been muted, it does turn up in Lismahago's gruesome adventures among the American Indians, on which Smollett lavishes an extraordinary amount of detail for a novel whose center is elsewhere. But this aggressive desire to destroy, to turn everything into chaotic violence, is always part of the Smollett dialectic and set against the opposing forces of moderation, status quo, even reaction. Knapp points out Smollett's almost compulsive need for order: "Like Dr. Johnson, Smollett was a firm believer in decorum, social order, and subordination. Following the aristocratic code he was scrupulously polite to his social equals or superiors, but disliked the rabble and was perhaps sarcastic and dictatorial at times toward his assistant literary hacks." (p. 305) His discipline *was* monumental, as attested to by his dogged work on projects such as the seven-volume *A Compendium of Authentic and Entertaining Voyages* (1756) and the five-volume *Continuation of the Complete History of England* (1760–5). Portraits show him scrupulously neat, in control, genteel.

Beneath this discipline and control, there were, as Knapp writes, "violent emotional tensions impossible wholly to account for or to analyze." (p. 305) Smollett noted these qualities in his letters: feelings of anger, vengefulness, sarcasm, even violence. These qualities surface in the vengeance of Fathom, the cruel practical jokes of Pickle, the scenes of cruelty in *Random*, Lismahago's Indian tales, in the excitement with which Smollett analyzes odd appearances, decrepitude, illness, invalidism, anything bizarre or different.

Clinker is not excessive in its violence or obsession with human misery–Smollett had mellowed–but this "other" aspect still does inform, though it is disguised. If Bramble is the controlling force, the element of noblesse oblige and societal moderation, symbolic of the status quo, then the other part of the dialectic is represented by Clinker, by Methodism, by the new democracy, by the ever-growing crowds at the watering spas, by the changes in taste, by the emerging "masses." While Bramble, and Smollett, reviled these changes–an outgrowth of shifting social values because of the industrialization and commercialization of England's middle class–the author Smollett recognized their presence and attempted to control them through his chief character. Such a resolution of the irresolvable is unsuccessful, however, as Smollett must have realized when he turned the group toward their travels in Scotland and revealed conciliatorily that Humphry was Bramble's bastard son.

That use of the father-son reconciliation is a curious device in Smollett's hands. Evidently, for lack of any adequate way of resolving the divergence of views between Bramble and Humphry, he created the blood tie. By so doing, he could glide over their differences and, apparently through a family alliance, reconcile a social rift. It is a devious device, of course, since what Humphry represents remains to be resolved with what Bramble represents, regardless of the disposition of the principals. Strikingly, Fielding, starting with quite different assumptions about man and society, concluded also that Tom could be brought into line only by revealing his well-born background. Apparently, the social consequences of accepting bastardy were too far-reaching for either Fielding or Smollett.

We are left, then, with Smollett's entrance into a muddy area which involved recognition of countermovements and counter-ideas, even if he deserted the area with an uneasy last-minute truce. Even the truce or reconciliation, however, cannot blind us to Smollett's awareness of opposites, within and without; and in this respect he shows his descent from Richardson, from the latter's use of Lovelace in the first edition as an attractive, disruptive force who must eventually be negated. If we ignore Smollett's uneasy resolutions, we read him, at his best, as a dialectician trying to strike a balance between the old and the new, the status quo and the budding forces of change. At stake are vast socio-economic and philosophical issues which bleed over from the literary matter, and it is to Smollett's credit that he saw such issues clearly in the 1760's, when the novel takes place.

"The pills are good for nothing," says Bramble at the beginning of the novel. Pills are a leitmotif in the novel. A pill is only a temporary restorative, if that, and it indicates that Bramble's hopes to hold back change will endure as long as the effectiveness of a pill. Withal, even pills fail to work; what ails him goes beyond a restorative prescribed by a sincere but speculative doctor. Since in the dedication of the novel to Henry Davis, Smollett indicates that the correspondence Davis prints is real documents, we can say that Bramble's letters indicating dyspepsia and constipation are historical facts–he is, indeed, hard to move. Medical information, history, and personal disposition come together, and Smollett has fused elements that in his previous work remained disparate.

A significant unifying device in *Humphry Clinker* is the presence of a family unit on the road. Individual picaresque has (shades of Thornton Wilder's *The Skin of Our Teeth*) given way to the journey of a family. Smollett stresses not its cohesiveness, however, but its broken elements—the bastard Humphry, the youthful libertinism of Bramble coming home to roost; the need for singles (Tabitha, Lismahago) to re-form into couples; the ballet between Lydia and "Wilson, the player"; the desire of Jery to maintain mastery in his own family unit; finally, the rounding out of Humphry's newly discovered upper-middle-class fortunes with marriage to the servant Winifred. It is indeed a curious family. While not in the state of disintegration of, say, the Karamazov clan, the Brambles and their circle are not at all a conventional family group.[5]

Initially, the family arrangement, before Humphry arrives on the scene, recalls *Clarissa*, and the part it recalls is precisely the family relationship that makes it impossible for Clarissa to remain with the Harlowes. Jery is, like James Harlowe, a brother who considers himself the defender of his sister's virtue, the director of female fortunes, and he has usurped the father's role. Also implicit is that the brother, the male, will direct the family's future by "choosing" his brother-in-law, ostensibly selecting someone who will not be a threat to his dominance. Jery is obviously less cruel and sadistic than James, but his intent is plain: to remain the dominant male in his sister Lydia's life, both in her own consciousness and in the consciousness of any man he permits her to marry. The carryover from *Clarissa* is pervasive, running as a variation through the novel until the so-called Wilson turns out to be the highly acceptable young George Dennison. By then, Jery has established his supremacy.

Even more apparent is the lack of parental guidance and of familial affection; no one really has interest in any one else. Bramble concentrates on his ills, although he means well by his niece and nephew; Tabitha is preoccupied with her problem of finding, enticing, and holding on to a mate; Jery is less interested in Lydia's happiness than in the family's fortunes, although he is neither cruel nor implacable; Lydia is busy with her own emotions; Clinker appears as a rank outsider who must constantly prove himself to gain an inside position, a foreigner in xenophobic territory, literally

[5] Ronald Paulson's "The Pilgrimage and the Family: Structures in the Novels of Fielding and Smollett," cited earlier, detects broken family relationships in Fielding, Richardson, Sterne, and Smollett, but does not stress *Clinker* in particular. It is, for what it does, an extremely valuable assessment of an aspect of Smollett that has been largely ignored.

naked in the family's eyes; Lismahago is also an outsider, even ranker than Humphry, a man whose sole attraction for the Brambles is the fact that he is an eligible male. Each character moves on his own file, parallel to the others in some places, but rarely crossing over or understanding others.

It is a curious pattern, doubly so because it appears a by-product of Smollett's other concerns, not central as in *Tristram Shandy* or *Tom Jones.* The central consideration, after all, is to bring a multiplicity of views upon a variety of scenes, so that we have the literary equivalent of a kaleidoscope. The most notable example of this effect comes in Volume I, when the expedition visits Bath. In Bramble's eyes, as we have noted, in the April 28 entry, Bath has deteriorated into a stinking sewer, a place not of purification but of plague, symbol of a dying England. From the young people's point of view, however, Bath is a place of variety and entertainment. Its diversity is a sign of health. We have already observed that Jery feels plebians will raise themselves by imitating their betters, while Bramble fears their presence will vulgarize all spheres of life. Both views apparently assume a certain unchangeable social order, but Jery's at least allows for some democracy and sharing.

In these diverging views, intense here, less intense elsewhere, we have only the lighter part of Smollett's dialectic. We should not, however, stop at this with Bramble; his preoccupations extend further and go deeper. Usually, we see him as a crusty, ill, aging man whose tendencies are decent and well meaning, even generous. But we should, I think, stress his obsession with degeneration, not only in the social sphere but in the physical. He dotes on decay. In the May 5 entry to Dr. Lewis, he re-creates for the good doctor a veritable "dance of death," skeletal figures celebrating the inevitable. Bramble's old chums, the colonel, the rear admiral, the baronet–what are they but nature's wrecks, and a hidden source of Bramble's joy? Bramble's interest in decay is, as we shall see, integral; it creates another dimension to the narrative; and it is, unfortunately, insufficiently accounted for by Smollett once the novel moves on to its travelogue sections.

The introduction of Humphry into the narrative in the May 24 entry created still another dimension and temporarily sidetracked Smollett from pursuing Bramble's dyspeptic view of mankind. Certainly, the emphasis shifts; for Humphry, from his entrance, is a source of life, a constant adversary to his benefactor and father, who sees death at the end of every passageway. Humphry's entrance is not unlike Tom Jones's—unclothed, of unknown origin, lacking friends or connections, isolated from all apparent aid, down on his luck or without any foreseeable chances. Such a character, whether mocked or presented seriously, is a bourgeois version of the mythical or ritualistic hero. If we examine the twenty-two qualities of such a hero as laid out by Lord Raglan,[6] we see that Humphry fits generally into the pattern, although as a bourgeois hero he will, of course, never attain his future kingdom or have to face a mysterious death. Nevertheless, his background and meeting with his father are strangely Oedipal, even though, to his credit, in the water episode Humphry saves his would-be father instead of dispatching him. They will never meet at a crossroads, but there are crossroad situations or longueurs.

Since Humphry is a bourgeois "hero," indeed almost a mock hero, he saves his father from death, all the while offering an alternative to him. We note an important movement here, not at all in a single direction. Humphry clearly wants to save what his father stands for, or at least the embodiment of him in the flesh, but at the same time he himself represents nearly everything Bramble has come to fear. Humphry preaches a strange religion, which is anti-establishment, subversive; he places his worth on inward serenity, not on outward trappings; he is without tradition, family, or fortune; he marries a servant from the Bramble household. Humphry is a Jacobin, not in his protestations of loyalty, it is true, but in his beliefs and actions. Yet, despite his opposition to Bramble's world, he wants to save the older man, preserve what is valuable in tradition.

In this play of near opposites, perhaps we have Smollett's own valiant attempts to understand what was occurring in the later eighteenth century. Forces were pulling the era apart. Reason was under attack from sentiment. Tradition was becoming less viable in the eyes of the commercial classes. Aristocracy was giving ground to money and ambition. Places of refuge like Bath were filling up with a new breed, and centers of entertainment were coming to reflect the new world. Unlikely as it may seem, Humphry and Bramble may represent the extremes of this world: a naked Methodist preacher and a crusty, physically depleted man of the world playing out large social and political movements.

[6] *The Hero: A Study in Tradition, Myth, and Drama*, pp. 174–5.

The arrival of Humphry, however, should not sidetrack us from our previous route: pursuing Smollett's preoccupation with the degenerative. Jery's description of Tabitha, in the May 6 entry, for example, is far in excess of what her kind calls for. She could be a Tabitha-type without Smollett's having elicited the particular kind of disgust he does. We recall he says:

> . . . she is tall, raw-boned, aukward, flat-chested, and stooping; complexion is sallow and freckled; her eyes are not grey, but greenish, like those of a cat, and generally inflamed, her hair is of a sandy, or rather dusty hue; her forehead low; her nose long, sharp, and towards the extremity, always red in cool weather; her lips skinny, her mouth extensive, her teeth straggling and loose, of various colours and conformation; and her long neck shrivelled into a thousand wrinkles . . . [Riverside edition, p. 56] [7]

When we add this description to that of Lismahago in the July 10 letter of Jery, we have possibly entered a new dimension. Lismahago's physical being is described as follows, this from a most sober observer:

> He would have measured above six feet in height, had he stood up right; but he stooped very much; was very narrow in the shoulders, and very thick in the calves of his legs, which were cased in black spatterdashes— As for his thighs, they were long and slender, like those of a grasshopper; his face was, at least, half a yard in length, brown and shrivelled, with projecting cheek-bones, little grey eyes on the greenish hue, a large hook-nose, a pointed chin, a mouth from ear to ear, very ill furnished with teeth, and a high, narrow fore-head, well furrowed with wrinkles. [pp. 170–1]

These two descriptions indicate more than an attempt to create originals. They indicate, on the contrary, a physical disgust that extends deeply into sexual matters. The bedding down of two such creatures leads not to laughter but to revulsion. Such descriptions, coming from the optimistic Jery and not the dyspeptic Bramble, signal an attitude on the part of the author that he could not suppress. The material must have represented an important aspect of Smollett's dialectic. In such terms, we can see how he has ideologically rejected Fielding's Shaftesburyism. For Fielding in his description of Blifil (in *Tom Jones*) makes it clear that physical abnormality makes marriage impossible. Smollett, on the other hand, suggests that the physical disgust embodied in the descriptions is no

[7] The standard text is that of the Oxford English Novels edition, but in matters of quotation, editions such as the Riverside are adequate and more accessible.

impediment to union, but indeed makes it plausible among one's fellows. Social humor here becomes overridden by certain vague excesses of Smollett's own temperament, his rejection of the physical appetite on such a huge scale that we must note Bramble's animadversions as not incidental but central to the overall disgust generated by the novel.

Part of this attitude toward physique, sex, union we may attribute to Smollett's ambivalence toward his female characters. Tabitha is a shrew and must be tamed; Lydia is emotionally unstable and must be held in check; Winifred, of the swivel-like head, has almost unbridled sexual appetites. Women are always spiders preparing their webs in order to ensnare a man. Women, writes Lydia to Miss Willis, "employ arts which are by no means to be justified . . ." (p. 236) Smollett's females, here and elsewhere, are almost always sources of man's decline and fall—well beyond what the century's literary conventions called for.

Late in the novel, in the tale of Baynard, a woman's frivolity and extravagance bring down the male, not the male's own character, which harbors the same weaknesses. The theme in this tale and elsewhere is that the male would choose to live differently if not for the female's insistence on ostentation. Woman snares man, is the incarnation of Eve. In still another entry, that for October 11, also from Bramble, Dennison's "country tale" tells of his attempts to live by country rules. He comments that "many others would have acceded to our society had they not been prevented by the pride, envy, and ambition of their wives and daughters." No wonder the young Dickens, in *Pickwick*, found Smollett so congenial, for the Pickwickians, if nothing else, are embodiments of male types found in the earlier writer.

These comments from *Humphry Clinker* conceal considerable resentments against women that are bound to have literary repercussions. Since Smollett's own marriage does not appear to offer any clues to particular anger, we can only conclude that in some area of his emotional life there was such resentment that it boiled over into nearly every reference to women. Unlike Defoe, Fielding, Richardson, and Sterne in this respect, he followed a line of reasoning which precluded any substantive feminine point of view. As a consequence, Smollett represents, for good or for ill, the most "masculine" traditions of the eighteenth-century novel.

When we return to technical matters, we can see that his use of multiple viewpoints, in which female characters are among the principal correspondents, serves little purpose in delineating his characters. Lydia and Winifred are, by their natures, caught up by trivial considerations; they can never hope to move in the world of doers and thinkers. They must be fairly passive, receptive to what others are doing for and around them. Lydia may try to reach out to Wilson, but Jery controls final things. Winifred may flirt outrageously, but her misspellings and solecisms—as later her social airs—place her in the world of underlings. In this sense, she is a foolish object. Consequently, the multiplicity of feminine views does not open up character or provide materials the reader may have himself missed. Smollett's limitations in regard to his female characters restrict his male figures as well. While they are often sharply and accurately observed, they do not by their ideas or actions move beyond what Smollett has established they are from the first. They do not grow.

Smollett's usage is almost diametrically opposite to Richardson's in his first edition of *Clarissa.* In the latter, the several correspondents create considerable ambiguity between what they profess and what they really think, and the multiple viewpoints help suggest dimensions. Clarissa is not yet sublime; Lovelace is not completely demonic; Miss Howe does not have perfect clairvoyance. Each character is caught, not only in circumstances, but in the web of his own assumptions and needs. In Smollett, the multiplicity of viewpoints, which should be a dynamic technique, serves mainly a static view of character and scene. As we suggested above, the narrators do not themselves demonstrate anything in their observations toward various phenomena the layman could not share. Smollett does not reveal depths in their perceptions or shrewd comments that the ordinary reader cannot also perceive. Lacking dimension, these are simply divergent viewpoints.

Even as Smollett attempted to move beyond his own practice of picaresque to something more "novelistic," he was snared by his own assumptions, or possibly by an inner rage he could not fictionally control. The point warrants pursuit. If we examine the experiential quality of the novel, we can see how Smollett's assumptions hobbled him. Nearly everything in the book before the long Scottish travelogue involves a society that is changing rapidly. We charted some of those variations above. Yet faced by this experiential variety, Smollett's characters, with the intermittent intrusion of the young people who see the entertainment value of Bath and London (cf. the May 29 and May 31 entries), refuse to react. Perhaps this is a sign of how change will become acceptable—through its ability to entertain. Such a point is trivial. The novel insists on the status quo. Even when the younger people "experience" new attitudes, their assumptions remain fairly constant, and their resolutions later are all acceptable within a traditional society.

There is, however, as we have stated, a dialectic. And we must ask once more where this sense of a dialectic touches the titular character, Humphry. In a sense, Humphry is the other side of Bramble—young, a Methodist, outside of traditional class and caste. While this opposition surely deserves further analysis, a clearer view of Bramble should precede it. Seemingly unresponsive, physically broken down, antisexual, indeed asexual, quick to anger, resentful of the world's folly, in this respect a true Welshman,[8] Bramble is comparable to Fielding's Squire Western, a rural Tory. Bramble attacks merchant classes (Whigs), as well as lords and gentlemen (London, urban Tories), as equally sources of folly and decadence. His values are seemingly conservative Tory views, disgusted as he is by both big-city Whiggery and Toryism, that is, both the commercial classes and those in power. In one letter after another, he attacks the press (an instrument of the new middle classes), the mixing of the classes (abetted by the press), all politicians, and the political process as well. He supports the older, more established writers, defends country life against the growing urban pollution, and backs tradition and custom.

By the June 14 entry, Bramble to Dr. Lewis, Humphry has begun to come increasingly to the fore. In his person and in his assumptions, he unwittingly challenges Bramble. And in the denouement, the revelation that Humphry is Bramble's son, we have, in one sense, an undoing of Bramble: the recognition on Smollett's part, for the moment, that a Bramble (a thorny, prickly aspect of nature) has secrets and underlife. Even Bramble has had to deal with matters

[8] Kahrl explains cogently why Smollett made his travelers Welsh: "Smollett's travelers are not Scottish, whom the English disliked, or French, whom Smollett abominated [see his *Travels Through France and Italy,* 1766], but Welsh, who were acceptable to the English and held in affectionate regard by the author." (p. 130) Smollett could contrast the simple life and manners of the Welsh with the ornate, fashionable, and false life of London and Bath, just as he used the digressions on Dennison and Baynard to vaunt rural life over contaminated urban waste.

that reason, cynicism, and disillusionment are unable to control; bits and pieces of his life break through unexpectedly. Thus, despite Smollett's own assumptions about past and present, a novelistic sense is apparent in his utilization of Humphry. For Humphry, in the denouement as well as elsewhere, disrupts and disturbs.

His Methodism, for example, is a source of much annoyance to Bramble, since it is a direct affront to Bramble's traditional religious views. Humphry's religion, however, is not only a theological threat, but implies social and political hostility. The growth of Methodism was, in one important sense, the growth of a new political bloc whose interests ran counter to Bramble's Toryism. Also, Humphry as an unrecognized son is disruptive in another sense, since his ability to get on *outside* the family structure is sufficient comment on the family itself: that it is superfluous for those capable of managing beyond it.

A social and political idea lies here, that of a new kind of society in which the traditional family is losing or has lost its functions. None of this can possibly aid Bramble's view of life. In a third sense, Humphry's eventual marriage to Winifred is a social disaster for Bramble, and yet it must be countenanced on other grounds. The marriage itself threatens what Bramble holds valuable, since its implicit democratic assumptions pre-empt class and undermine the hold of the rural Tories. The social point obtains, even though once the marriage is consummated, Winifred puts on airs and demands the respect due a country gentlewoman.

In virtually every phase of his activities, Humphry threatens Bramble's world, in time will make it impossible to hold on to, all the while protesting loyalty and respect. Here is the other part of the dialectic. Even the "rebirth" of Humphry has within it Smollett's ambivalent attitude toward what he represents. If we recall the episode (the major information comes in Jery's undated letter, falling between October 4 and 8, to Sir Watkins Phillips), Humphry saves Bramble from death by water. Although Humphry does not know Bramble is his father, he enters into a near-mythical-ritual process. Fishing Bramble up from the bottom, like Aeneas with Anchises he carries the older man on his back. His descent into the depths is itself a re-enactment of the birth process, and as a consequence of his deed, Humphry is figuratively reborn, first as Bramble's surrogate son, then as his real son.

Humphry's descent into the water is fraught with social and political overtones, none of which Smollett draws out. In a sense, once Humphry is reborn as legitimate, he usurps the father and the father's role. Methodism, marriage to Winifred, growth outside the family, self-education—these are all part of the dialectic, as much as Bramble himself, with his thorny Toryism and distrust of all forms of active life. Two kinds of life clash in a way we do not find in *Tom Jones.* At the end of that novel, Tom fits very well into the world of Squire Allworthy; through guilt and repentance, all distinctions have been purged. Having come through the test and demonstrated innate virtue, Tom is now ready for respectability.

By contrast, Humphry can never be like Bramble, nor can he be a rural Tory in his social and political assumptions. Even Smollett's predictions of future happiness differ from Fielding's resolutions. For the latter, life with Sophia will be bliss; for Smollett, married life is a snare one only discovers when passion wears off. In the November 8 entry, Jery writes: "Thus all the widgeons enjoy the novelty of their situations; but, perhaps their note will be changed, when they are better acquainted with the nature of the decoy." This is followed shortly by Winifred's letter of November 20, which she signs W. Loyd (a Bramble family name) and warns she has reached a higher sphere and must therefore keep a proper distance from the servants. Thus, through marriage, she has been turned into everything Bramble despised at Bath and London, and now his kind can see her kind multiply. Despite his evident sympathies for Bramble's type and his world, Smollett was true to his observations of society.

For the student of the novel, the travelogue part of *Humphry Clinker* is of minimal interest. Smollett here, as we have noted, is trying to capitalize on the popularity of travel literature in the 1760's, including his own *Travels Through France and Italy* and Sterne's *A Sentimental Journey*, as well as Drummond's *Travels* and Anstey's *New Bath Guide*, already referred to. The travels incorporate Smollett's continuing interest in *Don Quixote*, especially in the inn adventures and the slapstick. Lismahago is himself physically akin to the Don—cavernous, elongated, an El Greco-like figure; but the comparison ends rapidly. Cervantes's novel grows in humanity as the Don comes to embody several ideals; while Smollett's travel sections lack any overriding idea, and Lismahago's adventures among the Miamis are simply exploits in cruelty and sadism.

While Lismahago is a memorable character, his adventures do not serve any clear function or unify the novel as it wobbles its way through northern England into Scotland. His exotic past establishes, as Smollett himself recognized (see July 13 letter), a kind of ironic Othello-Desdemona theme in a novel that is moving in quite different directions. Even Lismahago's "common sense," a reflection of the Scottish common-sense school, does not key into the novel in any meaningful way, providing instead a kind of external banter based on Scottish contrariness.

Accordingly, these later sections, even though they contain the resolution of the Bramble-Clinker relationship, dissipate whatever force the multiple viewpoints may have had. Such material as we find in the travel sections does not require a sophisticated technique; a third-person narrative could do as easily. Matter does not justify method, and method does not broaden or intensify matter. Further, the digressions on Baynard and Dennison are only vaguely related to the ideology of the novel, since it has already established these points without the digressions. Nor does the revelation that young Wilson is actually young Dennison justify the variation. In these sections, Smollett is evidently harking back to the episodic method of the picaresque, even though the novel started out as something quite different.

In speaking of Smollett in his *Lectures on the English Comic Writers*, William Hazlitt compares him with Fielding, pointing up Fielding's superiority in his ability to maintain "the constant development of that character [at hand] through every change of circumstance." Hazlitt is referring to flaws in *Roderick Random*, specifically, but the point is well taken; for it suggests Smollett never broke with the randomness of character and event in the picaresque. And even in *Humphry Clinker*, where the attempt was valiant, we sense that Smollett felt more at home with caricature, with peculiarities of physical appearance, with eccentricities of behavior than he ever did with the sustained planning and structuring of a novel running more than three hundred pages. Hazlitt also speaks of what Fielding "leaves in the dark," and here, too, Smollett breaks down. We are left with little in the dark, with little mystery not only about plot but about character and motives; and it is precisely here that multiple viewpoints should technically have proven useful.

6

Tristram Shandy, *the Sentimental Novel, and Sentimentalists*

Too much criticism of *Tristram Shandy*[1] has concentrated on what is new about the novel and too little on what is old, traditional, foreseeable.[2] The novel is, in fact, directly related to the picaresque

[1] The novel was published as follows: Volumes I and II (December 1759, in York–January 1, 1760, in London); III and IV (January 1761); V and VI (December 1761); VII and VIII (January 1765); IX (January 1767). The "sources" for *Tristram Shandy* are well known and involve Sterne's favorite authors and books, among them: Rabelais, Cervantes, Burton's *Anatomy of Melancholy*, Locke, Montaigne's *Essays*, Bacon, Swift, Shakespeare. Of these, Locke determined much of the structure, Burton the manner, Rabelais the tone, Cervantes the sentiment, Montaigne the wisdom, and Shakespeare the phrasing and cadences. The edition of James A. Work (Odyssey Press, 1940), pages xxiii ff., discusses this material; see also Wilbur L. Cross, *The Life and Times of Laurence Sterne*, pp. 139 ff.

[2] Dorothy Van Ghent (*The English Novel: Form and Function*), for example, speaks of the novel as having "a new type of structure . . . of singular importance for the development of the modern novel." (p. 83) Gerald Weales (in *Twelve Original Essays on Great English Novels*, ed. Charles Shapiro) calls his essay "Tristram Shandy's Anti-Book," which suggests experimentation and ignores traditional elements. The best argument for "newness," however, comes from Wayne C. Booth ("The Self-Conscious Narrator in Comic Fiction," *PMLA,* pp. 163–85), surely because his essay so closely examines the conventions and modes Sterne utilized from previous fiction.

Booth speaks of Sterne's taking earlier materials, particularly from Marivaux, and "carrying everything to extremes." He says: "The methods of Marivaux have been carried beyond their original intent, and have produced something which is, however difficult to describe and however closely derived from earlier experiments, new." (p. 175) Booth qualifies the "novelty" of Sterne's book somewhat when he says that it "is not really an explosion of all formal canons but only seems to be so. Sterne takes the

narrative and, further, relies upon literary ideas that were not at all unique in the 1760's. We can, of course, read Sterne's work in several ways, but the one possibly conforming best to the text is to view it as part of a dialectic of conflicting elements in which certain parts are thrown rather violently against other parts, so that the *resolution* seems something very new, though the parts do not. Sterne, like Joyce after him, established a unity or order upon disparate materials that was not anything substantially new but that *appears* new because every synthesis creates different shapes.

If we take as an analogy a form very different from Sterne's book—Gerard Manley Hopkins's definition of Counterpoint Rhythm—we can perhaps see the kind of dialectic the novel offers. Hopkins speaks of Counterpoint as consisting of the "*mounting* of a new rhythm upon the old," which is accomplished by the poet's placing a syllabic stress where a slack is expected, and a slack where the stress would be. This reversal of expectation creates counterpoint, for "the new or mounted rhythm is actually heard and at the same time the mind naturally supplies the natural or standard foregoing rhythm." Accordingly, two rhythms are "in some manner running at once, and we have something answerable to counterpoint in music."

Hopkins's point is suggestive of an archetypal artistic process, for it presupposes not something terribly new, although the new is involved, and not something terribly difficult, although difficulties are present, but a dialectic of elements in which old and new combine to create the semblance of something very different from the component elements. In Sterne, as in Rabelais, the "old" is the picaresque form of the narrative, which is basic to the plan of the novel. Another convention, overlaid by verbal byplay, recalling Burton's *Anatomy*, is the biographical element, in a sense the work of the literary historian, the title being *The Life and Opinions of Tristram Shandy, Gentleman.*[3]

---

novel beyond the lines always carefully avoided by earlier novelists, but the line is not a line between unity and chaos. Rather it is a line between one kind of unity and another kind of unity, itself a fusion of various cohesive forces at work in the older 'facetious' and 'chaotic' traditions." (p. 85)

[3] The picaresque, biographical elements are suggested in Stephen Croft's comments, quoted by Work, on his recollection of Sterne's first plan for the book: ". . . to travell his Hero Tristram Shandy all over Europe and after making his remarks on the different Courts, proceed with making strictures and reflections on the different Governments . . . and at length to return Tristram well informed and a compleat English Gentleman." Evidently, Sterne's interests changed during the writing, but aspects of the original plan remain even while "opinions" prevail over "life."

The picaresque form, however disguised, is apparent in several ways. First, Tristram's birth and early years involve alienation from a family preoccupied with its own systems and peculiar energies. His is a mock-epical "birth of a hero," and his apprenticeship is to a much harder form of life than circumstances at first appear to warrant. Second, *Tristram Shandy* is of potentially limitless length; the form allows for the addition of innumerable episodes and innumerable characters. If Sterne had begun writing it at an earlier age, we might have had any number of volumes, any number of characters and episodes, for he himself indicated that he wanted to write a volume or more each year for the rest of his life. The sole control on length was the life of the author, not the nature of the material itself. While we could possibly say the same of *Clarissa*—one million words could have become two million—nevertheless the material contains its own end game once the rape is perpetrated. Third, Sterne's cast of characters includes high and low, several different elements and professions, civilians and military, lay and medical, masters and servants, agnostic and religious—the usual variety one expects in the picaresque. Fourth, one discovers in *Tristram Shandy* the sense of chance that rules also in the picaresque.

Sterne's picaresque depends strongly on happenstance, balanced, we assume, by an eighteenth-century reliance on providence. Fortune or chance lies at the center of any work that relies so heavily on the association of ideas; a self-aware consciousness or narrator whose circuitry is unlimited is an uncontrollable element or force, unlike the omniscient author, who is shaping and controlling at every step. A fiction based on the characters' consciousness, such as Sterne's, Joyce's, or Woolf's, is bound to make chance appear primary. In these novels, the usual elements of control are missing or minimized. In some final sense, of course, any novel is controlled, or else its shapelessness would recall life, not art. In a long fiction, our expectations for structure derive from plot and characterization of a particular kind, narrative arrangements of a certain organizing type. Even in the most wildly experimental work—*Finnegans Wake*, the later novels of William Burroughs, Thomas Pynchon's *V*, Michel

---

Both in plan and execution, one can see how Sterne differed from Thomas Amory's *The Life and Opinions of John Buncle, Esq.* (2 vols., 1756 and 1766), with which it has some affinities. Amory's volumes, however, are a hodgepodge of curious learning, the novelistic equivalent of Burton's *Anatomy of Melancholy*, without Sterne's sense of a shaping force or his ability to limn character consistently.

Butor's *Degrees* or *Passing Time*—we search beneath seeming confusion for those signals of order on which we can anchor our reactions; and such "signals" are the recognizable elements of plot, character, and narrative.

A central consciousness, we have noted, disturbs these assumptions, as it should;[4] and therefore any long work shaped by an individual's consciousness is giving itself over to seemingly fortuitous events. Its "structure" will have, as Dorothy Van Ghent says, "the form of a mind," in which the internal is externalized. Now all this is well within the province of the picaresque—chance, a distant ruling providence—although the element of individual consciousness may not be primary. Even here, however, Sterne is following the picaro's main line of development, to impose his person and his self on an aimless world.

Thus the rootedness of *Tristram Shandy* in existing practices. What makes the novel appear new and different from traditional sources is Sterne's use of the association of ideas along with a different sense of time. The combination is an important one. William V. Holtz touches on this connection. "The problem of personal identity, then, can be said to be a central, if implicit, concern in *Tristram Shandy*, and it is so directly related to the problem of time that one can be said to be a function of the other." (p. 137)

Many writers had tried to handle an association of ideas, even a ruling individual consciousness—Cervantes is a ready example—but all had tried it against a prevailing time sequence based on clock and calendar. We may think of Cervantes's use of the episode in the cave of Montesinos, in which the Don's sense of his having spent three days in the cave is played off against Sancho's assertion that it was about an hour. Sancho explains the discrepancy by falling back on the enchanters, who change our assumptions of time: ". . . perhaps what seems to us an hour may seem three days and nights down there." Cervantes, however, fudges the issue, for he returns time to

[4] Using his notion of Sterne as a novelist treading a thin line between writing and painting, William V. Holtz reaches somewhat similar conclusions: "The novel was, in fact, a hypothesis offering an image of reality intelligible in terms of plot and action and requiring certain conditional manipulations cf time. Sterne, conscious of what this hypothesis left out, sought to broaden it by making the conditional freedom absolute and achieved an image of reality intelligible in terms of the mind of a single character. The radical disruptions in narrative by which Sterne attempts to convey Tristram's unified awareness of his entire past are implicit in Tristram's request that he be allowed to stop a moment to give us a picture." (*Image and Immortality: A Study of Tristram Shandy*, p. 114)

our clock sense of temporal matters and sees the episode as one of the Don's typical aberrations; "rigmarole," Sancho calls it.[5]

Sterne has tried to stay closer to time sequences based on consciousness. Clock time gives way, in the mind, to a different ordering, what Bergson was later to call *durée*—the amount of time something seems to take, regardless of clock time. In Bergson's world, time is heterogeneous and fluid, and things in it are indistinguishable; while space is the opposite: homogeneous, measurable, separable. Bergson's time theory assumes a kind of experience impossible to measure, moments of consciousness which interpenetrate each other, mental reactions always in a process of distortion, and ideas unable to be projected without alteration.

In Sterne's conception of the little made great, the paltry raised to heroic stature, the ordinary intensified to epical proportions, such a time theory helps to blur the process of transformation. Metamorphosis is as crucial to Sterne's methodology as disguise is to Defoe's; it is central to an association of ideas in which one item leads not only to another, according to the individual's consciousness, but to a process in which ordinary distinctions between large and small are blurred. Bergson's time theory asserts a disbelief in surface reality, stressing a time that denies the clock and makes the mind supreme arbiter of all temporal dimensions. As defined by Bergson, what occurs is not controlled by the normal order of consciousness. One is intuitive, not rational.

With this scheme, Bergson broke out of Victorian mechanical timing. His "system" is anti-intellectual, anti-mechanical, anti-scientific; it seizes the moment. If we work back to Sterne from Bergson, we observe in rudimentary shape several of his main assumptions, whose presence in Sterne's work makes it appear so new and so different from that of his earlier contemporaries. For such "timing" invokes, as well, a different conception of life. It stresses existence for its own sake; it counters the Puritan thrust of Defoe and Richardson; it offers a more romantic view of life than that afforded by Fielding's

[5] In her essay on *Tristram Shandy*, Dorothy Van Ghent mentions the Montesinos episode, but with a different stress. Her emphasis is upon the merging of time past with time present, whereas mine is upon the playing off of the Don's psychological time against Sancho's clock and calendar time. Van Ghent's line of argument about Sterne surely cuts across my own when she says that "clock-time appears only intermittently as a felt factor," and that "any time-past may be time-present, or several times-past be concurrently present at once." (*The English Novel: Form and Function*, p. 85)

"indulgence with moral prudence." It stresses the relativity of all experience; ultimately, the triviality of all experience except that which is meaningful to the individual—thus, the personalized "hobbyhorse" theory is an intrinsic part of the time sequencing. For example, the siege of Namur in 1695 is not significant to Tristram as a historical event in the struggle between England and France; its importance lies in Uncle Toby's having been wounded there on July 27.

In this way, Sterne's sense of the paramount place of the individual experience appears startlingly innovative: time, narrative, the stress itself all point toward a new order, away from social resolutions, away from moral ordering, away from received assumptions of man and his society. Through time sequencing and mental circuitry, Sterne has apparently broken out of history, conventional morality, and traditional modes of thinking.

Time in the novel, as in drama, always creates a conflict of mental associations in the reader or viewer. It is, of course, an extremely complex subject, and we are here concerned only with those aspects touching upon Sterne's method of working. His dissociation of time is, we have seen, the key to his seeming newness; for with time he has broken up the narrative according to idiosyncrasies that thereby become the substance of the novel. His time method gave him the opportunity to observe his characters from a strategic point of vantage and to develop them through an accretion of detail rather than by means of a more limiting chronological narrative.

Sterne's utilization of Tristram as a central, self-aware narrator should not disguise the fact that the novel essentially does not concern him; and here we depart from the main line of picaresque. Wayne C. Booth speaks of Tristram as giving the book its form, the "secret of its coherence," and as being indistinguishable from what he relates, thus approaching Henry James's "ideal of a seamless web of subject and treatment . . ." (*The Rhetoric of Fiction*, pp. 223–4) We must, however, recognize that the dissociation of time, a feature of Sterne and not of James, pushes Tristram off to the side of the stage. Despite his "centrality" as the conscious narrator, the book is not about him but about a number of things. If there is a shaping power, it is not the synthesizing power of Tristram's consciousness but the formative power of an idea based on association, in which dissociation of time is not dysfunctional but functional, not the cause of disorientation but organizational at a different level. Time is, as it were, the consciousness, Tristram the coordinator.

We usually think of a "time scheme" as predominantly modern, belonging to Proust, Faulkner, Woolf, Joyce, and their epigoni. We also normally think of modern theories of physics and mathematics, the quantum theory, for example, as having had a profound influence on our concern with literary time. But literature—and not only fiction—almost from its beginnings has been preoccupied with time, from the point of the author's recognition that his narrator or his own omniscience operates in a different time scheme from that of his reader; a realization that the written word moves at a different pace from the spoken or the understood word.

A preoccupation with time accompanied the early development of the novel. Even in *Robinson Crusoe*, there is such an incipient pattern, with Robinson's diary of "prisoner time" on his island contrasted with time for those who live in the outside world. As noted, A. A. Mendilow, in *Time and the Novel*, has observed, in the fifty years between *Robinson Crusoe* and *Tristram Shandy*, we have "the unities of time, place, and action, strict sequence, selective causality, and associationist irregularity, intercalated, preliminary, and distributed exposition, continuity, and selection, immediacy and the time-shift." Had Dr. Mendilow extended his period another few years, to *Humphry Clinker*, he would have found another set of time sequences based on multiple narrators viewing similar materials. The preoccupation of the eighteenth-century novelists with time can be found, not only in the novels themselves, but in critical prefaces, introductions, digressions within the narrative, letters of intentions, dedications, even epigraphs. The epigraph to *Tristram Shandy*, for example, from Epictetus' *Enchiridion*, is translated as: "It is not actions, but opinions concerning actions, which disturb men." Actions would be spatial, part of an ordinary time sequence that works itself out chronologically; while "opinions" suggests a temporal dimension, an individual consciousness, an associationist order of mental activity.

There is always a conflict between the time sequences that the novel imposes on its materials and the wholeness of human experience that the novel attempts to suggest. More than any other artist, the novelist must compress his material, for his narrative usually spans a calendar duration of several years, even several lifetimes and generations. Yet his presentation of that duration is limited to scattered moments, scenes that would in fact take seconds or minutes, conversations that fill entire chapters but would fill only an hour or less, and so forth.

The novelist, from the beginning, was involved in a deception with almost infinite variations, for he had to juggle simultaneously: (1) the reader's expectation of certain time sequences; (2) the moment of time for his characters; (3) the characters' sense of passing time and how *that* affects their moments; (4) reading time, what we may call the differentiated pacing of the action for both characters and reader; (5) the novelist's own sense of passing time, which he must adjust to the fictional time; (6) events in the narrative itself and how they are affected by the internal "time ruboff" from other events and characters; (7) adjustments, within a character himself, between psychological and clock time; (8) the entire relationship between parts and whole, as a new, differing sense of time accrues from the merging of elements with each other.

From even a cursory examination of the beginning of *Tristram Shandy*, we can see how complicated the matter is. The last paragraph of Volume I, chapter I reads:

> *Pray, my dear,* quoth my mother, *have you not forgot to wind up the clock?— Good G—!* cried my father, making an exclamation, but taking care to moderate his voice at the same time,— *Did ever woman, since the creation of the world, interrupt a man with such a silly question?* Pray, what was your father saying?— Nothing. [*Tristram Shandy*, ed. James A. Work, p. 5]

This paragraph is in a sense a microcosm of both the method and matter of the novel. The central idea is *coitus interruptus,* the beginning of the theme of incompleteness or impotence which pervades the narrative. Specifically, the passage refers to Walter Shandy's habit (explained in chapter IV) of winding a "large house-clock" on the first Sunday night of every month, and on that same Sunday having sexual intercourse with Mrs. Shandy; thus in one swoop getting them "all out of the way at one time, and be no more plagued and pester'd with them the rest of the month." Two particular kinds of time, then, are immediately associated: the clock time mentioned in the winding and human time in the sexual act and the begetting. Mrs. Shandy, a creature lacking Walter Shandy's "rationality," confuses the two times, the time of intercourse and the time of winding, for one sets off in her "irrational" mind the idea of the other.

Her interruption of the sexual act to remind her husband of the winding of the clock, however, is only the beginning, a begetting in several ways. For Sterne then whimsically ventures the idea that the parents' thoughts at the moment of conception are significant in the development of the fetus. That is, ideas, thoughts, attitudes, tendencies, predilections are passed on with the homunculus or sperm; a theory that, by combining medieval humors with pseudo-genetics, makes a mockery of an entire genre.

Mrs. Shandy's interruption affects every aspect of Tristram's begetting, birth, and development as a child, for she creates hesitation, incompleteness, and "nothing." (We recall that, like the circular *Finnegans Wake, Tristram Shandy* ends with a cock-and-bull story, which is a narrative equivalent of the "nothing" that begins the novel.) The associational circuitry is suggested early on, for her role is to connect two skew events, clock winding and intercourse, an indication of how far afield an association may take one. The linking has just begun, however, for Uncle Toby is introduced, the source of the explanation to Tristram of his begetting, and then, through various literary sources (Bunyan, Montaigne, and Horace), the narrative winds back to an analysis of Walter Shandy's mind in reference to the first Sunday in every month, and ends, all within six pages, with the "sagacious Locke," whose ideas of sensation and association strongly influenced Sterne's way of proceeding.[6]

The microcosm (one is tempted to say the homunculus) establishes both the temporal dimensions of the novel and its method based on *interruptus.* The use of sensations and associations—all part of an anti-rational system comically based on Walter Shandy, an arch-rationalist—carries us one step further, into a world of chance and fortune, which by implication brings us to one of the major elements in the picaresque novel. We note, then, that all of Sterne's experimentation with time is still part of the old narrative method, now made more sophisticated and varied. Sterne may speak of a

[6] Sterne was attracted by the subjective potential of Locke's universe. According to the *Essay concerning Human Understanding* (1690), things in their primary qualities are solid, shaped, at rest; while the secondary qualities—such as color, sound, taste, smell—are in the beholder. While nothing is purely innate, things have the power to affect us or to produce the idea of themselves; and thus the subjectivity inherent in sensation, reflection, memory, with their implied associational or correspondent aspects. Professor Work, in his edition of *Tristram Shandy*, quotes a well-known passage from Locke that bears repeating, to the effect that associated ideas "always keep in company, and the one no sooner at any time comes into the understanding, but its associate appears with it; and if they are more than two which are thus united, the whole gang, always inseparable, show themselves together." (Locke's *Essay,* 2.33.5)

false pregnancy leading to a country laying-in the following year; he may speak of wind or water causing the sensation of the false pregnancy; and he may, further, speak of town and country as being part of a crazy marriage settlement; he may even show how all of these elements merge with each other, so that when Tristram is born, Dr. Slop is in attendance, and the result is the loss of the bridge of his nose.[7] The matter is quaint, the method is circuitous and tortuous; but the substance is the mock-heroical birth of an anti-hero, recognizable in terms of questions of origin, begetting, birth, and later development, all the stuff of the picaresque romantic novel. Locke may be the conductor of Sterne's contrapuntal symphony or the grand master of ceremonies at this extended "happening," but if we look deep enough, we see familiar materials.

The question then arises: What is *Tristram Shandy*? What is it about? What are its ingredients? Once we cut through the method, can we, unlike the widow Wadman, put our finger on the real trouble spot(s) and say that we have located the center?

If we seek order, we can find it in the image of art. Virtually every image and scene has its parallel or analogy with the world of art, the bringing forth of an inchoate work that will both develop its own terms and take on its own kind of life. And like the components of art, the materials of *Tristram Shandy* are attempting to find their own order, rather than to perpetrate disorder. In this respect, Sterne's heritage from *Don Quixote* is apparent: the Don spins out his metaphors, illusions, and symbolic acts, which become the order of a para-artist, and, comparably, Tristram tells a story full of disorderly material that he, now old and near death from consumption, is trying to shape.

In a book cited above, William V. Holtz sees *Tristram Shandy* as the coming together of literary and pictorial materials toward the creation of a "word-picture":

> Three things are worth noting . . . The first is that Tristram's dilemma is basically a matter of narrative technique, of selection and arrangement of

[7] Sterne may even extend noses, and indirectly penises, to such huge capers as "Slawkenbergius's Tale," which opens Volume IV. The mock-epical Slawkenbergius fingers his nose constantly, so that both "picking" and masturbation are interchangeable, and his power to beguile and bewitch is sensory and sexual. ". . . 'twas for ever in his hands,—you would have sworn, Sir, it had been a canon's prayer-book,—so worn, so glazed, so contrited and attrited was it with fingers and with thumbs in all its parts, from one end even unto the other." (p. 241) All of this serves a threefold scheme: as a commentary on Walter Shandy's obsession with noses and sexual play (or lack of it), on Tristram's loss of bridge and foreskin, on the Rabelaisian epic which Sterne was both utilizing and mocking.

the parts of his tale. The other two are the metaphors, common in *Tristram Shandy*, that intersect here: the narrative as a journey in one instance, as a painting in another. Together these embody the essence of a major problem Sterne explored in the pages of *Tristram Shandy*: how to capture in a narrative form the sense of total and simultaneous representation inherent in a painting, how to achieve static effects in the medium of time—in short, how to paint the picture of Tristram's journey through life. [*Image and Immortality*, p. 93]

Perhaps more important than Sterne's achievement as a word painter is his attempt to bring into completion a work of art from its basically primitive materials. One may argue that *all* first-person narrative, all semi- or quasi-biographical fiction, takes the shape of a work in the process of completing itself as art. To a certain extent, this is true. The first-person, self-aware narrator, whether Pip or Stephen Dedalus, is attempting to find cohesion in a wild disarray of experience and images, much as the artist shaping his clay into an urn. With Sterne's Tristram, however, a degree of difference creates the distinction. Tristram's materials have the patina of the very disarray in which they are disgorged. The shaping takes place beyond the consciousness of the narrator, who is trying to understand his experience; the reader must find the order, such as it is, somewhere in a nether land between the narrator, who is presenting the material, and the author, who is controlling that presentation.

As a consequence, dissociation is a new type of order, not a display of disorder; and interpolation, intercalation, dislocation are a new awareness of organization, not a quest for disorganization. Such devices only *seem* disorderly or innovative because of certain cultural assumptions we have made about the eighteenth-century novel in particular and the eighteenth century in general; but once we grant the variety of any age and note its alternate or adverse culture as a viable force, they are normalizing procedures. What, then, are these materials?

1. Like the artist, Tristram is obsessed with conception. The novel begins on this note, and conception and all its ramifications (from the marriage contract concerned with city or country laying-in to the homunculus theory or whimsy) remain central. All of which leads to:

2. Begetting. The first line of Volume I indicates the direction: "I wish either my father or my mother, or indeed both of them, as they were in duty equally bound to it, had minded what they were about

when they begot me . . ." The images are of a bringing-forth, distantly analogous to Joyce's bringing-forth of Stephen Dedalus in the first few paragraphs of *A Portrait of the Artist.*

3. Incompletion (*coitus interruptus*). The analogy to an art work is here the lack of completion in life which the art work must either suggest or make explicit. Incompleteness is a natural consequence of conception and begetting, since it implies a constant striving for what is unattainable except through death—which is completion, the final, resolutory line on the canvas. Holtz's comments on the limits of Sterne's art are appropriate:

> Hence, then, the many tableaux and minutely detailed, static figures that clog and halt the flow of Tristram's narrative: somehow the sequential march of verbal abstractions must be made to mark time and admit to their ranks a detailed image of the actor, not merely a broad outline of his action. Against the dilemma of language that Locke had discerned, Sterne invokes a vision of individualized humans, suspended in postures indicative of their unique personalities and their highly personal, yet sympathetically understandable, relations to the flux of life. Herein is the source of Walter Shandy's grotesque, grief-stricken figure sprawled across the bed and across page after page of the narrative of his family's misfortune until Toby's silent, beaming countenance melts his sorrow. The situation is comically expressive in itself, yet stands as an ironic commentary on the limits of his art, as Sterne attempts by an essentially pictorial technique to compensate not only for the abstract and arbitrary nature of language but also for the deficiencies of a narrative form. [*Image and Immortality*, p. 74]

4. Midwifery. While the subject appears to be midwifery, and is foreshadowed by the marriage contract, the real topic is the question of country vs. city, nature vs. nurture, folkways vs. "civilized" medicine. Midwife suggests Dr. Slop, and Dr. Slop is a combination of all evils for Sterne, as he would also have been for Fielding. The matter is one of natural (Shaftesburian) procedures contrasted with the artificiality and false knowledge of a stupid medical practitioner. Sterne's method being what it is, midwifery becomes not only malpractice but Popery, noses, bridges, penises, impotence, normal development, and so on into virtually every socio-sexual aspect of the fiction.

5. Naming. This is the novelist's need—whether Defoe's or Sterne's—to make concrete in the work of art that which is undefined, unnamed, indistinct in life or in imagination. Van Ghent, in her

essay on *Tristram Shandy*, speaks of Sterne's awareness of the concrete moment: ". . . we could say that it is because of his awareness of the preciousness of the concrete moment, that he is so acutely aware of time, which destroys the moment." (*The English Novel*, p. 93) Naming is close to medieval nominalism, which insisted that for the sake of convenience of thought and language we give names to universals or abstractions; but we must beware of confusing such names (or nominalisms) with realities, which possess an objective existence. Naming goes far beyond Walter Shandy's obsessive hatred for "Tristram" and moves to the heart of the philosophical issues behind Sterne's method; for naming involves the nature of reality, the question of universals with their own separate existence, and these issues lead into Locke, with his insistence upon sensations and their empirical basis in the particularities of experience.

6. Catastrophes. Disaster is as indigenous to the Shandy experience as it is essential to the comic thrust of the narrative. "True *Shandeism* [now a coinage]," Sterne writes, "think what you will against it, opens the heart and lungs, and like all those affections which partake of its nature, it forces the blood and other vital fluids of the body to run freely thro' its channels, and makes the wheel of life run long and cheerfully round." (Work edition, pp. 337–8) This passage is at the end of Volume IV, more or less at the center of the disasters, with Bobby's death announcement yet to come and Tristram's unplanned circumcision in the window-sash episode only a few pages off. Catastrophe is essential to both tragedy and comedy, but in Sterne's comedy, wherein the little is made to appear great, catastrophe becomes a form of mock-heroic: names, bridges of noses, and foreskins are all expendable. Nevertheless, death, loss, threat of sexual impotence, severe disappointment, frustration—all never far from Sterne's own debilitating consumption—are part of the comic mix.

7. Time. Discussed above.

8. Narration. A basic theme, as well as device, of the novel is the self-aware narrator, the character commenting on his own role as that role is developing. An examination of this process is the subject of a long essay by Wayne C. Booth, cited above. "Our attention," he writes, "must be centered on the self-conscious narrator who intrudes into his novel to comment on himself as writer, and on his book, not

simply as a series of events with moral implications, but as a created literary product . . . the crucial task is to determine the history and uses of the narrator who, like Tristram, not only makes explicit for the reader the technical decisions which in 'normal' fiction are carried on completely behind the scenes, but also portrays the activity of constructive response which successful readers must always make to the offerings of any author." (p. 165)

The "self-conscious narrator" is, evidently, connected to the stress Sterne places upon sensation, experience, association of ideas. It is, however, thematic, not solely technical. That is the main distinction we must make between Sterne's handling and that (let us say) of Defoe. And it reveals the process of art as it unfolds to fill out its own potential.

9. Hobbyhorses. Idiosyncrasies, obsessions—call them what you will, hobbyhorses are the product of Sterne's display of individual consciousness. They are anti-medieval, anti-rational, anti-establishment (any establishment), anti-state, and anti-societal. The hobbyhorse theory goes to the center of Sterne's universe: atomistic, individualistic, quirky, eccentric, bizarre, and, basically, trivial. Hobbyhorses make the small appear big, the trivial seem significant; they are a conception as well as a technique.

We could argue that the hobbyhorse, which exists without any basis in reason, is Sterne's bridge between Locke's two worlds of the real and the ideal. According to Locke, we can ascertain our ideas but can never be certain of data external to our own minds. There is a gap or paradox here, between ideas and reality. The hobbyhorse also suggests such a paradox, for whether the matter is noses, bridges, battles, placement of guns, strategies and logistics, or names, it is an idea of the world originating from within and lacking any firm sense of external reality. The somnambular quality of *Tristram Shandy*, the reverie-like quality of the narrator, is the consequence of ideas imposing their own kind of reality, while facts remain debatable, relative, molding themselves to human will.[8]

10. Love and romance. These are qualities which assert themselves by their marked absence. Much as Dickens's *Pickwick, Tristram Shandy* virtually excludes females. A woman is a strange creature from

[8] For an argument that suggests similar conclusions, see "The Shandean Comic Vision of Locke" by John Traugott, from his *Tristram Shandy's World: Sterne's Philosophical Rhetoric*, 1954.

another world. Tristram's mother, despite her mindlessness, insists on marriage contracts and laying-in agreements; she is more legalistic than sexual and is a once-a-month romantic object. The widow Wadman is a seductress who is trying to entrap the embattled Uncle Toby. Woman, however, is not powerful enough to be Eve. The male is not powerful but innocent, and untrappable because he is asexual. He is able to carry on marriage functions at a minimal level (Walter) or unable to function except in a pre-female world (Toby). The latter, perhaps more innocent than Hemingway's Jake Barnes, uses his groin injury as protection against women altogether. Young Tristram is himself moving toward this condition, with the circumcision at five, an accident that appears to Walter Shandy as castration, and his later consumption, which drains away his physical energy.

Because love and romance are so low-keyed, or nonexistent, *Tristram Shandy* reduces all male characters to childishness. Once again, the little (child) juxtaposed to the great (adult world) provides the humor. Women serve marginal functions—Mrs. Shandy listens in, described by Sterne as: ". . . she listened with all her powers:—the listening slave, with the Goddess of Silence at his back, could not have given a finer thought for an intaglio." (Work edition, p. 357) Yet among the comic paradoxes of the novel is the fact that even while women are offstage or strangely foreign figures, they dominate every aspect of the book. The men seemingly make the decisions, carry on the conversations, and determine the course of their lives; but the men have only the idea of rule, and the substance of rule lies elsewhere.

11. *Tristra-poedia.* Like Meredith's *The Ordeal of Richard Feverel*, the novel incorporates in its narrative a training manual, a self-conscious system based on theory, not human fact. Perhaps basing his idea on Xenophon's *Cyropaedia*, Walter Shandy plans a system of education for his son, so as "to form an INSTITUTE for the government of [Tristram's] childhood and adolescence." (p. 372) More immediately, the influence is Rabelaisian, specifically "How Gargantua was instructed by Ponocrates," so that he "lost not one hour of the day." Rabelais was, of course, outlining a study program for the education of a Renaissance prince, while Walter Shandy is setting forth a system which, day by day, becomes obsolete. As Mr. Shandy labors over the terms of his son's upbringing, Tristram is "abandoned" to his mother's care, which is the very thing the system is supposed to

avoid, and suffers through his misfortunes of misnaming, nose, and geniture.

Walter Shandy's educational system is a mélange of pseudo-scientific theory (the secret of health is finding a balance between the "radical heat and radical moisture within us") and certain imposed disciplines (Tristram shall "be made to conjugate every word in the dictionary, backwards and forwards the same way," so that every word is "converted into a thesis or an hypothesis"). While seemingly a "system," it is actually an association of unrelated ideas held together only by the vagaries of an individual consciousness, as discrete and disparate in its details as the fortuitous events of Tristram's misfortunes.

Father and son, then, are locked into comparable worlds, each one given over to happenstance, although while Tristram drifts, Walter believes he is imposing order. There is none. On the contrary, events occur according to their own unforeseen logic, like the activities of Panurge in the Abbey of Thélème, with their own propositions, consequences, and conclusions. Thus, a *Tristra-poedia* is a denial of the life force, which has its own undesigned logic, with only intimations of providence lurking in the shadows.

12. Sentiment, sentimentality, sensibility. In one way, the entire novel—through a series of individual stories, such as Le Fever's, Marie's, Slawkenbergius's—is an expression of Sterne's "benevolist" attitudes toward man and society. The benevolists, roughly parallel in England to the Rousseauists in France, insisted on man's natural goodness. Their social theories were optimistic, based on ideas of individual and social progress, and they tended to be secularists rather than religionists. They were anti-Hobbesian, just as their later followers were to be anti-utilitarian. In this respect, in his attachment to benevolist ideals, Sterne foreshadows Carlyle (in part), Dickens, and Ruskin.

The Sentimental Novel and Sentimentalists

The novel of sentiment or sensibility developed in Richardson and Fielding as a positive response to anti-Hobbesian, pro-Shaftesburian developments in philosophy and social theory. It was a precursor of aspects of romanticism in that it stressed feeling *without* any perjorative taint attached to emotionalism. Not surprisingly, sentimentality developed parallel with Methodism. The consequences of the literary development of sentiment were several, all tending toward that leveling process which was a concomitant of the Industrial Revolution and the growth of Methodism. Individual expression, on occasion, is carried to extremes. The value of experience is measured in its own terms, not for its social or religious ramifications. Indeed, didacticism, hitherto funneled through allegory, is forsaken and the individual embodies social morality. Instinct, intuition, the sense of things are all stressed, rather than learning, fixed values, the old hierarchies. There is the growth of pity and compassion for others, part of the "feelingness" each individual was expected to have toward his fellow sufferers; similarly, characters are judged by their ability to feel, not solely by their achievements or lineage. One finds a lessening of puritanical repression. (Victorianism, of course, reversed this aspect, disguising, however, rather than eliminating feeling.) Openness gives way to some dissembling, but one must simply read the conventions to find the equivalent passions. There is less seeking after dramatic effect; we experience routine, ordinary realism, a flattening out of events. At the same time, we note a growth of pictorial poetry—painting with words—what Lessing deplored in *Laocoön*. The dramatic effects—tragedy in particular—move into Gothic, where they blow themselves out after about three decades; the mainstream novel is free to modify or rechannel melodrama into a comic vision.

Basically, the movement or subgenre known as the novel of sensibility or sentimentality runs roughly parallel with the publication of *Tristram Shandy* through the 1760's and extends another decade or so until about 1780. We note some of its precursors in the 1750's, directly after the publication of *Clarissa*, especially in a book such as Charlotte Lennox's *The Female Quixote* (1752).[9] Intermixed

[9] Near the conclusion of *The Female Quixote*, Arabella, having sufficiently recovered from a great illness, must now be disabused of fanciful notions based on the romances she has been reading. "Your Imaginations, Madam, reply'd the Doctor, are too quick for Language; you conjecture too soon, what you do not wait to hear; and reason upon Suppositions which cannot be allow'd you." (Oxford edition, p. 370)

While Mrs. Lennox's ostensible point is a mockery of the romances and romantic novels which have sustained Arabella, nevertheless the young heroine's behavior has much in common with the later heroes and heroines of sensibility. Chiefly, all such protagonists are anxious to believe, not what experience tells them, but what their reading or philosophies have prepared them to accept. Their reactions are never empirical—which is the way of common sense—but based on reading, emotions, or preconceived attitudes. In their inability to accept what mind and senses should tell

with the "sentimental" turn is a group of novels that employed *Don Quixote* as their model, *The Female Quixote* as well as Smollett's *Sir Launcelot Greaves* (1762), Richard Graves's *The Spiritual Quixote* (1773),[10] and Clara Reeve's *The Champion of Virtue, a Gothic Story* (later renamed *The Old English Baron*, 1777). We should add that novels at the very heart of the sentimental movement owe a good deal of their existence to the Don, idealistic, benevolent, ready to believe the best about mankind.

For our purposes, the basic text for the movement is Goldsmith's *The Vicar of Wakefield* (1766), with secondary consideration given to Henry Brooke's *The Fool of Quality* (1766–70) and Henry Mackenzie's *The Man of Feeling* (1771), to which we can add the various satires and burlesques in the Cervantes tradition named above, novels by Lennox, Smollett, later Graves and Reeve. Always in the immediate background is *Tristram Shandy* itself, and *A Sentimental Journey Through France and Italy* (1768).

For the modern reader, Goldsmith's novel is evidently something different from what it was for an eighteenth-century audience. For the latter, its homiletic nature was just what endeared it, while for the former, its homiletics make it appear not only excessively innocent but also dull. Withal, *The Vicar of Wakefield* has an importance of its own in the development of prose fiction, although reading it today we must struggle hard to locate its virtues. Goldsmith found relatively "neutral" ground for his novel at a time when prose fiction was dividing and subdividing into numerous subgenres. After the deaths of Fielding and Richardson, and with Smollett's own contribution to the novel sporadic, prose fiction from about 1750 to 1775 fell into several byways. Proliferating in this period, without any major novelist to put together the pieces, were the romance, the anti-romance, Gothic, sensibility, parodies of

---

them, they build up a store of assumptions and sentiments far in excess of what they would normally have; and their subsequent behavior, founded on precisely this excess, marks the beginning of the novel of sensibility.

[10] Graves's novel glances off the sentimental subgenre, rather than reflecting it directly. Graves's ostensible purpose was to write a picaresque satire, modest in practice, based on Fielding's comic epic in prose. His Geoffry Wildgoose is a Fieldingesque Quixote, and the novel follows the "open road" pattern, which means interpolated episodes, a large cast of characters from high and low life, a respect for nature and for natural living, an openness about sex and sensuality, a comic perspective, and a general heartiness of manner and treatment. Implicit in such a novel is a benevolist philosophy which touches upon the sentimental novel. Incidentally, Graves began his novel in 1756 or 1757, so that its fifteen-odd years of composition straddle the entire development of the sentimental subgenre.

Cervantes, support of Cervantes, novels of one kind of excess or another.

Such diversity was not necessarily health. On the contrary, prose fiction was becoming faddish and facetious; excesses were becoming substantive. Sterne, the outstanding figure of this period, was not a "novelist," in that he had no developing career. He did one thing superbly, but he did only one thing; in that sense, he unknowingly helped contribute to the uncertainties of the genre in the second half of the century. We are not, incidentally, suggesting that the novel had to become anything in particular or lead to any predetermined conclusion. The period, however, is characterized by the single, broad success rather than by developing careers. There was a succession of hit-or-miss fiction. Horace Walpole, a Gothic novelist, did not have a continuing career in prose fiction. Mackenzie's *The Man of Feeling* is another good example, a novel published anonymously which did well without becoming part of a larger body of meaningful work. Thus, in a very special sense, Goldsmith's novel became an anchor amid diversity and uncertain change. Although leaning toward "sentimentality," *The Vicar of Wakefield* manages to slough off most excesses.

We should approach this novel in such a context: not as a work of intrinsic literary merit, but as one whose timing and general tone allow it to transcend its shortcomings. As a first-person narrative, with all events observed through the eyes of the Reverend Primrose, the novel has a connective link or sensibility it would not have had from a third-person narrator. While the method may appear to encourage excesses—of feeling and sentiment—in practice, it forces the novelist to moderate them to avoid jeopardizing the credibility of his protagonist. Since we know Goldsmith attacked Sterne for the latter's formlessness and salacious wit, we should expect *The Vicar of Wakefield* to diverge rather sharply from Sterne's novel. It does and it does not. As Cross points out, ". . . one is impressed more by real similarities than by surface differences." (*The Life and Times of Laurence Sterne*, p. 233)

Goldsmith's view, starting from sources such as *Pilgrim's Progress* and the Book of Job, is basically benevolist and ameliorist. Primrose steps rather lightly through a world of evil: his gains turning into losses (à la Job), his daughter seemingly lost to Thornhill (à la Richardson), his son George a victim of picaresque adventures. Nearly every novelistic strain passes through the novel, so that

Primrose, it would appear, must handle novelistic themes as much as he must handle life itself. Nevertheless, in an age of fads, transient movements, and superficial feelings, he remains steadfast, accepts providence, and never loses his benevolist attitudes.

Although cut from the same fabric as the other mild-mannered sentimental protagonists, Primrose is not so passive as they ordinarily are. He has married, fathered a family, adapted to numerous changes of fortune, shown considerable mobility, and tested out his philosophy against adversity. Unlike Harley, Mackenzie's "man of feeling," for example, Primrose is rarely merely an observer of his own fortunes. He participates actively, reacts to what he considers to be injustice, and fills out his space.

Once we have said this, we must note how Goldsmith uses sentiment or the sentient experience as the "connecting" link for all the episodes. While Primrose may be the first-person narrator, in actuality *he* is not so much the force for continuity as is a tone or attitude associated with the "sensibility" subgenre. Time and again, for example, when fortune has seemed, with the aid of God's wrath, to have turned completely against the Primrose family, the father offers faith, providence, benevolence as a way of meeting such adversity *personally.* In other words, he demonstrates, not how to grapple with changing phenomena, but how the individual must develop attitudes toward change. That is, through sentiment or feeling, one learns only how to *accept* adversity, not how to fight it.

This is the key distinction between the logistics of the sentimental novel and both the Gothic strain paralleling it and the realistic strain antedating it in Fielding and Richardson. Much of the passivity implicit in the viewpoint of the sentimentalists can be attributed to an acceptance of what is. It is truly a counter-reaction to Gothic and realistic conflicts, which are based on attempts to overcome what is. For the sentimental author, decisions are not attuned to the realities of one's situation but to the realities that prepare one for the afterlife.

Perhaps critics of the novel have failed to stress sufficiently the characteristic male protagonist of the fiction of sensibility. Mackenzie's Harley is not at all atypical. Essentially, a man such as Harley has substituted good feeling and benevolence for any sexual activity; analogously, Walter and Toby Shandy—part of that low-sexed Shandy heritage—have either turned sex into a game or else eschewed it altogether. Harley's relationship with Miss Walton is a good example of a diffidence that appears to result from impotence. Although Harley is perceived as one who feels rather than does, nevertheless his relationship to Miss Walton is fraught with unintentional defensive gestures.

Incapable of marrying her, he is almost literally killed by the sight of her. His already weakened heart fails him when Miss Walton appears. Mackenzie may present such a scene as an excess of feeling on Harley's part—he feels too much for his heart to bear the overload—but that effect could result as much from the low-voltage circuitry of his heart as from his high-voltage passion. James's Marcher, in "The Beast in the Jungle," has lived as an observer and dies still trying to hold on to life vicariously. Harley is in the same mold: full of sentiment, but essentially fearful of emotions.

In this respect, Harley is part of that weakly sexed male world that serves the same function in the sentimental novel that the Italianate, highly sexed male serves in the Gothic novel. Put another way, we can say that Lovelace in *Clarissa* spawned two character types: the sadistic, overbearing symbols of maleness we find in Gothic fiction, and the anti-Lovelace type represented by Harley, who substitutes feeling for doing. For such men, a woman is idealized, worshipped from a distance, and rarely, if ever, touched. Like Miss Atkins or Miss Walton, she is either a whore or a madonna, sometimes both. And like the type she represents, she has no life outside of the role the worshipping male has given her. The fear of sex, here, is equivalent to the excess of it in the Gothic frame of reference. Frequently, sex in the sentimental novel is based on whimsical observation, a kind of gentle voyeurism, unlike Ambrosio's fierce, masturbatory voyeurism.

Inset into *The Man of Feeling* is a short chapter called "The Pupil: A Fragment." In keeping with the "scattered" quality of the material, it is unconnected to the main narrative. In itself a trifle, it contains the two main strains we have observed: the Italian Count Respino, who has a "criminal passion" for a married woman, and the charitable benefactor, who eschews sex in favor of good deeds. The chapter is inset as a joke in the *Tristram* tradition, since the parting shot is pure Sterne, turning solemnity into farce by asking the Italian, " 'Do you eat macaroni—' "

What can we make of this strain of mild-mannered, inactive, really passive males who populate an entire subgenre: the Shandy brothers, Harley, Primrose, Yorick of *A Sentimental Journey*, Smollett's Greaves, Graves's Wildgoose? Can we settle for this as a literary convention and nothing more—a radical reaction to the raping, ravishing, rampaging male of the Lovelace type? Or is there, perhaps, another reason for their appearance, a reason attached to the gradual shaping of eighteenth-century society from one of openness and roughness to one of a more genteel type associated with the later novel of manners? Fanny Burney's *Evelina* (1778) is the next step in that evolution: the rejection of Gothic, the transformation of sentimental types, and the introduction of the mild, dignified, but virile protagonist who operates best in a drawing room. In brief, we are involved in another of those alternate styles pushing out against the period, beginning to establish still another mode, even while the mainstream and its tributaries appear to be something else.

Harley goes through life, like the Don, untouched by its baseness and ingratitude. His philosophy, however, is not the Don's, that is, not founded on transformation of baseness into gold, but on a Candide-like belief in this as the best of all possible worlds. At the conclusion of a tale of stress, his advice is: " 'Let me entreat you, sir,' " he says, to " 'hope better things. The world is ever tyrannical; it warps our sorrows to edge them with keener affliction. Let us not be slaves to the names it affixes to motive or to action. I know an ingenuous mind cannot help feeling when they sting. But there are considerations by which it may be overcome. Its fantastic ideas vanish as they rise; they teach us to look beyond it.' " (Norton edition, p. 51)

While such advice may lead to peace of mind, it could have killed the novel. The close reader may note that the "pure" sentimental novel is virtually a throwback to allegory, away from the kinds of conflict and decision-making which have marked the advent of the novel and which are necessary for the support of a lengthy narrative.

Henry Brooke's *The Fool of Quality* (1766–72) is another excellent example of the pure sentimental novel. Rambling, digressive, virtually unreadable nowadays, it is constructed like a snowball accumulating bits of moss and weeds and twigs as it lurches its way down an embankment. As shapeless as Thomas Amory's *The Life and Opinions of John Buncle* (1756, 1766), which it superficially resembles, it has little of the involuted narrative of *Tristram Shandy*, which it also superficially resembles. However unreadable it is now, the novel played on many tender chords, resisted an early death, and extended its influence into the Victorian era, becoming the favorite novel of Charles Kingsley. That may say a good deal about it.

In its tedious way, it plowed new ground, even while remaining at the center of the sentimental fad. Despite its heroic Christianity, the book touched on important matters. It anticipated Disraeli's "two nations," it argued for innate virtue, and it helped undermine a view of England based on privilege. It demonstrated the injustice of the upper classes and the impotence of the lower because of poverty. It became part of that wave of protest, faint and otherwise, which ran parallel to many of the ideals embodied in the French Revolution.

The novel has the basic structure of the apprenticeship-to-life, birth-of-a-hero type, the *Bildungsroman*, with bits and pieces from *Tom Jones*, *Roderick Random*, *Tristram Shandy* in the background; but the narrative of his life is not so much of deeds as it is of good deeds. The young hero, Henry Moreland, second son of the Earl of Moreland, is Christian making his pilgrimage through life, scattering his money wherever it is needed. Henry or Harry is a robust combination of Tom Jones and Don Quixote, without the sensual nature of the former and the overindulgent romanticism of the latter.

Using Harry's fortunes as his basic thread, Brooke weaves many tales, eleven major ones, which appear at regular intervals, as well as innumerable minor stories, which occur whenever a new character appears. The import of these tales in the picaresque style is to stress the emotional life. The stories—usually of woe and Job-like misfortune—are accompanied by weeping, breakdown, and suffering, all of which are verbalized at great length. In most instances, such intense suffering brings about a certain spiritual awareness, which then gives way to a monetary resolution. One can see why the novel remained popular in Victoria's day.

A recurring element in the main and subsidiary tales is man's Christian pilgrimage from original sin to salvation. Brooke's didactic purpose was to combine the idea of the Christian hero with a Rousseauistic educational process. Early in the novel, Mr. Fenton, Harry's mentor and beneficiary, lectures Vindex, a typically brutal schoolmaster, on his pedagogical duties: "When you, Mr. Vindex, iniquitously took upon you to chastise my most noble and most incomparable boy, you first whipped him for his gallant and generous avowal of the truth; and next, you barbarously flayed him because he refused to betray those who had confided in his integrity." (Routledge Library of Early Novelists, p. 67) The book's stress, like that of *Tom Jones*, is upon Harry's natural or innate qualities: truth, refusal to betray others, generosity of spirit.

Later, Mr. Fenton, in one of many lectures to the growing boy, informs him that "every man has a right in his person and property; and that his right is natural, inheritable, and indefeasible. No consent of parties, no institution, can make any change in this great and fundamental law of right; it is universal, invariable, and inalienable, to any man or system of men." (p. 264) This is English Rousseauism: yeomanry, Lockean inalienable rights, and Rousseau's belief in innate virtue, all intermixed to convey the kind of heroic Christian socialism we have associated with Charles Kingsley.[11]

After we have observed the generous and charitable nature of Harry and leave him as a young man ready to set out to reform an iniquitous world, we note that the novel's purpose is not only to chart Harry's fortunes but to inculcate a way of seeing. Brooke wishes to subsume intellect, religion, guidance, wisdom itself under the aegis of the individual's emotional reaction. If the individual can cry, emote, react without restraint, he has opened himself to God. Put another way, if he is unable to feel strongly, he is unable to receive divine grace. This is a position diametrically opposite to that taken in Gothic, where to feel too strongly is to open oneself to the temptations of Satan.

Many of these fictions, including *The Fool of Quality*, *The Man of Feeling*, Sterne's *A Sentimental Journey*, appear to form a subgenre of their own. The first two, which we have characterized as novels, are really novels only because they do not fit easily into any other category. Their conflicts, as we suggested above, are of little validity, since tension is established to reach a preresolved moral point, which is the real focus of the narrative. They are closer to allegory, for the essential element is not the fictional quality, however we may define that, but the moral lesson. In the 1780's, such fiction proliferated among the later contemporaries of Brooke and Mackenzie, until the subgenre exhausted its limited possibilities. By the time of Jane

[11] For the masochistic reader, there is a wealth of fiction in the Brooke tradition, perhaps the best known being Thomas Day's *History of Sandford and Merton* (3 vols., 1783, 1786, 1789), which is a loose combination of Rousseau's *Emile*, *Don Quixote*, and Brooke's *Fool of Quality*. In line with the last, he focuses on the conflict between two boys, including one educated along Rousseauistic "natural" lines. The rivalry, roughly paralleling that of *The Fool of Quality*, pits a rich against a poor boy, with a background of tears, emotional scenes, and moralizing. The rich boy learns from the poor one what innate virtue means, and the novel "resolves" on moral grounds the economic divisions separating the "two nations."

Austen's *Sense and Sensibility* (begun in 1797), the novel of sentiment had run its course, and its emotiveness, its excesses of feeling, its stress upon the natural passed into Gothic, which made use of these qualities in its own obsessive way.

Although not a "sentimental" novel in any strict sense, *Evelina* serves as an excellent bridge between sentimental fiction and the later novel of manners in that relatively undefined period of the 1770's and 1780's. Published anonymously in 1778, it drew on several earlier strains in the novel while managing to reject the excesses of some and modify others. Early in her preface, Fanny Burney (Madame d'Arblay) cited a number of writers, most of them novelists, who had saved the novel from revilement:

> Yet, while in the annals of those few of our predecessors, to whom this species of writing is indebted for being saved from contempt and rescued from depravity, we can trace such names as Rousseau [*Eloïse*], Johnson [*Rasselas*], Marivaux, Fielding, Richardson, and Smollett, no man need blush at starting from the same post, though many, nay most men, may sigh at finding themselves distanced.

Lest her own goals seem inflated—she was only twenty-six at the time of publication—she cites her unpretentious aim:

> To draw characters from nature, though not from life, and to mark the manners of the times, is the attempted plan of the following letters . . .
>
> Let me, therefore, prepare for disappointment those who, in the perusal of these sheets, entertain the gentle expectation of being transported to the fantastic regions of Romance, where Fiction is coloured by all the gay tints of luxurious Imagination, where Reason is an outcast, and where the sublimity of the Marvellous, rejects all aid from sober Probability. The heroine of these memoirs, young, artless, and inexperienced, is
>
> No faultless Monster, that the world ne'er saw,
>
> but the offspring of Nature, and of Nature in her simplest attire.

Yet, while rejecting Gothic and other romantic excesses, Fanny Burney helped create another kind of romance, that based on probability within improbable events. Her subject is ostensibly "A Young Lady's Entrance into the World" (the subtitle), but, in actuality, she eschews that realism in favor of the "romantic" potential that accrues from Evelina's situation. If we think of what Evelina is, and of what her fortunes involve, we can understand that

Fanny Burney was not winnowing out previous strains in the novel but consolidating them under a different aegis.[12]

She accepts, unquestioningly, the benevolist view of the individual and society; in this respect she is quite solidly within sentimentalist orthodoxy. At the same time, she has tried to preserve the epistolary form of Richardson, with some carryover of Clarissa's trapped situation, mild though her application may be. Her employment of the epistolary style, however, gains her little or no psychological detail. It differs only superficially from a third-person narration, since the letters are employed to carry the weight of the plotting, not to provide insights into character or to create dramatic tension. In this respect, she is a throwback to the Richardsonian tradition rather than to Richardson.

In other respects as well, we note Miss Burney's use of older novelistic traditions even while she recognizes they are no longer fully viable. Fitting herself into Fielding's benevolism, she blunts most of his antisocial drive, transforming his love of the natural into a drawing-room atmosphere, yet all the while reviling high society as corrupt and decadent. To a limited extent, she gives us Fielding's world through a woman's eyes, but the angle of vision is more limited and less lively than Fielding's. As a male protagonist, Tom Jones had a mobility and range denied to a seventeen-year-old young lady, particularly one as fastidious as Evelina. Even with his mobility, however, Evelina, thirty years later, would appear to move in

[12] Although the didactic spirit is only implicit in *Evelina*—particularly in her heroine's display of virtue victorious over vice—Fanny Burney's later fiction explicitly manifested the didacticism of near-allegory. In *Cecilia, or The Memoirs of an Heiress* (1782) and *Camilla, or A Picture of Youth* (1796), for example, her characters become stereotypical, her situations fixed, her intentions to edify. An initiator in the movement toward didacticism, she was also swept away by it.

We should stress that of the generation of female novelists that included Fanny Burney—Clara Reeve, Ann Radcliffe, Charlotte Smith (especially in *The Old Manor House*, 1793), Elizabeth Inchbald, Sophia Lee (*The Recess*, 1785), and numerous others—nearly all attempted to define certain ground in the novel that would distinguish them from the male novelists. Briefly, they derived from Richardson, possibly more from *Sir Charles Grandison* than from *Clarissa*; they utilized the epistolary technique, although sparingly and simplistically; they found in Gothic a way of presenting women and their problems sympathetically, not as the "victims" found in "male Gothic"; they explored the Don Quixote character as a way of softening the arrogance of the male; and they moved the novel from the outdoors into the drawing room, from the open road toward the marriage bed and family. They were, in all, a great force for realism. (For a survey of this material, see "The Female Novelists," *The Popular Novel in England 1770–1800* by J. M. S. Tompkins, pp. 116–71; and *Frail Vessels: Woman's Role in Women's Novels from Fanny Burney to George Eliot* by Hazel Mews, especially pages 9–41.)

another world. Miss Burney pays only lip service to nature and the natural. Her real aim, unlike Fielding's, is not to vaunt rural life at the expense of London "civilization," but to demonstrate that London for all its corruption and foppishness is capable of being natural. Discreet and without artifice, Lord Orville has himself been untouched by the socially artificial life he has led; again, the contrast with Tom, who becomes a reflection of his environment, is apparent.

Only in Captain Mirvan do we find some of the raucousness of Squire Western or of Smollett's characters. Involved, further, is a good deal of social commentary, for the captain reacts whenever he senses artificiality, even if in a so-called gentleman or lady. Capping the social theme is the monkey episode he arranges for Mr. Lovel, a particularly foppish and false character. Making a monkey out of Lovel may reveal Mirvan's vulgarity, but at the same time it establishes his basic democratic spirit, however socially offensive the form of it may take. His raillery at Madame Duval's expense, while not approved by the author, does provide balance for the madame's own pretensions. Mirvan is one part of that "new world" that Bramble in *Humphry Clinker* detested and feared. The mocking captain, with typical picaresque bite, marks the contempt large elements of English society, on the virtual eve of the French Revolution, held for the upper classes; and the freedom they felt they had to abuse those who had the advantage of birth. Such matters, however, are only part of the whole, and we must seek elsewhere for the real spirit of the novel.

Its real quality, as we have already suggested, lies in Burney's ability to draw on past strains of the novel. Her utilization of the "unknown birth" theme, for instance, is a clear carry-over from Fielding and Smollett, among others. Her variations, however, carry her somewhat past previous authors. When Tom Jones discovers his background, it is to work out the final piece in the puzzle, not to establish any further point about him or his fortunes. The discovery makes him a well-born, rather than a low-born, bastard, and that marks him as eligible for Sophia Western. When Evelina's real birth is recognized, she enters into a fairy-tale setting, for she is not only well-born but high-born, the daughter of a wealthy lord. Marginally, we experience the discovery of a brother, Macartney, as well. Her background, moreover, is a tangle of intrigue—an incorrectly recognized daughter, the dispossession of the rightful heiress, and so on—what we ordinarily associate with a Dickensian rather than an eighteenth-century plot. In these and related matters, Fanny Burney has drawn on rough-and-ready past usage and carried such elements into fairy tale, Freudian "family romance," domestic and drawing-room situations.

Similarly, we have noted her indebtedness to Richardson. In her application of Sir Willoughby's forged letter, she is using a Richardsonian technique. Willoughby's forgery, however, is a refinement of Lovelace's, since his purpose is to forge a vulgar letter from Orville so as to turn Evelina against the latter. But once again the device is not intrinsic, although it does lead into the kind of plot complication that looks ahead to Elizabeth Bennet and Darcy, when Elizabeth is deceived by the language and tone of Darcy.

In a more subtle Richardsonian way than the above, however, Fanny Burney has conceived of a girl whose destiny is to be "completed" not by herself but by the men in her circle. Like Clarissa, she is surrounded by men—father, brother, uncle, suitors. For Evelina, fortunately, the males are complaisant, although, in the Richardson manner, she must come to terms with father, brother, and suitor, not with mother, sister, or girl friend.

When we turn to Evelina herself, the seventeen-year-old heroine, we are disappointed both by her derivativeness and placidity. Despite Burney's light hand with the didactic-allegorical element, Evelina is still close to a symbol of virtue at bay, waiting for St. George to rescue her from the social dragons. We find in Evelina almost no ability to define herself, and, possibly, at seventeen and at the mercy of a predatory society, she has had little opportunity. She exists, not for any goal of her own, but to be worthy of the man she loves, Orville. Her life is defined, then, not by any end or goal that derives positively from herself, but by her ability to fit into the right niche. None of this would in itself be unusual, since the female novelists of the period took their values and judgments of themselves from the society at large, except that Fanny Burney was herself evidently dissatisfied with this resolution of female conflict.

As Hazel Mews points out, in her final novel (*The Wanderer*, 1814) Fanny Burney demonstrated considerable conflict as to female roles and attempted much more diversity in the woman's world, offering possibilities hardly hinted at in *Evelina*. Evelina, to repeat, is not upset by her role; she is only disturbed by the chance that she may not be able to fulfill it. By the time of *The Wanderer*, even the subtitle (*or Female Difficulties*) indicates some disruption in the domestic resolutions offered in the earlier novel. By 1814, while a deus ex machina in the form of acknowledgment of family and rank provides a solution for the upper-echelon female, the questions remain unanswered for the lower-class woman who has neither family nor rank with whom to identify.

Evelina, however, has minimized these questions of female role and goal. The area in which Fanny Burney has resolved her material clearly is in her movement of a young lady, already uncertain of class and background, into a social arena populated by diversified types: domesticated picaresque, as it were. In so doing, she caught themes and tones that link her with the great novelists before her and Jane Austen shortly after. The Reverend Mr. Villars is a pillar of respectability; he looks back to Squire Allworthy, on whom he is apparently modeled, and ahead to the somewhat astringent Mr. Knightley, of *Emma*. He is incapable of change or variety; he simply exists as the norm. Around him, however, revolve all those who represent temptation, instability, or power. The Branghtons, for example, reflect the vulgar middle-class values of the new era, a family outside of either good breeding or considerate behavior. Lacking high sense but full of their own pretentiousness, they turn everyone into objects for their consumption and fail to make the human distinctions necessary for civilized relationships.

If the Branghtons represent the new element, then Willoughby, Lovel, Smith, and Madame Duval reflect the excesses of established classes. While variations exist in their stations and roles, they are all, nevertheless, moral failures. Since they proceed without any sense of their larger role, they have no sense of their effect upon others. Having given up the moral reins of responsibility, in Burney's eyes, they will eventually be displaced by the Branghtons and those like them, while Orville and Evelina strive to preserve the status quo represented by Villars. We are well into Jane Austen's world.

Although Evelina herself lacks variability and the potentiality for change, she nevertheless moves through a society full of threats and alternate possibilities. Even so, Fanny Burney has extracted her heroine's situation from its background. There is almost no awareness of the larger society, of politics, history, even England in the midst of a struggle with one of its colonies (America) or fighting an intermittent war with one of its oldest foes (France). The characters themselves, as in the novels of Austen and James, must bear the entire weight. And while Evelina is incapable of working out more than her own slender destiny, the other characters move readily through social roles that help define a diverse, predatory society and, in turn, suggest a new stage in the development of the novel.

In this decade of *Evelina*, from 1770 to 1780, fiction moved forward in four major areas: Gothic, which was yet to peak; the sentimental trend, which was almost exhausted by the end of the decade; the "Don Quixote" theme, which had nearly run its course; and Fanny Burney's domestic comedy, which foreshadowed a major thrust in the genre. Picaresque had been almost completely absorbed into other subgenres. The two major novelists hovering in the future, Scott and Jane Austen, were to pick up the threads of these elements, for a period of retrenchment and stabilization. With *Northanger Abbey* (drafted in the late 1790's), Jane Austen would re-establish the main lines of the novel, away from excesses toward the probabilities of domestic realism.

7

Gothic, Gothicism, and Gothicists

In every literary epoch, as in every period of history, there appears to be a dominant tone or motif: Spenserianism in the late sixteenth and early seventeenth century, Augustanism or neoclassicalism in the eighteenth, Victorianism in the nineteenth. This dominant tone is often the quality that gives the name to the period, even though running parallel and counter to the leading element are adversary forces, tones, motifs themselves developing toward dominance. None of this development is linear, and frequently the emerging force is disguised. Like the manifest quality of a dream, the still-unformed motif or idea is often seemingly irrational, counterproductive, buried in its own growth materials, fragile, and concealed to all but the creative eye.

The essential quality of such a force or idea is its counterthrust to what appears to be the dominant culture. Such forces are revolutionary in a true sense. They aim at overthrow, and they have the same savage need at their heart that the son has in his desire to overthrow the father. In political terms, these countermovements are forms of assassination; in social terms, they are a new order of thought, style, and tone. In the eighteenth century, Gothic is a rubric for many kinds of forces that were gathering together to chip away at the Augustan ideal. Not surprisingly, in many Gothic tales, fathers and sons are, often literally, at each other's throats.

We must recognize that philosophical, social, and literary forces are disparate and discrete. They appear to coalesce only in retrospect, and we can justify their existence only if we tentatively accept the notion of a *Zeitgeist* (or spirit of a time). A *Zeitgeist* is a complex, broadly disputed idea not to be used carelessly, but if we understand it as something constantly embodying conflict, we can accept its usage. That is, the *Zeitgeist* is different for every moment in history, obviously, but what is constant about it is the sense of confrontation of forces it involves.

In the eighteenth century, the dominant *Zeitgeist* would appear to have been that engendered in the first two thirds of the century by its arbiters of taste, morality, and general culture: Pope, Swift, Johnson, the *Spectator*, and those who accepted their Tory vision of England. A more nearly valid view of the *Zeitgeist*, however, would recognize that antithetical elements were already eating into that vision. The age was, in fact, one of a balancing of those elements which appeared dominant and those which lay concealed.[1]

Among the hidden forces were those that eventually surfaced in the Gothic novel. It would be simplistic to think that the Gothic novel sprang ready-made from Horace Walpole (*The Castle of Otranto*, 1764) or even from Smollett's earlier *Ferdinand Count Fathom* (1753); or to believe it manifested uniform qualities. Prior to and contemporaneous with these works was a considerable body of literature that had Gothic overtones:

[1] From Walter Jackson Bate's comments in *From Classic to Romantic*, we can see such elements hidden in eighteenth-century philosophy and aesthetics. While empiricism appeared at first to reinforce Augustan rationalism, it was at the same time preparing the foundation for quite an opposing philosophy and aesthetic. Bate writes:

> A previous chapter mentioned the extent to which British experimental empiricism, in its earlier stages, joined with and helped to augment the anti-emotional and anti-imaginative bias of extreme neo-classic rationalism generally. Yet its direction is almost diametrically opposed to that of classicism: to the empiricist, knowledge comes wholly from sensation, or from reflection upon that sensation; insofar as we actually reason at all, therefore, "we reason," said Locke, "about particulars"; and for insight into the objectively general, empiricism substitutes the mere term "generalization," with its connotation of a subjective act of mind. In its opposition to the universal, and in its emphasis upon sensory and experiential proof, it is also essentially anti-rationalistic . . .
>
> The aesthetic and critical reverberations of these tendencies of British empiricism become pronounced and then extend widely throughout western Europe by the latter half of the eighteenth century; and, in doing so, they form the groundwork for the somewhat heterogeneous body of assumptions, inclinations, and values which is called romanticism. For European romanticism, as it emerged historically, may perhaps be most generally defined as a turning away, in whatever direction, from the classical standard of ideal nature, and from the accompanying conviction that the full exercise of ethical reason may grasp that objective ideal. [pp. 93–4]

The supernatural element of the ballad
The primitive, primeval quality of the epic
The extravagance and violence of Elizabethan drama (then being revived)
The wildness of pagan Europe caught in Ossian (1760–3) and slightly later in *Percy's Reliques* (1765)
The exoticism of Oriental and Near Eastern tales (Johnson's *Rasselas*, 1759; later, Beckford's *Vathek, An Arabian Tale*, 1786)
The excesses of the chivalric romances
The death-gloom of graveyard poetry (Young's "Night Thoughts," 1742; Blair's "The Grave," 1743; Gray's "Elegy Written in a Country Churchyard," 1751; and their forerunner, Thomas Parnell's "Night-Piece on Death," 1722)
The influence of Rousseau in terms of the natural, the primitive, the irrational
The stress on the sublime—primitive, sensuous, anti- and non-intellectual, playing on awe, ecstasy, and disorder
The rise of Methodism, chiefly the antiestablishmentarianism of the Wesleys, and the more elemental character of its form of worship as compared with that of the Church of England
The admiration for frenzied and disordered nature—part of the stress on the sublime
The Rousseauistic heritage, manifest, among other places, in the planned irregularities of the English garden

All these forces and interests operated as emotional counters to the main tradition of the realistic novel in Fielding, Richardson, and Smollett, even though Smollett's own *Count Fathom* furnished something of a link between realism and Gothic; and Richardson himself, as we have noted, suggested the darkness, gloom, and terror peculiar to the Gothic form in *Clarissa*. As the novel in its realistic forms was something of a revolution in eighteenth-century cultural terms, so Gothic was a further refinement of that counter or alternate motif, undermining the realistic novel even as the latter was subverting a more traditional sense of literature. Accordingly, to locate the *Zeitgeist* in 1750–60, when Gothic was shaping itself, we must find it in antitheses: between the development of the novel and the exhaustion of traditional forms (epic, drama, satire, burlesque, et al.), and then, in turn, between the realistic novel and a subgenre based on extravagance, disorder, frenzy, and the irrational.

Gothic challenged the novel internally within twenty years of the firm establishment of the genre, which we can date in the 1740's. And lest we think that Gothic itself was uniform and constant, we can cite vast differences between Mrs. Radcliffe's "romantic" Gothic and the psychologically harrowing Gothic of Matthew Lewis and Charles Maturin; or between the fruity, exotic Gothic of a sensualist like Beckford and the more realistic, pre-Dickensian Gothic of social thinkers like William Godwin or Mary Shelley. Mrs. Radcliffe's genteel scenes of eerie but sedate fright contrast sharply with Lewis's and Maturin's sado-masochistic images of torture and brutality. In *The Gothic Flame* (1957), Devendra Varma, drawing on the work of Montague Summers (*The Gothic Quest*, 1938), distinguishes among several kinds of Gothic.[2] Although his distinctions tend to oversimplify the development of Gothic, Varma's outline is nevertheless useful for its demonstration of the major points of movement, if we recognize that they are not necessarily chronological or progressive developments:

The main stream of Gothic Romance which issued from Walpole's *Otranto* diverged into three parallel channels: first, the Gothic-Historical type developed by Clara Reeve and the Lee sisters [especially Sophia Lee's *The Recess*], finally culminating in the Waverley Novels of Sir Walter Scott, where historic supernatural agents disport themselves against an authentic background of chivalrous pageantry; secondly, the School of Terror initiated by Mrs. Radcliffe and maintained by a host of imitators, perhaps the most extensive Gothic type in which superstitious dread is aroused by constant, dim suggestions of the supernatural—as constantly explained away; and lastly, the works of the Schauer-Romantiks [Lewis, Maturin] or the School of Horror, distinguished by lurid violence and crudity. Walpole adumbrated the machinery and characters of a Gothic story; Miss Reeve designed the characteristic Gothic ghost in an English setting; while Mrs. Radcliffe spread over all the warm colours of her romantic imagination. The later Schauer-Romantik writers were less concerned with atmosphere and suggestion than the bold machinery of animated corpses. Eventually the two Gothic streams of "terror" and "horror" met in the genius of Charles Robert Maturin. [p. 206]

[2] Summers locates the word itself: "The word 'Gothic,' which was to play so important a part in later days, and which now has so very definite and particular a meaning (especially in relation to literature) originally conveyed the idea of barbarous, tramontane and antique, and was merely a term of reproach and contempt. From its application to architecture—and Gothic building, as we shall see, was long enough held in very low esteem—it came to connote almost anything medieval, and could be referred to almost any period until the middle, or even the end, of the seventeenth century." (p. 37)

The one theme that cuts through virtually all Gothic is that of the "outsider," embodied in wanderers like Frankenstein's monster and Maturin's Melmoth, monks such as Lewis's Ambrosio and Mrs. Radcliffe's Schedoni, and so on. The outsider, like Cain, moves along the edges of society, in caves, on lonely seacoasts, or in monasteries and convents. While the society at large always appears bourgeois in its culture and morality, the Gothic outsider—like the earlier picaro—is a counterforce driven by strange longings and destructive needs. While everyone else appears sane, he is insane; while everyone else appears bound by legalities, he is, like Laocoön, trying to snap the pitiless constrictions of the law; while everyone else seems to lack any peculiarities of taste or behavior, he feels only estrangement, sick longings, terrible surges of power and devastation. He is truly countercultural, an alternate force, almost mythical in his embodiment of the burdens and sins of society.

Even after the main body of Gothic was dissipated, this sort of outsider remained as a type, turning up in various guises in Dickens, the Brontës, Poe, Hawthorne, Dostoevsky, Stevenson, Collins, Greene, Faulkner. He runs the gamut from tortured iconoclast to pure criminal, from saintly psychopath to vicious murderer, from overburdened penitent to an uncontrollable schizophrenic, from a sacrificial Isaac to a son intent upon parricide. In his subsequent development, as in his origin, the Gothic outsider is very much a commentary on everything the Augustan Age ostensibly represented.

The essential line of development of Gothic is psychological; and we note that in its short, almost orgasmic spurt of fifty to sixty years, it suggested the main arc of development of the novel itself. The point toward which the nineteenth-century novel was striving appears, in hindsight, to be a psychological interpretation of realistic events, comparable to the rather vague goal of Gothic. By fits and starts, Gothic was moving from the supernatural as part of a romantic view of phenomena to the supernatural as part of the mind's surrealism, the mind's sub- and unconscious. If our checkpoints are Lewis, Mary Shelley, and Maturin, we must conclude that Gothic reached both its fruition and its demise at the moment it attained the psychological; at that point, other forms of fiction could assimilate it, mainly Dickens's and the Brontës' novels, which clearly strove toward ends beyond realism.

Before we plunge into Walpole, Mrs. Radcliffe, Lewis, Godwin, Maturin, and Mary Shelley, however, it may prove instructive to see how the subgenre of Gothic was to be plowed under even as it flowered in the 1790's. Jane Austen's *Northanger Abbey* signaled the end.

Northanger Abbey burlesques contemporary fiction in much the same way that Cervantes's *Don Quixote* and Charlotte Lennox's *The Female Quixote* mocked contemporary romances. While Austen's achievement is youthful and slight contrasted with Cervantes's, it nevertheless falls within the same genre of parodic literature. Catherine Morland, consumed by fantasies with analogies to both novels of terror and novels of sensibility, must be disabused of her visions and dreams. Conceived as an anti-heroine—at first, thin, awkward, with a sallow complexion, lank hair, strong features—she has a mind as confused as her appearance is lackluster. Even in her confusion, however, we observe Catherine as a forerunner of later Austen heroines, and we recognize that the literary elements—the burlesque, parody, mock-heroic—are grafted onto a light romance. The connection with Cervantes is, at that point, completely severed.

Northanger Abbey is not simply a run-through and parody of the "horrid books" mentioned in chapter VI, centering on Mrs. Radcliffe's *The Mysteries of Udolpho*, but a critique of and commentary upon nearly all popular fiction of the later eighteenth century. In that respect, it is a catalogue novel, taking up at one point Fanny Burney's work, then Richardson's, especially his tepid and soporific *Sir Charles Grandison*, followed by *Tom Jones*, Lewis's *The Monk*, and so on.

Gothic bears the chief burden of Catherine's fantasies, and it is Gothic she must personally efface before she goes from anti-heroine to heroine. Once she comes out of the "dark" of Gothic, her own appearance comes out of the dark and she becomes an attractive young lady. Even while stressing burlesqued elements, we should never lose sight of this side of Catherine, that is, the sobriety beneath the fantasies. She may confuse Blaize Castle with Udolpho, a laundry bill with a lost manuscript, and General Tilney himself with the Montoni of Mrs. Radcliffe's novel; but she is essentially a forerunner of the more sober Elizabeth Bennet, Fanny Price, and Emma. If we doubt that, we need only contrast her with Isabella and John Thorpe. The latter, themselves foreshadowings of the urbane Crawfords of *Mansfield Park*, are typical "contrast" people, characters against whom one measures the better qualities of the hero and heroine. Keeping them in mind, we can see Catherine's sobriety beneath her frivolity; in matters that really count—and Gothic visions evidently do not—she makes sharp social distinctions, is well behaved, and measures herself correctly.

What concerns us here, however, is how the countermovement to Gothic is already in full operation in Jane Austen's youthful novel (generally attributed to 1797–8, readied for publication in 1803), *at a time* when Gothic was reaching its apotheosis with Mrs. Radcliffe, Matthew Lewis, Charlotte Smith (*The Old Manor House*), William Godwin's *Caleb Williams*, and all their following. We should also remember that Gothic at this stage had developed from Walpole's "pure" form and from the novel of sensibility as well; so that Jane Austen's counternovel is moving against an entire wave of fiction dominant in the 1780's and 1790's, to be joined later by Scott's own interpretation of "regional Gothic."

Without stretching a point, we can see in Catherine Morland's transformation not only a miniature of Jane Austen's own career but a microcosm of fictional change as it was going to occur during the early nineteenth century. Catherine moves from an excess of feeling, derived from the Gothic and sentimental novel, with both genres carried to their logical extremes, to a sober young lady, suitable, ultimately, to be General Tilney's daughter-in-law. With that, fiction has found a new basis for development, even as Gothic has reached its most intense moments.

Although we have charted the rise and fall of Gothic, we have yet to locate its chief practitioners. They are, as follows:

Horace Walpole—*The Castle of Otranto* (1764)
Mrs. Ann Radcliffe—*The Italian* (1797)
Matthew Lewis—*The Monk* (1796)
William Godwin—*Caleb Williams* (1794)
Mary Shelley—*Frankenstein* (1818)
Charles Maturin—*Melmoth the Wanderer* (1820)

Horace Walpole—The Castle of Otranto (*1764*)

So much of *The Castle of Otranto* seems nonsensical today that it is hard to believe it was taken seriously and still should be. Walpole, in his way, was a genius of the large and the outlandish, and we can say that with him a subgenre came into being. Although we must be careful not to make him the sole founder of Gothic,[3] we can agree with Varma that Walpole brought together the various elements that we now identify as typical: "the Gothic machinery, the atmosphere of gloom and terror, and stock romantic characters." (*The Gothic Flame*, p. 57)

Even more, Walpole had the supremely romantic turn of mind which demanded that the supernatural appear natural. In his preface to the first edition, he speaks of belief as relative to an age; so that "belief in every kind of prodigy was so established in those dark ages [ca. twelfth century] that an author would not be faithful to the manners of the times who would omit all mention of them." Walpole asks the reader to excuse "the air of the miraculous" and "allow the possibility of the facts." Thus, Walpole is very careful to turn the unusual into realistic detail. Through it all, he speaks of himself as no more than a translator of a manuscript found in the library of "an ancient Catholic family in the north of England," written at some undetermined time and printed at Naples in 1529. In this way, too, Walpole preserves realistic appearances, placing this bizarre undertaking within the mainstream of the eighteenth-century novel as an edited manuscript, a true history, a journal or series of letters, all authentic. We should stress this point lest Walpole's novel appear too much of an aberration in the eighteenth century. On the contrary, it is closer to the center than we are often led to suppose.

Walpole also associates his work with the drama, and we recall the revival of interest in Elizabethan drama. In his preface to the second edition, Walpole defends his method as a combination of low-comedy scenes and high tragedy based on no less authority than Shakespeare's own practice in *Hamlet* and *Julius Caesar.* And Sir Walter Scott, in his introduction to a later edition, speaks of Walpole's structuring as suitable to the modern novel, although we recognize his remarks as appropriate to the drama: "It was," Scott

[3] Montague Summers reminds us that the "tendencies of taste which culminated in the Gothic novel had origins wider and deeper than any one book, even *The Castle of Otranto*, could develop. The dominant elements in the terror novel of the 1790's, of which the most famous exemplar is *The Monk*, came from Germany; the historical romance, which we have just examined, accounts for much; the French influence of Baculard d'Arnaud and his 'drames monacles' [monastic] are of the first importance." (*The Gothic Quest*, p. 180) See also my comments on the "atmospherics" of Gothic, pp. 236–7.

wrote, "his object to unite the marvellous turn of incident, and imposing tone of chivalry, exhibited in the ancient romance, with that accurate exhibition of human character, and contrast of feelings and passions, which is, or ought to be, delineated in the modern novel."

Walpole's Gothic is, really, close to a special type of drama, what developed contemporaneously in Mozartian opera buffa and in later Italian opera. The contrasts of low comedy and high tragedy are the stock-in-trade of the operatic composer; and the machinery of Gothic that Walpole employed allowed necessary modulation from low to high to low. In fact, one of the oldest devices of both the early novel and of opera is the low-born young man—here Theodore—who turns out to be well-born, indeed princely. This is part of opera's "fabulous" heritage, and, curiously, one of the stock devices of the realistic novel—consider Tom Jones, Humphry Clinker, et al. Thus, within the protagonist himself, we find this characteristic movement between high and low.

The point warrants further exploration. Although the Gothic novel would appear by its trappings and major interests to be completely outside the realistic social frame of reference, there is, in fact, considerable overlap. And that overlap occurs in its modulation of movements from low to high and back again to low, or a comparable sequence, as embodied in a major character. The device is not, of course, new—it is part of the romance and fairy tale. But when it appears in the eighteenth-century novel, it becomes something else, the representative of an idea not yet ready for acceptance, but nevertheless ready for testing.

The ancient romance does become wedded to the modern novel in certain social assumptions. Theodore, for example, makes his mark as a "virtuous" young man while his social role is low; and though he turns out to be an aristocrat, the testing out of social roles indicates that innate virtue is as significant as birth. This is surely the conclusion of Fielding and Smollett, with Tom and Humphry, respectively, although as novelists they failed to resolve the social idea fully. Walpole is in this tradition, although his novel is not realistic; and it is precisely in this tradition that we find a good deal of Italian opera, as an amalgam of ancient romance and modern social ideas.

It is necessary to see Walpole, then, in the line of the eighteenth-century novel before proceeding to his deviations from it. In both his resemblance to the novel and his departures from it, he was moving toward alternate assumptions about man and his milieu, away from a settled, rational view toward other aspects of the human being which the romantics were to explore.[4] Likewise, the Methodist movement parallels the literary development of emotionalism, and the belief in redemption through faith finds its counterpart in certain Gothic trappings that Walpole helped to make famous.

First of these is the Gothic castle, whose atmosphere thins the line between supernatural and natural. The castle, if we wish to extend the analogy, provides a kind of religious experience based on awe, fear, and transcedence. Second are the climatic conditions, of storm, wind blasts, moonlight–all of which act as suitable background for the awesome castle. The climate creates sound for the castle's visual effects; we have here, really, the stage sets for Italian opera. Third in this swirl of events and effects is the melancholy young man who seems to carry a weight on his heart and shoulders–the Byronic hero of later years. He is, of course, perfectly suitable for the melancholy castle and weather, and his apotheosis as a figure of morbid gloom is Emily Brontë's Heathcliff. Once again, as in opera, the three elements of castle, weather, and moody, sullen protagonist are completely wedded, virtually indistinguishable, so that character, scene, and sound seem part of one single development. Such an

[4] It was this development that Clara Reeve had in mind in her preface to *The Old English Baron* (1780; originally published in 1777 as *The Champion of Virtue, a Gothic Tale* and dedicated to Richardson's daughter). A disciple of Richardson's novel of sensibility, she was worried about the excess of feeling in Walpole's novel: ". . . the machinery is so violent that it destroys the effect it is intended to excite. Had the story been kept within the utmost *verge* of probability the effect had been preserved, without losing the least circumstance that excites or detains the attention." She then speaks of the "limits of credibility," citing, for example, the sword and helmet as destroying the imagination because of their monstrosity. "I was both surprised and vexed to find the enchantment dissolved, which I wished might continue to the end of the book . . ." She gives her own plan, which is to combine Richardsonian sensibility with Gothic trappings which will never become excessive:

"In the course of my observations upon this singular book, it seemed to me that it was possible to compose a work upon the same plan, wherein these defects might be avoided; and the *keeping* [harmony among parts], as in *painting,* might be preserved."

In this way, she hoped to achieve her end of exciting the attention and directing it to some useful end; that is, to entertain and to instruct. However, as a counter to her realism, Varma observes, Miss Reeve makes extensive use of dream material. Dreams, as we shall see, became common in Gothic novels and often served to provide the fantasy side to novels that purported to be realistic. Further, the utilization of dream material helped the novelist explore the unknown, dark, fearful, subterranean, or "psychological" side of human behavior, all of which characterized the Gothic aspect of Gothicism.

achievement on a meaningful scale was, evidently, beyond Walpole's powers as a novelist, but it was clearly the aim of Gothic, as Scott's comments on the uniting of elements would appear to indicate.

If we view *The Castle of Otranto* as a vision of certain elements rather than as a novel in any traditional sense, we can gauge Walpole's achievement more effectively. As a novel, it is nonsense; as a vision (dream, nightmare, prophecy), it gains significance. Primarily, it is an observation of a life teeming with emotional crises denied in the contemporary literature of the period. It is a vision of omens, curses, extravagant stage sets (the helmet which crushes, the sword of monstrous size); a lustful, domineering father (Walpole's own was Fielding's model for Jonathan Wild) who goes well beyond the Harlowes; a devout, compliant, priest-ridden wife; a vision of doom, blood, terrified servants, apparitions, vengeance, and sadism. The novel suggests an imaginary, dreamlike state, one of ecstasy, in which the author stands "outside" normality and surveys the terrain of his own fantasies.[5]

There is, in this vision, something of the Sadean view of man. Manfred is the resident tyrant who uses his strong will to dominate men and his sexual power to overwhelm his weakling son, Conrad. (Cf. Heathcliff and *his* weakling son, whom he drives into an arranged, unconsummated marriage.) As a tyrant, Manfred is a man of violent extremes, a man who assumes that whatever he is, nature is also, a man whose libido is so strong it must manifest itself in every

[5] William Beckford's *Vathek* (written in 1782 in French, published, in English, 1786) fits loosely into this literature of vision and fantasy. Although *Vathek* in a few of its aspects recalls Johnson's *Rasselas*, it is, actually, a very different sort of thing—operatic in its way, certainly theatrical, a musical extravaganza directed by Busby Berkeley or Tom O'Horgan.

Beckford's Vathek is, to some extent, a thousand-and-one-nights version of Walpole's Manfred. Although Beckford appears to be satirizing Vathek's lust for power and his sensuality, the reader senses, behind the satire, a distinct feel for the exaggerated event, a sympathetic indulgence in sadistic acts and savage murder—the feeding of fifty innocent young men to the Giaour, for example. While such acts are purportedly part of the satirical exaggeration, they are described lovingly as elements of the author's own sexual fantasies.

Ostensibly, the tale is a moral one, pointing up the abuses of power; but the filigree work of the narrative focuses, instead, on the pleasures derived from such abuses. Never distant from sight or mind are the capricious tastes, the sexual content of the rich descriptions, the indifference to human life.

If we pull together the pieces, *Vathek* is a homoerotic fantasy, comparable in this respect to many aspects of *The Castle of Otranto*. Its chief victims are young men, its man of power (Vathek) is mother-ridden, its splendors are extravaganzas of design and indulgence.

situation. The cruelty of such a man is obvious if anyone attempts to interfere with his plans, needs, or lusts.

It is more than coincidence that Walpole's father figure, Manfred, should so closely resemble Fielding's interpretation of Sir Robert Walpole in *his* portrait of Jonathan Wild as a man of uncontrollable hands. Or that the son, Conrad, should be portrayed as a weakling, crushed under a helmet, while another, Theodore, eventually usurps the young man's role and marries his intended, Isabella. The vision is a fantasy of family life carried to its extravagant extremes, a medievalism that has little relationship to eighteenth-century reality but considerable connection to a view of family life by one who sits outside normality and can turn his personal vision into opera.

When Clara Reeve, Mrs. Radcliffe, and others rejected, in part at least, the extravagance of Walpole's tale and tried in their own work to be more realistic, they missed an essential factor: Walpole's entire scheme rested on the very aspect they rejected, on a vision or fantasy of his inner life posing as a medieval document. Summers quotes from a letter Walpole wrote to George Montagu: "Visions, you know, have always been my pasture; and so far from growing old enough to quarrel with their emptiness, I almost think there is no wisdom comparable to exchanging what is called the realities of life for dreams." (*The Gothic Quest*, p. 409). We also recall that Walpole claimed that *The Castle of Otranto* began with a dream. Writing to the Reverend William Cole, on February 28, 1765, he said: "Shall I even confess to you what was the origin of this romance? I waked one morning, in the beginning of last June, from a dream, of which all I could recover was, that I had thought myself in an ancient castle (a very natural dream for a head like mine filled with Gothic story) and that on the uppermost banister of a great staircase I saw a gigantic hand in armour. In the evening, I sat down, and began to write . . ."[6]

If we accept Walpole's romance as fantasy, then we are no longer troubled by extravagance and not worried about its purely novelistic qualities. While utilizing typical eighteenth-century devices also found in the realistic novel—the blending of social types, the use of the unknown young man who turns out to be well-born, the testing out of social roles, et al.—Walpole made his mark by his departure from the realistic novel then establishing itself. And he did so by

[6] Quoted by Summers in his introduction to *The Castle of Otranto*, 1924, pp. xxvi–vii.

moving from fiction based on a social vision to a fiction founded on a private vision, which is impervious to the usual criticism employed with novels. A fantasy life, and all its accouterments, is always true in its own terms, valid at every stage of its development; precisely as a schizophrenic's version of reality is *the* version, held on to tenaciously as *the* truth.

Thus, that strong, overwhelming father figure, Manfred, arranging everyone's destiny and then being brought down, indeed being unmanned by his signing his abdication from the principality, has significant psychological overtones. For when Manfred is forced from power, is made to take on "the habit of religion," the new prince is Theodore, a young man who has overthrown the father and gained power. The play of events suggests Freud's short essay "Family Romances" (1909), in which the child fantasizes about his background, sees himself as secretly allied to the aristocracy (born to a prince, etc.), and, through his dreams, hopes to replace his actual parents with others of different quality. Such a replacement, or an Oedipal variation thereon, occurs in Walpole's tale, all under the guise of a medieval document discovered by the teller. Even here, in the documentation, as in the substance of the tale itself, we have the elements of a fantasy life attempting to manipulate reality in order to further its own needs, in order to reinforce and implement its own vision: of a strong father brought down, despite a weakling son himself incapable of doing the deed.

Mrs. Ann Radcliffe—The Italian (*1797*)

By the time she published *The Italian*[7] in 1797, Mrs. Radcliffe had established her fame with *A Romance of the Forest* (1791) and *The Mysteries of Udolpho* (1794). While her two earlier books, *The Castles of Athlin and Dunbayne* (1789) and *A Sicilian Romance* (1790), did little to create her reputation, the two novels preceding *The Italian* made her the legitimate successor of Walpole and even gave her claim as the heiress of Richardson. It is generally agreed, however, that *The Italian* is her best work, and certainly it is for the modern reader who is attuned to the psychological implications of Gothic.

The purely Gothic element centers on the Italian Schedoni, whose conflict between irrational passion and ironlike outer control we find

[7] The full title is: *The Italian or the Confessional of the Black Penitents: A Romance.*

also in Lewis's monk, Ambrosio (*The Monk*, 1796), whose career fluctuates between severe self-denial and satanic indulgence. Ambrosio, however, is a more sexual creature than Schedoni, although the theme of repressed sex runs through both novels. Mrs. Radcliffe, more reticent, closer to bourgeois views of sex than the homosexual Lewis, tempered Schedoni's sensuality with a degree of conscience and compassion. Unlike Ambrosio's career, which spurts orgasmically, Schedoni's works by checks and balances. And Mrs. Radcliffe, besides, was much closer to the sentimental heritage of Richardson, whereas Lewis was interested in exploiting the satanic, sadistic elements implicit in Richardson's persecution of the innocent.[8]

About one quarter through *The Italian*, we have a good view of Mrs. Radcliffe's use of mixed Gothic and Richardsonian materials. Ellena, the maiden persecuted by the Marchesa di Vivaldi, has been secreted in a convent deep in the Abruzzi Apennines, but she is discovered by her admirer, the marchesa's son, Vincentio. Although the convent is fearsome (like Clarissa's home, it is full of destructive parental figures), it is a refuge of sorts from even worse dangers. When Vincentio appears, Ellena must choose between a hateful lair and the even worse possibility of running off with a potential Lovelace, who may toy with her affections. "It was true that Vivaldi had discovered her prison, but, if it were possible, that he could release her, she must consent to quit it with him; a step from which a mind so tremblingly jealous of propriety as hers, recoiled with alarm, though it would deliver her from captivity." (Oxford edition, p. 122)

The conflict is a real one, because at this stage Ellena is unaware that Vincentio is not a Lovelace. And there is the evident impropriety in her running off with a young man she barely knows. What saves Ellena, and at the same time weakens the novel, is Vincentio's innate decency, his purely romantic attachment to Ellena, and his lack of irrational passion. Vincentio is the opposite of Schedoni, who has, like Shakespeare's Claudius, used his position to poison his own brother and draw his sister-in-law into marriage. Mrs. Radcliffe's novel blunts the greater horrors of the Gothic genre and leads into Jane Austen's realistic romances. While Schedoni dominates much of the novel, which takes its title from him, nevertheless Mrs. Radcliffe is striving to transform Gothic romance

[8] See Mario Praz's "The Shadow of the Divine Marquis," *The Romantic Agony*, pp. 95–7.

into novel; that is, to transmute supernatural elements into the more reasonable, and practical, conflicts of the emerging novel.

One of her common devices is the use of chiasmus, a term usually applicable to poetry but one that can equally apply to a reversal of terms or fortunes in the novel when characters or elements appear to be crisscrossing. Through this device, which recurs repeatedly, Mrs. Radcliffe is clearly attempting to go beyond the supernatural, although that, too, is part of her fictional equipment. What Mrs. Radcliffe gains from the use of chiasmus is the conflict of elements, the reversal of needs, the irony between individual desire and external forces. In chapter V of Volume II, for example, a good deal turns on Ellena's refusal to marry Vivaldi until his family, dead set against the marriage, agrees to the union. Her refusal is very important, for without it all impediments are removed. Yet her desire to win the favor of the marchese and marchesa comes precisely at the time that the marchesa has resolved to have Ellena murdered (with Schedoni's active help) and dropped into the Adriatic. While such violence is surely not alien to Gothic, what is at stake here is the realistic plotting germane not to the romance but to the novel.

At another level, which merges Gothic romance with novelistic realism, Mrs. Radcliffe goes into great detail over Schedoni's plan to murder Ellena, as she rightfully should, since his scheme gives us our first full insight into his character. The plotting here, as elsewhere, employs chiasmus, several reversals of fortune which, in turn, are linked implicitly to social themes. Going ahead with his plans for the murder, Schedoni discovers, as he thinks, that Ellena is his own daughter and is appalled that he has almost done the bidding of the Marchesa di Vivaldi. This sets off a train of thought in which all the terms of his previous existence are upset, in which a compassion he has never before felt tempers his innate violence. Further, he recognizes that every step he had taken with the marchesa to advance his ambitions was retrograde; that by opposing the marriage of Vivaldi and Ellena, he was opposing a rise in his own fortunes, since Ellena's marriage would have meant an alliance between the families.

Suddenly the romance, with its overtones of Gothic murder, Richardsonian child "murder," and sadistic maidenly persecution—suddenly, all that is blown away and Schedoni thinks of social advancement. His mind becomes like Pip's, in *Great Expectations*, aware of his ambitions, alliances, furthering his career. And this severe, murderous, repressed priest begins to take on the shape of a young man on the make, afraid of an incorrect social move. Only, since this is Gothic, his moves are in dark places, on the shores of the Adriatic, in caverns and dungeons, where he is cowled in constant disguise, his dark motives hidden beneath centuries of repression. His motives, however, are socially oriented, and Mrs. Radcliffe, fully aware of reversals and how intrinsic they are to the novel, moves Schedoni out into the open.

This, of course, is not sufficient. Saved by Schedoni's "discovery," Ellena—now somewhat like Magwitch's daughter, Estella, in Dickens's novel—must move in the shadow of a father who reputedly poisoned his brother and married his sister-in-law, whom he later allegedly murdered. If that is her background, then what chance does she have of ever gaining the Vivaldi approval of her marriage? A reversal has occurred once again, and it is clearly more than purely Gothic disguise being torn aside. These aspects of the plot have social consequences, something untrue of pure Gothic, in which disguise, darkness, the supernatural, and terror exist for themselves. Here we are in the midst of social maneuvering, and the divulgence of Schedoni's past moves at the multiple levels of the novel rather than with the singular impulse of the romance. As it turns out, a further reversal occurs, one now familiar in the eighteenth-century novel: Ellena is the daughter, not of Schedoni, but of his dead brother, and her mother is Olivia, the brother's wife, whom Schedoni had married, stabbed, and left for dead.

The incidents are melodramatic, of course, but the import is novelistic, what with such insistent questions of identity and past history. Keep the melodrama and one glimpses Dickens; eliminate the violence but keep the deception and one foresees *Middlemarch.* We should not overstate the continuity of English fiction, or try to wrench it into consistency, but we should not lose sight of Mrs. Radcliffe's position in fiction as a writer of the 1790's and as a female novelist, a contemporary of Jane Austen and Fanny Burney. Implied in her work is a social statement, inchoate as yet, that has at its roots snobbery, vanity, family position, upward mobility, all appearing in the melodramatic terms of the genre.[9]

[9] In *The Mysteries of Udolpho*, the Richardsonian overtones are apparent. Emily, not unlike Ellena, is an innocent cast to the tigers of desire and willfulness. She must choose between two equally distasteful forces, one represented by Count Morano, an

The Italian is something of a riposte to Lewis's extremely popular *The Monk*, published the year before. Lewis had himself been influenced by Mrs. Radcliffe's earlier work, especially *The Mysteries of Udolpho*, but, with quite different intentions, moved Gothic toward the demonic and sadistic. *Her* reaction to *The Monk* was to transform Ambrosio's self-destructive impulses, his bottled-up anger and sexual rage, into Schedoni's "Byronic" qualities of severe gloom intermixed with pride. Schedoni, not Ambrosio, leads us into Manfred and Heathcliff. In still another way, Ambrosio's impulses toward self-gratification, his surge toward a life of orgasmic pleasure went well beyond Mrs. Radcliffe's own imagination, or else never got beyond her inhibitions. She saw Ambrosio as the embodiment of unbridled destructiveness, a sexual fiend, while her own Schedoni, with terrible crimes behind him, is torn by conscience, still capable of moral choices.

In other ways as well, we can observe Mrs. Radcliffe's attempt to move Gothic from horror to social terms. *The Italian* is set in 1758, the year that Vivaldi catches his first glimpse of Ellena, not the time of old moldering manuscripts, medieval castles, or musty, tortuous passageways. Although she recalls the Inquisition (as it had not been in Italy for almost a century) and the Catholic Church as a medieval institution, she has moved her story into modern times.

Further, she utilizes a narrative form that is very much a picaresque tradition: the presence of a closely knit duo, Vivaldi and his servant Paulo, who recall the Don and Sancho, Tom Jones and Partridge, Random and Strap, Uncle Toby and Trim, et al. Such a narrative apparatus forces a social point, since in these relationships master and servant lines break down. In *The Italian*, for example, Paulo shows as much courage as Vivaldi, the same devotion to honor and integrity; and the point is clearly a late-eighteenth-century class idea rather than a medieval one.

The comparison has been made before, but bears repeating, between Mrs. Radcliffe's final novel and Elizabethan drama, not

---

impetuous suitor, and the other by her aunt's husband, Montoni. The parellelism to Lovelace and the Harlowe family, despite the melodramatic setting, is apparent.

We can also find a comparable situation in *The Romance of the Forest*, in which Adeline is caught between La Motte, her apparent benefactor, and the Marquis de Montalt, who controls La Motte's fate. This novel is almost completely Richardsonian in its conception, since the major conflict involves the fortunes of Adeline entrapped by both "family" (La Motte) and dissolute suitor (the marquis). The Gothic elements are, as it were, grafted on, so as to turn Richardsonian realism into Gothic romance.

only Shakespeare (Schedoni and Iago, for example), but Webster, Massinger, Ford, Tourneur, and Marston. The poisonings, the revenge motifs, the stress upon knives and swords, the imminence or actuality of bloody scenes—all of these recall Elizabethan and Jacobean conventions. The point is significant, because it reminds us that Mrs. Radcliffe, like the later Elizabethans, was moving toward a realistic view of human behavior by means of melodramatic conventions. It tells us, also, a good deal about her Schedoni, who influenced a generation or more of novelists and poets. For if Schedoni resembles the Iago-type, he cannot be dismissed as a fiend or as a sexually repressed madman, or even as particularly aberrant. His "wound" or criminal instinct is part of his complexity, and his crimes are as much against himself as against others. He strives after a tragic view, the flawed individual who tries to rise above his sinful nature, the man aware of his difference from others, cognizant of the distance he must keep, sensible, as well, of the tremendous violence implicit in his rage.

Ambrosio, evidently, shares some of these characteristics, but his behavior, once he has made his Faustian pact, is irreversible; he has gone over to the devil. Schedoni is closer to the tragic protagonist; everything is bottled up, he has nothing to give, and even treachery is unfulfilling. It is surely his inability to find any firm ground that made him so attractive to the romantic writers. In his depiction, if we view the novel as a whole, Mrs. Radcliffe was evidently straining after another kind of statement; and, although she provided a Jane Austen-like happy ending, she also tried to wed tragedy to melodrama, bringing Gothic toward its epitome even while signaling its absorption into other forms.

Matthew Lewis—The Monk (*1796*)

Influenced by Mrs. Radcliffe's early Gothic novels, Matthew Lewis in *The Monk* tried to move Gothic toward the mainstream of the novel, although his stress, unlike hers, involved chiefly a psychological orientation for hitherto romantic material. The epigraph to the novel is a curious one, from *Measure for Measure* (I, 3, 50–3):

> Lord Angelo is precise;
> Stands at a guard with envy; scarce confesses
> That his blood flows, or that his appetite
> Is more to bread than stone . . .

What is at stake in Shakespeare is a transfer of power to Angelo, whose first act of command is to punish licentiousness. Lewis, also, uses the comment to refer to inward command, not to external power, so that the words stand for contrasting images of self-indulgence and denial, or life and death. Thus, to pursue the epigraph's imagery, Lewis's Ambrosio presents a façade of stone (as a monk), but within, his "blood flows" and his appetite "is more to bread," to something soft and giving.

The novel, then, establishes its theme as one of passion in a man who is as rigid as the cathedrals in which he preaches. It is a tale of opposites, of conflicting forces, of terrible juices running within Ambrosio which he must dam up to survive. In a sense, the novel is about sex, but it is concealed, disguised, shameful, and destructive—not normal intercourse between men and women who willingly admit to desire. Sexual activity takes place in the hidden chambers of underground passages, in settings of stone and dungeons, with corpses never distant, with chains and torture tools within reach. Essentially, concealment, which is such a significant factor, allows for a form of subversive, forbidden sex, and we can see Lewis, himself a homosexual, grappling with sexual appetites and tastes that had to be screened or disguised. Sex is itself painful and repressed. Denial is as necessary as indulgence, indeed interchangeable with it.

Images of concealment run the gamut: atmospheric, locational, psychological. We first learn that Ambrosio, a famous monk, had been found by Capuchins "while yet an infant at the abbey," so that his origin is unknown—the typical background of the would-be hero. Ambrosio's birth is characteristic of him; an unknown, he follows some concealed path of motivation and virtue and his practices are "secret." In one passage, Lewis notes that while Ambrosio spoke, "his rosary, composed of large grains of amber, fell from his hands and dropped among the surrounding multitude." (Grove Press edition, p. 46) This is a curious image, full of sexual potential (masturbation) and unconscious unfolding of character (loss of religious ideals). It is a symbolic act for Ambrosio, suggesting the dropping away of layers and layers of protective skin, until, like a peeled onion, he stands revealed.

Then, precisely when we are keenly aware of Ambrosio, he is removed, concealed, and the scene changes to a different set of actors. As a consequence, he recedes into shadows now as part of the narrative, as before part of his own life style. We recognize that

Ambrosio survives only *because of* what he hides and represses; for him, revelation is self-destructive. Ambrosio's struggle is to dam up what will drown him, virtually the very sexual juices that ultimately pour out and pollute the self.

Like a Verdi opera, the novel proceeds through various disclosures. At the center is a shameful, ambiguous secret, a mask of self, a passion that can be controlled only by denying all passion, a destructiveness that can be resisted only by denying all life. The religious counterpart of such superhuman control and psychological disturbance is the satanic pride of Lucifer, who tries to challenge God's command of his resources. Before we can judge the quality of Ambrosio's pride in "holding back," we must consider what he is hiding. At the beginning, potentially, and, later, actually, he is a voyeur, a rapist, a sadist, a masochist, a necrophiliac, a matricide, as well as incestuous; at his best, a profaner and a masturbator. Lewis is toying with the Sadean notion of man's almost infinite potential for evil and, in effect, making evil a way of life. Defiance first of self and then of mankind is a form of survival that depends on moral degradation. Ambrosio is most vital when he commits crimes against others, most devious when he controls himself.[10]

In religious terms, the control Ambrosio exercises is equivalent to

[10] In *The Romantic Agony*, Praz charts Ambrosio's fictional ancestors, among others Montoni from Mrs. Radcliffe's *The Mysteries of Udolpho* and the "German villains put into circulation by the 'Stürmer und Dränger,' villains, incidentally, who found their way into Schiller, Lamartine, Sue, and Byron as well as into Lewis." (p. 61)

A more direct source of *The Monk*, according to Lewis, was Addison's "Santon Barsisa" in *The Guardian* (No. 148), a Turkish tale translated into English as part of the general Oriental revival in the eighteenth century. In the advertisement to *The Monk*, Lewis also gives several other sources (such as the *Bleeding Nun*, the *Water-King*, *Belerma and Durandarte*), but none is so important as the tale of Barsisa. Montague Summers gives a synopsis, as follows:

> Satan, enraged by the surpassing holiness of Barsisa, contrives that the daughter of a king shall be sent to him to heal of her sickness. The beauty of the princess tempts the santon to violate her. Afterwards, at the fiend's suggestion, he kills his victim, burying her in his grotto, where the body is found. Barsisa is seized, and upon the gallows he adores the Evil One who promises in return to save him from death, but who immediately mocks and abandons his wretched prey. [p. 223]

According to J. M. S. Tompkins (*The Popular Novel in England 1770–1800*), Lewis took "two-thirds of the book . . . almost word for word, from a German romance, *Die Blutende Gestalt* . . ." In this, the "two themes of the devil's compact and spectral nun are already united, though the hero of the former is an old nobleman, not a monk." (p. 245, n. 1) For a more nearly complete list of the numerous influences on *The Monk*, see Louis F. Peck's *A Life of Matthew G. Lewis*, 1961, pp. 292–3, n. 4.

obedience to God, while his dammed-up passions involve the temptations of the devil. Human sexuality, the ballet of superego and id, becomes the traditional battleground between the dictates of God and the seductions of the devil. To carry the conflict directly into sexual imagery, one is reminded of outpourings, emissions, masturbation, all barely withstood by acts of will.

On several levels of activity, Ambrosio fills out the Faustian theme—a theme, incidentally, often woven into the fabric of the Gothic novel. The reasons are apparent, for the Faustian pact involves a basic conflict identifiable as sexual, social, political, psychological. As a universal pattern, it fits well into Gothic, which incorporates sweeping, panoramic views of man, nature, and society.

In chapter VII, Matilda, the young girl disguised as the monk Rosario, reveals herself as a witch of sorts. She tells Ambrosio her guardian had instructed her in the uses of magic potions based on a complete understanding of the laws of the elements. As a result, he "could reverse the order of nature . . . and the infernal spirits were submissive to his commands." (p. 265) Such opposition to nature was considered a crime against the universe (a curious idea in an age that had considered nature as secondary to man's rational control of it). Matilda then offers Ambrosio a pact with the devil, for which he is certain to receive Antonia (the Gretchen-Marguerite of Faust's desires). Ambrosio resists, asserting that Antonia will be his, but "by human means."

The shrewd Matilda, however, plays on one of Ambrosio's sexual secrets, his voyeurism, and with a magic mirror she shows him Antonia undressing to bathe herself. It is a typical masturbatory fantasy for Ambrosio, indicating that his "secret vice" was perhaps the only way he could keep his passions under control. The Monk, in a frenzy, smashes the mirror on the ground and, asking Matilda for the real thing, not the image, sells his soul for love of Antonia.

He must, consequently, follow Matilda into St. Clare's sepulcher. His descent into the tomb is here symbolic of his descending scale of morality and, as well, his literal descent into the tomb of his own desires, the Gothic approximation of the Freudian subconscious. This descent into the dark, dripping, clammy, vaginal tomb is, of course, the end of Ambrosio's control, for it involves a succession of images which confuse the sexes, confound the senses, and arouse the passions, a whole panorama of masturbatory fantasies.

At the first application of magic, a naked youth of eighteen appears, evidently a messenger from Lucifer, marking Matilda's success; she then warns Ambrosio that henceforth he must invoke supernatural aid himself, for which he must pay the price, the loss of his soul. She then promises Ambrosio his immediate desire, satisfaction with Antonia, which will come, like Lovelace's with Clarissa, while she is drugged. Thus, the would-be rapist is revealed to be a necrophiliac.

With this, Ambrosio is lost, and the novel, by and large, loses its tonal variety. Before, Ambrosio, hiding his secret needs, is Spanish steel; Ambrosio revealed is ordinary. Our awareness of the Inquisition, the ever-present, hard, unyielding surfaces of cathedrals, tombs, stone slabs, the softness of wronged women like the unfortunate Agnes and the naïve Antonia, the alternating rigidity and passionate intensity of Ambrosio himself—all these contrasting textures help establish the theme of conflicting forces and elements. The novel depends, formally, on contrasts: not only the contrast between what seems to be and what is, but between opposing forces within the same person, between social roles and private needs, between the disguise one has selected and the developing person beneath. Mythically, the supporting figure is Proteus.

A little more than halfway through (pp. 230 ff.), we see how façades have hidden substance. The novice Rosario stands revealed as Matilda, the devout Matilda is a witch, and the devoted Ambrosio now hides his present indulgence beneath renewed religiosity. Meanwhile, the victimized Agnes is perishing in the dungeon, and Ambrosio has rejected her pleas. Sexual roles take on dubious identity. Rosario-Matilda, already bisexual in appeal to Ambrosio, turns masculine in her command of the Monk: "Now she assumed a sort of courage and manliness in her manners and discourse." The Prioress is herself a figure of severity and command, turning her nuns into slaves to her needs for power, asserting in every way her authority over them. Like de Sade's men and women, Lewis's do not distinguish sexual roles from power roles.

This probing of the subconscious is Lewis's forte. Along the way, he exploits nearly every aspect of Gothic suggested by Walpole and developed by Mrs. Radcliffe. There is a prophecy or curse, the device Gothic used as a parallel to the fated quality of ancient tragedy. Early in the novel (p. 62), the Gypsy reads Antonia's palm and sees nothing but distress, warning her as Clarissa was warned of

Lovelace: "Though he seem so good and kind, / Fair exteriors oft will hide / Hearts that swell with lust and pride." Yet the dire warning applies also to the Monk and to Agnes. The Gypsy's prophecy is turned directly into Agnes's curse when Ambrosio denies her appeals: " 'Then when you yield to impetuous passions . . . think upon Agnes, and despair of pardon.' "

The prophecies and curses are fate, and as in all Gothic, they establish the pattern of narrative and character. Here, they lead directly into the theme of the persecuted maiden. This, the Richardsonian heritage, is apparent in all mainstream Gothic: the maiden is soft, white, clinging, vulnerable, innocent, while her persecutor is dark, Italianate, passionate, corrupted, the spirit both of manhood and of destruction. He moves amid heavy materials—stones, slabs, iron gratings, a steel-like desire—while she is a creature of laces and silks, bedrooms, sitting rooms, draped with fine, expensive materials. Further, the woman tends to be natural in her affections, direct in her sympathies, whereas the male is rarely what he seems: an engaging manner disguises a power-seeking master.

The sadistic possibilities are evident, and the sexual play, such as it is, is structured on seizure and rape. Persecuting the maiden whets the male's appetite; he can function only when opposed. He desires the woman only when he can terrorize her, reduce her emotional defenses, and strike when she is either drugged or distraught. Even while such action temporarily establishes the male as supreme, it undermines his pretensions to superiority.

In Lewis, the convent serves the function of the castle in other Gothic fiction. As soon as sexual roles are disguised or reversed, the convent, with its sexually ambiguous prioress, its untouchable nuns and monks, its potential for a power structure, is a suitable locale for the treachery, torture, and deception carried over from the castle. Also, like the castle, a convent or monastery has twisting stairways, tombs, dungeons, hidden rooms, slimy walls, secret passages, unknown treasures and horrors. In another sense, it is forbidden territory, Kafkaesque in its possibilities for the occult, magic, unknown. It is medieval, foreign, alien to reason, and it is Roman Catholic—*The Monk* takes place largely in Madrid during the Inquisition. The potential for hypocrisy is highest when ideals are involved, and a convent contains the highest possible ideals—abnegation, continence, marriage to Jesus. Further, for the Protestant Englishman, Roman Catholicism can become the villain; comparably, for the "white" Englishman, the dark Mediterranean type—whether Italian, Spanish, or Moorish—is the defiler of womankind. Religiously, ethnically, racially, the Englishman remains superior.

The bleeding-nun episode, which Praz connects to numerous images of profanation of the Madonna, is a key element in the development of *The Monk*, for it embodies a curselike dimension and simultaneously provides mystery, contrast, revolt. A "bleeding nun" is itself a contrast in terms, for blood of a virgin denotes the breaking of the chastity vow. Further, blood drawn on a field of white or purity is a sharper image than blood drawn from a brawny arm. Lewis's bleeding nun provides both a premonition of Agnes's fate and a parallel to Ambrosio's licentious, amoral career, and is herself a typically driven Gothic character who embraces sexual gratification, atheism, and depravity. Her fate is treacherous death; and, then, like a ghost or specter, she appears every five years in full bloody regalia, a figure of guilt, penance, vengefulness, and solitary pride.

There appears to be little or no psychological "side" to the bleeding nun, but she does help sustain that confusion of the senses, that constant presentation of the bizarre, that embodiment of nightmarish materials which both Lewis and, later, Maturin brought to the Gothic tale. Ambrosio's end, however, is standard fare—the final act of blasphemy, the selling of his soul for removal from prison, the treachery of Lucifer, and the final revelations of Ambrosio's matricide and incest before the tortures of Prometheus, Tantalus, and Oedipus are visited upon him. He is now carrion for insects and birds of prey, a religious resolution of crime and punishment.

For the reader, however, Lewis's legacy is quite otherwise: a yearning, burning monk, a fierce desire to break out of self-imposed bonds, the revelation of secret practices and desires, the need for self-expression even at the expense of self-destruction, the numerous "graveyard" scenes of rot, slime, filth, waste, life writ large as death. In these respects, Lewis, like the Elizabethan dramatists, has conveyed a melodramatic process that carries far more weight than his hastily conceived resolution.

William Godwin—Caleb Williams (*1794*)

With Godwin's *The Adventures of Caleb Williams or Things as They Are*, we find still another novel both incorporating and blunting aspects of Gothic, even while Gothic is still flourishing in its purer state. Godwin's Gothic is not that of Walpole's castle, nor that of Mrs. Radcliffe's romantic forests. It is, rather, the dark interior of a man's mind. Godwin has assimilated terror into psychological realism, absorbed darkness and bleakness into the mythical chase, and merged most of the modes of eighteenth-century fiction with philosophical inquiry.

Caleb Williams is a catchall of eighteenth-century themes and techniques. As narrative, it owes a good deal to the picaresque novel, although it is considerably more tightly conceived and executed. In the attempt at narrative ambiguity, Smollett is echoed—although presented as the narrative of Mr. Collins, the story is put together from various quarters. In Falkland's similarity to Squire Allworthy and his patronage of the young Caleb, we recall *Tom Jones. Clarissa* enters in the dilemma of Miss Melville, who is caught between her unbending benefactor, Mr. Tyrrel, and a suitor, Grimes, whom she detests. She even has a dream of violence comparable to Clarissa's foreseeing of her own rape and death. Miss Melville "imagined she saw Mr. Tyrrel and his engine Grimes, their hands and garments dropping with blood . . ." (Holt edition, p. 98)

Despite these echoes, and actual borrowings, Godwin created his own novel and infused it with ideas distinctly his own. *Caleb Williams*, ultimately, is concerned with the nature of tyranny and with a definition of individual human rights. Written shortly after the French Revolution, the novel is, in a sense, an extension of the ideas of the rights of man. Godwin argues that man has the right to fulfill himself without interference from tyranny; that the individual must always seek the maximum amount of choice in an oppressive society; that a person must never let himself be governed by circumstance (the latter an eighteenth-century assumption); that human dignity demands each responsible individual break the master-slave relationship wherever he finds it; that responsible people can together create an enlightened world conducive to freedom; that man is, indeed, Faustian in his positive ability to throw off the old and assume the mantle of the new.

In Godwin's philosophy, which saturates *Caleb Williams*, we recognize many aspects of the romantic movement. As Shelley's father-in-law, he was evidently an influence and parallel force for the poet. Shelley aside, however, we see Godwin's ideas as running parallel to many other elements in the 1790's: Wordsworth's Preface to the second edition of *Lyrical Ballads*, with its insistence on a new type of poetry and a new readership; Robert Burns's poems celebrating the lowly and downtrodden; Blake's insistence on the emotional life, on energy and vitality as stemming from the entire being rather than simply from the mind; Byron's protagonists endlessly searching for some clue to human existence, some way to grapple with experience. Once we recognize how close Godwin is to these other thinkers, we can understand the truly Faustian quality of his novel: its use of Caleb as a bridge between the old, bookish, but demonic world of Falkland and the newer world of human rights and individual dignity.[11]

Representing courtliness, decency, scholarship, Falkland is clearly an exponent of the Old World. In one respect, at least, he embodies the world of art, tied as it was in the eighteenth century to traditional values and modes of behavior. Opposed to him in the early parts of the novel (which Godwin wrote last) is Tyrrel, something of the new man in his insolence, but, for Godwin, unrepresentative of the new values as they should be. Tyrrel stands for Mars or war—his standards are physical, his interests power, control, rule. His confrontation with Falkland is the classic confrontation of art and war, with art the temporary victor.

For Godwin, however, Falkland is himself a false representative of the world of art. He is duplicitous, manipulative, and ruthless in pursuit of his own values. His attractiveness holds within it too many traps for the unsuspecting and the innocent. Behind the façade of culture and traditional values hides a man who will suppress every manifestation of human dignity if it interferes with his own plans. Falkland, then, is a false prophet. His cultivated mind is only one part of him; the other part is the tyrannical aspect of England and Europe, which, before the French Revolution, terrorized all those who failed to accept traditional hierarchies and customary chains of being.

The truly new man is Caleb Williams—his name alone would

[11] A lesser-known writer, Robert Bage, a Midlands industrialist turned novelist, moved in and out of Godwin's "revolutionary" themes. Like Godwin, Bage, in his own *Hermsprong, or Man as he is not* (1796), believed that the novel could serve a social and political function. Hermsprong is cut in the mold of Caleb Williams—that is, honest, independent, hardy—whereas his antagonist, Lord Grondale, like Falkland, is puffed by privilege and position in a traditional, hierarchical society. In his six novels, Bage helped create the liberal political atmosphere of the 1790's that we usually associate with Godwin and the youthful Wordsworth and Coleridge.

appear to indicate his newness as a post-revolutionary hero. Although gifted with a bookish mind, a good memory, and an easy manner, he is ordinary. The hunting down of Caleb, both mythical and symbolic, is indicative of the play of forces: the new man chased by the old, hounded by the footsteps of authoritarianism, dogged by traditional values. One recalls a later chase in literature, in Hugo's *Les Misérables*, but there the values involved are clearly social rather than cultural. Godwin is moving toward new political assumptions about man, and the novel is his vehicle of philosophical inquiry.

Since the chase is so intrinsic to the novel—we note that Godwin wrote Part III first, where the chase is in its simplest form—we should examine its potential. As a narrative structure, the chase recalls picaresque fiction. In picaresque, however, the protagonist aims at acceptance, wherever he can find a suitable niche. In Godwin, the chase is more suggestive of ultimate values. Without belaboring a difficult and knotty point, we can see his utilization of such a narrative device as existential. Godwin's protagonist is caught at his outside extremities of survival: he is not running to seek a niche but to survive. He is naked man against both the elements and active opposition. He is stripped of all support; indeed, all the old props are in the hands of his enemy. The secret he carries in his breast—his knowledge that Falkland has killed Tyrrel and let the Hawkinses swing for it—has made him vulnerable to all traditional authority. Caleb is, indeed, the enemy of normal society, although his is the only moral position. The situation is familiar to us in modern literature, but in the eighteenth century it was rare.

Williams runs. When he falls into the hands of outlaws, he is treated by some of them better than by the legal authorities, who have made an outlaw of him. In his naked state, Williams sees that these outlaws have a certain energy that the state wastes, an energy lacking in traditionalists like Falkland. Thus, the chase broadens to include those living on the margins of society and the law. The captain of the outlaws, Raymond, counsels civil disobedience: "Which was most meritorious, the unresisting and dastardly submission of a slave, or the enterprise and gallantry of the man who dared to assert his claims?" (p. 256) He argues that if, as a result of the laws, innocence can be punished as well as guilt, then what courageous man will fail to defy the law?

Williams rejects this formulation. Nevertheless, the idea does temporarily establish a kind of anarchy or suggest an unsettled world in which values are blown asunder, in which law is outlaw, in which outlaw establishes its own laws. It is in this type of world that the chase occurs, and Williams must survive with only his own wits as weapon. Like Defoe's Moll, he assumes disguises, becomes protean to escape his oppressors. A tramp's appearance, a clownish gait—these are the expedients of a man seeking to remain "erect and independent." Comfortless, homeless, hungry, oppressed on every side, hounded by his persecutors, Williams cries out: " 'Here I am, an outcast, destined to perish with hunger and cold. All men desert me. All men hate me . . . Accursed world! that hates without a cause . . . Why do I consent to live any longer? Why do I seek to drag on an existence, which, if protracted, must be protracted amidst the lairs of these human tigers?' " (p. 292)

Such a cry against circumstance and fate recalls Robinson Crusoe's; but Crusoe turns to a religious resolution. Williams must seek his within himself, not within tradition. And what he seeks is more than sustenance on his "island"; he seeks justice. Up to the point of his defiance, Williams is assessing an existential experience; his ultimate aim, however—to make society responsive to the individual—is Godwin's own conception and takes Williams well outside the existential experience. For a short while, nevertheless, Godwin has caught an alternate type of society; and, despite his borrowings here and there from Defoe, Gay's *Beggar's Opera*, Fielding's *Jonathan Wild*, the Gothic of Mrs. Radcliffe, despite these, he entered for a time into a true alternate experience of philosophical anarchy.

The basis of Godwin's thought is the goodness of man: even though man can no longer live idyllically, he can live justly. This is Godwin's premise. Then what about Falkland, in whose evil character courtliness, gentleness, the chivalric code find such a large part? Godwin has attempted something very large in Falkland, the man perhaps modeled on Richardson's Sir Charles Grandison—that is, useful, considerate, helpful at every turn—who is, nevertheless, a person of demonic pride, of destructive urges, of an overpowering need for vengeance. Falkland, in outline, recalls the later Byronic duality, like Cain a man who can live for a time peacefully, but who, when provoked, must assert the anarchy lying beneath respectability.

We must be careful in assessing Falkland, for Godwin intended him in the novel to represent certain social values: specifically, the man who uses his high social position to impose his own kind of justice, in disregard of real justice. A modern reading will tend to see Falkland in psychological terms as a man repressing violence under a cloak of respectability. Neither reading excludes the other. Indeed, we can say that the psychological theme merges with the social when Godwin establishes his point that only social justice can control the murderous streak within Falkland; that until social justice controls it, a Falkland by virtue of his position is free to move as his own will dictates. It is a subtle vision and one not duplicated by any other writer in the eighteenth century except the Gothic novelists, and their aim was not really justice but an exploration of the demonic, bestial, and sadistic within a seemingly normal man.

A chase, however, usually has further psychological dimensions, which are the peculiar affinity the hunter has for the hunted—indeed, the special need each has for the other. There is, we recognize, no woman in the story in relationship to either Williams or Falkland. Miss Melville is a plaything of Tyrell's and Grimes's, unimportant in the novel and destined as a victim anyway. There is, in addition, the "infernal Thalestris," the savage woman associated with the outlaws, the "execrable hag" who attempts to chop up Williams with a butcher's cleaver. Women, thus, are at the extremes of the scale, timid and victimized like Miss Melville, or Amazonian like the murderous hag. This is, in effect, a society without women; and within such a society, the male bond becomes predominant.

Falkland appears to have supplanted in Williams's mind most of the feelings normally associated with a woman. He reveres the man even after Falkland has revealed himself as capable of any crime. He always tries to live up to Falkland's view of him; his ideal for the male sex is Falkland, an ideal that continues well into the pursuit. What I am suggesting, then, is a psychological offshoot of Godwin's political and social theme. And this aspect, involving the deepening relationship between the two men, carries with it a sexual freight, an undefined homoerotic attachment maintained by means of the chase. Although the chase is primarily of social significance, its personal or psychological level allows the two men to create a relationship based on sadism, masochism, the taking of alternate masculine roles—all sanctioned by society as long as the chase provides the façade. Once again, we recall, Part III stresses the chase, and that is the part with which Godwin began, moving then to II and, finally, to I.

The sexual content of Gothic and near-Gothic is, of course, apparent, as Mario Praz has so amply demonstrated. Sado-masochism is a key ingredient. When Gothic peaks in the 1790's, with Mrs. Radcliffe and Monk Lewis, its concerns nearly always border on the sexually bizarre. While Godwin is not Lewis in his tastes or stresses, he nevertheless joins his contemporary in exploring, however tentatively, the psychological outer reaches of Gothic, where the line between normality and abnormality becomes blurred. It is this line, from Godwin on, that defines where Gothic will go in a writer like Dickens, in whom sexual eccentricities are intermixed with sociopolitical themes; whereas it is from Lewis that the line extends to the Brontës, especially to Emily's *Wuthering Heights*, in which eroticism dominates.

Mary Wollstonecraft Shelley—Frankenstein (or The Modern Prometheus) (*1818*)

Even without the dedication of *Frankenstein* to William Godwin, her father, Mary Shelley would appear to be working in a vein similar to *Caleb Williams*: that is, more preoccupied with moral issues than with Gothic horrors themselves.[12] This is not to deny the evident dimension of horror in the novel; but it is to note that by 1818, when the novel was published, Gothic had turned from its earlier preoccupations—even those of Lewis—toward a romantic concern with larger questions of morality. Like Godwin, Mary

[12] Varma, however, sees *Frankenstein* as part of the "horror" school of Gothic: "Mary Shelley's *Frankenstein* (1818) is another Gothic novel which falls within the orbit of the Schauer-Romantik, not so much for her treatment of horror, as for the individuality of her theme. While not the inventor of the scientific romance, she was the first to adapt its methods to the peculiar purposes of the novel of horror. *Frankenstein* carried horror into the pseudo-scientific: a proof that the Schauer-Romantiks carefully sought their inspiration in a succession of unfamiliar themes capable of being given a 'Gothic' tone." (p. 154)

The circumstances leading up to the writing of the novel were Gothic in themselves. On a cold, wet evening in 1816, Mary Shelley, Shelley, Byron, Lewis, and Polidori were sitting around a fire in the Villa Deodati, near Geneva, telling ghost stories. By the end of the evening, Mrs. Shelley relates in her introduction to *Frankenstein*, each had decided to write a ghost story. That night she had a waking dream: "My imagination, unbidden, possessed and guided me, gifting the successive images that arose in my mind with a vividness far beyond the usual bounds of reverie. I saw—with shut eyes, but acute mental vision—I saw the pale student of unhallowed arts kneeling beside the thing he had put together. I saw the hideous phantasm of a man stretched out, and then, on the working of some powerful engine, show signs of life, and stir with an uneasy, half vital motion." (Dolphin edition, p. 11)

Shelley was concerned with an individual's responsibility for his actions. Caleb Williams's view of his own fortunes is quite different from the role Falkland has chosen for him; analogously, Frankenstein's role for his creation is quite distinct from the monster's own view of himself. Mrs. Shelley is testing out a new dimension, where science and the scientific mind end and social responsibility begins.

Thus, it appears that Mrs. Shelley's novel is a focal point of several different elements: (1) the moral and ethical concerns of Godwin; (2) the Faustian strain common to both her work and Maturin's—like Melmoth, Frankenstein has sold his soul, not for longer life, but for his special gift of learning the secret of human creation (in another respect, too, *Frankenstein* has certain affinities to *Melmoth*, which was to be published two years later, in that both see the battle for a man's soul panoramically, no longer within the confines of castle and moat); (3) a realistic strain from the main novelistic tradition; that is, once we accept the unlikely idea of the monster, we move into mundane concerns with family, mate, home, et al.—not unlike the orchestration in Kafka's *Metamorphosis*, in which once we accept the transformation of Gregor, we are involved in an intense family drama; and (4) certain philosophical ideas that, carrying over from the eighteenth century, merge with those of the romantic movement, specifically, her husband's.[13]

Consider one or two areas in which these strains merge with each other. Gothic fiction, as we have observed, is concerned with the outsider, whether the stationary figure who represses his difference, or the wandering figure who seeks for some kind of salvation, or else the individual who—for whatever reason—moves entirely outside the norm. In any event, he is beyond the moderating impulses in society, and he must be punished for his transgression. Frankenstein's monster obviously straddles these categories. He wanders through wastelands, mountain aeries, the far North, lurks in caves and

[13] Unlike Varma, Robert Kiely stresses the relationship of the moral theme to the preoccupations of the romantics, that is to say, with questions of idealism, egoism, personal morality. He writes: "Her novel, like almost everything else about her life, is an instance of genius observed and admired but not shared. In making her hero the creator of a monster, she does not necessarily mock idealistic ambition, but in making that monster a poor grotesque patchwork, a physical mess of seams and wrinkles, she introduces a consideration of the material universe which challenges and undermines the purity of idealism. In short, the sheer concreteness of the ugly thing which Frankenstein has created often makes his ambitions and his character—however sympathetically described—seem ridiculous and even insane." (*The Romantic Novel in England*, p. 161)

caverns, in places no one else dare go. He seeks a mate, a complement to his own loneliness. He is gloomy and melancholy, full of self-pity and self-hatred. Like Cain, he is the perpetual outsider, marked by his appearance, doomed to wander the four corners of the earth, alone and reviled.

As an outsider, he argues with Frankenstein that he needs a female monster with the same defects, so that he will not have to go through life alone. He desires completion in monstrosity—still well within the Gothic orbit. This argument, however, becomes intermixed with several eighteenth-century strains existing outside of Gothic. In a curious turn, the monster sees himself as capable of all kinds of beautiful behavior, but because of his ghastly appearance, no one will allow him to develop his propensities for good. A product of ill treatment and society's horror, he can only indulge in revenge and cruel acts against the innocent.[14] The monster's plaint comes directly from the eighteenth-century belief in the *tabula rasa* and Godwin's sense of the individual's innate right to develop at his own rate. At the same time, this point is well within the idealism and political beliefs of Shelley's circle.

In still another aspect of the novel recalling non-Gothic practices, the technique is epistolary—however weakly developed. The basic form is a series of letters from Robert Walton, an explorer, to his sister. Within Walton's epistles appears Frankenstein's own story as related to Walton, and within the latter a further narration from the monster to its creator. With its rudimentary burrowing technique of tales within tales, the novel once again anticipates *Melmoth*; and with its epistolary style, the book revives the eighteenth-century practice. Mrs. Shelley, however, is less interested in technique than in presenting the moral dilemma of her "modern Prometheus."

Frankenstein himself requires some attention as an eighteenth-century man and scientist, as well as a romantic idealist. He, too, falls into Gothic; at the same time he manifests the qualities of a

[14] The monster, for instance, has just saved a young girl from drowning when a rustic approaches. " 'On seeing me, he darted towards me, and tearing the girl from my arms, hastened towards the deeper parts of the wood. I followed speedily, I hardly knew why; but when the man saw me draw near, he aimed a gun which he carried, at my body, and fired. I sunk to the ground, and my injurer, with increased swiftness, escaped into the wood.

" 'This was then the reward of my benevolence! . . . The feelings of kindness and gentleness which I had entertained but a few moments before gave place to hellish rage and gnashing of teeth.' " (p. 126)

"normal" man. Ordinarily, critics handle Frankenstein simplistically, and yet he appears to possess much of the dualism implicit in more openly Gothic characters. His creation of the monster certainly demonstrates another side to him, and his use of the monster to eliminate Elizabeth suggests some of the necrophilia we have already observed in purer forms of Gothic. While Frankenstein often appears the dedicated man of science, he demonstrates a terrible pride in his desire to manipulate nature. As a "modern Prometheus," he plays God with man and nature; he crosses paths with Faust and, in the act, recalls other Gothic protagonists: Ambrosio, Melmoth, the Italian.

Frankenstein is a great dreamer—to wrench nature into line with mind is the basis of his schemes—but his dream lacks moral content. He creates without considering the full consequences. His monster remains unnamed, unmated, lacking everything that the maker himself seems to consider important for human life. Not only has the creator overreached himself, he has also demonstrated the moral void in his own plans, even while he considers himself the most moral of men. The psychological implications here are unlimited, perhaps more so than in the more-evident Gothic protagonists; because here we have a man whose repressed feelings and ideas can only emerge in the form of the monster. And yet even after their emergence, he must retain his innocence and naïveté.

A character like Frankenstein—who would have fitted easily into a Jane Austen drawing room—suggests terrible things about human morality. Despite a gentlemanly, kind façade, he is driven by a Promethean ego; behind his idealism is the need to express himself at any cost, even if his fiancée and friends are sacrificed—or more surely *because* they will be. Whatever his precise motivation, Mrs. Shelley has charted a strange territory, so that Gothic materials, Faust, Prometheus, subterranean acts, and Austen gentlemen come together in one last Gothic convulsion.

Charles Robert Maturin—Melmoth the Wanderer (*1820*)

Charles Maturin, an Irish Protestant clergyman, gave the Gothic novel a maturity and complexity it never had as "pure Gothic." Maturin is to the Gothicness of Walpole and Mrs. Radcliffe what Dostoevsky is to the detective novels of Wilkie Collins. *Melmoth the Wanderer*, in fact, is possibly the only English novel between *Clarissa* and the work of Dickens which tries to be all things to all men. It is, at once, existential, psychological, indeed pathological, mythical, religious, and, even, political. *Caleb Williams* is an earlier attempt at syncreticism, but Godwin's effort is vitiated by the relative thinness of his narrative line and the pragmatic bent of his imagination.

Maturin, on the contrary, possessed a fertile imagination, comparable to the ever-proliferating visions of Coleridge's "Kubla Khan" and "Ancient Mariner." Like Coleridge's visions, Maturin's was often near-mad, insightful *because* pathological. The method itself is that of tunneling—Kafka's burrow comes to mind—the examination of dark passages which conceal even further reaches of darkness, and so on through a series of Chinese boxes, tales within tales, lives, like those in Plato's cave, that will never see the light. The psychological dimension becomes apparent: the tunneling is back into some dark pre-conscious, into the birth passage and trauma, where the author explores darkness as symbolic of death, fear, the world of nightmare and night journeys. The method is, of course, perfectly suitable for the subgenre that Praz called the "tale of terror" school.

The first and longest of the tales situated within the larger tale of Melmoth is the novella of the Spaniard's story. Despite its length, the Spaniard's tale is actually peripheral to the main story, which is that of old Melmoth wandering the earth seeking someone to share his fate so that he can escape damnation.[15] The younger Melmoth—descendant of the wanderer—has been called to attend his dying uncle, at whose house he discovers the manuscript of the older Melmoth. While there, the young man becomes caught in the wild violence of a shipwreck offshore, a scene whose Bosch-like riot of images foreshadows the tale of the persecuted Spaniard, Alonzo Monçada. The description of the shipwreck is typical of Maturin's almost pathological sense of pain, torture, anguish, agony in life and death:

> The whole shore was now crowded with helpless gazers, every crag and cliff was manned; it seemed like a battle fought at once by sea and land, between hope and despair. No effectual assistance could be rendered,—not a boat could live in that gale,—yet still, and to the last, cheers were heard from

[15] The older Melmoth has, many years before, bargained away his soul in exchange for longer life; in this variation of the Faustian pact, he can only avoid eternal damnation by finding one person to join or relieve him. His eyes, like the Ancient Mariner's, are terrible to behold, for in their depths one can observe the doom and damnation of his bargain as well as his need to compromise one other soul.

rock to rock,—terrible cheers, that announced safety was near and—impossible;—lanthorns held aloft in all directions, that displayed to the sufferers the shore all peopled with life, and the roaring and impassable waves between;—ropes flung out, with loud cries of help and encouragement, and caught at by some chilled, nerveless, and despairing hand, that only grasped the wave,—relaxed its hold,—was tossed once over the sinking head,—and then seen no more. [Bison edition, p. 49]

Stunned by the events and by a mysterious "Gothic" laugh that seems to emanate from the devil himself, Melmoth falls from the cliff and would have drowned except for the Spaniard, who rescues Melmoth and tells his lengthy story by means of Maturin's typical method of convolution, inversion, chronological foreshortening, time within time, interpolation of episodes. The story involves a theme common in Gothic fiction: the Church as ultimate authority and repressor, as repository of nightmares. The Spaniard's story, in a sense, suggests Dostoevsky's parable of the Grand Inquisitor: a submissive Christian, the narrator, confronted by the mightiness of an unyielding institution, the Church, whereas ultimate truth is expressed by a frail Jesus on the cross. The Spaniard tries to explain his attitude toward the Church:

Truth may be horrible to the inmates of a convent, whose whole life is artificial and perverted,—whose very hearts are sophisticated beyond the hand even of Heaven (which they alienate by their hypocrisy) to touch. But I feel I am at this moment an object of less horror in the sight of the Deity, than if I were standing at his altar, to (as you would urge me) insult him with vows, which my heart was bursting from my bosom to contradict, at the moment I uttered them. [p. 75]

While the Spaniard's tale of religious horror is not really the main element of the novel—Melmoth eventually is—his episode does take almost 100,000 words. And it contains a potpourri of materials which, like the horrors in Dostoevsky's fiction, become transcendent because of the intensity of the psychological detail and the vision projecting them. The Spaniard's story has a psychological realism that justifies Balzac's comparison of it with both Goethe's *Faust* and Byron's *Manfred.* Of particular interest is Maturin's insight into despair and how such despair becomes turned into crime. To follow up on the Spaniard's situation: his is the result of a father more than willing to sacrifice his son to the Church; once caught in its net, the young man's salvation comes only as a result of a plan which involves a parricidal monk. The parricide is, apparently, the hidden side of the Spaniard; the monk's murder of his father equivalent to the Spaniard's desire for revenge on his.

The fact of the "doubling" relationship is evident. Maturin has involved the reader in the parricide's intense madness, which looks ahead to both Dickens[16] and Dostoevsky. Yet, with typical authorial irony, the Spaniard's freedom depends on this madman, this unrepentant Oedipus; and we are encoiled in the fortunes of two men, completely different on the surface, joined together in a common quest. The images are of chewing, gnawing, tearing, biting, suffocating, nearly dying. "We lay beside each other like two panting dogs that I have read of, who lay down to die close to the animal they pursued, whose fur they fanned with their dying breath, while unable to mouthe her." (p. 151) The Spaniard must follow and obey a being he despises: ". . . I felt that his presence was at once an irrepealable curse, and an invincible necessity." (p. 153)

While lying together waiting for rescue or death, the parricide relives his moments of father-murder, which he committed for money; he describes the killing, the knife, the blood on the hilt, the hair mixed with blood on the blade, all this while the two are surrounded by darkness and stone and despair. While lacking the Russian novelist's metaphysical dimension, the scene is nevertheless of Dostoevskian grandeur. Shortly after, the madman offers his philosophy, which is close to Melmoth's in the major episode to follow: "One physical want, one severe and abrupt lesson from the tintless and shrivelled lip of necessity, is worth all the logic of the empty wretches who have presumed to prate it . . ." (p. 165) The parricide speaks as a man beyond salvation, whose crimes have been so great that only further crimes can sustain him—unless the Church offers him release. This it does, but only if he betrays Monçada. The parricide, while seeming to lead the Spaniard to safety from the reaches of the Church, has really led him into the hands of the Inquisition.

This betrayal leads to further episodes of violence and brutality,

[16] In *Great Expectations*, for instance, we note how Dolge Orlick's murder of Mrs. Joe manifests Pip's hidden desire to commit "matricide" on a mother figure he despises. In Dickens, the sequences are embedded logically in the fabric of the novel, whereas Maturin, with picaresque abandon, has used the episode only as shadowing for Melmoth's own crimes.

finally to a Zolaesque sequence in which a mob reduces the parricide to a "bloody formless mass." Through seemingly disjointed scenes of crime, terror, and treachery, Maturin has now readied us for the main episode, which will complete the second half of the novel: the tale of the wandering Melmoth. This Gothic creature is an amalgamation of the Wandering Jew, Cain, Milton's Satan, Faust, the Byronic hero, the Ancient Mariner; later, Ahab, Raskolnikov, the anti-hero, and every other figure who seeks salvation through degradation and suffering. Melmoth is a figure of agony, forced by his dealings with Mephistopheles to lead a dual existence, involved in disguises, lies, in tortuous journeys down dark passages, all of which is the very substance of Maturin's narrative method, a passage "as long and intricate as any that ever an antiquarian pursued to discover the tomb of Cheops in the Pyramids . . ." (p. 201)

The section on Melmoth (itself well over 100,000 words) involves the classic encounters implicit in the Faustian situation, between innocence, represented here by Immalee, and the slouching, hurrying, possessed figure of evil, Melmoth himself. Praz astutely compares the Immalee of the early episodes with Haidée in Byron's *Don Juan* and then Isidora (Immalee's "double," as it were) of the later episodes with Goethe's Gretchen. (p. 118) The encounter between Immalee and Melmoth is less sexual than redemptive. The entire novel, including each episode tunneled within other episodes, is concerned with those saved and those damned, and this most important section is no exception. Melmoth's depravity is such that he cannot fully comprehend the saving nature of Immalee's love for him, and therefore her innocence is insufficient to save this doomed, despairing wanderer.

Melmoth represents one side of the later Dostoevskian "tortured" anti-hero, and it is vastly to Maturin's credit that he refused to bend to romantic notions of "redemption after struggle," as Goethe did in *Faust.* Because he can never be saved, in his torment he has insight into all nightmares. Damned and doomed, he can project personal bitterness and pain into a universal vision. Like the later Underground Man, Stavrogin, Raskolnikov, Ivan Karamazov, he can use his own imbalance as a way of reading all the horrors that exist in "normal" society. He has the clairvoyance of the epileptic who feels the fit upon him, and he has the constant awareness of self of the man who knows a cancer is obliterating his flesh. In a way, Melmoth already has the eagle chewing away at his liver; like the Underground Man, he is preternaturally sensitive to every physical and emotional nuance.

If Maturin were fully Dostoevskian, Melmoth would have had another, redemptive side. For the Russian, Immalee's purity would have worked upon Melmoth and saved him through self-knowledge, renewed loyalties, personal resurrection. But for Melmoth there is no redemption. On the contrary, Melmoth tries to entice Immalee into his own visions of evil and cruelty. If he can make her despair, then he has won a convert and can avoid eternal damnation. Immalee, however, refuses to despair. She believes in moral order, and she tries to show that obsessive love of self can be transformed into universal love and redemption.

The scene then shifts from the idyllic interlude between Immalee and Melmoth to Madrid and the Inquisition. The novel becomes a curious combination of *Faust* and *Clarissa.* Melmoth courts Isidora (the "civilized" Immalee) as a Lovelace, over the protestations of her "pious mother, and angry brother, and all your relatives, testy, proud, and ridiculous as they may be." (p. 267) The analogy with *Clarissa* holds even to the suitor provided by the father, the duel of Lovelace-Melmoth with the brother (whom Melmoth kills), on to a secret marriage. Mixed in with these aspects of the tale, in which Melmoth tries to forestall his doom—much as the driven Lovelace "tries on" respectability while courting Clarissa—is the technical apparatus to which Maturin constantly calls our attention. At this moment, the story is the result of still further manuscript materials about old Melmoth, owned by the Jew Adonijah, and discovered and narrated by the Spaniard Alonzo Monçada to the young Melmoth. The insistent need to provide sources recalls the eighteenth-century concern with historicity and harks back to Cervantes and the manuscripts of the Moor Cid Hamete as the basis for *Don Quixote.*

The apparatus would not in itself warrant attention except that it is one of the few attempts after Sterne to find a technical or methodological equivalent to the substantive matter. Since the theme involves tortured, anguished individuals at the time of the Inquisition, deceit and conspiracy are at every turn. The narrative method, accordingly, twists, curves, and re-establishes itself, like a railroad line with numerous sidings. *Nothing* is linear, from Melmoth's intentions, to Immalee's scheming father; from the help the parricide appears to be giving the Spaniard, to the deception he is actually practicing. So the method follows the winding recesses of a Gothic chamber of horrors.

After Immalee's secret union with Melmoth, even while her father is arranging a suitable marriage, the narrative moves off into parallel segments, the stories of the Walbergs and Mortimers, for example, in which the wanderer Melmoth is peripheral and yet tonally central to the sense of doom that overlays their fortunes. These stories of greed, children sacrificing themselves for their parents, forsaken brides, near-parricide, all cut across the despairing cynicism of the wanderer. And Melmoth actually encounters them, if only to pierce them with a glance from his terrible eyes. The stories, as the scenic description of the union with Immalee, are pure Gothic. Moonlight, gravestones, coldness, crosses: all combine to furnish the kind of world in which Melmoth is doomed to move. He is defined by darkness, not light; he moves in shadows.

Even confessing his crimes is insufficient to save him. He admits that his was "the great angelic sin—pride and intellectual glorying! It was the first mortal sin—a boundless aspiration after forbidden knowledge!" (p. 380) Every attempt to find a fellow sinner is frustrated, and even Immalee, her infant dead, her brother murdered by Melmoth, forsaken by all, refuses to give over her soul to him. With that, the strands of the narrative come together, and the young Melmoth recognizes that the old wanderer has thrown himself into the ocean, moving now eternally among the waters as he had once moved on earth.

Maturin's vision, ultimately, is of man's doom, salvation, redemption—the great issues of Christianity. Despite all his evident borrowings from *Faust* (Part I of *Faust* was published in 1808), Maturin brought an intensity, indeed an awareness of madness, that looks ahead to Emily Brontë, parts of Dickens, and, above all, to Dostoevsky. Gothic, finally, worked itself out in the mad visions of anti-heroic Jesus Christs, epileptic princes of the Church, demonic murderers and wanderers, underground creatures. It is often difficult to distinguish Maturin's keen sense of psychopathology from his religious vision; and, to his credit, as the novel developed later in Europe, the distinction between the two no longer held. The anti-hero of our time, like Melmoth, is the wandering, isolated, suffering individual who will never find another to share his fate.

Melmoth the Wanderer is by far the greatest achievement of the

Gothic subgenre, coming when the novel had already turned from Gothic toward domestic comedy (Austen) and historical romance (Scott). Not until Dickens and the Brontës are these various strands brought together, and by then Gothic was to become something else.

8

Near-Novels

In the introduction I discussed at length those elements or categories that appear to make up the novel. As we have seen, they comprise a number of directions rather than a resolution. We come upon the novel without ever knowing for sure that we are there. And while the novel form is itself being defined—however it *is* defined—numerous other kinds of fiction are appearing, which may or may not be novels.[1] Such an unfolding of the new form characterized not only the period associated with the pre-novel—that is, the late sixteenth and entire seventeenth century—but the period in which we agree the genre developed and flourished, the eighteenth century.

Thus, while Defoe was beginning to write what we have agreed to call novels, Swift was penning *Gulliver's Travels*, about which we are uncertain. While Smollett was in full career, Johnson was preparing *Rasselas*, which may or may not be a novel. Similarly, at mid-century, with the publication of *Clarissa* and *Tom Jones*, John Cleland was publishing *Memoirs of a Woman of Pleasure* (or *Fanny Hill*), which, like all pornography, creates problems in the novel's genealogy. And, finally, just before the flowering of Gothic fiction, which we have characterized as novels, there appeared Beckford's *Vathek*, a fiction

[1] No such distinction appeared to trouble Clara Reeve, for in *The Progress of Romance* she listed all of the following as novels: *The Tale of a Tub, Gulliver's Travels, Pilgrim's Progress, Pilgrim, Don Quixote, Modern Don Quixote, Robinson Crusoe, Gaudentio di Lucca, Peter Wilkins, Voyage to the Moon, Arsaces, Prince of Betlis, Life of John Buncle, Tristram Shandy, The Citizen of the World, The Spiritual Quixote,* and *The Castle of Otranto.*

that is not quite Gothic, not quite Oriental tale, and not quite novel.

Perhaps presumptuously, I have called these four works near-novels because, while they appear to have strong affinities with the emerging genre, they do not have the feel or sense of novels. Attempts at such distinctions are, of course, tentative; they may, in fact, be foolhardy. It may nevertheless be instructive to examine them as near-novels in the hope that the distinctions we thereby discover will help to isolate the novel's characteristics. Such categorization is not final in any sense; for when we have finished, we cannot be expected to answer all objections as to why one fiction is a novel and another is not, when we cannot even agree on what makes a clear-cut novel a novel.

We should, possibly, begin with a review of the process of *becoming* that distinguishes the genre. Since we suggested in the introduction that the novel consists of several "sides," some of them novelistic, running parallel with others from earlier, traditional practices, we can perhaps isolate the strain of the novel by noting how it *becomes* something else. Rather than stress only the realism of the novel, it may be preferable to note its social base, so that we see the genre as founded on a profane view of man and his role in society. Such a man (and such a society) is devoted to materiality, even though he may remain or become pious, showing parallel allegiance to aspects of his secular self, even while attempting to transcend it. Such a man requires options. He is apt to make mistakes, but he also has the sense that he can correct them. He nearly always believes that he directs his own life and can predict his future. That is, no matter how tightly the novelist spins the web, his characters seek hopefully for an outlet, whether material or spiritual. This sense of openness and choice helps set the novel apart from allegory on the one hand and satire on the other.

In line with individual free choice and openness, the novel insists on certain assumptions that threaten the status quo. Whereas *Rasselas* strengthens the status quo and allays desire for change, novels pursue the threat of altering conditions much further, often balancing radical change against the security of the status quo. The novel appeals to a psychological need in respectable people for exposure to danger—if not in life, then in literature. The early novel stressed pirates, rapists, robbers, muggers, radical and anarchic figures who roamed the cities and the countryside, and who, in their ideas and practices, belied everything a respectable society stands for. And yet this was the type of reading offered up to a middle-class, predominantly female audience. In such terms, there can be no equation between the audience and the materials of the novel, since our conclusions would be almost certainly contradictory. Rather, we posit that the novel developed along the lines of its own secularity, instead of appealing *directly* to its audience.

In nearly all respects, the four near-novels we have cited explore "fantasy worlds" of one kind or another, lacking that hard, often brutal exposure to the secular world in which the individual must insistently define his relationship to the community and society. Matters such as social justice, the growth of the individual (not collective) self, the possibility of valid alternate styles of existence, the potential of a more open life, the awareness of loneliness and even alienation, the willingness to suffer personally for one's point of view—most or all of these characteristics are missing from the near-novels, while the majority are present in the "becoming" quality of more identifiable novels.

Erich Auerbach makes distinctions that are valuable for our understanding of the novel, although, once again, we must stress that no single distinction accounts for the development of the genre. We are trying to locate the almost imperceptible stages of a mutation, when the very idea of a mutation suggests a process inaccessible to precise analysis. In distinguishing between the Homeric and Old Testament styles respectively, Auerbach writes:

> The two styles, in their opposition, represent basic types: on the one hand fully externalized description, uniform illumination, uninterrupted connection, free expression, all events in the foreground, displaying unmistakable meanings, few elements of historical development and of psychological perspective; on the other hand, certain parts brought into high relief, others left obscure, abruptness, suggestive influence of the unexpressed, "background" quality, multiplicity of meanings and the need for interpretation, universal-historical claims, development of the concept of the historically becoming, and preoccupation with the problematic. [*Mimesis*, 1953, Anchor edition, p. 19]

If we add to Auerbach's emphasis on "becoming" a somewhat different conception of language than had hitherto obtained in literature, we can perhaps isolate the reasons why some novels become "near" while others achieve self-definition. In one of the paradoxes that have always typified the genre, the language of the novel is increasingly denotative and precise even as the novel itself stresses openness, possibility, potential. As against the romance, whose language is "poetic" while its realistic options are few or predetermined, the novel moved in the opposite direction, demanding a stricter, more reified prose to balance out, potentially, the greater openness of the material. At the same time, the use of a denotative language does not imply homogeneity. We note once more the paradox of the writer seeking an informative, commonsensical language at the same time he had to differentiate among characters and events. The prose style of novel writing, consequently, allowed for great diversity, even while it called for a loose agreement as to its function.

The language of the novel was not, fundamentally, ceremonious. Nor was it embellishment or rhetoric. If we can adopt Roland Barthes's conception of "the zero degree of writing," we can view the development of what he labels a "negative momentum," which is to say a prose accountable to people and things. Such a prose is non-literary, non-poetic, a verbal posture that is a mirror image of the bourgeoisie even while it recounts the frailties of this class.

The novelist is anxious to thrust his protagonist(s) into the modern world, into "now." For such a writer, man is not part of the homogeneous sacred world but a discrete, isolated element with a private view of phenomena. Such a man owes his loyalties, not to God, not even to king, but to himself and to things. Only the novel reflects this protagonist's world; only the novel mirrors *his* kind of existence. The genre, therefore, gains its distinction from what it can distinctly do. In most instances, it posits a relationship between the individual and his society or community that reveals the divisions between the two, not their similarities. The individual rarely "fits," nor is he meant to. The novel concerns itself with conflict. Implicit in the novel is a sense of range or breadth, as well as the depth we assume for all literary endeavor.

Matters of realism, such as I listed on pages 13–14 of the introduction, are relevant, but they are, perhaps, secondary to other considerations, such as those of life as a process; the novelist's awareness of life as a huge, undefined, alien atmosphere; the protagonist's sense of himself as distinct from anyone and anything else; the relativity of the happiness principle even while the novelist leads hero and heroine into happiness. The novel, in brief, settles for few certainties, while the near-novel, like allegory and sermon, seeks surety.

Jonathan Swift—Gulliver's Travels (*1726*)

Because both Defoe's *Robinson Crusoe* (1719) and Swift's *Gulliver's Travels* (1726) belong to that genre of prose narrative involving travel, shipwreck, abandonment, exotic adventures, strung-together episodes, and similar complications through the length of their narratives, we are struck with an immediate question: Why is the first book labeled, without any difficulty, a novel and the second treated rather warily as a kind of mutation, neither novel nor not-novel?

For all its variety of imaginative invention and its intimations of a real, historical world, *Gulliver's Travels* fits loosely into the same subgenre of utopian and pseudo-utopian literature as *Rasselas*, both of which depend on general principles rather than on the nature of experience as their guide. About midway through the "Voyage to Lilliput," Gulliver comments on the Blefuscu conquest, in which he is requested to enslave an entire people under the Lilliputian monarch. He responds:

> This open bold Declaration of mine was so opposite to the Schemes and Politicks of his Imperial Majesty, that he could never forgive me: He mentioned it in a very artful Manner at Council, where, I was told, that some of the wisest appeared, at least by their Silence, to be of my Opinion; but others, who were my secret Enemies, could not forbear some Expressions, which by a Side-wind reflected on me. And from this Time began an Intrigue between his Majesty, and a Junta of Ministers maliciously bent against me, which broke out in less than two Months, and had like to have ended in my utter Destruction. Of so little Weight are the greatest Services to Princes, when put into the Balance with a Refusal to gratify their Passions. [Norton critical edition, p. 35]

Gulliver's response, balanced and worthy of an Augustan, turns a potentially novelistic situation into one embedded in general, philosophical principles. The demands of Swiftian satire pre-empt the fictional response. The two—satire and novel—are evidently at odds. As we have already suggested, satire assumes established, conservative values, while the novel represents the innovative and opportunistic. The first is founded on God's rightness in the creation, the latter on man's desire to challenge that very creation. Ronald Paulson demonstrates that the novelist accepts "the assumption (with which the satirist could never agree) that man is basically good" and "the belief in progress," which the satirist is anxious to disprove.[2]

There is, nevertheless, a rather large area of overlapping between the novelist and satirist. While their assumptions and motives may be considerably different, their field of operation is, perforce, less distinct. Repeatedly, we note Gulliver falling into Robinson Crusoe's attitudes and situations: from the several voyages out, each of which leads to an unforeseen end, to the distaste each displays for family connections, culminating in their need to distance themselves from supposedly loved ones. Each protests his feeling for close relatives—Robinson for parents, Gulliver for wife and children—but each, apparently, needs to fulfill something within himself quite distinct from familial affection.

Once we have said this—and this accounts for a good many of the experiential parts of both narratives—then we observe how different motives lead them to separate accounts. Defoe related a single event in depth, providing that accumulation of detail, both inner and outer, which we associate with the processes of the novel. His Robinson is a man alone, caught by a situation from which there is no miraculous escape. Gulliver, on the contrary, is provided with an escape from each of his episodes whenever Swift decided to terminate his various satirical attacks, whether political, social, scientific, philosophical, or theological. The latter, *the attack itself,* has assumed the thrust of the narrative; all else is subsumed under it.

Further, the frequent shifts in physical scale work to the detriment of any novelistic purpose. The novel appears to operate only in areas where dimensions remain steady. When metamorphosis does occur in the eighteenth-century novel, it is usually within a scale or frame of reference that does not allow the realistic dimension to deteriorate. We see frequent metamorphic transpositions in the early novel, but such alterations are less Ovidian than they are modes of disguise. In brief, change does not alter the scale, whereas in *Gulliver's Travels*, change of scale always forces problems in credibility, so that satire pre-empts novel. In satire, we are attuned to believe anything, and

[2] The reader interested in investigating the relationship between the novel and satire should consult Paulson's first chapter, called "Satire and the Conventions of Realism," in *Satire and the Novel in Eighteenth-Century England.*

man made little or large, horsy or otherwise, does not disturb our basically realistic frame of reference. We can say, therefore, that the distortions in scale that satire demand are counter to our sense of the novel, in which elements are identified by their ordinariness. Gulliver would never agonize for pages over a single footprint in the sand.

In still another, related respect, Swift reveals his dualism in the narrative: his use of Gulliver, the individual, to assert general principles. In chapter V of "A Voyage to the Houyhnhnms," for example, Gulliver speaks of "the following Extract of many Conversations I had with my Master." These conversations involve a rundown of English affairs of the last forty years, with a stress on the stupidity of human behavior. Such stupidity—as we have noted in picaresque—is all to the good as far as the novel is concerned. For purposes of the satire, however, Swift must handle stupidity in a linear, singular way and must, also, exclude his own conservative view from the same stain of stupidity. If *all* ideas or attitudes had been offered up for evaluation or criticism, then the generalizations that occur here would not have been so detrimental, in novelistic terms, to Swift's presentation of Gulliver.

Gulliver always loses his particularity whenever he comes up against the larger plan. Of considerable interest to us is Gulliver's lack of an inner life. In our discussion of Robinson Crusoe, we saw how important were Robinson's home life and his relationship to his father. Swift, however, is clearly not concerned with this aspect; disdain and contempt replace the kind of detail that would have struck a balance between Gulliver's particularity—the nature of his fears, motivations, physical courage—and the generalizing purposes of the narrative. There is some attempt at this, especially along the lines of Gulliver's misanthropy, but not enough to dilute the didactic function of the satire.

The final chapter of the fourth section is, of course, intended to drive home the salient point: that the principal design of Gulliver's narrative "was to inform, and not to amuse thee." The disproportion lies here, the disproportion so necessary for satirical or utopian literature and yet so delicately detrimental for the novel.[3] Swift's

[3] Such an argument is not teleological. That is, we are not arguing back from our attempted definition of the novel and those works that fulfill it while denying this status to those that somehow fail the definition. We are, on the contrary, arguing that the loose form we have called the novel makes its own kind of demands, and that

satire is one of the last and, clearly, best instances of the tenacity of old forms—allegory, satire, utopian narrative—the very thing the novel was to supersede in its uneasy quest for different priorities of experience.

John Cleland—Memoirs of a Woman of Pleasure (*1749*)

The publication of John Cleland's *Memoirs of a Woman of Pleasure* (popularly known as *Fanny Hill*) calls up its associations with other books published at mid-century, especially *Tom Jones*, *Roderick Random*, and *Clarissa.* It demonstrates certain carry-overs from those novels, as well as from *Pamela*, *Moll Flanders*, picaresque fiction, and the society novel which flourished earlier in the century. Its patina of soft pornography has disguised the fact that *Fanny Hill* is very much a hybrid fiction, a composite of previous techniques and familiar substances.

Like *Pamela*, it is rooted in the Cinderella tale; like Richardson's novels, its method is epistolary—although consisting of only two long letters; like Fielding and Smollett, Cleland employs the picaresque narrative style without being specifically picaresque; like *Moll Flanders*, it leads its heroine through a predatory London in which danger lurks in every kindly smile. And yet it never achieves the quality we have associated with the novel. It is a near-novel, and its failure to achieve novel status we can attribute to the nature of Cleland's conception of his heroine and to his reliance on sexual detail as a substitute for the detail of a more varied experience. Moreover, Cleland has not found a language flexible enough for the novel. It is homogeneous, only occasionally graphic, but without the quality of sufficient distinction. Of course, filtering all experience through the eyes and mouth of an adolescent girl helps create the lack of variety; or, contrariwise, forces us to exclude language and expression as serious considerations.

These are relative issues, however, and I am certain that most future historians of the novel will include *Fanny Hill* alongside *Pamela* in the genre. The best way to illustrate my exclusion of the book

Gulliver's Travels, like all satirical-utopian literature before and after it, sets up different ones. We are in the position of Gotthold Lessing, who, while recognizing the overlapping categories of poetry and painting in his *Laocoön*, tried to define their distinctive features, not to assert the superiority of one over the other, but to clarify each one's potentialities.

from the novel genre is in the area that has made it most famous, as a sexual novel and as a sexual experience. Here it limns a fantasy world, the fantasy world of the pornographic adventure. In the main, Fanny's experiences with sex are all toward fulfillment. Her chief worry in most of her experiences is whether or not she is internally large enough to sheath an exceptionally preponderant male organ. The sexual "resolution," so to speak, is often one of logistics rather than experience; that is, of the maneuverability of an engorged penis into an area that appears too small to house it.

Such an adventure is humorous, since it appears to have analogies to military maneuvers; but Cleland treats it seriously, albeit lightly. There is no mockery of the situation. Instead, there is a serious commitment to the solving of the problem—adjusting the female buttocks, propping up the thighs, moistening the tip of the attacking penis, hitting the target at a particular angle, driving ahead despite hymenal resistance. One thinks of a mortar attack rather than of the rather complicated nature of two people experiencing an intimate act. Put another way, if there are complications, they exist solely in bringing the event about. Few complications exist in the nature of the experience, since it is always successful.

Sex is nearly always sweet and never truly unpleasant, even when the male is not to Fanny's liking or has special tastes which are not particularly hers. Her distaste quickly turns to acceptance; she is a compliant female, waiting to be molded. And molded (and kneaded) she is. If the male requires special attention, she gives it without any loss of vitality. If he requires birching, for example, she enters into it and allows herself to be birched—at a time when she no longer needs the money. Moll Flanders would never have permitted that; she may have accepted birching, but only as a way of making her fortune, not for the pleasure of the experience. The point here, however, is not Fanny's openness to experience, which is certainly necessary for a novel, but her compliance in any scheme and her acceptance of other people's plans for herself. She has no will of her own, no scheme or pattern of her own needs. Allowing herself to be shaped, she gives herself up to what she assumes will be a completely benevolent nature. She trusts those who will direct her fortunes as much as she trusts the hand of nature, which has turned her into an appealing young woman. Inner and outer are indistinguishable for her.

Fanny's experience of sex is instinctual, primitive, without complication, while Pamela's attitude to sexuality is full of the fears and tensions of the potential experience. Although Fanny's attitude is certainly more enjoyable, Pamela's lends itself to the conflict implicit in the novelistic treatment of experience. She is caught between whatever she feels and the demands of a society that rewards abstinence; whereas Fanny has placed no restrictions on her reactions and yet is never punished for her innocence in a world that requires caution and discretion. When Pamela denies herself any sexual involvement, we may react adversely to her primness and hypocrisy; but, at the same time, we must recognize that self-denial leads her into other possibilities, so that sex and sexual experience become allied to the larger world that Pamela, for whatever reason, wants to join.

For Fanny, the sexual adventure always leads to orgasm, her own and the male's—and strikingly always at the same instance, a matter of timing that is indeed based on a benevolent nature. Sexuality is not attached to productivity in the larger world, to station, ambition, movement beyond one's physical sense of oneself. And yet that is the very thing the novel explores, the very ground on which the novel exists. The other is fantasy, an Oriental vision appropriate to the harem experience and surely not viable for the mid-eighteenth century, which was harsh, realistic, full of contradictory and cautionary warnings.

Like Cinderella, Fanny has her cake and eats it, too. She enjoys her initiation into sex, and its monetary rewards, and still gains her beloved Charles. And it has all come to her without effort or any change in her nature; the sole change is within her groin—her vagina has become more distended than her sensibilities. It is this lack of the experiential process which marks Cleland's effort, and the book, consequently, falls into that nether world of prose narrative which is neither fish nor fowl, neither good pornography nor novel.

Samuel Johnson—Rasselas (*1759*)

Rasselas starts out from a general principle: that it is possible to discover the nature of happiness. Although the form of the narrative is very loosely that of the *Bildungsroman*—the initiation of the young man into life and self-discovery—Johnson made no use of experience that was not already preordained by the general principle. In this respect, he was pursuing an allegorical plan in which not even the illusory sense of experience was present. We can compare *Rasselas* to Voltaire's *Candide*, which appeared the same year (1759); both of which, in turn, recall the philosophical dialogue. Both lack that free play of choice or direction which, although it may later be resolved by a traditional ending, gives the experiential sense we expect from the novel.

Johnson, for example, often draws on the picaresque tradition, in that he takes Rasselas from episode to episode by means of which the young prince of Abyssinia hopes to discover what constitutes the happy life. Such an endeavor has intimations of *Don Quixote* and other utopian or pseudo-utopian literature, in which the mythical Golden Age informs the background. In chapter XVI, Rasselas, in his quest, enters Cairo, an area where Johnson could have been "novelistic" in confronting his protagonist with experiences that would alter his preconceptions about life. This change in sensibility or in attitude would suggest the process which we have associated with novel-making.

Yet all such experience is related as a third-person narrative, either through the golden philosopher Imlac or through the author. As a consequence, we meet such materials after the fact, as outside the direct experiential line. Recounted are particulars of narrative such as could be related in an expository essay driving toward a resolution of ideas. From such particulars, further, Imlac draws general conclusions, which now supersede the very materials that they draw upon. Imlac's point, reiterated repeatedly, is that a realistic assessment of life, and only that, can overcome false hopes. Imlac's conclusions are, actually, based on the premises of the first lines of *Rasselas*:

> Ye who listen with credulity to the whispers of fancy, and persue with eagerness the phantoms of hope; who expect that age will perform the promises of youth, and that the deficiencies of the present day will be supplied by the morrow; attend to the history of Rasselas prince of Abissinia. [Rinehart edition, ed. Bertrand H. Bronson]

With Imlac's conclusions before us—that is, with the experiential aspect of the narrative concluded—Rasselas now meets various types, all of whom will illustrate Imlac's wisdom. These types are, in their way, analogous to the vices and virtues Pilgrim meets in Bunyan's book. They include a philosopher whose philosophy is insufficient in time of need; a prosperous man who is fearful; a hermit who finds solitude almost unbearable; a confused philosopher who argues that men should live according to nature. No one is happy because no one has realistically assessed himself and his situation. All are types; all live without any particularity of felt experience. When change does occur within them, it occurs in all instances as the result of doctrine, not from a sense of life.

Such a development or sequence of events would not in itself preclude a novelistic quality, except that it pre-empts the entire narrative. In his short book, *Johnson and Boswell* (1969), E. L. McAdam, Jr., points out that nothing is concluded, that no loose ends are tied up, reminding us that the final chapter is called "The conclusion, in which nothing is concluded." The very point, however, is *not* the ambiguity of the chapter but its explicitness, the fact that the conclusion is implicit in every aspect of the narrative: which is that the prince and princess will return to Abyssinia, made wiser by Imlac's advice. Although they may not obtain their personal desires, such as Rasselas's wish for a little kingdom and his sister's for a college of learned women, nevertheless they will understand the boundaries of happiness and their expectations will be more in alignment with reality. Like Candide, they have learned to cultivate their garden and seek in themselves a balance between inner and outer.

The route to such a conclusion, not the conclusion itself, is what determines the "novelistic" quality of a narrative. Johnson's route, via Imlac, is toward "transcendental truths." The poet and, by analogy, the individual must "disregard present laws and opinions, and rise to general and transcendental truths, which will always be the same: he must content himself with the slow progress of his name; contemn the applause of his own time, and commit his claims to the justice of posterity." (p. 629) This is homiletic, didactic, anagogic in its plea for a higher self. It belongs more to religion or loose philosophizing than to the novel.

Johnson himself lacked that openness to change that characterizes the novelist, even when the latter, like Goldsmith, argues for traditional values and fears change. Implicit in Goldsmith's gentle novel is the sense of alternate experiences, of a counterlife, no matter how mutedly and disadvantageously these qualities may be presented, no matter how fiercely they are attacked. In Johnson, that sense of the "other"—whatever it is—is rejected *before* it is experienced. Once outside the Happy Valley, the prince and princess are made to reject the content of their adventures before they have even experienced the hazards of such encounters.

In his praise of Richardson, Johnson chose not to see how the former, through the strength of his presentation of a counter, forbidden life, was trying it out for its potential, giving it a stature of its own, throwing the reader into an alternate process, before finally rejecting it as destructive of a "normal" society. Johnson seized on Richardson's conclusion without granting that in the novel everything is in the process, the route, the getting to the end, not the end.

William Beckford—Vathek (*1786*)

Although I discussed *Vathek* briefly in the chapter on Gothic, where Vathek is viewed as a thousand-and-one-nights version of Walpole's Manfred, this type of prose fiction belongs more narrowly to near-novels than to novels. There is, admittedly, a broad overlapping here, for if we refuse novel status to *Vathek*, why admit *Otranto*? Do we exclude Beckford's narrative because it owes more to the subgenre of the Oriental-foreign tale, which became a popular form in eighteenth-century England, than it does to the main lines of the developing novel?

Taking the opposite position is Robert Kiely, who, in *The Romantic Novel in England*, comments: ". . . Beckford's *Vathek*, when not dismissed as Asian Gothic, is often regarded as the last remnant of this pseudo-Oriental literary fashion which had reached its peak nearly thirty years earlier [with the following English and French versions: *The Vision of Mirzah*, 1711; *Lettres Persanes*, 1721; *Voyage to Abyssinia*, 1735; *Candide*, 1759; *Rasselas*, 1759; *The Citizen of the World*, 1760–2; *Contes Moraux*, 1761–5]. Nothing could be less true." (p. 44) Later, however, Kiely mentions some of the sources for *Vathek*, indicating *The Arabian Nights, Persian Tales, Mogul Tales,* and *The Adventures of Abdalla Son of Hanif.* Such sources and Beckford's inability to go beyond them would place him close indeed to the very pseudo-Oriental subgenre which Kiely has denied for him. If we measure Beckford against other novelists, he would certainly appear to fit more comfortably in the "tale" than in the novel tradition.

Without complicating our argument unduly, we can note that the tale involves a somewhat different set of criteria from those applied to the novel. Implied in the tale is a fantasy life for the characters which differentiates this subgenre from the more realistic processes of the novel. A fantasy life, whether satirical, moralistic, or otherwise, not only affects the development of the protagonist, but cuts deeply into modes of language and scenic arrangements. As we see in *Vathek*, the scenic effects are panoramic, involving hordes of people and dramatic, sweeping dioramas, such as the chasm in which fifty youths are sacrificed to the Giaour, so that the individual life and the individual consequence are lost in the larger orchestration. When this occurs, the ambience is closer to that of allegory, whose intent is to dwarf the individual and to strengthen the general and universal.

The caliph Vathek is in search of power, ultimate and forbidden, willing to sacrifice anyone and anything in his quest. His search, however, is really for himself, and the narrative becomes tangled in the web of Vathek's own narcissism. In everything he does, he wishes to see himself, to view his grandeur, "to adore himself," as Beckford writes. "He consoled himself, however, for this intruding and unwelcome perception of his littleness with the thought of being great in the eyes of others, and flattered himself that the light of his mind would extend beyond the reach of his sight and extort from the stars the decrees of his destiny." (Scribner's edition, p. 130)

The very quest for power, consequently, does not result in the kinds of conflict we associate with the novel, but with what we can relate to myth and allegory. Vathek may be questing for his self, but it is a self he wishes to see reflected in the eyes of others, not in his own. He looks for the mirror image, not for the thing itself. Vathek's narcissism, which appears excessive even for a romantic and pre-romantic age, is allowed free rein. There is no censoring element either in the men around him or in God or in Vathek himself; lacking conscience, wanting restrictions, he is not disallowed whatever his tastes lead him to. As Kiely writes: "He is not therefore a Faustus, but a child's fantasy Everyman who fills the whole world with amusing toys and good things to eat." (p. 60)

Such unrestricted appetites, without either personal denial or societal punishment, place Vathek in the hands of divine judgment, the area where allegory, not the novel, operates. Vathek dies, the victim of his own voracious, amoral designs, but he dies impersonally, because *all men must die.* In the novel, a man dies not only because his body has given out, as all bodies fail, but because he has himself taken a course of action which leads to death. The distinction is significant.

Vathek's doom is spelled out by an oracle, deriving from the lips of

Mahomet himself. The decree is irrevocable. Yet the conjunction of Vathek and the voice of doom is not embedded in the nature of the material, nor is such a development intrinsic to what we know of Vathek. The doom at the finale is a curtain scene, a way to allow the secondary characters to exit into their lives unimpeded by the tyrant. Dramatically, the final scene does not derive from preconditions implicit in the material. Once again, the grandiosity of the production has pre-empted the very areas in which the novel can function. Without restrictions of character, scene, conception, and development, without consideration for these elements of probability and realistic process, Beckford has pursued a vision, somewhat like Vathek's, of childish fantasies wrapped in a tall tale.

9

The Development of Technique in the Eighteenth-Century Novel[1]

While we tend to view the eighteenth-century English novel as somewhat rudimentary, in reality, during a thirty-year period from *Robinson Crusoe* through *Clarissa* and *Tom Jones*, the novel was more or less fixed technically for the next 150 years. The strategical problems that Defoe, Fielding, and Richardson grappled with in terms of narrative technique, plot and character, time considerations, nature of the narrator were the fundamental difficulties facing the genre. This does not suggest that they in any way solved such matters. Their attempts were not resolutions but part of the developing process of novel-making; and while they searched for subjects that would attract an audience, they also sought the most effective packaging for their ideas. We have, perhaps, overstressed the relationship of these writers to an audience without taking into account the fact that they were also craftsmen and artists, men with canniness and know-how in several areas of accomplishment, crude as some of their methods may appear in the later light of Flaubert, James, and Conrad.

We can trace the development of novelistic technique in many

[1] This chapter will chart the ways in which the early novelists, in practice and theory, came to grips with technical matters. For the reader who has approached this book sequentially, there will be some superficial repetition of earlier sections. For the most part, however, this discussion is not duplicated either in this study or elsewhere.

areas: the dependence on different aspects of point of view, away from the omniscient narrator toward the self-aware or self-conscious narrator; the employment of a time technique to upset the linear time sequences of more elementary narratives; the widespread acceptance of the epistolary technique, a form developed and exhausted within the eighteenth century; the growing distinction made by critics and novelists between the romance or epic and the narrative coming to be known as the novel; the further distinction, made chiefly by the novelists, between the novel and satire; the move away from historical narrative toward new forms of narrative; the incorporation of burlesque, caricature, ridicule, and satire within the new developing form; the emergence of plot structures from the very different ideas about plot of Fielding, Richardson, and Sterne; the expansion of narrative devices to create multiple points of view, as well as to distance narrator from narrative; the growing awareness that the author must, somehow, vanish, so that the novel could take on its own hues and colors as an independent entity; and, most important, the growing rejection of picaresque, although it never disappeared and was not *necessarily* a negative factor in the novel's development.

The last point provides us with our overview. That is, all these experiments in technique amount to stratagems for blunting the thrust of picaresque, for relieving its stranglehold on the long prose narrative. As the novel became more responsive to domestic life, so did the need grow to tame its narrative, to close down on the openness of an early form and a previous time. Picaresque only partially reflected the needs and ideals of a middle-class society; and so we note the development of a technique that will control the novel's materials, in line with the bourgeoisie's own growing control over the materials of its life.

Technique, therefore, is not only literary, it is social. It reflects what is happening in a society as much as it mirrors what is happening in a genre. Put another way, a genre as socially responsive as the novel—as distinct from poetry or even drama—will not develop without taking social change into account. An audience demands a certain form as well as content. In the later nineteenth century, when *an audience* split into *audiences,* when a general audience became coteries, technique also divided, so to speak, into the more specialized and abstruse kind for the "serious" reader and the more available kind for the general reader. Thus, James, Conrad, and

Joyce co-existed with Wells, Bennett, and Galsworthy. In the eighteenth century, although "serious" and "popular" novelists also co-existed, the genre did not have quite that diversity, because the demands upon it were less diverse. The one area, however, that both serious and frivolous novelists appeared to agree upon was diverting picaresque from its episodic, somewhat unfocused conception of prose fiction.

Why, we ask, was picaresque inadequate to represent the mid-century view of life? All novelists after Defoe recognized that the picaresque form, while containing sufficient realism, as well as sufficient elements of probability and probable characters, lacks a center; for its idea is based on moving through an endless variety of time, place, and event. Under such conditions, there is no stopping place in the fiction itself. In picaresque, there is little or no sense of a society or a community, only a sense of boundaries or limits for the individual protagonist. There is no opportunity for the protagonist to measure himself against more than his own goals. The question of existence, which is essentially a matter of measurement of oneself against an "other" (person, group, force, cosmos), is at its most primitive in picaresque. The "other" is always a physical being, rarely an idea; a pressure, rarely a philosophical issue or a loss of purpose or will. Only *Don Quixote* combines picaresque with the range of ideas listed above; later novelists could not match Cervantes's achievement in the picaresque form. Clearly, then, picaresque would have to disappear as the novel turned toward tragic possibilities, domesticity, and domestic comedy, away from on-the-road adventures and from romance.

Fielding spoke of the scene "opening itself by small degrees," and we are amazed by the sophistication of the conception, although we are not at all certain how Fielding meant it. We are equally amazed by Clara Reeve's perception when, in 1785, she saw the novel clearly enough to write: "The Novel gives a familiar relation of such things as pass every day before our eyes, such as may happen to our friend or to ourselves; and the perfection of it is to represent every scene in so easy and natural a manner, and to make them appear so probable, as to deceive us into a persuasion (at least while we are reading) that all is real, until we are affected by the joys or distresses of the persons in the story as if they were our own." (*The Progress of Romance*, p. 111)

Similarly, a lesser novelist such as Mrs. Manley could say as early as 1705:

He that writes a true History ought to place the accidents as they naturally happen, without endeavouring to sweeten them for to procure a greater credit, because he is not obliged to answer for their probability; but he that composes a History to his fancy [a fiction, really] gives his heroes what characters he pleases, and places the accidents as he thinks fit, without believing he shall be contradicted by other Historians; therefore he is obliged to write nothing that is improbable. 'Tis nevertheless allowable that an Historian shows the elevation of his genius when, advancing improbable actions, he gives them colours and appearances capable of persuading. [preface to *Queen Zarah*, 1705]

Such clear statements of motives about novel, romance, history, probability, narrative technique (epistolary, picaresque, and others) must obviously be translated into their technical equivalents. Further, each utilization of an appropriate technique involves some awareness of a time technique; that is, some recognition that time in history and time in romance differ from time in the novel. Our novelists verbalized little of this, although implicit in every shift away from picaresque is a temporal shift away from clock and calendar time toward complications we do not normally associate with the eighteenth-century novel.

It is worth pausing a moment to show how temporal considerations become part of any technical development away from picaresque. We have already indicated, in the introduction, how prefaces, asides, forewords, digressions in the body of the novels, and essays all indicate a preoccupation with time. As early as *Robinson Crusoe*, we are confronted by fairly sophisticated time considerations. Defoe has, in effect, two time sequences—internal and external—running side by side, although such sequences rarely become obtrusive or substantive. Robinson's journal is a crude attempt to capture internal time; while his awareness within that journal of time passing in the outside world approximates external time. Robinson, consequently, is always responding to two kinds of awareness: the island time, in which he is, as it were, imprisoned indefinitely, and his sense of another time outside his immediate frame of reference. Although he must live, be vital, within his journal time, it is that external time into which he wishes to fit himself—it is in *that* time he will find the real center of his existence and hope for the future.

While Defoe does not use this dichotomy or conflict substantively, nevertheless such time considerations are rarely far from Robinson's thoughts. He marks off outside time in his journal even as he insists on his inner life on the island. He will survive physically on the island, if successful in his endeavors, but he lives, and succeeds, psychologically, in terms of the outside. As a further dimension to what is already a complex consideration, Defoe presents the entire matter in his preface as a "true" story, with himself as editor, not author. Thus, in a vague way, we have still another temporal dimension, that of the "author" standing outside his work, editing what purports to be a historical narrative.

None of this has the conscious complications it has in Conrad, James, Proust, or Faulkner. With the same casual ingenuity with which he stumbled onto so many projects, Defoe stumbled on all kinds of novelistic problems, although stumbling here means passing on without emphasis. His glancing involvement with temporal considerations makes time appear as a prism reflecting different kinds of light: the outside author, in his time, as editor; the narrative that is not yet journal, reflecting an external time that is "real time" for a man imprisoned on an island for twenty-eight years; the inside time of the journal itself—a journal, moreover, that will end when his supply of ink runs out; the additional fact that the journal catches time past—it is written once Robinson has settled in and can afford the leisure of writing a journal. With that factor, we have premonitions of the epistolary narrative, of the character *writing down his life* as a parallel of, or substitute for, external events. Inner and outer join here in some curiously symbolic way, even though Defoe was not making conscious use of any or all of these considerations. Yet in this conception he clearly has broken with picaresque.

Apparently, picaresque was disturbing for the eighteenth-century novelist because it no longer reflected society. Something comparable occurred in the early twentieth century when novelists and poets recognized that traditional styles no longer had the tones and rhythms of modern life. These are extraliterary perceptions, evidently, but they are reflected almost immediately by the novel. The response is an adjustment in technique and content, then a refinement of the changes, and so on, in a dialectic of seemingly opposing elements working toward a temporary synthesis. Kenneth Burke, in another context, called these shifts and changes "strategies" or symbolic actions.

In the long essay "The Philosophy of Literary Form," for instance, Burke speaks of critical and imaginative works as "answers to questions posed by the situation in which they arose. They are not merely answers, they are *strategic* answers, *stylized* answers." He goes on to say: "So I should propose an initial working distinction between 'strategies' and 'situations,' whereby we think of poetry (I here use the term to include any work of critical or imaginative cast) as the adopting of various strategies for the encompassing of situations. These strategies size up the situations, name their structure and outstanding ingredients, and name them in a way that contains an attitude towards them." (*The Philosophy of Literary Form: Studies in Symbolic Action*, 1973, p. 3) Burke adds that the "situations are real: the strategies for handling them have public content; and in so far as situations overlap from individual to individual, or from one historical period to another, the strategies possess universal relevance."

We have no intention of measuring the early novel against so sophisticated a yardstick, especially one that appears to have more relevance for drama and poetry than for the novel. But if we are dealing with strategists such as Defoe, with his endless projects, or Fielding, with his background in theater, or Richardson, with his long interest in drama, or Smollett, with *his* background as a failed playwright—if these writers are our major materials, then we can assume that their literary endeavors reflect a concern with strategies, symbolic actions, and formalistic solutions for situational dramas.

All of them strive for unity, even minor writers like Thomas Holcroft. In his preface to *Alwyn; or, the Gentleman Comedian* (1780), Holcroft used "romance" to designate an episodic, picaresque structure, and retained the term "novel" for a narrative sequence of unified design. The goal for the novelist was a sense of wholeness, while the romancer could work without the interrelationships of the various parts of his narrative. Like many of his predecessors, Holcroft was also trained in the theater.

Let us then take up in a loosely sequential way some of the strategies devised to blunt the episodic narrative and note, through these strategies, how the eighteenth-century novelists created mirror images of their society, not only in content, but in technique. Our concerns are in four large, overlapping areas:

1. The development, even earlier than Defoe, of "point of view," in narrative terms[2]
2. The development of the epistolary technique, a form characteristic of, and unique to, the eighteenth century. My remarks on the epistolary method will overlap with comments in the chapters on Richardson and Smollett, which the reader should also consult
3. The development of the domestic plot in Richardson and of the episodic plot in Fielding. These are twin developments occurring at mid-century, both intended to neutralize the strung-out quality of picaresque, Richardson working in time, Fielding still working in space, but struggling toward a more cohesive formal technique to approximate theatrical process. Critics have spoken of Fielding playing with the form, an anti-novelist toying with something that was already established, but before we consider how he "sported" with the novel, it is more important to see how he tried to become a novelist
4. Connected to all three above, the employment of a time technique to upset the linear time sequences of picaresque. The most obvious utilization of this technique occurs in Richardson and Sterne, but aspects of it exist in nearly all authors who experiment with narrative

We could extend these four to include many other topics, but to discuss them all would require a book in itself. Three, however, are important enough to merit mention, even if a full discussion is impossible:

—The expansion of all kinds of narrative devices, not only epistolary, but multiple levels of narration, interrupted narrative, distancing of the narrator, and so on, all toward revising the lineality of the picaresque narrative.

—An examination of how a given narrative device affects charac-

[2] In *To the Palace of Wisdom: Studies in Order and Energy from Dryden to Blake*, Martin Price speaks of the eighteenth-century "narrator" even in forms other than the novel: "No age has made more striking use of a fictitious narrator or speaker whose peculiar slant of vision is critical to an understanding of the whole work. Swift is the most conspicuous ironist of the age in his use of Lemuel Gulliver and the insouciant teller of *A Tale of a Tub*. Pope's Socratic use of the Horatian or Juvenalian satirical speaker, Fielding's complex use of the self-conscious narrator, Sterne's Tristram Shandy, and Blake's dramatization in *Songs of Innocence and of Experience* of 'the two contrary states of the human soul' are all instances of a literature that demands that we take account of a voice, of a point of view, of a state of the soul that may also imply a world view and a religion." (p. 15)

terization; the changes in the types of character we find in the novel as against those in previous prose fiction.

—The modulation of a comic point of view; the absorption of satire, burlesque, caricature, and ridicule, among others, into the novel form. Paulson notes that after 1730, Fielding, Smollett, and Sterne "were the only first-rate satiric temperaments to emerge in England and all three turned to the novel." In the process, he says, "they transformed satire beyond recognition and left the mark of satire upon the novel." (p. 9) Other forms of comedy also became absorbed into the novel, so that by the end of the century the novel had pre-empted all comedy except that still upon the stage. Such an absorption is as much a matter of technique as it is one of content.

Point of View

Critics after James and Conrad have regarded point of view as if it were the salvation of the novel. The development of point of view in the eighteenth century and earlier, however, was more casual, simply one of many things the early novelists stumbled upon unawares. The point is important: we should not deify point of view as if it were *the* crucial stage in the mutation of the novel from crude beginnings.

In distinguishing between novel and romance, the writer starts from certain assumptions that are reflected in his handling of point of view. Point of view, primarily, takes into account several narrative possibilities or opportunities. In his *PMLA* article "Point of View in Fiction: The Development of a Critical Concept," Norman Friedman asks four basic questions about the narrator:

1. Just who is he or she? That is, is he the author himself, in the first or third person, is he an inset character in the first person, or is he, possibly, no one at all?
2. In what relationship to the story is the narrator when he tells it? Friedman asks: Is he "above, periphery, center, front, or shifting?"
3. Specifically, what does the narrator channel to the reader?—the author's words and thoughts? the characters' words, thoughts, and actions? a combination of these? A corollary of the above is: How does the reader receive information about "mental states, setting, situation, and character"?

4. What about the distancing of the reader in relationship to the narrator? Is the reader placed within the story, far from it, or in a shifting perspective?[3]

The above is a purely literary response to the materials. We must, I think, handle point of view in a somewhat larger perspective. Until considerations of point of view pre-empted most other assumptions about narrator and narrative, point of view was itself embedded in a paraliterary dimension of novelistic development, attached to a distinction between novel and romance. As we have already noted, Clara Reeve catches the sense of the change from one genre to another, writing in 1785, when a large body of novels existed to provide an inductive definition:

> The Romance is an heroic fable, which treats of fabulous persons and things. The Novel is a picture of real life and manners and of the times, in which it is written. The Romance, in lofty and elevated language, describes what never happened nor is likely to happen. The Novel gives a familiar relation of such things as pass every day before our eyes, such as may happen to our friend or to ourselves; and the perfection of it is to represent every scene in so easy and natural a manner, and to make them appear so probable, as to deceive us into a persuasion (at least while we are reading) that all is real, until we are affected by the joys or distresses of the persons in the story as if they were our own. [I, 111–12]

Translated into point of view, this distinction reminds us that romance comes from a society given over to privilege, a society in which an overviewer, an "omniscient narrator"—whether man or God—is a natural outgrowth of politics and society as well as a reflector of a traditional sacred outlook. In the romance, we expect the author to be superior in word and command to any one of his characters. The authorial narrator is magisterial in his control. For the novel, such control, if not outmoded or superseded, is at least questioned.

We can see this fundamental distinction, which translates into narrator and narrative process, almost one hundred years before Clara Reeve, in Congreve's preface to the reader of *Incognita* (1692).

[3] *PMLA*, LXX (December 1955), 1168–9. Friedman's piece is valuable chiefly for the potentialities it demonstrates in the later nineteenth-century concern with narrative processes. Except for the outline of materials cited above, it has less application to the early development of the novel, which placed only limited emphasis on point of view.

He speaks there of the novel being "of a more familiar nature," which delights us with "odd events" which are not "wholly unusual or unpresidented." The romance, on the contrary, conveys wonder. Congreve then places this point in a further perspective, which is that all traditions must "give place to the drama." He goes on to say he resolved "to imitate dramatick writing, namely, in the design, contexture, and result of the plot . . ." His point is not precisely clear, but we can assume that Congreve's move toward the dramatic was a repudiation, in principle at least, of the tyrannical overview of romance and an attempt, instead, to disperse responsibility among a diversity of characters. At a time when romance was still flourishing, Congreve called *Incognita* a novel, although the term was not yet at all fixed for what later came to be known as the novel.

Similarly, Mrs. Manley, thirteen years after Congreve, but still eighty years before Clara Reeve, reiterated the need for verisimilitude in the relationship between the sexes, in the handling of individual characters, in the author's attitude toward "time and sense" as connected to incidents, in matters of motivation as well as conclusion and resolution. While Congreve saw everything subsumed under "dramatick writing," Mrs. Manley was anxious to define her own kind of "true History," whose cornerstone is verisimilitude. Nevertheless, they were both moving toward something comparable, which is a cultural shift that, in literary terms, becomes translated into a narrative shift; into a shift, finally, in point of view.

This movement from romantic omniscience to other methods of narration involves, then, shifts in cultural sensibility: in the slow growth of the individual's social and political awareness; in the increasing atomization of a population; in the movement away from an authoritarian, despotic hierarchy; in the development of a secular spirit and a gradual repudiation of the sacred; in the shift from authority passed down from above to authority and responsibility shared—even when messy irresponsibility results.

In an analagous way, Lessing argued in *Laocoön* that art was capable of generating its own forms, its own responses to the world; that rules as handed down were no longer applicable in themselves; that critics ought not to make *a priori* rules but to explore and analyze art as a way of discovering its laws of operation. Although Lessing's study comes in 1766, it was actually a summary of many already-existing tendencies; and what it says about painting and literary form is meaningful for the development of the novel as a counter- or adversary force early in the century.[4]

Thus, Defoe's development of narrative technique in *Robinson Crusoe* and *Moll Flanders* is not happenstance, or a solely literary phenomenon. His method, as well as his content, is embedded in something as broad as the dimensions of his own life. When Moll says, in her own voice, as the creator of her own fate, that "I was a great fortune" (Riverside edition, p. 113), we find an extremely complex but natural development of an early-eighteenth-century narrative device. Except for some editing of Moll's story, which Defoe tells us he did to make it more modest, the novel bypasses the omniscient author in favor of the direct language and thoughts of Moll.[5] Narrative technique immediately becomes part of the shift in power in the society as a whole; the narrator is herself part of that shift, away from the authoritarian author, who has, however, forsaken his prerogatives reluctantly. A further concession is that the author must, as it were, "rewrite" *his* way of saying something in favor of her way of saying it. Language itself, then, becomes part of the transference of power and rights.

The words themselves are full of cultural connotations. The metaphorical phrasing transforms the person into the thing—the "great fortune"—which is what the narrator and her narrative are all about: money and power. The vulgarity of the expression indicates a realignment of language and social position: if Moll were indeed a great fortune, she would not be in her present situation. Further, it is not necessary to have the fortune, only necessary to be thought to

[4] Joseph Frank's influential essay "Spatial Form in Modern Literature" carries the above considerations into an examination of modern literature. Although his stress is different, his point is similar: that "changes in aesthetic form always involve major changes in the sensibility of a particular cultural period." ("Spatial Form," originally published in *Sewanee Review*, but more available in *The Widening Gyre: Crisis and Mastery in Modern Literature*, pp. 9 ff.) This argument is no mere restatement of a Hegelian *Zeitgeist* theory; it is, rather, a recognition that literary form (and not only "content") is interwoven into a cultural period, not as resolving anything, but as a sensitive indicator of the various mutations occurring in that society.

[5] A further *caveat:* we must remember that Moll is recounting her life from the vantage point of repentant old age, and adding moral feelings that she did not have in her youth. This "gap," if it can be called that, exists also for Tristram Shandy, whose memories have been filtered through the mind of the sick man, closer to death than to birth. The self-conscious narrator, from Moll to Proust's Marcel, is almost always involved in such narrative "straining." Richardson tried to reduce the gap by using the epistolary method, just as others did with journal styles and, recently, stream of consciousness.

have it. The accent is distinctive of the speaker and revelatory of Defoe's motives in writing and creating. The author, nevertheless, remains outside. Moll is sufficient to say it all for him, for he has discovered the true accent of his narrator. As long as she can reveal herself in this way, his omniscience is unneeded. He can "vanish," which is a word and a strategy we associate with a much later, more sophisticated period in the development of the novel.

Reviewing Moll's standing as a narrator, we see her as an inset character in the first person, at the very beginning of the book, channeling to the reader a combination of her words, thoughts, and actions, all directly related, with the reader placed near the narrative line but shifted as necessary further back. The omniscient novelist is present, but Defoe has removed himself directly from Moll's tale by means of an ingenious preface to the novel, and *there* he works his hand, as it were, as the godlike novelist.

First, he establishes himself as the editor of the narrative, which he has put into "modester words than she told it at first." Second, he warns the reader to be more "pleas'd with the moral than the fable, with the application than with the relation, and with the end of the writer more than with the life of the person written of." Third, he tells the audience that because of his sifting of the original, none can find fault or "cast any reproach upon it." He satisfies the reader that the wicked are punished or made penitent, that "there is not an ill thing mention'd but it is condemn'd," not a "just thing but it carries its praise along with it." Finally, and most importantly for narrative purposes, Defoe informs us he has excised two parts of the narrative; that is, the life of Moll's governess, whose career sounds suspiciously like Moll's, and the life of Moll's transported husband, whose adventures, we assume, would be the typical "Newgate" highwayman's tale, "twelve years of successful villainy."

With these few remarks, Defoe has, with incredible skill for a still-rudimentary form, ostensibly removed himself from the narrative and held to Moll as the primary source of the reader's knowledge. The device of the first-person revelation is not the element that should impress us. Far more impressive is Defoe's use of the prefatory material to make his pitch as the omniscient novelist, reminding us there rather than in the text that he has not forsaken the reader to a vile, sinful tale. The removal of the novelist in this way is not in every instance so important. In *Moll Flanders* it is significant because Moll's narrative style is of a piece, *sui generis,* and interference or interruption, especially along homiletic lines, would disrupt its tone and rhythm.

For Fielding, on the other hand, such interruptions fit well into the comic line of *Joseph Andrews* and *Tom Jones.* Fielding's comic approach to his material, as well as his variety of means and techniques, opens it up and allows him to enter the narrative in ways denied to novelists like Defoe and Richardson, who circumscribed the authorial role. In *Joseph Andrews*, for example, we are constantly aware of the omniscient novelist, *always* there, insistent about his presence, very much the opposite of the dramatist. Fielding insists upon himself in a variety of ways: in the prefatory material to books and chapters of the novel, in phrasing such as "to return to," in the extended similes that act as comic comment upon the inset material, in direct remarks upon qualities in the characters.

Yet, at the same time, Fielding tried something more sophisticated, although not always successfully: in Andrews and Adams he created for himself, so to speak, posts of observation. This is not quite so apparent as it may appear, since Fielding was trying to combine novelistic omniscience with theatrical omniscience. He has his drama within—that is, characters who define themselves through their own words and actions—and his novel without, the externals presented through the author's words.[6] We can attach such contrasting methods to Fielding's inherent interest in opposing elements, to the fact that his play of opposites in content is nearly always translated directly into contrasts and opposites in technique. The opposing drives of the man himself, as we suggested in the Fielding chapter, become part of the dialectic of techniques.

In *Joseph Andrews*, Fielding rarely settles on one method. He moves in and out of the dramatic and non-dramatic, at one time leaving the characters to themselves, at another time giving us both information and point of view that must derive from the interrupt-

[6] Writing about parallel matters, Wayne C. Booth touches on this point: "A curious ambiguity in our notions of 'omniscience' is ordinarily hidden by our terminology. Many modern works that we usually classify as narrated dramatically, with everything relayed to us through the limited views of the characters, postulate fully as much omniscience in the silent author as Fielding claims for himself." (In "Distance and Point of View: An Essay in Classification"—an expanded version of chapter VI of *The Rhetoric of Fiction*, which the reader should also consult; originally published in *Essays in Criticism*, XI [1961], reprinted in *The Theory of the Novel*, ed. Philip Stevick, 1967, p. 102.)

ing, intruding novelist. Unlike Defoe, he does not allow his characters to define themselves fully, although he tries to convey the illusion of their so doing. Even this procedure, however, shifts within the novel itself. At the beginning, when Fielding is intent on satirizing Richardson's *Pamela*, authorial commentary is at its maximum; when Fielding allows his story its own play, authorial interruptions become somewhat less frequent. Since Adams is relatively unconnected to the burlesque of *Pamela*, he appears to be given more of his own lead than Joseph and Fanny, who are more directly involved in the original satire.

None of this is quite consistent—Fielding is not James, nor does he intend to be. In chapter XIV and those following, for example, with Adams and Parson Trulliber, we have scenes examining their respective Christian values that are almost completely dramatic in their objective reporting. On the other hand, in a satirical chapter just preceding, one that features Mrs. Slipslop with Fanny and Joseph on the periphery, we have narrative interfused with authorial intrusions. Such intrusions, here as well as elsewhere, comment not only on the plot and characters but also on the style, mentioning practices from traditional literature in order to make the novel appear more respectable.

Fielding, in *Joseph Andrews*, is playing many different games, and it is impossible, as well as undesirable, to pin him down.[7] In *Tom Jones*, however, he has become his own man, turning from burlesque and satire of literary matters to life itself, but even here his manner is uncertain. He tries out many different things—almost as many as Melville in *Moby-Dick*, who moves in and out of his "I," Ishmael, in and out of the consçiousness of others, tries to provide sources for his materials, gives up frequently to enter scenes without witnesses, holds the narrative together with an omniscient author, while denying his

[7] Friedman, in the *PMLA* article cited above, agrees tacitly with the Jamesians that the artist fulfills his material only by "working within limits, albeit self-imposed, and any lapse thereof is in all probability the result either of not establishing a limiting frame to begin with or of breaking the one already established." (p. 1180) Such a Jamesian judgment, however, cannot and should not be applied to a novelist like Fielding, whose work was not completed but in the process of becoming. We would not say the same of Richardson in *Clarissa*, for there material has found its method; however, for Fielding, whose four novels are all different, the "becoming" is far more important. In his haste to produce a novelistic career, he experimented with forms as he went along, without having the time, or inclination probably, to work out his theories ahead of time. Had he lived beyond *Amelia*, he might have consolidated his methods, but since we lack such works, we can only deduce from existing materials that for Fielding method was a changing process, always in the making. From such an approach, there can be no sense of lapse or even of a "limiting frame."

omniscience, all the time looking longingly at his inadequate central consciousness.[8]

The "I" of *Tom Jones* is often Tom and it is often Fielding. Tom is, in a sense, Fielding's post of observation, but, unlike James with Strether (in *The Ambassadors*), he cannot trust his own creation, for he realizes how fragile all categorization is when history, romance, and novel still appear undifferentiated. A good part of Fielding's difficulty with method, with hewing to his post of observation, is connected to the point he is making. His allegiance to Tom's self-awareness can never be complete, because while Tom *will* work out satisfactorily, he must be chastised. Tom is not what he seems to be to the others, nor is he to be accepted fully by his readers for what he appears to be to them. Fielding is a referee standing between Tom and the reader, Tom and the other characters in the book, making up the rules as he goes along and at each stage cajoling and judging the characters as well as the reader.

When such a double and triple game is translated into method, we cannot expect the intense simplicity of James's Strether, whose sensibility is ours and whose rising awareness is also ours. Characters in Fielding's novel who see Tom for what he is are often mistaken; those who don't see him for what he is are also mistaken; and the reader who wants to accept him must wait until he changes before embracing him. Tom moves within a simplified illusion-reality axis, Fielding's heritage from *Don Quixote.* Since concealment—of background and origin—is the major plot element, and since definition of genre is another major element, we should expect Fielding to leap from one method to another. Neatness of method is not the aim.

If we isolate a relatively small matter (in Book VIII, chapter IX) in a dialogue between Tom and Benjamin, now revealed as Partridge, ostensibly Tom's father, we can see how difficult it was for Fielding to hold to any single method of narration. In this scene, Partridge tells Tom about Prince Charles Stuart, the Catholic Pretender to England's throne. He assures Tom, as he has himself been assured by a Catholic priest, that Charles is "as good a Protestant as any in England." Now Tom is no Jacobite, although

[8] We recall that in chapter I of Book II, Fielding warns the reader: ". . . for as I am, in reality, the founder of a new province of writing, so I am at liberty to make what laws I please therein." While he is evidently jesting good-naturedly, jests nevertheless contain divine wisdom, and Fielding here is both justifying and cajoling. We recognize he feels he is on to something new, and, like Wordsworth in his Preface, he must shape the tastes of his audience even while appealing to it.

Partridge is, and in defense of his religious views, Tom supports the cause of King George II as "the cause of liberty and true religion."

We have assumed from early on that Tom is the author's post of observation, since it is Tom's development which is the focus of the novel. If so, what ironies are involved in Tom's defense of George and how ambiguous Fielding's reliance on his protagonist's point of view must become! For a defense of George suggests a defense of the administration that threw Fielding off the stage when his dramatic career was moving smoothly. King George's wife, Caroline of Anspach, was a long-time advocate of Robert Walpole, and Walpole was Fielding's chief target and antagonist, the author of the 1737 Licensing Act that did in Fielding's theatrical career, the same Walpole who was the butt of *Jonathan Wild.* Later in the novel, Western calls the pack around the throne Hanover rats, a common phrase of the times; Fielding, who opposes Western on humanitarian grounds, agrees with his epithets against the throne. At the same time, while seemingly supporting Jones against Partridge, he must hide his own mixed feelings about the crown.

Given such a conflict of allegiances and loyalties, where can an author rest his method? Tom is evidently insufficient; unlike Sterne, Fielding did not wholeheartedly endorse the fragmentary nature of his protagonist's experiences. Further, even though Tom differs with Partridge's Jacobitism, he hides his feelings and goes along with the older man, as we see in subsequent narrative. Accordingly, Fielding relies on a post of observation even while diverging from it, shifting to Western—an unlikely post indeed—for some of his own views, using Partridge on other occasions, interrupting in his own voice when his various posts do not appear sufficient, forsaking his principles even as he was forging them.

Fielding becomes a supplicant for a kind of narrative he cannot himself maintain. His uneasiness with his principles derives, of course, from the novelty of his undertaking. Only Richardson, of mid-century novelists, was able to maintain a methodology in the face of shifting materials. And Richardson could do so because he had found, for then, the single element that served as a control—that is, his ability to move the narrative within the framework of writing itself, so that his materials became part of the novelistic process.

Point of view in Richardson shows experimentation along the lines of "multiple focusing," a term we normally use with Conrad and Gide. A. A. Mendilow, in *Time and the Novel*, refers to "multiple focusing" as part of the modern experimentation with *time* devices and strategies; but we can also see the term as a narrative device connected to point of view. The latter is, in turn, related to the epistolary technique. In a narrow sense, Richardson has explored more consistently what Fielding attempted in *Tom Jones*, seeking out various posts of observation within his materials. Richardson's method is neater because the epistolary technique lends itself to such a search; but, essentially, Fielding was aiming, however uneasily, at a comparable method.

For something as important as point of view in *Clarissa*, there is surprisingly little criticism that handles the subject as distinct from the epistolary technique. Booth barely touches upon it, and Watt discusses it only as part of other elements. Yet point of view deserves comment in itself, especially since the epistolary method depends on certain consistencies in the author's various posts of observation. Richardson's preface to the 1759 edition and his lengthy postscript to the novel are indirectly concerned with point of view. We must also keep in mind that there is not one novel called *Clarissa* but several, for Richardson revised substantially from one edition to the next. Point of view was a major part of these revisions, as Richardson tried to shift the balance of sympathy from Lovelace to Clarissa, or to set right what he felt had been misunderstood.

The overriding issue for Richardson appears to have been where to locate his center of intelligence, although he couches his meaning in terms of substantive stress rather than methodological procedure. In the 1759 preface, written when all the versions of *Clarissa* lay stretched out before him, he defends the epistolary style as the letters "written while the hearts of the writers must be supposed to be wholly engaged in their subjects . . . So that they abound not only with critical Situations, but with what may be called *instantaneous* Descriptions and Reflections . . ." The style of "those who write in the height of a *present* distress" is a dramatic style, not a "dry, narrative, unanimated Style of a person relating difficulties and dangers surmounted . . ." Such a method, further, is only justified as a vehicle for instruction, since it will disappoint all those who expect "a *light Novel*, or *transitory Romance;* and look upon Story in it . . . as its *sole end* . . ."

Such comments feed into point of view, as do the following remarks from the postscript, for they indicate a strategic concept distinct from the epistolary method and from considerations of temporal elements. In the postscript, Richardson speaks of refusing what would have been the "popular" resolution, a happy ending, "to wit, by reforming Lovelace, and marrying him to Clarissa." Richardson writes:

> To have a Lovelace for a series of years glory in his wickedness, and think that he had nothing to do, but as an act of grace and favour to hold out his hand to receive that of the best of women, whenever he pleased, and to have it thought, that marriage would be sufficient amends for all his enormities to others, as well as to her; he [the author] could not bear that. [v. IV, 553]

Goodness of heart, a fine face, even passion with sense as its object—none of these is sufficient for the reformation of the man except being touched by the "divine finger." Richardson says that as author he "had a great end in view."

Later in the postscript, he defends his method of presentation, responding to those who felt the "story had been told in the usual narrative way of telling stories designed to amuse and divert . . ." (v. IV, 562) He then quotes at length from a French critique of *Clarissa* (published in translation in June and August 1749, in the *Gentleman's Magazine*). The critique is concerned with the positive aspects of the epistolary style, with special comment on the advantages of "writing to the moment." It draws a distinction between the romance, in which the history is written after the fact and in which a "strength of memory beyond all example" is implied, and Richardson's method, in which particulars and contemporary detail are authentic.

Such remarks, however, move us into the uses and development of the epistolary technique, which is the next, not the present, step. As point of view, writing letters involves various emphases: timing of letters, repetition of comments and repetition of letters, stationing of the correspondent in a particular position, angle of vision, verbal stress, rapidity as well as type of response, choice of one's correspondent, chronological sequencing (for the author), questions of inclusion and exclusion of material, further questions of selection of materials for a given correspondent. This list is by no means exhaustive, and yet these are problems only touched upon in studies of the point-of-view aspects of the epistolary style.

Point of view enters in the character of Clarissa, for example, when we recognize that she is shaping reality as well as reacting to it. Each letter she writes changes her situation, although the letter is itself intended to hold the line or to make it easier for her to breathe. Each letter is even more complicated and its positioning more complex: for while she writes a letter to relieve her predicament, she also has to be sure it does not worsen it. She is different from such a post of observation as James's Strether, although he has analogous concerns vis-à-vis Mrs. Newsome. Clarissa's situation is more precarious, for at stake is the very quality of her existence, while for Strether, at stake is a certain pleasant or unpleasant future. He moves at less disadvantage, and in a less complicated world.

Always at stake in point of view is the question of the speaker's honesty and his awareness of his own intentions. When Lovelace, for example, has an interview with Miss Howe (related in the letter for Thursday afternoon, March 23, XLIX, v. I, 251 ff.), he tells her not to tell Clarissa about their conversation, which has shown extreme sympathy for Clarissa's situation with Solmes and with the Harlowes. At the same time, he intrudes a menacing tone, threatens to kill Solmes and James Harlowe—telling this to Miss Howe, but warning her not to pass it on, fully knowing she will. Thus, the letter acts circuitously as point of view; through Miss Howe's letter to Clarissa, Lovelace stations himself between the two correspondents and becomes the *chief inner voice* of the letters at that stage.

That, however, is only the begining of the device. Although Lovelace disavows to Miss Howe any intention of carrying out his threats, he has, meanwhile, planted an agent to turn the Harlowes and Mrs. Howe against Clarissa, clearly to force her into his protection. We know this from his earlier letter to Belford (March 13), which vows revenge on all women for his having been jilted in his "early manhood." He also says there that he intends to try out "stratagem and contrivance" to carry Clarissa off and see if she is indeed an angel.

With this letter, we are only about one fifteenth into the novel, and yet the potentialities of point of view are already immense. Embedded within Lovelace's strategic positioning of himself is more than conscious duplicity, more than contrivances to make Clarissa and all women bend to his needs. Also involved is Lovelace's own uncertain sense of himself. Although ostensibly he is out to ruin or try Clarissa, he desperately (if unconsciously) wants her to resist his machinations and thus convince him that one woman at least cannot be defiled. The countering need to ruin her—and prove all women can be ruined—is his need for her to withstand a monster of deception like himself. At least, such dualism is part of the Lovelace we meet before the 1751 alterations harden him for the reader.

By controlling the substance of the letters between Miss Howe and Clarissa, by making *his plans, not theirs,* the content of their correspondence, he has assumed a central position, not that different from Sterne's Tristram. He mediates between the omniscient author and the other characters, who take on their existence from the way he chooses to view them. While we could argue, as Richardson does, that Clarissa has divine purpose, we could counterargue that her position is always determined by Lovelace's plans for her and her family. They are puppets, he is puppet-master, in turn controlled by the author. Yet the magnificence of that first edition of *Clarissa* rests with Richardson's hands-off policy, his production of something gaining its own character *despite* what he thought he was doing. In that version, Lovelace mediates an entire world. He is less the great lover—we rarely, in fact, see him moving as a conqueror—than a great strategist, shaping his material so that the other characters as well as the reader must observe.

To follow up this point: Clarissa's letter of "Tuesday Morn." (XCII ff.), telling of her elopement with Lovelace, is her narrative reaction to his deception. That is, until she runs off with Lovelace, misled by his offer of help, she has had no way of responding actively to his manipulation of friends and family. Even Miss Howe has been caught in the uncertainty. When we come to Clarissa's description of the event—not written to the moment, incidentally, but after the event as a piece of history—we may feel that she is now Richardson's post of observation. In support of that view, we know she has his sympathy and her spirit will determine final things. Nevertheless, the narrative and development of point of view work against such a view, making her an agent of Lovelace's spider stratagems even while she appears to be acting out her own script.

We can say, in fact, that when Clarissa feels herself at the zenith of her free will, she has actually reached the nadir. Her description of her escape—with her fears, the threat of sword and sex, the menace of force and even of death, Lovelace's vows of violence while he swears eternal duty to her wishes—is the very stuff of Lovelace's world, of his desire for deception and conquest, by no means a part of Clarissa's own values. Accordingly, just when she thinks she is resolving the irresolvable, she has taken on Lovelace's way of seeing things, has become his woman rather than her own. Her vigilance to the contrary, he determines the substance of her world; and her "seeming" post of observation, what she has described to Miss Howe, all goes to naught. As she elopes with her doom, she has an insight into his manipulatory tactics, for she writes: ". . . it is plain to me now, by all his behaviour, that he had as great a confidence in my weakness as I had in my own strength . . . he has triumphed; for he has not been mistaken in me, while I have in myself!" (v. I, 486–7)

The reason Richardson's revisions for the 1751 edition, in reference to Lovelace in particular, are deleterious to the novel as a whole lies in his utilization of point of view. In the first edition, he had stationed Lovelace in the strongest narrative position; all else is subsumed, narratively speaking, under him. Richardson's readers reacted favorably to the "early" Lovelace in part because they accepted the male's dilemma unquestioningly, but also because they sensed Lovelace's central position among the major voices. When Richardson altered Lovelace's character in the 1751 and subsequent editions, he made more than ideological changes. He, in fact, weakened the narrative structure of the novel by undermining the credibility of his post of observation. Such considerations are extremely complex, no less complicated than Sterne's use of Tristram. One could argue that the potential of a million-word novel, in terms of point of view, will never be exhausted, and surely the subject in itself warrants a separate study.

Tristram Shandy differs from our previous examples of point of view in narrative technique because of its use of associational time. Critics almost always cite variations in temporal method as the "new" factor in Tristram's arrangement of phenomena, so that they discuss the self-conscious narrator and a time technique in tandem. Too often in such discussions, the novel appears to be about Tristram, when, in fact, it is about many things that include Tristram. In the chapter on Sterne, I quoted Booth's comment to the effect that Tristram gives the narrative its "secret of coherence." This is, in a sense, true: without Tristram's self-conscious, self-aware narrative, there could be no novel. Reliance on *that* aspect of the novel, however, may disguise something else, which is that the novel is dominated more by an idea than by a person, and that this novel which so appears to derive psychologically from the narrator really tells us very little about him and rather much about other things.

Paradoxically, the quality we most expect from a self-conscious narrator is knowledge of what he is, and yet in this very long novel, we learn relatively little about Tristram. We learn about unconnected episodes—implicit in the temporal structure of the narrative—but in the end we know far less about him than we do about Moll Flanders, Tom Jones, Clarissa, Lovelace, and other centrally located characters. In terms of the inner consciousness of Tristram, we have little sense of depth or insight into his experience. He is, chiefly, a filter for his observations of others; he does not, as it were, filter his own sensibility. In this respect, we cannot equate Tristram to the Joycean protagonists—the very young Stephen, the student Stephen, Bloom, Molly—who use interior monologues, various streams, and dissociation of temporal elements to define themselves. The technique reverberates upon them, whereas in Sterne the technique is a means of getting outside of him, to history, events, other personalities.

This distinction may seem obvious once made, but it is a point often blurred in discussions of the self-conscious narrator. Tristram's consciousness may be the organizing principle of the book; but his consciousness is not itself the center. In the later section on time, as well as in pages 208–14 of the Sterne chapter, I examine how time has pre-empted considerations of self-consciousness, so that it, time, not the narrator, becomes the manipulator.

The subject of *Tristram Shandy* is a family, not an individual; and the primary theme running through the depiction of the family is that of interruptions, of broken relationships, between father and son, husband and wife, mother and son, and so on. The only true relationship is fraternal, between Walter and Toby, but even they act at cross purposes and frequently with misunderstanding. Only Toby and Trim appear to transcend the broken family lines; that is, male bonding, to use an anthropological term, survives when every other form of connection is allied to disaster. Whatever we say of Tristram's role in putting these scenes together, what he finally links in the nine books is not self-revelatory. His stress upon conception and misconception, ennui, impotence, sublimation, his emphasis on still-born intellect, on whimsy, and on hobbyhorse all lead away from the substance of his own life toward the depiction of his environment. Events and circumstances impinge upon his life, but they do not tell us much about him. The chief disaster of his life, his middle-aged bout with consumption, which determines both his writing career and his future life, is not the result of earlier episodes filtered through his consciousness. He may be, as some have written, the product of various disasters, but we rarely gain his reaction to them.

In his excellent *PMLA* article on the Tristram syndrome, "The Self-Conscious Narrator in Comic Fiction before *Tristram Shandy*," Wayne C. Booth makes the best possible statement for Tristram's being a kind of impresario:

> . . . *Tristram Shandy* is not as chaotic a book as it seems; it is not really an explosion of all formal canons but only seems to be so. Sterne takes the novel beyond the line always carefully avoided by earlier novelists, but the line is not a line between unity and chaos. Rather it is a line between one kind of unity and another kind of unity, itself a fusion of various cohesive forces at work in the older "facetious" and "chaotic" traditions. What Sterne learned from Montaigne and Béroalde de Verville and "Gabriel John" and Dunton and Swift was not how to create a self-conscious narrator who could disrupt conventional fictional unity; he had been learning that from the novels of his own time [an upsurge of such "intrusion" novels in the 1750's]. What he learned was how to employ this kind of narrator to impose unity, of however "loose" or unconventional a kind, on seemingly disparate materials. Sterne's true achievement is in taking forces which had become more and more disruptive in comic fiction and synthesizing them, with the help of older models, into a new kind of fictional whole. [LXVII (March 1952), 185]

The distinctive element in Sterne, however, was not this ability to unify, although that is present, but his decision to create first-person narrative in which all material does *not* lead back to him, in which the "I" is not also the principal. In his essay on "Point of View in Fiction," Norman Friedman speaks of a novelist's need to find a narrator commensurate with the content he desires to convey: "Thus the choice of a point of view in the writing of fiction is at least as crucial as the choice of a verse form in the composing of a poem; just as there are certain things which cannot get said in a sonnet, so each of the categories we have detailed has a probable range of functions it can perform within its limits. The question of effectiveness, therefore, is one of the suitability of a given technique for the achievement of certain kinds of effects . . ." (p. 1180)

Sterne's "kind of effect" was not to portray Tristram. That would have been a different novel, focusing on Tristram's own development, his reaction to a superrational father, a fumbling but curiously strong mother, an impotent uncle, and so on. The sentimentality we find in the novel would, under these conditions, have been vitiated, even turned into resentment and antagonism. Instead, the comic tone requires Tristram to turn away from his own disasters toward a more impersonal view of misfortune in general and toward the broken elements of a family that appears to have had relatively little influence on his psyche or physical development. What do we know of Tristram's own love life? (After all, he lost only his foreskin in the window-sash accident, and his name *is* Tristram.) What do we know about the development of his writing talent? What do we know about how he feels toward war and peace, England and France, the power of government, the shift in society to a middle-class power structure, the movement from mercantile to capitalistic standards, and so on?

It is not essential that we answer any of these questions. Tristram and *Tristram* stand without further responses on our part. But our reaction to Sterne's narrative depends on what we expect. He has shifted to the "I" without probing the "I." His novelty lies in his manner of unification, through a central intelligence in the novel's structure who is not a central intelligence in the novel's meaning. Not until the much later novel, that of the early twentieth century, do we have the truly self-conscious narrator, conscious about himself, aware of the ironies and paradoxes of self-revelation, always evaluating himself in relationship to others and to himself.

The Epistolary Style

All methodology is interconnected and interpenetrated, what Kenneth Burke has obliquely referred to as the "dancing of an attitude," a symbolic act in which all parts, body and mind, correspond. The serious development of the epistolary style in the eighteenth century is, of course, related to the novelists' ideas about other technical matters—point of view, time, plot, narrative devices, and tone. The epistolary style had special advantages for pioneer novelists. It allowed the novelist to stay within the terms of ordinary events; it accepted the probable and the possible as the materials of the novel; it permitted the concentration of energy upon small matters that is so relevant to the early development of the genre. The epistolary method in Richardson's hands comes on as an irresistible wave of small things, the accumulation of which has occupied an entire society. It becomes the perfect bourgeois weapon.

In his "Notes on the Novel," Ortega y Gasset, although speaking specifically about Dostoevsky, makes a comment equally applicable to Richardson:

> Sometimes it takes two volumes to describe what happens in three days, indeed, in a few hours. And yet, is there anything more intense? It is an error to believe that intensity is achieved through an accumulation of occurrences. Just the opposite; the fewer the better, providing they are detailed, i.e. "realized." Here, as in many other instances, the *multum non multa* applies. Density is obtained not by piling adventure upon adventure but by drawing out each incident through a copious presentation of its minutest components. [*The Dehumanization of Art*, p. 67]

The epistolary method has widespread ramifications in nearly all technical areas.[9] As "point of view," it fits into what Booth has called the "narrator-agent" method, in which the narrator produces "some observable effect on the course of events." The epistolary narrator in a novelist such as Richardson serves a more sophisticated function than a comparable "narrator-agent" in a work where the omniscient author dominates *despite* the use of such a narrator. Conrad's Marlow, in two novels and two long stories, and Fitzgerald's Nick Carraway, in *The Great Gatsby*, are narrator-agents who add considerable complication and intensity to the narrative, but lack the full participation of a Richardsonian narrator-correspondent.

Marlow in *Heart of Darkness* acts as an intermediary of sorts between the events of the interior story, in which he participates, and the sensibilities of the reader, which he is, to some extent, manipulating. At no time, however, is he a *maker* of those interior events; he participates in what has already been shaped, and he acts as a filter, a stand-in, for the reader, trying to make the reader see what he has seen, experience what he has experienced. Despite his centrality, he has almost no effect on the events he reports. In *Lord Jim* also: although Marlow may here and there act as catalyst or agent for some of Jim's activities, he plays no role in the interior drama of the novel, where Jim's own psyche is supreme. There can be no intrusion on that conflicted area, because that is the arena where the novel chiefly—although not exclusively—works itself out, not in Marlow's mind or experience.

In Richardson, by contrast, the correspondents who narrate are at

[9] The reader interested in observing the operation of the technique more specifically in Richardson and Smollett should note the following: for Richardson, see chapter 3, on *Clarissa*; for Smollett, chapter 5.

the same time creating, through their choices, the story in which they are participants. They are never merely narrators or filters for events which have been created for their observation or experience to work upon. When they observe, they are co-equal participants in a drama whose materials they have helped select. Each of the narrator-agents in *Clarissa* is, of course, weighted differently. Lovelace is a far greater participant than Belford; Clarissa is also far more involved than Miss Howe. This is merely a matter of scale; the principle remains the same.

Accordingly, when we speak of one of Richardson's major characters as a narrator-agent, we are speaking of someone *turned in* upon the material in a particular way made possible by the writing of letters. This is not to imply that the characters' activities could not have taken place without letters. What it does mean is that their activities take on a particular shape and significance as a result of being related in letters. Letters virtually force a response in many areas in which the narrator might have declined a reaction if confronted solely by the activity itself and not by a letter insisting on a decision. Similarly, a letter written to another involves a reply, a forcing of reciprocation. The threat in a letter is almost more immediate than the direct threat to one's physical being. We can say that letters themselves shape experience as much as do decisions made in the correspondence.

As we have seen elsewhere, the matter becomes even more complicated. The letter may be simply a shield for whatever plan the correspondent intends, possibly for a plan he has no intention of carrying out. Or else the letter may be only partially true, the exact proportions of truth and falsity we cannot discover until later, in other letters. Once we enter into this kind of process, the epistolary method assumes dimensions the more normalizing use of the narrator-agent alone cannot begin to match. For in the latter, we have a single agent, whereas in the epistolary technique at its most sophisticated, we are involved in almost infinite combinations of responses and counterresponses, all depending on the number and inventiveness of the correspondents. And each response and counter-response is an element of narrative, point of view, and plot development.

Clara Reeve, who dedicated her *Old English Baron* to Richardson's daughter, spoke later in *The Progress of Romance* of the novel giving "a familiar relation of such things as pass every day before our eyes, such as may happen to our friend, or to ourselves." (I, 111) She apparently had Richardson in mind, and, by extension, the epistolary technique. Further on in her study, she has one of her disputants raise objections to Richardson's method, which her chief narrator and stand-in then refutes. The objections are: "1st. His insupportable prolixity.— 2dly. From his works have sprung up a swarm of paltry Novels in the letter-writing way to the great exercise of our patience.— And 3dly, they have taught many young girls to wiredraw their language, and to spin away long letters out of nothing." (I, 137) The reply is extensive, and it is expected to close the matter in favor of Richardson and his technique.

Miss Reeve, in effect, has applauded a style which underlies a "paralytic novel," a phrase Ortega y Gasset has used to describe Proust's method. Once we connect the epistolary method to the development of plot, we can see its conception of material is based on paralysis. Its function is to slow things down, bring them to a virtual halt, and then to demonstrate the potentialities of seemingly stagnant materials. Vitality, Richardson is suggesting in his epistolary-plot development, derives not only from the ordinary and trivial, but from lives immersed in repetition, boredom, tiny flickers of recognition and involvement. Not unlike Proust, he builds on these minutiae, and he builds toward great moments and great choices. The building process itself, however, is more vital to the novel—as narrative and plot development—than are the great moments in which resolutions occur. The latter are, as it were, almost irrelevant to the slow accretion of detail which the epistolary method makes possible in plot development.

Through letters Richardson not only brought the novel indoors, as we outlined in chapter 3, he also made plot development respond to the changing social and intellectual atmosphere of mid-eighteenth-century England. The secularity in the period is really a long transition from the medieval notion that individual actions derive from "being" to a conception in which "being" is no more than the summation of individual actions. As a figure himself caught between traditional and new modes of thought, Richardson created a "medieval" Clarissa, concerned with "being" in the old sense, against a background of the new, in which "being" gives way to stratagems and actions. There is in Richardson's technique both a reflection of social reality and the distorted refraction of individual motives. The epistolary technique intertwines with all other technical developments and suggests almost infinite potential.

We must distinguish Richardson's use of this technique from that of other writers before and after him. Day speaks at great length of the fragmentary and unsuccessful work of "epistolarians" before Richardson; and Black writes of the method after Richardson, in which the employment of letters does not advance upon his literary usage but instead breaks up into oddities and mannerisms. The post-Richardson "epistolarians" pursued their model with "tame imitation."

Smollett, for example, cannot match Richardson's complexity in his own attempts at multiple narration. In *Humphry Clinker*, multiple narration rarely becomes an intrinsic part of meaningful points of view in interaction with other points of view or of plot development, which remains basically picaresque. One must conclude that the complexity of cross-referral correspondence was antithetical to Smollett's temperament and way of responding to character and events. His vision was that of the picaresque novelist—linear, in space, with events built on cause and effect, characters explained by stimulus and response. Smollett's inability to understand his female characters (beyond caricature) placed him at an obvious disadvantage in the epistolary technique. His women can respond only with compliance or eccentricity, which implies authorial paternalism and condescension. Thus, the complexity implicit in the cross-referral of letters is immediately lost. The epistolary method should be dynamic, should allow growth, if only by accretion; but for Smollett at his best, the method solidifies what is static, denies growth wherever possible, and justifies the status quo while satirizing change. Unreconciled opposites work against the use of the method.

In Fanny Burney's *Evelina*, the method has moved toward its demise. That is, with its potential exhausted thirty years earlier, it has become part of the omniscient narration, although it purports to be the primary form of the narrative. The letters in *Evelina* carry the plot line, which an omniscient author could do as well, without providing the complications of internal motivation the epistolary method does at its best. Correspondence does not in itself create dramatic tensions in its post-Richardsonian development; and in that respect, it has become a technique absorbed and ready to be discarded. In a thirty-year period to the end of the century, it accounted for one third of the total novels published; its popularity was not a sign of health, however, but of the mechanical faddishness of its practitioners.

We recognize that the epistolary method was the sole way for the eighteenth-century novelist up to and even after Sterne to try to gain some *psychological* control over his characters. Notwithstanding, most attempts were inchoate, with little achieved except by Richardson himself, and that only because of the great length and intensity of *Clarissa.* In a simplified attempt such as *Pamela*, letter writing is almost another form of omniscient narration, since, except for the aspect of "writing to the moment," what the letters finally tell us is a narrated tale. And that tale is not too different from Moll's once we allow for all the differences of character, place, and situation. What *Pamela* does achieve, however, is the sense of interiors, of plot domesticated, so to speak, by letters, by the exclusion of the outdoors with its endless episodes and linear sequences.

As we have seen in the chapter on Richardson, letters in *Clarissa* serve the distinct function of any successful technique. Like Joyce's interior monologue and stream of consciousness, they tell us something in a way that makes us see and feel differently. Not only does the content become different from previous content, we are forced to react uniquely. The Harlowe family observed from letters becomes almost a mythical middle-class family, one that gains its stability by driving one of its members to madness or suicide, that proceeds as if nothing were wrong when in fact everything is amiss, that assumes it epitomizes stability and traditional values even as it is disintegrating, that hides from itself all its secret wishes and desires even while it applauds openness of view and manner. This type of family becomes the triumph of the Victorian novelists and would appear to fit Dickensian rather than Richardsonian specifications. Yet that mythical middle-class family does exist in Richardson because of his epistolary technique, and we could argue that no other technique at this time could give us the same feel for the Harlowes' tortured values.

Plot

Plot in the eighteenth-century novel appears to have been a response to the "plotlessness" of picaresque fiction and the equally episodic nature of the romance. If we weave together the various strands of criticism as found in prefaces, forewords, authorial intrusions, direct comments in letters, asides, et al., we find them overlapping at one broad point: the novel, or whatever, could only develop along lines somewhat different from those of picaresque and romance. Such lines involved everything we associate with "technique," but especially the structuring of plot, whether it is the plot of Defoe's *Roxana*, Richardson's *Clarissa*, Fielding's *Amelia*, Walpole's *Castle of Otranto*, Sterne's *Tristram Shandy*, or the domestic Gothic of Mrs. Radcliffe.

We see developing, in the main, two basic kinds of plots: those that accommodate the indoors (houses, drawing rooms, kitchens, city) and those that involve the outdoors (woods, nature, open road, travel, numerous and varied episodes). The two are not, of course, distinct; a novel like *Tom Jones* will combine both, although our primary memories of the novel nearly always rely on images of the outdoors, possibly because some of the strongest scenes occur early when Tom is an outdoorsman. Even there, however, Fielding, in his prefaces, was working against the outdoors episode, relating it to more classical plots, always moving the material within limits, even while his story is being defined spatially. Similarly, Smollett, especially in *Humphry Clinker*, tried to keep his episodic material from running on by compressing it with multiple narrators; so that in his hands the narrative process is itself a function of plot. We will see later in the section on time how temporal elements are themselves elements of plot, as we have already noted how the epistolary technique cannot be separated from point of view, time, or plot.

The eighteenth-century novelist nearly always saw plot as a form of control rather than as a thing in itself. The early novelists could never have conceived of plot as had the great tragedians: that is, if we follow Aristotle's definition, as the "first principle," as the "soul of tragedy." Such a deification of plot leads to a unity of purpose, in which, as Aristotle cautions, a disruption of "any one of them [parts]" will lead to the whole being "disjointed and disturbed." The early novelists were far more casual, far more subversive of the classical rules.

Aristotle warns that "of all plots and actions the episodic are the worst. I call a plot 'episodic' in which the episodes or acts succeed one another without probable or necessary sequence." As if foreseeing the dangers of picaresque as the basis for later fiction, Aristotle notes that "bad poets" frequently "stretch the plot beyond its capacity and are often forced to break the natural continuity." In further remarks on plot, he defines simple and complex plots, from which we can derive our view of the early novel structures as "simple": that is, when "the change in the hero's fortune takes place without reversal of the situation and without recognition." Since the early novelists were not concerned with tragedy, their rejection of the "complex plot," which does involve reversal and recognition, is understandable.

The area in which Aristotle's foreshadowing of fictional plot crosses the varied attempts of the eighteenth-century novelists comes in the passage in which he speaks of fear and pity. He says these qualities may be aroused by spectacular means; "but they may also *result from the inner structure of the piece,* which is the better way, and indicates a superior poet" (my italics). In defining plot as organic, Aristotle presages the fictional experimentation of the eighteenth-century novelists, their blunting of the episodic nature of picaresque and romance, their turning earlier forms toward what Mrs. Manley in 1725 called "one entire scheme or plot," in which "the other adventures are only incidental or collateral to it."

Plot in eighteenth-century terms developed more from characters' lives than from external events. As character turned inward, in what later became a psychological process, plot derived from character; events themselves became secondary to how the character would react. As major characters became secular and rebellious, and attempted to assert their uniqueness, character moved closer to Aristotle's view of it and plot derived increasingly from internal events. Albert Cook speaks of "plot as discovery" in later novelists such as Conrad, Dostoevsky, and Faulkner. His remarks, however, suggest how *all* plot progressed, although its early structure was shaky and uncertain. He writes: "Slowly, in the fine process of their small actions, the characters must be shown to arrive at a state of being that is likely to involve more discovery for us than for them. The plot is the discovery: it discovers the subtle center of the secret lives of all the characters." (*The Meaning of Fiction*, 1960, p. 202)

Such a process fits more technically sophisticated novels than most in the eighteenth century, but we can run down our major, and even minor, authors and see each striving toward some definition of plot, either directly or indirectly. Since most early criticism of the novel did not concern itself with plot as such, our conception of plot must derive from practices rather than from theories, from marginal remarks rather than from well-thought-out procedures, from a combination of tactics and strategies rather than from a clear-cut grappling with the Aristotelian categories.[10]

The very structure of the novels of Defoe demonstrates that turning from the external, picaresque conception of plot to plot as derivative of internal states of mind and feeling. Although the narrative line follows the picaresque development—we are always aware of an episodic progression—nevertheless, Defoe has lengthened normally picaresque scenes, given them additional coloring, to throw the stress from externals to internals. He draws the action from the impingement of the world upon the individual to action that projects from the individual's self-assertion, whether Crusoe on his island, Moll in London streets, or Roxana in her pursuit of wealth.

In *Roxana*, Defoe tried to advance the narrative by way of tensions or unresolved conflicts rather than solely by means of incidents or episodes. That is, he was attempting some kind of plot development by way of thematic tensions. The constant shapes and disguises Roxana assumes—far more than we find in *Moll Flanders*—are matters of plot, since they offer recurrences, balances, overlappings, rovings back and forth. While they do not fully blunt episodic picaresque, they do give us a sense of cohesion through familiar images and rhythms. The fact also that the novel is narrated in the first person

[10] Even such a driven Aristotelian as Frye, in his "Theory of Modes," presents fictional plot as developing under a social rather than a literary stress: "Myths of gods merge into legends of heroes; legends of heroes merge into plots of tragedies and comedies; plots of tragedies and comedies merge into plots of more or less realistic fiction. But these are change of social context rather than of literary form, and the constructive principles of story-telling remain constant through them, though of course they adapt to them." (*Anatomy of Criticism*, p. 51)

In his valuable survey of early criticism of prose fiction, J. H. Heidler demonstrates that even major literary figures in the first decades of the eighteenth century gave little thought to the novel as a developing genre, no less to plot or any other specific category. A study of the correspondence of Pope, Swift, Gay, and Arbuthnot shows some attention to particular novels, but "none of these men thought of prose fiction as a growing genre with definite attributes and possibilities." (*The History, from 1700 to 1800, of English Criticism of Prose Fiction,* p. 39) Heidler goes on to say that "they considered it worthy of consideration only as a convenient vehicle for political propaganda or social uplift." (p. 41) Criticism dealt not with the novel but with the epic, with matters of "truth to fact," with the function of prose fiction as an instructor of virtue (see, for example, Addison, *Tatler*, March 18, 1709). As Heidler sums it up, the "occasional allusions [in the period from 1719 to 1740] to the need for probability and truth to life were not followed by any broad, comprehensive statements of the function, technique, and possibilities of prose fiction." (p. 45) Even in the following decades, there are few allusions to novel structure and virtually no generalizing upon the style of the genre except in terms of its realism, its homiletic function, and the truthfulness of its characterization.

works toward the cohesiveness of a plot structure, for such narration organizes the individual's own experience and keeps it intimately in front of us. Lacking any real psychological sense, Defoe did strive to convey psychological realism through the first-person narrator. In this rudimentary way, he was applying a cohesiveness to his materials which we can identify as a plot element.

Among major novelists, Richardson gave the largest single boost to conscious plotting. Although the epistolary technique did not solve all the problems—it raised, in fact, as many as it solved—because of its very intensity, it forced a particular focus and specified each character's relationship to the central problem. Further, as a "plot device," the epistolary novel derived from the psyche of individual letter writers; letters are a flowing out from within, a subjective, personal statement. They reinforce the development of plot as an internal process. We can, in fact, say that Richardson's use of the epistolary technique, coming as it does at such a crucial time in the development of the novel, compels us to see plot as deriving from within. Without Richardson, the line of plot, at least in the eighteenth century, might have remained picaresque, at least until Sterne, if not after him. If, however, we look to Richardson's prefaces to *Pamela* or his preface and long postscript to *Clarissa* for any discussion or even mention of plot, we find, instead, references only to moral aspects of the novel and a complete eschewing of structural elements.

Fielding, too, whether in *Joseph Andrews* or in *Tom Jones*, was sufficiently uncertain of the new genre so that his copious remarks do not touch upon plot, except indirectly. With him, as with others, we must seek the emergence of a plot sense from his method of handling his materials rather than from statements of intention. One finds, of course, faint touches here and there, as in the introductory matter to Book XI of *Tom Jones.* There, amid an attack upon critics, he insists on the supremacy of the whole as against the fault of any given part. The merit of the whole should command the critic's attention, not the failure of a sentence or even a phrase. Like so much early and mid-century novel criticism, a point about structure or style is embedded in remarks concerning other matters. While Fielding was answering his potential and real critics, he did argue a very valuable point, the primacy of the whole art object, its organic nature rather than its diverse parts.[11]

[11] I am aware that in separating "plot" from all "plot elements"—that is, from plots of action, plots of character, and plots of thought—I am apparently going against R. S.

Similarly, his last novel, *Amelia*, may be closer to an attempt at that integration of elements which demonstrates an awareness of plot. There is little question Fielding was attempting something very different from his previous novels, all three of which resemble picaresque despite his attempts to cover his tracks with ironies, parodies, intrusions, and other means. *Amelia* is, undeniably, more concentrated, solidified, and interlocking. I discuss what I consider to be the failure of the novel in chapter 4. Here, where my stress is somewhat different, I should add that, whatever the novel's success or failure, the narrative method does demonstrate a distinct movement toward unification of elements. It and *Clarissa* are almost the only mid-century efforts at a plotted novel.

Mid-century critics of literature as a whole stressed the realism of the new genre, as well as the need for a high moral tone. (See *The Rambler* for March 31, 1750.) Somewhat later, in his depreciation of Fielding and vaunting of Richardson, Johnson pointed to the latter's ability to seek out the "kernel of life," while his coeval "was content with the husk." We can view Johnson's remark as applauding Richardson's psychological realism, along with his higher moral tone. We can assume that in Johnson's mind "psychological realism" was attached to an ordered plot structure, but even here we are trying to draw out comments that are little more than fragmentary *obiter dicta*.

Heidler, in his study of the criticism of this period, devotes an entire chapter to Sterne, for the latter's critical ideas on aspects of the novel. Sterne, however, like his earlier contemporaries, provides lean pickings. It is true that in various places in the early parts of *Tristram Shandy*—especially in the preface inset into chapter XX of Volume III—Sterne demonstrates some theoretical awareness of the fictional process; but even here his remarks are facetiae directed against critics. In no sense can they be called a considered response to the problems of the new genre, no less to matters of plot. He stresses wit *and* judgment as the cornerstones of his work, and these qualities, which James Work also traces to Locke, are never far from generalized eighteenth-century critical concepts, with little or no

Crane's essay on "The Concept of Plot and the Plot of *Tom Jones*." I am, in actuality, seeking the same awareness of cohesiveness, the same concentration, the same consciousness of interrelated elements that Crane emphasizes in his tripartite stress on *plots* rather than plot. In probing Fielding's own remarks, I am trying to discover his intentions in these combined areas, and in probing his novels, I am trying to unravel his practices.

specific application to the novel. It is true, as Heidler notes, that Sterne placed some limitations on individual expression in favor of an ordered progression of ideas (i.e., a plot structure), but even here Sterne is defending his digressions more than he is advancing an argument for overall order.[12]

If we wish to seek his ideas about plot, we must look for them in the internal workings of *Tristram Shandy* itself. Through his manipulation of time, for example, Sterne in his novel created a simultaneity of events which are actually stretched out over many years, from before Tristram's birth to his second trip to the Continent in his middle years. This simultaneity, achieved through paralleling and roved-back temporal sequences, contains a plot element, or a plot sense, somewhat comparable to Richardson's epistolary method, functioning to make large, seemingly disparate amounts of material cohere.

As we shall see later, it is difficult to distinguish temporal elements from plot; but there is really no need. A time scheme is essentially a plot scheme, as much as it is a character scheme, et al. Coleridge remarked that Fielding "unrealized" or unsettled his story, a way of conveying a more profound sense to his material; but we can more readily apply the term to Sterne, who started with Fielding's sense of his material and then played off novel elements against their antithesis.[13] That is, he carried plot thus far as a way of testing out

[12] In a parallel argument that touches on the novel only here and there, Alvin Kernan shows how difficult it is to apply ideas of plot to satire. Although Kernan believes satire does have a plot structure—in the sense that "any work of literature" with action, shifting scenes, and movement has plot—nevertheless, any application of a formal plot sense is doomed. In the following passage from *The Plot of Satire*, we can see how ideas of structure, or lack of it, in satire parallel those in novelistic picaresque and comedy: "Satire has been even more misunderstood than comedy, for the application of the Aristotelian plot formula to it can only result, and often has in fact, in the decision that the genre is deficient in plot or altogether plotless. It is possible to visualize *Antigone* or *Othello* as linear progressions, but to call to mind *The Acharnians*, Horace's *Sermones, The Satyricon, In Praise of Folly, Tale of a Tub, The Dunciad,* or *Don Juan* is to evoke an image of a mob of characters whirling about in a great variety of scenes, and a succession of seemingly loosely related events with little apparent development." (p. 97)

[13] Booth (*PMLA*) speaks directly to this point, suggesting a strong connection between Fielding's and Sterne's attitudes toward the novel. "Thus in a sense the novel never had any 'canons' of form established, even before Sterne, since Fielding's chief impact on the novel was to make it more diffuse, less unified than it had been in his own hands and in the hands of his immediate predecessors. The very devices Sterne uses to emphasize his ostensible chaos, and thus to 'explode the novel,' were merely extensions of what everyone was borrowing from Fielding. The whole tendency throughout the fifties was really one of increasing disorganization, with ornamental

plot, and he carried character thus far as a way of testing out character; and so on with time and intrusion and Chinese boxes—utilizing such means while extending them to seek their breaking point.

In coming to terms with the variousness of Sterne, for the first time in English fiction we really become aware of what Mark Schorer called "technique as discovery": that is, the use of a technique, whatever the form or rhythm, that enriches or renews "our apprehension of the world of action." Such a technical means is, of course, part of content and, in Sterne's novel, is plot itself. The so-called modernity of Sterne is attributable to his desire to unsettle existing modes by presenting in a different way the same old plot, actually, of a young man's apprenticeship to life, and by so doing creating a new sense of plot and plotting. To jump two centuries, we are reminded of Alain Robbe-Grillet's comment: "What is found in common between individuals, in each of the literary movements of our history, is chiefly the desire to escape a sclerosis, the need for *something else.* Around what have artists always grouped themselves, if not the rejection of the outworn forms still being imposed on them? Forms live and die, in all the realms of art, and in all periods they have had to be continually renewed . . ." (*For a New Novel: Essays on Fiction*, 1966, p. 135)

Plot is also a response to social change. A more coherent plot structure, based on consolidation, on trimming, on organization of elements, is itself a social idea, containing some of the inherent philosophy of the bourgeoisie. Contrariwise, a revolt against plot is the revolt against the bourgeois frame of reference. Sterne's utilization of plot elements, through time and other techniques, is one side of his novelistic-social need; while the breakup of these very elements into fragments with intrusion, disruption, and mockery is the other side of his need. Thus, in *its* development, plot can be responsive to non-literary elements—responsive to the needs of the writer, to the needs of society, and to the larger elements of the body politic. If we agree upon that, we can say that Sterne's disruption of plot, even while he is careful to create a plot line, is his response to social change; that his balancing act between picaresque episode and

intrusions used in ever more disruptive ways. Fielding was thus an important ancestor of Sterne, in this regard as in so many others, and he was himself a descendant of some of the ancestors Sterne was supposed to be using in rebellion against him." ("The Self-Conscious Narrator in Comic Fiction before *Tristram Shandy*," p. 176)

novelistic plot structuring is a precarious attempt to resolve what is basically irresolvable, since it is the dialectic of social movements.

Plot in Sterne, furthermore, is made more coherent by its reliance on a self-conscious narrator. All plot elements are, theoretically at least, sifted through a single narrator, even though much of the novel does not concern Tristram. The mere act of thus centralizing the material is an act of "plot thinking." Character, time shifts, intrusions, narrative roving back and forth, interpolated material—all of these qualities of a single consciousness become plot elements, and all demonstrate Sterne's manner of playing off the traditional against the innovative, *not to seek final resolutions,* but to create a process for "seeing." (For further comment on this and related points, see the following section on time and pages 215ff. of chapter 6, on *Tristram Shandy.*)

After Sterne, in the somewhat literarily impoverished 1770's and 1780's, we can discover little theoretical interest in plot. The novels of this period, early Gothic, novels of sentiment and social purpose, and domestic comedies, are not notable for their concern with form, either in theory or in practice. Most of the novelists as a matter of course, rather than of conscious thought, slid into a more coherent plot. Since their material often called for some thematic statement, plot organization and unity were more apparent than in the time when the novel was simply the sum of its episodic parts. As soon as the novel came to serve some function—of morals, manners, description, evocation, et al.—the novelist showed more attention to details of plot structure. Even here, however, we must be careful, because these very novelists were often so carried away by their function—as, say, Henry Brooke's pedagogical purpose in *The Fool of Quality*—that plot structure, like all other technical elements, becomes hostage to a nobler purpose.

Novel criticism and practice remained rudimentary. The major disruption of attitudes which the novel by mid-century had portended had become dissipated. With no major novelists recapitulating the past while introducing innovation, the novel temporarily lost its thrust, much as the Edwardian fiction of Galsworthy, Bennett, Wells, Hudson, and Gissing lies as a kind of valley between the Victorian and early-modern giants. Yet, at the same time, the novel was becoming an acceptable part of critical vocabulary; instead of aestheticians like Blair and Burnet making reference to drama for their literary examples, they refer to novels. Without any conscious development of novel theory, the novel had entered the literary consciousness.

Clara Reeve's study *The Progress of Romance*, in 1785, is instructive, for while she seems to be on the edge of a breakthrough in discussing form, in fact she has little to say about the genre that is useful today, except her distinction between novel and romance. Implied in her remarks are matters of plot, but once again, we see that implication prevails over actual statement. The novel has indeed entered her consciousness, but still as an inchoate form. And so it follows that the minor novelists Heidler cites in his study—forgotten writers such as Mrs. Francis Sheridan, George Coleman, John S. Leland—while concerned with a definition of prose fiction, also fell back on well-worn nostrums, reiterating their support of realistic depiction of character and event. Walpole himself, on the eve of a significant development in the genre, stressed the realistic elements in *The Castle of Otranto*, in his preface to the first edition in 1764. Other well-known figures, such as Goldsmith and Burney, placed a similar stress on realism and on the moral function of the new genre. Goldsmith's distaste for Sterne can be attributed to these feelings.

We are, accordingly, left with actual practices, not theories. At the same time, if we look to the immediate future, the later acceptance of the historical romance in Scott was going to strain any coherent theory of plot, since in the romance a unified plot becomes secondary to considerations of colors, setting, atmosphere. Not until the mature novels of Jane Austen do we find the essential plot elements of the eighteenth century drawn together consciously and coherently; and in her practices—she, too, provided no theories—we see a reliance on plot that was to prevail for nearly the remainder of the century.

Time

The eighteenth-century novelists did not often verbalize their conception of the novel and we must, as it were, put words in their mouths to understand their intentions. In their striving toward some kind of understanding of the novel, they would have nodded in agreement at Alain Robbe-Grillet's comment that "we do not know what a novel, a true novel, should be; we know only that the novel today will be what we make it, today, and that it is not our job to cultivate a resemblance to what it was yesterday, but to advance beyond." For those early novelists, the novel was a process going in a direction they could not chart, whose parameters they could not foresee, whose potential seemed still murky and unsafe. It was through a time technique that they moved toward the control of materials whose depth and breadth they were uncertain of. Conscious use of a time technique infuses nearly every segment of the developing genre.

Very early in *Tom Jones*, that adventurous exploration into the literary unknown, Fielding suggests, however lightly, some of the problems implicit in matters of time in the new genre. He remarks that the reader will find different qualities of time in his kind of history; on some occasions time will fly and on others it will appear to stand still. But since the form is really "a new province of writing," he is accountable to no one except himself for his vagaries and flights. (Book II, chapter I) Fielding says little more in this section, although simply his awareness of the problems becomes important to us. In the next book (chapter VIII), he refers to the foreshortening of time elements and repeats something of the same thing in Book V, where he takes up the argument of the unities of time and place. As I indicated in my comments on Fielding's prefatory criticism, the importance of his remarks lies not in their intrinsic value as theoretical statements but elsewhere: their significance in terms of Fielding's own procedures and their relevance as matters of novelistic awareness. With some exceptions, Fielding was touching on problem areas without full concern for their ultimate importance outside of his own work.

Awareness is forewarning. Time *was* intimately involved with the novel. Fielding, however, relied almost completely upon external time, that time in the novel which differs only intermittently from stretches of time in history and epic. Nowhere in his prefatory remarks is he aware of the more complicated sense of inner time, nor should we expect him to be. *Tom Jones*, after all, proceeds from without to within, not the other way, and therefore we should not expect time to thrust out, but to impinge upon other elements. With its external plot, its external characterization, its external benevolism, *Tom Jones* lacks the intensity for which "inner time" is so necessary an ingredient.

Defoe, also, showed an awareness of temporal elements, as we have already seen, but he was still so close to the picaresque narrative that, like Fielding later, he saw time in broad sweeps. This is not to deny Defoe's awareness. He uses simple time to provide foreshadowings of Robinson's fate; he suggests more complicated time differentiation in his employment of "island time," "journal time," "outside time," "reader's time." These are all present, although they are not probed. Further, in *Moll Flanders*, Defoe implies a more complex time technique by using the "humble and penitent" Moll as his central intelligence, through the medium of her story edited and revised by the author. Several temporal sequences are implicit in this arrangement: remembrance of things past (through conscious, voluntary memory), memories strained not only by time but by change of habits, with the consequent reshaping of past events as a result of age and penitence, the employment of present time in the author's revisions, and the reader's own present and past as he grapples with a past life related in the present and revised at some time in the recent past-present. Few of the implications are consciously developed; only a little of the method becomes substance or meaning. It is a narrative device first, a temporal method as a by-product. Nevertheless, as we indicated with Fielding, such early forays into temporal territory suggest some of the potential of the genre.

If we back up to *Don Quixote*, we can see a similar awareness, in the cave of Montesinos. In that scene (Part II, chapter XXIII), the Don must distinguish between outer time of about one hour and inner time of possibly three days. Although Cervantes was not concerned primarily with time—time, here, is actually a metaphor of the Don's overall condition—he glanced off a very revealing aspect of novel development: that is, time awareness of the experiencing character, as against the time sequences of (1) the other characters; (2) the historical background in which events occur; (3) the author, who stands outside; (4) the reader, who must put it all together in a different progression from characters, author, and era.

If we assume that Proust has been the only novelist in history who has successfully developed a fully coordinated, sequential, unified time technique, then we can see the dilemma of previous novelists who lacked his sense of an involuntary memory and yet were struggling to gain a time perspective. Through revelatory moments, Proust attempted to get outside of time, so that time itself is bypassed in favor of timelessness, where all elements cohere. Through *his* method, Proust achieved something akin to Pound's definition of the image: as an instant of time. That "instant of time" was possible in poetry, where the construct is words, and virtually impossible of attainment in the novel, where the construct is not only words but developing characters and situations. The novel cannot nourish itself from only metaphors and images; it exists in developing time. Therefore, only Proust's "discovery" of involuntary memory could approximate parallel developments in poetry, the growth of Imagism and the sense of the image, the rediscovery of the Metaphysicals and the sense of paradox, the creation of a new poetic language to reflect these shifts in sensibility.

The eighteenth-century novelist—even Sterne—lacked the means, or intent, to get outside of time. Forced to forgo revelation and to draw on voluntary memory, he grappled with the problem mainly from the outside. The eighteenth-century novelist's aim was to turn the spatial quality of the romance, epic, and picaresque narrative into the temporal quality of the new, developing form. For this early novelist, literary practices were still rooted in the historical imagination (from which the novelist was, of course, attempting to escape), not in the timelessness that characterizes myth or what Joseph Frank has called the "spatiality" of modern literature.

To use Auerbach's frame of reference, the eighteenth-century novelists in their employment of time were moving tentatively and uneasily between "Homeric" and "Old Testament" styles. In the former, realism dictated interconnected elements with a minimum of discontinuity and externalized descriptions, with "all events in the foreground"; in the latter, concern with the problematic, the "development of the historically becoming," unfathomable motivations and seemingly unmotivated reactions, "multiplicity of meanings and the need for interpretation." (In *Mimesis*, see his chapter on "Odysseus's Scar.") The first was almost literal; the second relied upon an imaginative thrust into unexplored areas involving point of view, plot, and, for our purposes here, a time scheme that both reflected and refracted.

Certainly the most successful pre-*Tristram* excursion into a complicated time technique resulted from Richardson's complex development of the epistolary method. Because of Richardson's refusal to simplify the technique—no matter how he simplified the motivations of his characters in later, revised editions of *Clarissa*—time considerations come to us with some intimation of Proustian "timelessness"; that is, with the merging of past with present time, so that past has the same immediacy and contemporaneity as present. As I mentioned in the introduction, Richardson's sliding in and out of background and foreground, his shifting among near past, far past, near present, and present all suggest a conscious approach to temporal elements, without, of course, having the deliberateness of a Bergsonian or Proustian time treatment.

The monumental size of his work creates a time element in itself. Because of its length, *Clarissa* impinges literally upon our lives, forcing us to reconsider our own time conceptions while we take on *its*. Richardson's decision to write such a long novel, we can speculate, was motivated by a desire to engage us entirely, to occupy all our time. More importantly, however, in the internal workings of the novel, Richardson sets up temporal shadings, fine gradations of narrative which resolve themselves into time levels. The narrative itself, which proceeds by accretion, is for the reader a slowing up of life into minute elements, into fragmentary details, causing a discontinuity with our normal expectations of a smoothly flowing narrative line in both fiction and our life.

Mendilow cites Richardson, as well as the more obvious Flaubert and James, as masters of "slow motion." His point indicates how a literary work, even early in the development of the genre, can manipulate us through its sense of time:

> By their detailed treatment the fictional time seems to go slower than the reader's clock. They make the writing correspond to what Proust called 'the unheeding fluidity of the days and years'. No gaps are left in the continuity, cause and effect are ruthlessly analysed, descriptions of states of mind abound, and the slow groping towards action predominates over the decisive action itself. They impress and sometimes oppress the reader by a sense of inevitability where the other novelists exhilarate him by continual surprise. [*Time and the Novel*, p. 127]

The "slow tempo," however, is only one element, and it is attached more to the conceptual whole than it is to the functioning of time *within* the novel itself. That is, the slow tempo is for the reader, while other internal time considerations proceed laterally across characters. Consequently, we have several time potentialities working in *Clarissa*: the tempo between novelist and reader, characters and reader; the tempo working laterally among the characters; the tempo working between novelist and characters; the tempo that belongs to history (the sense of passing time or the sense of an era). All of this in the novel comes to us with the force of a glacier moving irresistibly across a plain. The particular rhythms of the novel—

difficult enough to sustain in a work of such length—are probably attributable to subtle workings of time in the three or four areas specified above.

If we analyze the very beginning of the novel, with the succession of letters clustered from January 10 to January 20, we can see how time elements work, although the beginning only suggests the full complexity of the method. The first letter is almost a marginal one, from Miss Howe to Clarissa, not *from* but *to* a major character. The letter concerns a past event, murky to the reader but evidently well known to the principals involved and already incurring a reaction. In this sense, Richardson has begun his bourgeois epic *in medias res,* with the dim past yet to be brought up to the present.

This January 10 letter presents several factors: the relationship of Lovelace with Clarissa, faintly suggested; the prior relationship between Lovelace and someone else in the family, as yet unnamed (Arabella); the consequence of some conflict that resulted in the duel between Lovelace and Clarissa's brother, James; the opposition of the Harlowe family to further association between Clarissa and Lovelace, who is trying "to wade into her favour . . . through the blood of her brother" (Volume I, p. 2); the suggestion of some difficulty between Clarissa and her family, indicating a division between the mother on one side and sister and brother on the other; the opposition of Clarissa's Uncle Antony in particular, although to exactly what we do not yet know.

The point here is not that so many lines of development have come in a single seemingly marginal letter—although as a technique that might be remarkable in itself—but that Richardson, through arrangement of time strata, has achieved what Auerbach was to define as the "Old Testament style." He has, in fact, created layers of events, not within a strict interconnection, but embedded in a hidden past in which motivations and reactions will never be fully clarified, in which time itself appears to dissolve. Events and reactions to events will come to us through the author's cutting back and forth through the various strata of action in a slowly rising crescendo.

The entire novel, actually, is encapsulated in that first letter. All lines of conflict are suggested, and the blood drawn in the duel is to stain every character in the book. Furthermore, the novel is a working out of "bad blood," another kind of stain. A subsequent letter, the first from Clarissa (to Miss Howe), begins to explain part of the past conflict, especially the Lovelace-Arabella imbroglio. But we note that the explanation comes from a second party, Clarissa, and not from Lovelace, whose attempt at direct explanation comes in Letter XXXI, on March 13. In brief, we must wait for later letters to fill in earlier details; and as we move further away from the event—and all its complications have begun to pile up—we are still awaiting some explanation of what those earlier lines of conflict really were.

The line of temporal development, accordingly, is something like the more radical time methodology in *Tristram Shandy.* In both books, material recalled is never made fully clear before intervening material establishes further complications and further intrusions. Clarissa's attempt at explanation of events, in Letter II, is based on partially invalid information, taken from Arabella's point of view, which is that Arabella turned down Lovelace's offhand proposal in the expectation he would ask again more politely. From Arabella's defense of her position, we note she declined the mode of address, not the man, or so she says in order to rationalize an impossible situation. By the time Lovelace offers his point of view—which is intermixed with his own need to defend his motives, citing a previous jilting in which *he* was victim, not victimizer—Clarissa has become involved in his plans and the family is in arms. Violence is already in the air, from James and Mr. Harlowe on the one hand, from Lovelace seeking revenge upon Harlowes and upon women on the other.

Within this same early sequence of letters, all clustered within January, we have the main lines of the future action while we are still grappling with explanations of past events. Clarissa is embattled within her family, both in terms of suitors and in terms of property rights. She has, in a sense, been isolated by events which are becoming part of a mythical past—that is, impossible of clarification given the passions unveiled and the defenses raised. Rereading, we note Richardson has obfuscated time sequences so that past and present always impinge on each other; so that each evidence of disentanglement does not really clarify, but, instead, joins the mass of general evidence which makes the unraveling of motives almost impossible to achieve.

Some of this is point of view, some of it narrative method, some epistolary technique, but all of it is wrapped within time considerations. Too much hinges on the relationship of past and present events for us to relegate the complications to narrative method or epistolary technique alone. While methodologies are intertwined, time considerations cause a mythical, clouded past to exert pressures on the seemingly "open" present, until both past and present appear enwrapped in fateful, inexorable actions. Since this latter is the point of the novel, technique and matter have blended.

As we suggested above, Richardson's divulgation of past events only after still other events have intervened acts somewhat in the manner of Sterne's lengthy intrusions, which, so to speak, postpone the past as they attempt to recapitulate it. Although we are simplifying—all attempts at "discovering" the Richardsonian and Sternian method are simplifications—we can see a common attempt to create strata of past time (far, nearer, recent past) and to show how each stratum impinges upon the others. Since the strata cannot actually merge into one, except perhaps through the development of a special language (stream of consciousness, interior monologue, free association, et al.), Richardson and Sterne worked through intrusion, which is, as we have noted, as much a time technique as it is one of narrative and point of view.

It is well known that Sterne derived his plan of "associated ideas" from Locke, and also his stress on subjectivity—sensation, reflection, memory, the correspondence of things similar and dissimilar. A by-product of this reliance on Locke is a time technique: Sterne roves from sensation to experience, from particulars to universals, from *a priori* knowledge to experiential. Translated into a time technique, this allowed Sterne to flit back and forth between objective time, which is very logically worked out in the novel,[14] and subjective time, which appears to be haphazard. Thus, as reader, we are split, without and within, like two interpenetrating cones or gyres.

Yet even as we are made aware of the tight, ordered outer frame of reference—actual events, historical battles, real wounds, medical

[14] Mendilow demonstrates the methodical way in which Sterne went about the external time sequences: "There is scarcely an incident, no matter how slight, no matter where it occurs in the book, no matter how often it is interrupted and taken up again, but falls into its correct place in time in relation to every other incident. Slips in dating are very rare, one or two at most. Many of these incidents, especially those relating to Uncle Toby, can be checked against historical events. Every piece in the jig-saw puzzle is found to fit into its place." (*Time and the Novel*, p. 170)

In his edition of *Tristram Shandy* (Riverside), Ian Watt's useful side-by-side comparison of historical and fictional events, and where these are interrelated in the text, substantiates Mendilow's contention that Sterne had tight control indeed over external events.

mishaps, begettings and misbegettings, all—the world within, the subjective world of inner time, appears to have no order or logic. Locke's primary qualities are set, fixed, without, but then, as if Sterne were arguing Berkeley's own point, within the disordered time of the inner world he questions all primary qualities. Further, time within, the scene set inside another scene, the intrusion fixed within an intrusion, has its own point, its own dramatic reason for existence, separate and independent. Breakup of the story and narrative line exists for itself, without regard for the larger flow of events.

Such breakup and independence of elements within interdependence makes Sterne innovative. He felt no compulsion to justify an intrusion; it exists as firmly as an idea or thought seemingly exists in the conscious mind without regard for any other frame of reference. A feeling or attitude is, narratively and temporally speaking, its own justification. Time in such a frame of reference is bent, refracted, within and without. Sterne can move within his characters' minds (see pages 208–10 of the chapter on Sterne), in what Bergson called heterogeneous time, or he can move without to an infinite number of vantage points: that is, within other characters, events, incidents, trivalities, whims. Once he has established from the first pages his way of working, he has gained the novelist's license to strike his own pattern, and we, as reader, indulge his switches and vagaries. In this respect, we have accepted the dualism of his time sequencing, the dualism of his world. Time disordered becomes for us normal time; while historical and external time becomes secondary or arbitrary.

Possibilities are, like points of vantage, infinite; the novel may end, but it does not have to—ever. Such a time sequencing finds its narrative counterpart in Chinese boxes, an infinite sense of perspective, ever receding but never ending. Associations are also infinite, attached only to the energies of the creator, and time positioning within those associations is of limitless variety, of endless gradations of past never quite reaching present, or present straining to meet the future without ever actually doing so.

If the epistolary novel slows the tempo, so that fictional time predominates over clock time, so does Sterne's technique impose its own time philosophy. Even while he honors empirical knowledge, he questions it, indeed undermines it. With Richardson and Sterne, for the first time in English fiction, we are "within" the work: in Richardson because of *Clarissa*'s great length, but not less so because his fictional time subsumes clock time; in Sterne because subjective time has become a more effective mode of comprehending experience.

After these two writers, we do not have any other comprehensive time technique until the modern movement, although we do note the growth of subjectivity, which foreshadows the development of an inner time sense. Certainly not in other eighteenth-century novelists, whether those of the sentimental or Gothic school, can we expect to find serious interest in time considerations. For Smollett, Goldsmith, Burney, the Gothicists, "time" meant relatively simple narrative devices, occasional flashbacks, intrusions, interpolations, but all within an uncomplicated sense of past and present time. And even in the great pre-Victorian and Victorian novelists, we do not find anywhere the awareness of complicating time considerations; which is not to say we do not find an awareness of technique. Technique, there, was wedded to ideas of narrative, point of view, authorial intrusion, all apart from temporal complexity. In some paradoxical way, the experiment with time ended, for at least another century, almost with the beginning of the novel. If we look at the eighteenth-century English novel from the point of view of technique, we do not note any steady growth toward technical mastery, or toward a sophisticated time technique. We see, on the contrary, great achievements within sporadic starts and stops, little sense of developmental building, and even less conscious awareness of the novel's potential. If anything, at the end of the century, novelists were less technically sophisticated than their predecessors had been fifty years before. Beginnings brought innovation; while by the 1780's and 1790's, the novel, technically, had settled into middle age.

A Chronology of Eighteenth-Century Fiction and Near-Fiction

1705

Mrs. Mary Manley (1663–1724), *The Secret History of Queen Zarah and the Zarazians*

1709

Mrs. Manley, *The New Atalantis*

1710

Mrs. Manley, *Memoirs of Europe*

1714

Mrs. Manley, *The Adventures of Rivella*

1719

Daniel Defoe (1660–1731), *Robinson Crusoe*, Part I; *Robinson Crusoe*, Part II

1720

Defoe, *Robinson Crusoe*, Part III; *Captain Singleton*

1722

Defoe, *Moll Flanders*; *Colonel Jack*; *A Journal of the Plague Year*

1723

Mrs. Eliza Haywood (1693?–1756), *Lasselia*

1724

Defoe, *Roxana*

1726

Jonathan Swift (1667–1745), *Gulliver's Travels*

1727

Mrs. Mary Davys (1674–1733), *The Accomplished Rake*

1739

Mrs. Penelope Aubin (1674–1732), *A Collection of Entertaining Histories and Novels*

1740

Samuel Richardson (1689–1761), *Pamela*

1741

Henry Fielding (1707–54), *Shamela*

1742

Fielding, *Joseph Andrews*

1743

Fielding, *Jonathan Wild*

1744

Sarah Fielding (1710–68), *David Simple*

1748

Richardson, *Clarissa Harlowe*
Tobias Smollett (1721–71), *Roderick Random*

1749

Henry Fielding, *Tom Jones*
John Cleland (1709–89), *Fanny Hill*

1751

Fielding, *Amelia*
Smollett, *Peregrine Pickle*

1752

Mrs. Charlotte Lennox (1720–1804), *The Female Quixote*

1753

Smollett, *Ferdinand Count Fathom*

1753–4

Richardson, *Sir Charles Grandison*

1756–66

Thomas Amory (1691–1788), *John Buncle*

1759

Samuel Johnson (1709–84), *Rasselas*

1759–60–67

Laurence Sterne (1713–68), *Tristram Shandy*

1760–62

Smollett, *Sir Launcelot Greaves*

1764

Horace Walpole (1717–97), *The Castle of Otranto*

1766

Oliver Goldsmith (1730–74), *The Vicar of Wakefield*
Christopher Anstey (1724–1805), *New Bath Guide*

1766–70

Henry Brooke (1703–83), *The Fool of Quality*

1768

Sterne, *A Sentimental Journey*

1771

Henry Mackenzie (1745–1831), *The Man of Feeling*
Smollett, *Humphry Clinker*

1773

Richard Graves (1715–1804), *The Spiritual Quixote*

1777

Clara Reeve (1729–1807), *The Old English Baron*

1778

Fanny Burney (d'Arblay; 1752–1840), *Evelina*

1782

Burney, *Cecilia*

1783–9

Thomas Day (1748–89), *Sandford and Merton*

1785

Sophia Lee (1750–1824), *The Recess*
Reeve, *The Progress of Romance*

1786

William Beckford (1760–1844), *Vathek*

1790

Mrs. Ann Radcliffe (1764–1823), *A Sicilian Romance*

1791

Mrs. Radcliffe, *The Romance of the Forest*

1793

Charlotte Smith (1749–1806), *The Old Manor House*

1794

Mrs. Radcliffe, *The Mysteries of Udolpho*
William Godwin (1756–1836), *Caleb Williams*

1796

Matthew Lewis (1775–1818), *The Monk*
Robert Bage (1728–1801), *Hermsprong*
Burney, *Camilla*
Elizabeth Inchbald (1753–1821), *Nature and Art*

1797

Mrs. Radcliffe, *The Italian*

1799

Godwin, *Travels of St. Leon*

1818

Mary Shelley (1797–1851), *Frankenstein*

1820

Charles Maturin (1780–1824), *Melmoth the Wanderer*

Selected Bibliography[1]

INTRODUCTION AND CHAPTER 9
The Development of Technique in the Eighteenth-Century Novel

Abrams, M. H., *The Mirror and the Lamp*, 1953.
Akenside, Mark, *The Pleasures of Imagination*, 1744.
Alter, Robert, *Rogue's Progress*, 1964.
Altick, Richard D., *The English Common Reader*, 1957.
* Auerbach, Erich, *Mimesis*, 1953.
Babbitt, Irving, *Rousseau and Romanticism*, 1919.
Baker, Ernest, *The History of the English Novel*, vols. 3, 4, 5, 1929, 1930, 1934.
* Bate, Walter Jackson, *From Classic to Romantic: Premises of Taste in Eighteenth-Century England*, 1946.
Bayne-Powell, Rosamond, *Eighteenth Century London Life*, 1938.
———, *The English Child in the Eighteenth Century*, 1939.
Besant, Walter, *London in the Eighteenth Century*, 1903.
Birkhead, Edith, "Sentiment and Sensibility in the Eighteenth Century Novel," *Essays and Studies of the English Association*, XI, 1925.
Black, Frank G., *The Epistolary Novel in the Late Eighteenth Century*, 1940.
* Booth, Wayne C., *The Rhetoric of Fiction*, 1961.
———, "The Self-Conscious Narrator in Comic Fiction before *Tristram Shandy*," *PMLA*, LXVII (1952), 163–85.
Braudy, Leo, *Narrative Form in History and Fiction: Hume, Fielding, and Gibbon*, 1970.

[1] An asterisk indicates a significant work.

Burke, Edmund, *A Philosophical Enquiry into the Origin of Our Ideas of the Sublime and Beautiful*, 1757.
Cassirer, Ernst, *The Philosophy of the Enlightenment* [1932], 1951.
* Chandler, Frank W., *The Literature of Roguery*, 2 vols., 1907.
———, *Romances of Roguery*, 1899.
Collingwood, R. G., *The Idea of History*, 1946.
* Day, Robert Adams, *Told in Letters: Epistolary Fiction Before Richardson*, 1966.
Dobrée, Bonamy, *English Literature in the Early Eighteenth Century 1700–1740*, 1959.
Donovan, Robert Alan, *The Shaping Vision: Imagination in the English Novel from Defoe to Dickens*, 1966.
Fiebleman, James, *In Praise of Comedy: A Study in Its Theory and Practice*, 1939.
Foster, James R., "The Abbé Prévost and the English Novel," *PMLA*, XLII (1927), 443–64.
———, *A History of the Pre-Romantic Novel in England*, 1949.
* Frank, Joseph, "Spatial Form in Modern Literature" [1945], *The Widening Gyre*, 1963.
Friedman, Norman, "Forms of the Plot," *Journal of General Education*, VIII (1955), 241–53.
* ———, "Point of View in Fiction," *PMLA*, LXX (1955), 1160–84.
* Frye, Northrop, *Anatomy of Criticism*, 1957.
Gay, Peter, *The Enlightenment: An Interpretation* (Vol. I, *The Rise of Modern Paganism*; Vol. II, *The Science of Freedom*), 1967, 1969.
Gillie, Christopher, *Character in English Fiction*, 1965.
Gombrich, E. H., *Art and Illusion*, 1960.
Hammond, J. L. & Barbara, *The Town Labourer*, 1968.
* Heidler, J. B., *The History, from 1700 to 1800, of English Criticism of Prose Fiction*, 1928.
Highet, Gilbert, *The Anatomy of Satire*, 1962.
Hobsbawm, E. J., *Labouring Men: Studies in the History of Labour*, 1964.
Hume, David, *Essays*, 1854.
Johnston, Arthur, *Enchanted Ground: The Study of Medieval Romance in the Eighteenth Century*, 1964.
Jusserand, J. J., *The English Novel in the Time of Shakespeare*, 1890.
Kames (Home, Henry), Lord, *Elements of Criticism*, 1762.
Kany, Charles E., *The Beginnings of the Epistolary Novel in France, Italy, and Spain*, 1937.
Karl, Frederick R., "Picaresque and the American Experience," *Yale Review*, LVII (1968), 196–212.
Kermode, Frank, *The Sense of an Ending: Studies in the Theory of Fiction*, 1967.
Kernan, Alvin, *The Cankered Muse*, 1959.
———, *The Plot of Satire*, 1965.
Kiely, Robert, *The Romantic Novel in England*, 1972.
* Lessing, Gotthold Ephraim, *Laocoön*, 1766.

* Lovejoy, Arthur O., *Essays in the History of Ideas*, 1948.

———, *The Great Chain of Being*, 1936.

Lukács, Georg, *The Theory of the Novel* [*1920*], 1971.

McBurney, William Harlin, *A Check List of English Prose Fiction 1700–1739*, 1960.

McKillop, Alan, *The Early Masters of English Fiction*, 1956.

Mendilow, A. A., *Time and the Novel*, 1952.

Mews, Hazel, *Frail Vessels: Woman's Role in Women's Novels from Fanny Burney to George Eliot*, 1969.

Meyerhoff, Hans, *Time in Literature*, 1955.

* Monk, Samuel H., *The Sublime: A Study of Critical Theories in XVIII-Century England*, 1935.

Morgan, Charlotte, *The Rise of the Novel of Manners: A Study of English Prose Fiction Between 1600 and 1740*, 1911.

Muir, Edwin, *The Structure of the Novel*, 1928.

Ortega y Gasset, José, *The Dehumanization of Art and Other Essays on Art, Culture, and Literature*, 1948, 1968.

Paulson, Ronald, "The Fool-Knave Relation in Picaresque Satire," *Rice University Studies in English*, LI (1965), 59–81.

* ———, *Satire and the Novel in Eighteenth-Century England*, 1967.

Poirier, Richard, *The Performing Self*, 1971.

Poulet, Georges, *The Interior Distance*, 1959.

* Praz, Mario, *The Romantic Agony*, 1933.

Price, Martin, *To the Palace of Wisdom*, 1964.

Reynolds, Sir Joshua, *Discourses on Art*, 1769–90.

* Richetti, John, *Popular Fiction Before Richardson: Narrative Patterns 1700–1739*, 1969.

* Schlauch, Margaret, *Antecedents of the English Novel 1400–1600*, 1963.

Shapiro, Charles, ed., *Twelve Original Essays on Great English Novels*, 1960.

Sherwood, Irma Z., "The Novelists as Commentators," *The Age of Johnson: Essays Presented to Chauncey Brewster Tinker*, 1949.

Showalter, English, Jr., *The Evolution of the French Novel 1641–1782*, 1972.

Singer, Godfrey Frank, *The Epistolary Novel: Its Origin, Development, Decline, and Residuary Influence*, 1933.

Slagle, Kenneth Chester, *The English Country Squire as Depicted in English Prose Fiction from 1740 to 1800*, 1938.

Stephen, Leslie, *English Literature and Society in the Eighteenth Century*, 1904.

———, *History of English Thought in the Eighteenth Century*, 2 vols., 1902.

Taylor, John Tinnon, *Early Opposition to the English Novel: The Popular Reaction from 1760 to 1830*, 1943.

Thackeray, William Makepeace, *English Humourists of the Eighteenth Century*, 1853.

Tieje, A. J., "The Expressed Aim of the Long Prose Fiction from 1597 to 1700, *Journal of English and Germanic Philology*, XI (1912), 403–32.

———, *The Theory of Characterization in Prose Fiction Prior to 1740*, 1916.
* Tompkins, J. M. S., *The Popular Novel in England 1770–1800*, 1932.
Van Ghent, Dorothy, *The English Novel: Form and Function*, 1953.
* Watt, Ian, *The Rise of the Novel*, 1957.
———, ed., *The Augustan Age*, 1968.
Whitney, Lois, *Primitivism and the Idea of Progress in English Popular Literature of the Eighteenth Century*, 1934.
Willey, Basil, *The Eighteenth Century Background*, 1946.
———, *The English Moralists*, 1964.
Wright, Walter Francis, *Sensibility in English Prose Fiction 1760–1814*, 1937.
Young, Edward, *Conjectures on Original Composition*, 1759.

CHAPTER 1
Don Quixote as Archetypal Artist and Don Quixote *as Archetypal Novel*

* Auerbach, Erich, *Mimesis*, 1953.
Bell, Aubrey F. G., *Cervantes*, 1947.
Benardete, M. J. & Flores, Angel, editors, *The Anatomy of Don Quixote*, 1932.
Flores, Angel & Benardete, M. J., editors, *Cervantes across the Centuries*, 1947.
Levin, Harry, "The Example of Cervantes," *Contexts of Criticism*, 1957.
———, *The Myth of the Golden Age in the Renaissance*, 1969.
Mann, Thomas, "Voyage with Don Quixote," *Essays of Three Decades*, 1934, 1947.
Ortega y Gasset, José, *The Dehumanization of Art and Other Essays on Art, Culture, and Literature*, 1948, 1968.
* Riley, E. C., *Cervantes's Theory of the Novel*, 1962.
* Unamuno, Miguel de, "Don Quixote in the Contemporary European Tragi-Comedy," *The Tragic Sense of Life*, 1921.

CHAPTER 2
Daniel Defoe: The Politics of Necessity

Ayres, Robert W., "Robinson Crusoe: 'Allusive Allegorick History,'" *PMLA*, LXXXII (October 1967), 399–407.
Brooks, Douglas, *"Moll Flanders," Essays in Criticism*, XIX (1969), 46–59.
Columbus, Robert K., "Conscious Artistry in *Moll Flanders*," *Studies in English Literature*, III (1963), 415–32.
Donoghue, Denis, "The Values of *Moll Flanders*," *Sewanee Review*, LXXI (1963), 287–303.
Häusermann, Hans W., "Aspects of Life and Thought in *Robinson Crusoe*," *Review of English Studies*, XI (1935), 299–312, 439–56.

* Hunter, J. P., *The Reluctant Pilgrim: Defoe's Emblematic Method and Quest for Form in Robinson Crusoe*, 1966.

Karl, Frederick R., "Moll's Many-Colored Coat: Veil and Disguise in the Fiction of Defoe," *Studies in the Novel*, V (1973), 86–97.

Koonce, Howard L., "Moll's Muddle: Defoe's Use of Irony in *Moll Flanders*," *ELH*, XXX (1963), 277–88.

Martin, Terence, "The Unity of *Moll Flanders*," *Modern Language Quarterly*, XXII (1961), 115–24.

Moffat, James, "The Religion of Robinson Crusoe," *Contemporary Review*, CXV (1919), 664–9.

Moore, John Robert, *A Checklist of the Writings of Daniel Defoe*, 1960.

* ———, *Daniel Defoe: Citizen of the Modern World*, 1958.

* Novak, Maximillian E., *Defoe and the Nature of Man*, 1963.

* ———, *Economics and the Fiction of Daniel Defoe*, 1962.

Payne, William, ed., *The Best of Defoe's Review*, 1951.

Secord, A. W., *Studies in the Narrative Method of Defoe*, 1924.

Stamm, Rudolph G., "Daniel Defoe: An Artist in the Puritan Tradition," *Philological Quarterly*, XV (1936), 225–46.

* Starr, G. A., *Defoe and Spiritual Autobiography*, 1965.

Sutherland, James, *Defoe*, 1938.

Tillyard, E. M. W., "Defoe," *The Epic Strain in the English Novel*, 1958.

Woolf, Virginia, *"Robinson Crusoe," The Second Common Reader*, 1932.

CHAPTER 3
Samuel Richardson and Clarissa

Barbauld, Anna Laetitia, *The Correspondence of Samuel Richardson*, 6 vols., 1804.

* Carroll, John, ed., *Selected Letters of Samuel Richardson*, 1964.

Eaves, T. C. Duncan & Kimpel, Ben D., "The Composition of *Clarissa* and Its Revision Before Publication," *PMLA*, LXXXIII (1968), 416–28.

———, "Richardson's Revisions of *Pamela*," *Studies in Bibliography*, XX (1967), 61–88.

* ———, *Samuel Richardson: A Biography*, 1971.

Farrell, William J., "The Style and the Action in *Clarissa*," *Studies in English Literature, 1500–1900*, III (1963), 365–75. Reprinted in *Samuel Richardson: A Selection of Critical Essays*, ed. John Carroll, 1969.

Golden, Morris, *Richardson's Characters*, 1963.

Hilles, Frederick W., "The Plan of *Clarissa*," *Philological Quarterly*, XLV (1966), 236–48.

Kearney, A. M., "*Clarissa* and the Epistolary Form," *Essays in Criticism*, XVI (1966), 44–56.

———, "Richardson's *Pamela*: The Aesthetic Case," *Review of English Literature*, VII (1966), 78–90.

Kinkead-Weekes, M., "*Clarissa* Restored?" *RES*, X (1959), 156–71.

Kreissman, Bernard, *Pamela-Shamela: A Study of the Criticisms, Burlesques, Parodies, and Adaptations of Richardson's "Pamela,"* 1960.

McKillop, Alan Dugald, "Epistolary Technique in Richardson's Novels," *Rice Institute Pamphlet*, XXXVIII (1951), 36–54.

———, *Samuel Richardson: Printer and Novelist*, 1960.

Sale, William Merritt, "From *Pamela* to *Clarissa*," *The Age of Johnson*, ed. Hilles, 1949.

* ———, *Samuel Richardson: A Bibliographical Record of His Literary Career with Historical Notes*, 1936.

———, *Samuel Richardson: Master Printer*, 1950.

Sherburn, George, " 'Writing to the Moment': One Aspect," *Restoration and Eighteenth Century Literature: Essays in Honor of Alan Dugald McKillop*, 1963.

CHAPTER 4
Henry Fielding: The Novel, the Epic, and the Comic Sense of Life

Alter, Robert, *Fielding and the Nature of the Novel*, 1968.

* Battestin, Martin C., *The Moral Basis of Fielding's Art: A Study of Joseph Andrews*, 1959.

Blanchard, Frederic T., *Fielding, the Novelist: A Study in Literary Reputation*, 1926.

Coley, William B., "Gide and Fielding," *Comparative Literature*, XI (1959), 1–15.

* Crane, R. S., "The Concept of Plot and the Plot of *Tom Jones*," *The Journal of General Education*, IV (1950), 112–30.

* Cross, Wilbur, *The History of Henry Fielding*, 3 vols., 1918.

Digeon, Aurélien, *The Novels of Fielding*, 1925.

Dudden, F. Homes, *Henry Fielding: His Life, Works, and Times*, 2 vols., 1952.

Ehrenpreis, Irvin, *Fielding: Tom Jones*, 1964.

———, "Fielding's Use of Fiction: The Autonomy of *Joseph Andrews*," *Twelve Original Essays on Great English Novels*, ed. Shapiro, 1960.

Empson, William, *"Tom Jones," Kenyon Review*, XX (1958), 217–49.

Golden, Morris, *Fielding's Moral Psychology*, 1966.

Kermode, Frank, "Richardson and Fielding," *Cambridge Journal*, IV (1950), 106–14.

Kreissman, Bernard, *Pamela-Shamela*, 1960.

Sacks, Sheldon, *Fiction and the Shape of Belief: A Study of Fielding with Glances at Swift, Johnson, and Richardson*, 1964.

Sherburn, George, "Fielding's *Amelia*: An Interpretation," *ELH*, III (1936), 1–14.

Spilka, Mark, "Comic Resolution in Fielding's *Joseph Andrews*," *College English*, XV (1953), 11–19.
Thornbury, Ethel Margaret, *Henry Fielding's Theory of the Comic Prose Epic*, 1931.
Woods, Charles B., "Fielding and the Authorship of *Shamela*," *PQ*, XXV (1946), 248–72.
(Also see Kreissman listing under Richardson.)

CHAPTER 5
Smollett's Humphry Clinker: *The Choleric Temper*

Boege, Fred W., *Smollett's Reputation as a Novelist*, 1947.
Kahrl, George, *Tobias Smollett, Traveler–Novelist*, 1945.
* Knapp, Lewis, M., *Tobias Smollett: Doctor of Men and Manners*, 1949, 1963.
———, ed. *The Letters of Tobias Smollett*, 1970.
Martz, Louis L., *The Later Career of Tobias Smollett*, 1942.
* Rousseau, G. S. with Boucé, P. G., *Tobias Smollett: Bicentennial Essays Presented to Lewis M. Knapp*, 1971. (Especially recommended are essays by Butt, Paulson, Stevick, and Gassman.)
Strauss, Albrecht B., "On Smollett's Language: A Paragraph in *Ferdinand Count Fathom*," *English Institute Essays*, 1958.

CHAPTER 6
Tristram Shandy, *the Sentimental Novel, and Sentimentalists*

Baird, Theodore, "The Time-Scheme of *Tristram Shandy* and a Source," *PMLA*, LI (1936), 803–20.
* Booth, Wayne C., "Did Sterne Complete *Tristram Shandy*?" *Modern Philology*, XLVIII (1951), 172–83.
* ———, "The Self-Conscious Narrator in Comic Fiction before *Tristram Shandy*," *PMLA*, LXVII (1952), 163-85.
Boys, Richard C., "*Tristram Shandy* and the Conventional Novel," *Papers of the Michigan Academy of Science, Arts, and Letters*, 1951.
* Cross, Wilbur, *The Life and Times of Laurence Sterne*, 1909.
Curtis, Lewis Perry, ed., *Letters of Laurence Sterne*, 1935.
Fluchère, Henri, *Laurence Sterne*, 1961.
Hartley, Lodwick, *Laurence Sterne in the Twentieth Century: An Essay and a Bibliography of Sternean Studies, 1900–1965*, 1966.
* Holtz, William V., *Image and Immortality: A Study of Tristram Shandy*, 1971.
Jefferson, D. W., "*Tristram Shandy* and the Tradition of Learned Wit," *Essays in Criticism*, I (1951), 225–48.
Lehman, B. H., "Of Time, Personality, and the Author. A Study of

Tristram Shandy: Comedy," University of California *Publications in English*, VIII (1941), 223–50.

Moore, Robert E., *Hogarth's Literary Relationships*, 1948.

Piper, William Bowman, *Laurence Sterne*, 1965.

Stedmond, J. M., *The Comic Art of Laurence Sterne*, 1967.

* Traugott, John, *Tristram Shandy's World: Sterne's Philosophical Rhetoric*, 1954.

Tuveson, Ernest, "Locke and Sterne," *Reason and Imagination: Studies in the History of Ideas 1600–1800*, ed. Mazzeo, 1962.

(For the section on the sentimental novel, see Walter Francis Wright, *Sensibility in English Prose Fiction, 1760–1814*, cited above.)

CHAPTER 7
Gothic, Gothicism, and Gothicists

Birkhead, Edith, *The Tale of Terror*, 1921.

* Praz, Mario, *The Romantic Agony*, 1933.

Railo, Eino, *The Haunted Castle: A Study of the Elements of English Romanticism*, 1927.

* Summers, Montague, *The Gothic Quest: A History of the Gothic Novel*, 1938, 1964.

———, *The Vampire, His Kith and Kin*, 1928.

———, *The Vampire in Europe*, 1929.

Tarr, Sister Mary Muriel, *Catholicism in Gothic Fiction*, 1946.

* Varma, Devendra, *The Gothic Flame*, 1957, 1966.

CHAPTER 8
Near-Novels

There is no formal bibliography for "Near-Novels." Readers interested in questions of novel form and the nature of the genre should consult Frye, Booth, Watt, Auerbach, Paulson, Friedman, Van Ghent, Frank, et al., cited above. Also recommended are the essays collected by Philip Stevick in *The Theory of the Novel* (1967) and, to a lesser extent, by William Van O'Connor in *Forms of Modern Fiction* (1948) and John D. Aldridge in *Critiques and Essays on Modern Fiction, 1920–1951* (1952).

Index